WILLIAM MARSTON.

MARY MARSTON.

A NOVEL.

BY

GEORGE MACDONALD,

AUTHOR OF "ANNALS OF A QUIET NEIGHBORHOOD," "ROBERT FALCONER," ETC., ETC.

NEW YORK:

GEORGE ROUTLEDGE & SONS,

9 LAFAYETTE PLACE.

IN MEMORIAM

PR ━━ 7
M32
━ ━ ━
M.+N

CONTENTS.

MARY MARSTON.

CHAPTER I.

THE SHOP.

It was an evening early in May. The sun was low, and the street was mottled with the shadows of its paving-stones—smooth enough, but far from evenly set. The sky was clear, except for a few clouds in the west, hardly visible in the dazzle of the huge light, which lay among them like a liquid that had broken its vessel, and was pouring over the fragments. The street was almost empty, and the air was chill. The spring was busy, and the summer was at hand ; but the wind was blowing from the north.

The street was not a common one ; there was interest, that is feature, in the shadowy front of almost each of its old houses. Not a few of them wore, indeed, something like a human expression, the look of having both known and suffered. From many a porch, and many a latticed oriel, a long shadow stretched eastward, like a death-flag streaming in a wind unfelt of the body—or a fluttering leaf, ready to yield, and flit away, and add one more to the mound of blackness gathering on the horizon's edge. It was the main street of an old country town, dwindled by the rise of larger and more prosperous places, but holding and exercising a charm none of them would ever gain.

Some of the oldest of its houses, most of them with more than one projecting story, stood about the middle of the street.

The central and oldest of these was a draper's shop. The windows of the ground-floor encroached a little on the pavement, to which they descended very close, for the floor of the shop was lower than the street. But, although they had glass on three oriel sides, they were little used for the advertising of the stores within. A few ribbons and gay handkerchiefs, mostly of cotton, for the eyes of the country people on market-days, formed the chief part of their humble show. The door was wide and very low, the upper half of it of glass—old, and bottle-colored ; and its threshold was a deep step down into the shop. As a place for purchases it might not to some eyes *look* promising, but both the ladies and the housekeepers of Testbridge knew that rarely could they do better in London itself than at the shop of Turnbull and Marston, whether variety, quality, or price, was the point in consideration. And, whatever the first impression concerning it, the moment the eyes of a stranger began to grow accustomed to its gloom, the evident size and plenitude of the shop might well suggest a large hope. It was low, indeed, and the walls could therefore accommodate few shelves ; but the ceiling was therefore so near as to be itself available for stowage by means of well-contrived slides and shelves attached to the great beams crossing it in several directions. During the shop-day, many an article, light as lace, and heavy as broadcloth, was taken from overhead to lay upon the counter. The shop had a special reputation for all kinds of linen goods, from cambric handkerchiefs to towels, and from table-napkins to sheets ; but almost everything was to be found in it, from Manchester moleskins for the navvy's trousers, to Genoa velvet for the dowager's gown, and from Horrocks's prints to Lyons silks. It had been enlarged at the back, by building beyond the original plan, and that part of it was a little higher, and a little better lighted than the front ; but the whole place was still dark enough to have awaked the envy of any swindling London shopkeeper. Its owners, however, had so long enjoyed the confidence of the neighborhood, that faith readily took the place of sight with their customers—so far at least as quality was concerned ; and seldom, except in a question of color or shade, was an article carried to the door to be confronted with the day. It had been just such a shop, untouched of even legendary change, as far back as the memory of the sexton reached ; and he, because of his age and his occupation, was the chief authority in the local history of the place.

As, on this evening, there were few people in the street, so were there few in the shop, and it was on the point of being closed : they were not particular there to a good many minutes either way. Behind the counter, on the left hand, stood a youth of about twenty, young George Turnbull, the son of the principal partner, occupied in leisurely folding and putting aside a number of things he had been showing to a farmer's wife, who was just gone. He was an ordinary-looking lad, with little more than business in his high forehead, fresh-colored, good-humored, self-satisfied cheeks, and keen hazel eyes. These last kept wandering from his not very pressing occupation to the other side of the shop, where stood, behind the opposing counter, a young woman, in attendance upon the wants of a well-dressed youth in front of it, who had just made choice of a pair of driving-gloves. His air and carriage were conventionally those of a gentleman—a gentleman, however, more than ordinarily desirous of pleasing a young woman behind a counter. She answered him with politeness, and even friendliness, nor seemed aware of anything unusual in his attentions.

"They're splendid gloves," he said, making talk ; "but don't you think it a great price for a pair of gloves, Miss Marston ?"

"It *is* a good deal of money," she answered, in a sweet, quiet voice, whose very tone suggested simplicity and straight-forwardness ; "but they will last you a long time. Just look at the work, Mr. Helmer. You see how they are made ? It is much more difficult to stitch them like that, one edge over the other, than to sew the two edges together, as they do with ladies' gloves. But I'll just ask my father whether he marked them himself."

"He did mark those, I know," said young Turnbull, who had been listening to all that went on, "for I heard my father say they ought to be sixpence more."

"Ah, then!" she returned, assentingly, and laid the gloves on the box before her, the question settled.

Helmer took them, and began to put them on.

"They certainly are the only glove where there is much handling of reins," he said.

"That is what Mr. Wardour says of them," rejoined Miss Marston.

"By the by," said Helmer, lowering his voice, "when did you see anybody from Thornwick?"

"Their old man was in the town yesterday with the dog-cart.

"Nobody with him?"

"Miss Letty. She came in for just two minutes or so."

"How was she looking?"

"Very well," answered Miss Marston, with what to Helmer seemed indifference.

"Ah!" he said, with a look of knowingness, "you girls don't see each other with the same eyes as we. I grant Letty is not very tall, and I grant she has not much of a complexion; but where did you ever see such eyes?"

"You must excuse me, Mr. Helmer," returned Mary, with a smile," if I don't choose to discuss Letty's merits with you; she is my friend."

"Where would be the harm?" rejoined Helmer, looking puzzled. "I am not likely to say anything against her. You know perfectly well I admire her beyond any woman in the world. I don't care who knows it."

"Your mother?" suggested Mary, in the tone of one who makes a venture.

"Ah, come now, Miss Marston! Don't you turn my mother loose upon me. I shall be of age in a few months, and then my mother may—think as she pleases. I know, of course, with her notions, she would never consent to my making love to Letty—"

"I should think not!" exclaimed Mary. "Who ever thought of such an absurdity? Not you, surely, Mr. Helmer? What would your mother say to hear you? I mention her in earnest now."

"Let mothers mind their own business!" retorted the youth angrily. "I shall mind mine. My mother ought to know that by this time."

Mary said no more. She knew Mrs. Helmer was not a mother to deserve her boy's confidence, any more than to gain it; for she treated him as if she had made him, and was not satisfied with her work.

"When are you going to see Letty, Miss Marston?" resumed Helmer, after a brief pause of angry feeling.

"Next Sunday evening probably."

"Take me with you."

"Take you with me! What are you dreaming of, Mr. Helmer?"

"I would give my bay mare for a good talk with Letty Lovel," he returned.

Mary made no reply.

"You won't?" he said petulantly, after a vain pause of expectation.

"Won't what?" rejoined Miss Marston, as if she could not believe him in earnest.

"Take me with you on Sunday?"

"No," she answered quietly, but with sober decision.

"Where would be the harm?" pleaded the youth, in a tone mingled of expostulation, entreaty, and mortification.

"One is not bound to do everything there would be no harm in doing," answered Miss Marston. "Besides, Mr. Helmer, I don't choose to go out walking with you of a Sunday evening."

"Why not?"

"For one thing, your mother would not like it. You know she would not."

"Never mind my mother. She's nothing to you. She can't bite you.—Ask the dentist. Come, come! that's all nonsense. I shall be at the stile beyond the turnpike-gate all the afternoon—waiting till you come."

"The moment I see you—anywhere upon the road—that moment I shall turn back —Do you think," she added with half-amu▿ ▵ ▵ ▵ ▵ ▵ ll the gossips of Testbridge talk of my going out on a Sunday evening with a boy like you ?"

Tom Helmer's face flushed. He caught up the gloves, threw the price of them on the counter, and walked from the shop, without even a good night.

"Hullo !" cried George Turnbull, vaulting over the counter, and taking the place Helmer had just left opposite Mary ; "what did you say to the fellow to send him off like that ? If you do hate the business, you needn't scare the customers, Mary."

"I don't hate the business, you know quite well, George. And if I did scare a customer," she added, laughing, as she dropped the money in the till, "it was not before he had done buying."

"That may be ; but we must look to to-morrow as well as to-day. When is Mr. Helmer likely to come near us again, after such a wipe as you must have given him to make him go off like that ?"

"Just to-morrow, George, I fancy," answered Mary. "He won't be able to bear the thought of having left a bad impression on me, and so he'll come again to remove it. After all, there's something about him I can't help liking. I said nothing that ought to have put him out of temper like that, though ; I only called him a boy."

"Let me tell you, Mary, you could not have called him a worse name."

"Why, what else is he ?"

"A more offensive word a man could not hear from the lips of a woman," said George loftily.

"A man, I dare say ! But Mr. Helmer can't be nineteen yet."

"How can you say so, when he told you himself he would be of age in a few months ? The fellow is older than I am. You'll be calling me a boy next."

"What else are you ? You at least are not one-and-twenty."

"And how old do you call yourself, pray, miss ?"

"Three-and-twenty last birthday."

"A mighty difference indeed !"

"Not much—only all the difference, it seems, between sense and absurdity, George."

"That may be all very true of a fine gentleman, like Helmer, that does nothing from morning to night but run away from his mother ; but you don't think it applies to me, Mary, I hope !"

"That's as you behave yourself, George. If you do not make it apply, it won't apply of itself. But if young women had not more sense than most of the young men I see in the shop—on both sides of the counter, George—things would soon be at a fine pass. Nothing better in your head than in a peacock's !—only that a peacock *has* the fine feathers he's so proud of."

" If it were Mr. Wardour now, Mary, that was spreading his tail for you to see, you would not complain of that peacock ! "

A vivid rose blossomed instantly in Mary's cheek Mr. Wardour was not even an acquaintance of hers. He was cousin and friend to Letty Lovel, indeed, but she had never spoken to him, except in the shop.

" It would not be quite out of place if you were to learn a little respect for your superiors, George," she returned. " Mr. Wardour is not to be thought of in the same moment with the young men that were in my mind. Mr. Wardour is not a young man ; and he is a gentleman."

She took the glove-box, and turning placed it on a shelf behind her.

"Just so !" remarked George, bitterly. " Any man you don't choose to count a gentleman, you look down upon ! What have you got to do with gentlemen, I should like to know ? "

" To admire one when I see him," answered Mary. " Why shouldn't I ? It is very seldom, and it does me good."

" Oh, yes !" rejoined George, contemptuously. " You *call* yourself a lady, but—"

"I do nothing of the kind," interrupted Mary, sharply. " I should *like* to be a lady : and inside of me, please God, I *will* be a lady ; but I leave it to other people to call me this or that. It matters little what any one is *called*."

"All right," returned George, a little cowed ; "I don't mean to contradict you. Only just tell me why a well-to-do tradesman shouldn't be a gentleman as well as a small yeoman like Wardour."

"Why don't you say—as well as a squire, or an earl, or a duke ?" said Mary.

"There you are, chaffing me again ! It's hard enough to have every fool of a lawyer's clerk, or a doctor's boy, looking down upon a fellow, and calling him a counter-jumper ; but, upon my soul, it's too bad when a girl in the same shop hasn't a civil word for him, because he isn't what she counts a gentleman ! Isn't my father a gentleman ? Answer me that, Mary."

It was one of George's few good things that he had a great opinion of his father, though the grounds of it were hardly such as to enable Mary to answer his appeal in a way he would have counted satisfactory. She thought of her own father, and was silent.

"Everything depends on what a man is in himself, George." she answered. "Mr. Wardour would be a gentleman all the same if he were a shopkeeper or a blacksmith."

"And shouldn't I be as good a gentleman as Mr. Wardour, if I had been born with an old tumble-down house on my back, and a few acres of land I could do with as I liked ? Come, answer me that."

"If it be the house and the land that makes the difference, you would, of course," answered Mary.

Her tone implied, even to George's rough perceptions, that there was a good deal more of a difference between them than therein lay. But common people, whether lords or shopkeepers, are slow to understand that possession, whether in the shape of birth, or lands, or money, or intellect, is a small affair in the difference between men.

"I know you don't think me fit to hold a candle to him," he said. "But I happen to know, for all he rides such a good horse, he's not above doing the work of a wretched menial, for he polishes his own stirrup-irons."

"I'm very glad to hear it," rejoined Mary. "He must be more of a gentleman yet than I thought him."

"Then why should you count him a better gentleman than me?"

"I'm afraid, for one thing, you would go with your stirrup-irons rusty, rather than clean them yourself, George. But I will tell you one thing Mr. Wardour would not do if he were a shopkeeper: he would not, like you, talk one way to the rich, and another way to the poor—all submission and polite-ness to the one, and familiarity, even to rudeness, with the other! If you go on like that, you'll never come within sight of being a gentleman, George—not if you live to the age of Methuselah."

"Thank you, Miss Mary! It's a fine thing to have a lady in the shop! Shouldn't I just like my father to hear you! I'm blowed if I know how a fellow is to get on with you! Certain sure I am that it ain't *my* fault if we're not friends."

Mary made no reply. She could not help understanding what George meant, and she flushed, with honest anger, from brow to chin. But, while her dark-blue eyes flamed with in-dignation, her anger was not such as to render her face less pleasant to look upon. There are as many kinds of anger as there are of the sunsets with which they ought to end: Mary's anger had no hate in it.

I must now hope my readers sufficiently interested in my narrative to care that I should tell them something of what she was like. Plainly as I see her, I can not do more for them than that. I can not give a portrait of her; I can but cast her shadow on my page. It was a dainty half-length, neither tall nor short, in a plain, well-fitting dress of black silk, with linen collar and cuffs, that rose above the counter, standing, in spite of displeasure, calm and motionless. Her hair was dark, and dressed in the simplest manner, without even a re-minder of the hideous occipital structure then in favor—es-pecially with shopwomen, who in general choose for imitation and exorbitant development whatever is ugliest and least lady-like in the fashion of the hour. It had a natural wave in it, which broke the too straight lines it would otherwise have made across a forehead of sweet and composing proportions. Her features were regular—her nose straight—perhaps a little

thin ; the curve of her upper lip carefully drawn, as if with
design to express a certain firmness of modesty ; and her chin
well shaped, perhaps a little too sharply defined for her years,
and rather large. Everything about her suggested the repose
of order satisfied, of unconstrained obedience to the laws of
harmonious relation. The only fault honest criticism could
have suggested, merely suggested, was the presence of just a
possible *nuance* of primness. Her boots, at this moment unseen of any, fitted her feet, as her feet fitted her body. Her
hands were especially good. There are not many ladies, interested in their own graces, who would not have envied her such
seals to her natural patent of ladyhood. Her speech and manners corresponded with her person and dress ; they were direct
and simple, in tone and inflection, those of one at peace with
herself. Neatness was more notable in her than grace, but
grace was not absent ; good breeding was more evident than
delicacy, yet delicacy was there ; and unity was plain throughout.

George went back to his own side of the shop, jumped the
counter, put the cover on the box he had left open with a bang,
and shoved it into its place as if it had been the backboard of
a cart, shouting as he did so to a boy invisible, to make haste
and put up the shutters. Mary left the shop by a door on the
inside of the counter, for she and her father lived in the house ;
and, as soon as the shop was closed, George went home to the
villa his father had built in the suburbs.

CHAPTER II.

CUSTOMERS.

The next day was Saturday, a busy one at the shop. From
the neighboring villages and farms came customers not a few ;
and ladies, from the country-seats around, began to arrive as
the hours went on. The whole strength of the establishment
was early called out.

Busiest in serving was the senior partner, Mr. Turnbull. He was a stout, florid man, with a bald crown, a heavy watch-chain of the best gold festooned across the wide space between waistcoat-button-hole and pocket, and a large hemispheroidal carbuncle on a huge fat finger, which yet was his little one. He was close-shaved, double-chinned, and had cultivated an ordinary smile to such an extraordinary degree that, to use the common hyperbole, it reached from ear to ear. By nature he was good-tempered and genial; but, having devoted every mental as well as physical endowment to the making of money, what few drops of spiritual water were in him had to go with the rest to the turning of the mill-wheel that ground the uni-verse into coin. In his own eyes he was a strong churchman, but the only sign of it visible to others was the strength of his contempt for dissenters—which, however, excepting his part-ner and Mary, he showed only to church-people; a dissenter's money being, as he often remarked, when once in his till, as good as the best churchman's.

To the receptive eye he was a sight not soon to be for-gotten, as he bent over a piece of goods outspread before a customer, one hand resting on the stuff, the other on the yard-measure, his chest as nearly touching the counter as the pro-testing adjacent parts would permit, his broad smooth face turned up at right angles, and his mouth, eloquent even to so-lemnity on the merits of the article, now hiding, now disclos-ing a gulf of white teeth. No sooner was anything admitted into stock, than he bent his soul to the selling of it, doing every-thing that could be done, saying everything he could think of saying, short of plain lying as to its quality: that he was not guilty of. To buy well was a care to him, to sell well was a greater, but to make money, and that as speedily as possible, was his greatest care, and his whole ambition.

John Turnbull in his gig, as he drove along the road to the town, and through the street approached his shop-door, showed to the chance observer a man who knew himself of importance, a man who might have a soul somewhere inside that broad waistcoat; as he drew up, threw the reins to his stable-boy, and descended upon the pavement—as he stepped down into the

shop even, he looked a being in whom son or daughter or
friend might feel some honest pride ; but, the moment he was
behind the counter and in front of a customer, he changed to
a creature whose appearance and carriage were painfully contemptible to any beholder who loved his kind ; he had lost the
upright bearing of a man, and cringed like an ape. But I
fear it was thus he had gained a portion at least of his
favor with the country-folk, many of whom much preferred
his ministrations to those of his partner. A glance, indeed,
from the one to the other, was enough to reveal which must
be the better salesman—and to some eyes which the better
man.

In the narrow walk of his commerce—behind the counter,
I mean—Mr. Marston stood up tall and straight, lank and lean,
seldom bending more than his long neck in the direction of the
counter, but doing everything needful upon it notwithstanding, from the unusual length of his arms and his bony hands.
His forehead was high and narrow, his face pale and thin, his
hair long and thin, his nose aquiline and thin, his eyes large,
his mouth and chin small. He seldom spoke a syllable more
than was needful, but his words breathed calm respect to every
customer. His conversation with one was commonly all but
over as he laid something for approval or rejection on the
counter : he had already taken every pains to learn the precise
nature of the necessity or desire ; and what he then offered he
submitted without comment ; if the thing was not judged
satisfactory, he removed it and brought another. Many did
not like this mode of service ; they would be helped to buy ;
unequal to the task of making up their minds, they welcomed
any aid toward it ; and therefore preferred Mr. Turnbull, who
gave them every imaginable and unimaginable assistance, grov-
eling before them like a man whose many gods came to him
one after the other to be worshiped ; while Mr. Marston, the
moment the thing he presented was on the counter, shot
straight up like a poplar in a sudden calm, his visage bearing
witness that his thought was already far away—in heavenly
places with his wife, or hovering like a perplexed bee over some
difficult passage in the New Testament ; Mary could have told

which, for she knew the meaning of every shadow that passed or lingered on his countenance.

His partner and his like-minded son despised him, as a matter of course ; his unbusiness-like habits, as they counted them, were the constantly recurring theme of their scorn , and some of these would doubtless have brought him the disapprobation of many a business man of a moral development beyond that of Turnbull ; but Mary saw nothing in them which did not stamp her father the superior of all other men she knew.

To mention one thing, which may serve as typical of the man: he not unfrequently sold things under the price marked by his partner. Against this breach of fealty to the firm Turnbull never ceased to level his biggest guns of indignation and remonstrance, though always without effect. He even lowered himself in his own eyes so far as to quote Scripture like a canting dissenter, and remind his partner of what came to a house divided against itself. He did not see that the best thing for some houses must be to come to pieces. "Well, but, Mr. Turnbull, I thought it was marked too high," was the other's invariable answer. "William, you are a fool," his partner would rejoin for the hundredth time. "Will you never understand that, if we get a little more than the customary profit upon one thing, we get less upon another ? You must make the thing even, or come to the workhouse." Thereto, for the hundredth time also, William Marston would reply: "That *might* hold, I daresay, Mr. Turnbull—I am not sure—if every customer always bought an article of each of the two sorts together ; but I can't make it straight with my conscience that one customer should pay too much because I let another pay too little. Besides, I am not at all sure that the general scale of profit is not set too high. I fear you and I will have to part, Mr. Turnbull." But nothing was further from Turnbull's desire than that he and Marston should part ; he could not keep the business going without his money, not to mention that he never doubted Marston would straightway open another shop, and, even if he did not undersell him, take from him all his dissenting customers ; for the junior partner was deacon of a small Baptist church in the town—a fact which, although like vinegar to the teeth and smoke to the eyes of John Turnbull in his villa, was invaluable in the eyes of John Turnbull behind his counter.

Whether William Marston was right or wrong in his ideas about the rite of baptism—probably he was both—he was certainly right in his relation to that which alone makes it of any value—that, namely, which it signifies ; buried with his Master, he had died to selfishness, greed, and trust in the secondary ; died to evil, and risen to good—a new creature. He was just as much a Christian in his shop as in the chapel, in his bedroom as at the prayer-meeting.

But the world was not now much temptation to him, and, to tell the truth, he was getting a good deal tired of the shop. He had to remind himself, oftener and oftener, that in the mean time it was the work given him to do, and to take more and more frequently the strengthening cordial of a glance across the shop at his daughter. Such a glance passed through the dusky place like summer lightning through a heavy atmosphere, and came to Mary like a glad prophecy ; for it told of a world within and beyond the world, a region of love and faith, where struggled no antagonistic desires, no counteracting aims, but unity was the visible garment of truth.

The question may well suggest itself to my reader—How could such a man be so unequally yoked with such another as Turnbull ?—To this I reply that Marston's greatness had yet a certain repressive power upon the man who despised him, so that he never uttered his worst thoughts or revealed his worst basenesses in his presence. Marston never thought of him as my reader must soon think—flattered himself, indeed, that poor John was gradually improving, coming to see things more and more as he would have him look on them. Add to this, that they had been in the business together almost from boyhood, and much will be explained.

An open carriage, with a pair of showy but ill-matched horses, looking unfit for country work on the one hand, as for Hyde Park on the other, drew up at the door ; and a visible wave of interest ran from end to end of the shop, swaying as well those outside as those inside the counter, for the carriage was well known in Testbridge. It was that of Lady Margaret

Mortimer; she did not herself like the *Margaret*, and signed only her second name *Alice* at full length, whence her *friends* generally called her to each other Lady Malice. She did not leave the carriage, but continued to recline motionless in it, at an angle of forty-five degrees, wrapped in furs, for the day was cloudy and cold, her pale handsome face looking inexpressibly more indifferent in its regard of earth and sky and the goings of men, than that of a corpse whose gaze is only on the inside of the coffin-lid. But the two ladies who were with her got down. One of them was her daughter, Hesper by name, who, from the dull, cloudy atmosphere that filled the doorway, entered the shop like a gleam of sunshine, dusky-golden, followed by a glowing shadow, in the person of her cousin, Miss Yolland.

Turnbull hurried to meet them, bowing profoundly, and looking very much like Issachar between the chairs he carried. But they turned aside to where Mary stood, and in a few minutes the counter was covered with various stuffs for some of the smaller articles of ladies' attire.

The customers were hard to please, for they wanted the best things at the price of inferior ones, and Mary noted that the desires of the cousin were farther reaching and more expensive than those of Miss Mortimer. But, though in this way hard to please, they were not therefore unpleasant to deal with; and from the moment she looked the latter in the face, whom she had not seen since she was a girl, Mary could hardly take her eyes off her. All at once it struck her how well the unusual, fantastic name her mother had given her suited her; and, as she gazed, the feeling grew.

Large, and grandly made, Hesper stood "straight, and steady, and tall," dusky-fair, and colorless, with the carriage of a young matron. Her brown hair seemed ever scathed and crinkled afresh by the ethereal flame that here and there peeped from amid the unwilling volute rolled back from her creamy forehead in a rebellious coronet. Her eyes were large and hazel; her nose cast gently upward, answering the carriage of her head; her mouth decidedly large, but so exquisite in drawing and finish that the loss of a centimetre of its length would to a lover have been as the loss of a kingdom ; her chin a trifle large, and grandly lined ; for a woman's, her throat was massive, and her arms and hands were powerful. Her expression was frank, almost brave, her eyes looking full at the person she addressed. As she gazed, a kind of love she had never felt before kept swelling in Mary's heart.

Her companion impressed her very differently.

Some men, and most women, counted Miss Yolland *strangely* ugly. But there were men who exceedingly admired her. Not very slight for her stature, and above the middle height, she looked small beside Hesper. Her skin was very dark, with a considerable touch of sallowness ; her eyes, which were large and beautifully shaped, were as black as eyes could be, with light in the midst of their blackness, and more than a touch of hardness in the midst of their liquidity ; her eyelashes were singularly long and black, and she seemed conscious of them every time they rose. She did not *use* her eyes habitually, but, when she did, the thrust was sudden and straight. I heard a man once say that a look from her was like a volley of small-arms. Like Hesper's, her mouth was large and good, with fine teeth ; her chin projected a little too much ; her hands were finer than Hesper's, but bony. Her name was Septimia ; Lady Margaret called her Sepia, and the contraction seemed to so many suitable that it was ere long generally adopted. She was in mourning, with a little crape. To the first glance she seemed as unlike Hesper as she could well be ; but, as she stood gently regarding the two, Mary, gradually, and to her astonishment, became indubitably aware of a singular likeness between them. Sepia, being a few years older, and in less flourishing condition, had her features sharper and finer, and by nature her complexion was darker by shades innumerable ; but, if the one was the evening, the other was the night . Sepia was a diminished and overshadowed Hesper. Their manner, too, was similar, but Sepia's was the haughtier, and she had an occasional look of defiance, of which there appeared nothing in Hesper. When first she came to Durnmelling, Lady Malice had once alluded to the dependence of her position—but only once : there came a flash into rather than out of Sepia's eyes that made any repetition of the insult impossible, and Lady Malice wish that she had left her a wanderer on the face of Europe.

Sepia was the daughter of a clergyman, an uncle of Lady Malice, whose sons had all gone to the bad, and whose daughters had all vanished from society. Shortly before the time at which my narrative begins, one of the latter, however, namely Sepia, the youngest, had reappeared, a fragment of the family wreck, floating over the gulf of its destruction. Nobody knew with any certainty where she had been in the interim : nobody at Durnmelling knew anything but what she chose to tell, and that was not much. She said she had been a governess in Austrian Poland and Russia. Lady Margaret had become reconciled to her presence, and Hesper attached to her.

Of the men who, as I have said, admired her, some felt a peculiar enchantment in what they called her ugliness ; others declared her devilish handsome ; and some shrank from her as if with an undefined dread of perilous entanglement, if she should but catch them looking her in the face. Among some of them she was known as Lucifer, in antithesis to Hesper : they meant the Lucifer of darkness, not the light-bringer of the morning.

The ladies, on their part, especially Hesper, were much pleased with Mary. The simplicity of her address and manner, the pains she took to find the exact thing she wanted, and the modest decision with which she answered any reference to her, made Hesper even like her. The most artificially educated of women is yet human, and capable of even more than liking a fellow-creature as such. When their purchases were ended, she took her leave with a kind smile, which went on glowing in Mary's heart long after she had vanished.

"Home, John," said Lady Margaret, the moment the two ladies were seated. "I hope you have got *all* you wanted. We shall be late for luncheon, I fear. I would not for worlds keep Mr. Redmain waiting.—A little faster, John, please."

Hesper's face darkened. Sepia eyed her fixedly, from under the mingling of ascended lashes and descended brows. The coachman pretended to obey, but the horses knew very well when he did and when he did not mean them to go, and took

not a step to the minute more : John had regard to the splen-
did-looking black horse on the near side, which was weak in
the wind, as well as on one fired pastern, and cared little for
the anxiety of his mistress.   To him, horses were the final peak
of creation—or if not the horses, the coachman, whose they are
—masters and mistresses the merest parasitical adjuncts.   He
got them home in good time for luncheon, notwithstanding—
more to Lady Margaret's than Hesper's satisfaction.

Mr. Redmain was a bachelor of fifty, to whom Lady Margaret was endeavoring to make the family agreeable, in the hope
he might take Hesper off their hands.   I need not say he was
rich.   He was a common man, with good cold manners, which
he offered you like a handle.   He was selfish, capable of picking up a lady's handkerchief, but hardly a wife's.   He was
attentive to Hesper ; but she scarcely concealed such a repugnance to him as some feel at sight of strange fishes—being at
the same time afraid of him, which was not surprising, as she
could hardly fail to perceive the fate intended for her.

"Ain't Miss Mortimer a stunner ? " said George Turnbull
to Mary, when the tide of customers had finally ebbed from the
shop.

"I don't exactly know what you mean, George," answered
Mary.

"Oh, of course, I know it ain't fair to ask any girl to admire another," said George.   "But there's no offense to you,
Mary.   One young lady can't carry *every* merit on her back.
She'd be too lovely to live, you know.   Miss Mortimer ain't
got your waist, nor she ain't got your 'ands, nor your 'air ;
and you ain't got her size, nor the sort of hair she 'as with
her."

He looked up from the piece of leno he was smoothing out,
and saw he was alone in the shop.

CHAPTER III.

THE ARBOR AT THORNWICK.

THE next day was Sunday at last, a day dear to all who do anything like their duty in the week, whether they go to church or not. For Mary, she went to the Baptist chapel ; it was her custom, rendered holy by the companionship of her father. But this day it was with more than ordinary restlessness and lack of interest that she stood, knelt, and sat, through the routine of observance ; for old Mr. Duppa was certainly duller than usual: how could it be otherwise, when he had been preparing to spend a mortal hour in descanting on the reasons which necessitated the separation of all true Baptists from all brother-believers ? The narrow, high-souled little man—for a soul as well as a forehead can be both high and narrow—was dull that morning because he spoke out of his narrowness, and not out of his height; and Mary was better justified in feeling bored than even when George Turnbull plagued her with his vulgar attentions. When she got out at last, sedate as she was, she could hardly help skipping along the street by her father's side. Far better than chapel was their nice little cold dinner together, in their only sitting-room, redolent of the multifarious goods piled around it on all the rest of the floor. Greater yet was the following pleasure —of making her father lie down on the sofa, and reading him to sleep, after which she would doze a little herself, and dream a little, in the great chair that had been her grandmother's. Then they had their tea, and then her father always went to see the minister before chapel in the evening

When he was gone, Mary would put on her pretty straw bonnet, and set out to visit Letty Lovel at Thornwick. Some of the church-members thought this habit of taking a walk, instead of going again to the chapel, very worldly, and did not scruple to let her know their opinion : but, so long as her father was satisfied with her, Mary did not care a straw for the world besides. She was too much occupied with obedience to trouble her head about opinion, either her own or other people's. Not until a question comes puzzling and troubling us so as to paralyze the energy of our obedience is there any necessity for its solution, or any probability of finding a real one. A thousand foolish *doctrines* may lie unquestioned in the mind, and never interfere with the growth or bliss of him who lives in active subordination of his life to the law of life : obedience will in time exorcise them, like many another worse devil.

It had drizzled all the morning from the clouds as well as from the pulpit, but, just as Mary stepped out of the kitchen-door, the sun stepped out of the last rain-cloud. She walked quickly from the town, eager for the fields and the trees, but in some dread of finding Tom Helmer at the stile ; for he was such a fool, she said to herself, that there was no knowing what he might do, for all she had said ; but he had thought better of it, and she was soon crossing meadows and cornfields in peace, by a path which, with many a winding, and many an up and down, was the nearest way to Thornwick.

The saints of old did well to pray God to lift on them the light of his countenance : has the Christian of the new time learned of his Master that the clouds and the sunshine come and go of themselves ? If the sunshine fills the hearts of old men and babes and birds with gladness and praise, and God never meant it, then are they all idolaters, and have but a care-less Father. Sweet earthy odors rose about Mary from the wet ground ; the rain-drops glittered on the grass and corn-blades and hedgerows ; a soft damp wind breathed rather than blew about the gaps and gates ; with an upward springing, like that of a fountain momently gathering strength, the larks kept shooting aloft, there, like music-rockets, to explode in showers of glowing and sparkling song ; while, all the time and over all, the sun as he went down kept shining in the might of his peace ; and the heart of Mary praised her Father in heaven.

Where the narrow path ran westward for a little way, so that she could see nothing for the sun in her eyes, in the middle of a plowed field she would have run right against a gentleman, had he been as blind as she ; but, his back being to the sun, he saw her perfectly, and stepped out of her way into the midst of a patch of stiff soil, where the rain was yet lying between the furrows. She saw him then, and as, lifting his hat, he stepped again upon the path, she recognized Mr. Wardour.

"Oh, your nice boots!" she cried, in the childlike distress of a simple soul discovering itself the cause of catastrophe, for his boots were smeared all over with yellow clay

"It only serves me right," returned Mr. Wardour, with a laugh of amusement. "I oughtn't to have put on such thin ones at the first smile of summer."

Again he lifted his hat, and walked on.

Mary also pursued her path, genuinely though gently pained that one should have stepped up to the ankles in mud on her account. As I have already said, except in the shop she had never before spoken to Mr Wardour, and, although he had so simply responded to her exclamation, he did not even know who she was.

The friendship which now drew Mary to Thornwick, Godfrey Wardour's place, was not one of long date. She and Letty Lovel had, it is true, known each other for years, but only quite of late had their acquaintance ripened into something better; and it was not without protestation on the part of Mrs. Wardour, Godfrey's mother, that she had seen the growth of an intimacy between the two young women. The society of a shopwoman, she often remarked, was far from suitable for one who, as the daughter of a professional man, might lay claim to the position of a gentlewoman. For Letty was the orphan daughter of a country surgeon, a cousin of Mrs. Wardour, for whom she had had a great liking while yet they were boy and girl together. At the same time, however much she would have her consider herself the superior of Mary Marston, she by no means treated her as her own equal, and Letty could not help being afraid of her aunt, as she called her.

The well-meaning woman was in fact possessed by two devils—the one the stiff-necked devil of pride, the other the condescending devil of benevolence. She was kind, but she must have credit for it; and Letty, although the child of a loved cousin, must not presume upon that, or forget that the wife and mother of long-descended proprietors of certain acres of land was greatly the superior of any man who lived by the exercise of the best-educated and most helpful profession. She counted herself a devout Christian, but her ideas of rank, at least—therefore certainly not a few others—were absolutely opposed to the Master's teaching : they who did least for others were her aristocracy.

Now, Letty was a simple, true-hearted girl, rather slow, who honestly tried to understand her aunt's position with regard to her friend. "Shop-girls," her aunt had said, "are not fitting company for you, Letty."

"I do not know any other shop-girls, aunt," Letty replied, with hidden trembling ; "but, if they are not nice, then they are not like Mary. She's downright good ; indeed she is, aunt !—a great deal, ever so much, better than I am."

"That may well be," answered Mrs. Wardour, "but it does not make a lady of her."

"I am sure," returned Letty, bewildered, "on Sundays you could not tell the difference between her and any other young lady."

"Any other well-dressed young woman, my dear, you should say. I believe shop-girls do call their companions young ladies, but that can not justify the application of the word. I am scarcely bound to speak of my cook as a lady because letters come addressed to her as Miss Tozer. If the word 'lady' should sink at last to common use, as in Italy every woman is Donna, we must find some other word to express what *used* to be meant by it."

"Is Mrs. Cropper a lady, aunt ? " asked Letty, after a pause, in which her brains, which were not half so muddled as she thought them, had been busy feeling after firm ground in the morass of social distinction thus opened under her.

"She is received as such," replied Mrs. Wardour, but with doubled stiffness, through which ran a tone of injury.

"Would you receive her, aunt, if she called upon you ? "

"She has horses and servants, and everything a woman of the world can desire ; but I should feel I was bowing the knee to Mammon were I to ask her to my house. Yet such is the respect paid to money in these degenerate days that many a

one will court the society of a person like that, who would
think me or your cousin Godfrey unworthy of notice, because
we have no longer a tithe of the property the family once possessed."

The lady forgot there is a Rimmon as well as a Mammon.

"God knows," she went on, "how that woman's husband
made his money! But that is a small matter nowadays, except to old-fashioned people like myself. Not *how* but *how
much*, is all the question now," she concluded, flattering herself she had made a good point.

"Don't think me rude, please, aunt : I am really wishing
to understand—but, if Mrs. Cropper is not a lady, how can
Mary Marston not be one ? She is as different from Mrs. Crop-
por as one woman can be from another."

"Because she has not the position in society," replied Mrs.
Wardour, enveloping her nothing in flimsy reiteration and self-
contradiction.

"And Mrs. Cropper has the position ?" ventured Letty,
with a little palpitation from fear of offending.

"Apparently so," answered Mrs. Wardour. But her inquiring pupil did not feel much enlightened.

Letty had not the logic necessary to the thinking of the
thing out ; or to the discovery that, like most social difficulties,
hers was merely one of the upper strata of a question whose
foundation lies far too deep for what is called Society to perceive its very existence. And hence it is no wonder that Society, abetted by the Church, should go on from generation to
generation talking murderous platitudes about it.

But, although such was her reasoning beforehand, heart had
so far overcome habit and prejudice with Mrs. Wardour, that,
convinced on the first interview of the high tone and good influence of Mary, she had gradually come to put herself in the
way of seeing her as often as she came, ostensibly to herself
that she might prevent any deterioration of intercourse ; and
although she always, on these occasions, played the grand lady,
with a stateliness that seemed to say, "Because of your individual worth, I condescend, and make an exception, but you
must not m··· ' J · · · · · T' · ' ' " 'e had

almost entirely ceased making remarks upon the said class in
Letty's hearing.

On her part, Letty had by this time grown so intimate with
Mary as to open with her the question upon which her aunt
had given her so little satisfaction ; and this same Sunday afternoon, as they sat in the arbor at the end of the long yew
hedge in the old garden, it had come up again between them ;
for, set thinking by Letty's bewilderment, Mary had gone on
thinking, and had at length laid hold of the matter, at least
by the end that belonged to *her.*

"I can not consent, Letty," she said, "to trouble my mind
about it as you do. I can not afford it. Society is neither my
master nor my servant, neither my father nor my sister ; and
so long as she does not bar my way to the kingdom of heaven,
which is the only society worth getting into, I feel no right to
complain of how she treats me. I have no claim on her ; I do
not acknowledge her laws—hardly her existence, and she has
no authority over me. Why should she, how could she, con-
stituted as she is, receive such as me ? The moment she did
so, she would cease to be what she is ; and, if all be true that
one hears of her, she does me a kindness in excluding me.
What can it matter to me, Letty, whether they call me a lady
or not, so long as Jesus says *Daughter* to me ? It reminds me
of what I heard my father say once to Mr. Turnbull, when he
had been protesting that none but church-people ought to be
buried in the churchyards. 'I don't care a straw about it, Mr.
Turnbull,' he said. 'The Master was buried in a garden.'—
'Ah, but you see things are different now,' said Mr. Turnbull.
—'I don't hang by things, but by my Master. It is enough
for the disciple that he should be as his Master,' said my father.
—'Besides, you don't think it of any real consequence yourself, or you would never want to keep your brothers and sisters
out of such nice quiet places !'—Mr. Turnbull gave his kind of
grunt, and said no more."

After passing Mary, Mr. Wardour did not go very far before he began to slacken his pace ; a moment or two more and
he suddenly wheeled round, and began to walk back toward
Thornwick. Two things had combined to produce this change

of purpose—the first, the state of his boots, which, beginning
to dry in the sun and wind as he walked, grew more and more
hideous at the end of his new gray trousers; the other, the
occurring suspicion that the girl must be Letty's new shopkeeping friend, Miss Marston, on her way to visit her. What
a sweet, simple young woman she was! he thought; and
straightway began to argue with himself that, as his boots were
in such evil plight, it would be more pleasant to spend the
evening with Letty and her friend, than to hold on his way to
his own friend's, and spend the evening smoking and lounging
about the stable, or hearing his sister play polkas and mazurkas
all the still Sunday twilight.

Mary had, of course, upon her arrival, narrated her small
adventure, and the conversation had again turned upon Godfrey just as he was nearing the house.

"How handsome your cousin is!" said Mary, with the
simplicity natural to her.

"Do you think so?" returned Letty.

"Don't *you* think so?" rejoined Mary.

"I have never thought about it," answered Letty.

"He looks so manly, and has such a straightforward way
with him!" said Mary.

"What one sees every day, she may feel in a sort of take-
for-granted way, without thinking about it," said Letty. "But,
to tell the truth, I should feel it as impertinent of me to criti-
cise Cousin Godfrey's person as to pass an opinion on one of
the books he reads. I can not express the reverence I have for
Cousin Godfrey."

"I don't wonder," replied Mary. "There is that about
him one could trust."

"There is that about him," returned Letty, "makes me
afraid of him—I can not tell why. And yet, though everybody, even his mother, is as anxious to please him as if he were
an emperor, he is the easiest person to please in the whole
house. Not that he tells you he is pleased; he only smiles;
but that is quite enough."

"But I suppose he talks to you sometimes?" said Mary.

"Oh, yes—now. He used not: but I think he does now

more than to anybody else. It was a long time before he began, though. Now he is always giving me something to read. I wish he wouldn't ; it frightens me dreadfully. He always questions me, to know whether I understand what I read."

Letty ended with a little cry. Through the one narrow gap in the yew hedge, near to the arbor, Godfrey had entered the walk, and was coming toward them.

He was a well-made man, thirty years of age, rather tall, sun-tanned, and bearded, with wavy brown hair, and gentle approach. His features were not regular, but that is of little consequence where there is unity. His face indicated faculty and feeling, and there was much good nature, shadowed with memorial suffering, in the eyes which shone so blue out of the brown.

Mary rose respectfully as he drew near.

"What treason were you talking, Letty, that you were so startled at sight of me?" he said, with a smile. "You were complaining of me as a hard master, were you not?"

"No, indeed, Cousin Godfrey!" answered Letty energetically, not without tremor, and coloring as she spoke. "I was only saying I could not help being frightened when you asked me questions about what I had been reading. I am so stupid, you know!"

"Pardon me, Letty," returned her cousin, "I know nothing of the sort. Allow me to say you are very far from stupid. Nobody can understand everything at first sight. But you have not introduced me to your friend."

Letty bashfully murmured the names of the two.

"I guessed as much," said Wardour. "Pray sit down, Miss Marston. For the sake of your dresses, I will go and change my boots. May I come and join you after?"

"Please do, Cousin Godfrey ; and bring something to read to us," said Letty, who wanted her friend to admire her cousin "It's Sunday, you know."

"Why you should be afraid of him, I can't think," said Mary, when his retreating steps had ceased to sound on the gravel. "He is delightful!"

"I don't like to look stupid," said Letty.

"I shouldn't mind how stupid I looked so long as I was learning," returned Mary. "I wonder you never told me about him!"

"I couldn't talk about Cousin Godfrey," said Letty; and a pause followed.

"How good of him to come to us again!" said Mary. "What will he read to us?"

"Most likely something out of a book you never heard of before, and can't remember the name of when you have heard it—at least that's the way with me. I wonder if he will talk to you, Mary? I should like to hear how Cousin Godfrey talks to girls."

"Why, you know how he talks to you," said Mary.

"Oh, but I am only Cousin Letty! He can talk anyhow to me."

"By your own account he talks to you in the best possible way."

"Yes; I dare say, but—"

"But what?"

"I can't help wishing sometimes he would talk a little nonsense. It would be such a relief. I am sure I should understand better if he would. I shouldn't be so frightened at him then."

"The way I generally hear gentlemen talk to girls makes me ashamed—makes me feel as if I must ask, 'Is it that you are a fool, or that you take that girl for one?' They never talk so to me."

Letty sat pulling a jonquil to pieces She looked up. Her eyes were full of thought, but she paused a long time before she spoke, and, when she did, it was only to say:

"I fear, Mary, I should take any man for a fool who took me for anything else "

Letty was a rather small and rather freckled girl, with the daintiest of rounded figures, a good forehead, and fine clear brown eyes. Her mouth was not pretty, except when she smiled—and she did not smile often. When she did, it was not unfrequently with the tears in her eyes, and then she looked lovely. In her manner there was an indescribably taking charm, of which it is not easy to give an impression; but I think it sprang from a constitutional humility, partly ruined into a painful and haunting sense of inferiority, for which she imagined herself to blame. Hence there dwelt in her eyes an appeal which few hearts could resist. When they met another's, they seemed to say: "I am nobody; but you need not kill me; I am not pretending to be anybody. I will try to do what you want, but I am not clever. Only I am sorry for it. Be gentle with me." To Godfrey, at least, her eyes spoke thus.

In ten minutes or so he reappeared, far at the other end of the yew-walk, approaching slowly, with a book, in which he seemed thoughtfully searching as he came. When they saw him the girls instinctively moved farther from each other, making large room for him between them, and when he came up he silently took the place thus silently assigned him.

"I am going to try your brains now, Letty," he said, and tapped the book with a finger.

"Oh, please don't!" pleaded Letty, as if he had been threatening her with a small amputation, or the loss of a front tooth.

"Yes," he persisted; "and not your brains only, Letty, but your heart, and all that is in you."

At this even Mary could not help feeling a little frightened; and she was glad there was no occasion for her to speak.

With just a word of introduction, Godfrey read Carlyle's translation of that finest of Jean Paul's dreams in which he sets forth the condition of a godless universe all at once awakened to the knowledge of the causelessness of its own existence. Slowly, with due inflection and emphasis—slowly, but without pause for thought or explanation—he read to the end, ceased suddenly, and lifted his eyes.

"There, Letty," he said, "what do you think of that? There's a bit of Sunday reading for you!"

Letty was looking altogether perplexed, and not a little frightened.

"I don't understand a word of it," she answered, gulping back her tears.

He glanced at Mary. She was white as death, her lips quivered, and from her eyes shot a keen light that seemed to lacerate their blue.

"It is terrible!" she said. "I never read anything like that."

"There *is* nothing like it," he answered.

"But the author is a Unitarian, is he not?" remarked Mary—for she heard plenty of theology, if not much Christianity, in her chapel." •

Godfrey looked at her, then at the book for a moment

"That may merely seem, from the necessity of the supposition," he answered; and read again:

"'Now sank from aloft a noble, high Form, with a look of uneffaceable sorrow, down to the Altar, and all the Dead cried out, "Christ! is there no God?" He answered, "There is none!" The whole Shadow of each then shuddered, not the breast alone; and one after the other all, in this shuddering, shook into pieces.'—You see," he went on, "that if there be no God, Christ can only be the first of men."

"I understand," said Mary.

"Do you really then, Mary?" said Letty, looking at her with wondering admiration.

"I only meant," answered Mary—"but," she went on, interrupting herself, "I do think I understand it a little. If Mr. Wardour would be kind enough to read it through again!"

"With much pleasure," answered Godfrey, casting on her a glance of pleased surprise.

The second reading affected Mary more than the first—because. of course, she took in more. And this time a glimmer of meaning broke on the slower mind of Letty: as her cousin read the passage, "Oh, then came, fearful for the heart, the dead Children who had been awakened in the Churchyard, into the temple, and cast themselves before the high Form on the Altar, and said, 'Jesus, have we no Father?' And he answered, with streaming tears: 'We are all orphans, I and you; we are without Father!'"—at this point Letty gave her little cry, then bit her lip, as if she had said something wrong.

All the time a great bee kept buzzing in and out of the

arbor, and Mary vaguely wondered how it could be so careless.

"I can't be dead stupid after all, Cousin Godfrey," said Letty, with broken voice, when once more he ceased, and, as she spoke, she pressed her hand on her heart, "for something kept going through and through me; but I can not say yet I understand it.—If you will lend me the book," she continued, "I will read it over again before I go to bed."

He shut the volume, handed it to her, and began to talk about something else.

Mary rose to go.

"You will take tea with us, I hope, Miss Marston," said Godfrey.

But Mary would not. What she had heard was working in her mind with a powerful fermentation, and she longed to be alone. In the fields, as she walked, she would come to an understanding with herself.

She knew almost nothing of the higher literature, and felt like a dreamer who, in the midst of a well-known and ordinary landscape, comes without warning upon the mighty cone of a mountain, or the breaking waters of a boundless ocean.

"If one could but get hold of such things, what a glorious life it would be!" she thought. She had looked into a world beyond the present, and already in the present all things were new. The sun set as she had never seen him set before; it was only in gray and gold, with scarce a touch of purple and rose; the wind visited her cheek like a living thing, and loved her; the skylarks had more than reason in their jubilation. For the first time she heard the full chord of intellectual and emotional delight. What a place her chamber would be, if she could there read such things! How easy would it be then to bear the troubles of the hour, the vulgar humor of Mr. Turnbull, and the tiresome attentions of George! Would Mr. Wardour lend her the book? Had he other books as good? Were there many books to make one's heart go as that one did? She would save every penny to buy such books, if indeed such treasures were within her reach! Under the enchantment of her first literary joy, she walked home like one intoxicated with opium—a being possessed for the time with the awful imagination of a grander soul, and reveling in the presence of her loftier kin.

CHAPTER IV.

GODFREY WARDOUR.

THE property of which Thornwick once formed a part was then large and important; but it had, by not very slow degrees, generation following generation of unthrift, dwindled and shrunk and shriveled, until at last it threatened to disappear from the family altogether, like a spark upon burnt paper. Then came one into possession who had some element of salvation in him; Godfrey's father not only held the poor remnant together, but, unable to add to it, improved it so greatly that at length, in the midst of the large properties around, it resembled the diamond that hearts a disk of inferior stones. Doubtless, could he have used his wife's money, he would have spent it on land; but it was under trustees for herself and her children, and indeed would not have gone far in the purchase of English soil.

Considerably advanced in years before he thought of marrying, he died while Godfrey, whom he intended bringing up to a profession, was yet a child; and his widow, carrying out his intention, had educated the boy with a view to the law. Godfrey, however, had positively declined entering on the studies special to a career he detested; nor was it difficult to reconcile his mother to the enforced change of idea, when she found that his sole desire was to settle down with her, and manage the two hundred acres his father had left him. He took his place in the county, therefore, as a yeoman-farmer—none the less a gentleman by descent, character, and education. But while in genuine culture and refinement the superior of all the landed proprietors in the neighborhood, and knowing it, he was the superior of most of them in this also, that he counted it no derogation from the dignity he valued to put his hands upon occasion to any piece of work required about the place.

His nature was too large, however, and its needs therefore too many, to allow of his spending his energies on the property; and he did not brood over such things as, so soon as they become cares, become despicable. How much time is wasted in what is called thought, but is merely care—an anxious idling over the fancied probabilities of result! Of this fault, I say, Godfrey was not guilty—more, however, I must confess, from healthful drawings in other directions, than from philosophy or wisdom: he was *a reader*—not in the sense of a man who derives intensest pleasure from the absorption of intellectual pabulum—one not necessarily so superior as some imagine to the *gourmet*, or even the *gourmand:* in his reading Godfrey nourished certain of the higher tendencies of his nature—read with a constant reference to his own views of life, and the confirmation, change, or enlargement of his theories of the same; but neither did he read with the highest aim of all—the enlargement of reverence, obedience, and faith; for he had never turned his face full in the direction of infinite growth—the primal end of a man's being, who is that he may return to the Father, gathering his truth as he goes. Yet by the simple instincts of a soul undebased by self-indulgence or low pursuits, he was drawn ever toward things lofty and good; and life went calmly on, bearing Godfrey Wardour toward middle age, unruffled either by anxiety or ambition.

To the forecasting affection of a mother, the hour when she must yield the first place both in her son's regards and in the house-affairs could not but have often presented itself, in doubt and pain—perhaps dread. Only as year after year passed and Godfrey revealed no tendency toward marriage, her anxiety changed sides, and she began to fear lest with Godfrey the ancient family should come to an end. As yet, however, finding no response to covert suggestion, she had not ventured to speak openly to him on the subject. All the time, I must add, she had never thought of Letty either as thwarting or furthering her desires, for in truth she felt toward her as one on whom Godfrey could never condescend to look, save with the kind-

ness suitable for one immeasurably below him. As to what
might pass in Letty's mind, Mrs. Wardour had neither curiosity nor care : else she might possibly have been more consider-
ate than to fall into the habit of talking to her in such swelling words of maternal pride that, even if she had not admired
him of herself, Letty could hardly escape coming to regard
her cousin Godfrey as the very first of men.

It added force to the veneration of both mother and cousin
—for it was nothing less than veneration in either—that there
was about Godfrey an air of the inexplicable, or at least the
unknown, and therefore mysterious. This the elder woman,
not without many a pang at her exclusion from his confidence,
attributed, and correctly, to some passage in his life at the
university ; to the younger it appeared only as greatness self-
veiled from the ordinary world : to such as she, could be vouch-
safed only an occasional peep into the gulf of his knowledge,
the grandeur of his intellect, and the imperturbability of his
courage.

The passage in Godfrey's life to which I have referred as
vaguely suspected by his mother, I need not present in more
than merest outline : it belongs to my history only as a compo-
nent part of the soil whence it springs, and as in some measure
necessary to the understanding of Godfrey's character. In the
last year of his college life he had formed an attachment, the
precise nature of which I do not know What I do know is,
that the bonds of it were rudely broken, and of the story nothing remained but disappointment and pain, doubt and distrust. Godfrey had most likely cherished an overweening notion of the relative value of the love he gave ; but being his, I
am certain it was genuine—by that, I mean a love with no
small element of the everlasting in it. The woman who can
cast such a love from her is not likely to meet with such another. But with this one I have nothing to do.

It had been well if he had been left with only a wounded
heart, but in that heart lay wounded pride. He hid it carefully, and the keener in consequence grew the sensitiveness,
almost feminine, which no stranger could have suspected
beneath the manner he wore. Under that bronzed counte-

nance, with its firm-set mouth and powerful jaw—below that
clear blue eye, and that upright easy carriage, lay a faithful
heart haunted by a sense of wrong : he who is not perfect in
forgiveness must be haunted thus ; he only is free whose love
for the human is so strong that he can pardon the individual
sin ; he alone can pray the prayer, "Forgive us our trespasses,"
out of a full heart. Forgiveness is the only cure of wrong.
And hand in hand with Sense-of-injury walks ever the weak
sister-demon Self-pity, so dear, so sweet to many—both of
them the children of Philautos, not of Agape. But there was
no hate, no revenge, in Godfrey, and, I repeat, his weakness
he kept concealed. It must have been in his eyes, but eyes are
hard to read. For the rest, his was a strong poetic nature—a
nature which half unconsciously turned ever toward the best,
away from the mean judgments of common men, and with positive loathing from the ways of worldly women. Never was peace
endangered between his mother and him, except when she
chanced to make use of some evil maxim which she thought experience had taught her, and the look her son cast upon her stung
her to the heart, making her for a moment feel as if she had
sinned what the theologians call the unpardonable sin. When
he rose and walked from the room without a word, she would
feel as if abandoned to her wickedness, and be miserable until
she saw him again. Something like a spring-cleaning would
begin and go on in her for some time after, and her eyes would
every now and then steal toward her judge with a glance of
awe and fearful apology. But, however correct Godfrey might
be in his judgment of the worldly, that judgment was less inspired by the harmonies of the universe than by the discords
that had jarred his being and the poisonous shocks he had
received in the encounter of the noble with the ignoble. There
was yet in him a profound need of redemption into the love of
the truth for the truth's sake. He had the fault of thinking
too well of himself—which who has not who thinks of himself
at all, apart from his relation to the holy force of life, within
yet beyond him ? It was the almost unconscious, assuredly the
undetected, self-approbation of the ordinarily righteous man,
the defect of whose righteousness makes him regard himself as

upright, but the virtue of whose uprightness will at length disclose to his astonished view how immeasurably short of rectitude he comes. At the age of thirty, Godfrey Wardour had not yet become so displeased with himself as to turn self-roused energy upon betterment; and until then all growth must be of doubtful result. The point on which the swift-revolving top of his thinking and feeling turned was as yet his present conscious self, as a thing that was and would be, not as a thing that had to become. Naturally the pivot had worn a socket, and such socket is sure to be a sore. His friends notwithstanding gave him credit for great imperturbability; but in such willfully undemonstrative men the evil burrows the more insidiously that it is masked by a constrained exterior.

CHAPTER V.

GODFREY AND LETTY.

GODFREY, being an Englishman, and with land of his own, could not fail to be fond of horses. For his own use he kept two—an indulgence disproportioned to his establishment; for, although precise in his tastes as to equine toilet, he did not feel justified in the keeping of a groom for their use only. Hence it came that, now and then, strap and steel, as well as hide and hoof, would get partially neglected; and his habits in the use of his horses being fitful—sometimes, it would be midnight even, when he scoured from his home, seeking the comfort of desert as well as solitary places—it is not surprising if at times, going to the stable to saddle one, he should find its gear not in the spick-and-span condition alone to his mind. It might then well happen there was no one near to help him, and there be nothing for it but to put his own hands to the work: he was too just to rouse one who might be nowise to blame, or send a maid to fetch him from field or barn, where he might be more importantly engaged.

One night meaning to start for a long ride early in the

morning, he had gone to the stable to see how things were; and, soon after, it happened that Letty, attending to some duty before going to bed, caught sight of him cleaning his stirrups: from that moment she took upon herself the silent and unsuspected supervision of the harness-room, where, when she found any part of the riding-equipments neglected, she would draw a pair of housemaid's gloves on her pretty hands, and polish away like a horse-boy.

Godfrey had begun to remark how long it was since he had found anything unfit, and to wonder at the improvement somewhere in the establishment, when, going hastily one morning, some months before the date of my narrative, into the harness-room to get a saddle, he came upon Letty, who had imagined him afield with the men: she was energetic upon a stirrup with a chain-polisher. He started back in amazement, but she only looked up and smiled.

"I shall have done in a moment, Cousin Godfrey," she said, and polished away harder than before.

"But, Letty! I can't allow you to do things like that. What on earth put it in your head? Work like that is only for horny hands."

"Your hands ain't horny, Cousin Godfrey They may be a little harder than mine—they wouldn't be much good if they weren't—but they're no fitter by nature to clean stirrups. Is it for me to sit with mine in my lap, and yours at this? I know better."

"Why shouldn't I clean my own harness, Letty, if I like?" said Godfrey, who could not help feeling pleased as well as annoyed; in this one moment Letty had come miles nearer him.

"Oh, surely! if you like, Cousin Godfrey," she answered; "but do you like?"

"Better than to see you doing it."

"But not better than I like to do it; that I am sure of. It is hands that write poetry that are not fit for work like this."

"How do you know I write poetry?" asked Godfrey, displeased, for she touched here a sensitive spot.

"Oh, don't be angry with me!" she said, letting the stirrup fall on the floor, and clasping her great wash-leather gloves together ; " I couldn't help seeing it was poetry, for it lay on the table when I went to do your room."

" Do my room, Letty ! Does my mother— ? "

" She doesn't want to make a fine lady of me, and I shouldn't like it if she did. I have no head, but I have pretty good hands. Of course, Cousin Godfrey, I didn't read a word of the poetry. I daredn't do that, however much I might have wished."

A childlike simplicity looked out of the clear eyes and sounded in the swift words of the maiden ; and, had Godfrey's heart been as hard as the stirrup she had dropped, it could not but be touched by her devotion. He was at the same time not a little puzzled how to carry himself. Letty had picked up the stirrup, and was again hard at work with it ; to take it from her, and turn her out of the saddle-room, would scarcely be a proper way of thanking her, scarcely an adequate mode of revealing his estimate of the condescension of her ladyhood. For, although Letty did make beds and chose to clean harness, Godfrey was gentleman enough not to think her less of a lady— for the moment at least—because of such doings : I will not say he had got so far on in the great doctrine concerning the washing of hands as to be able to think her *more* of a lady for thus cleaning his stirrups. But he did see that to set the fire-engine of indignant respect for womankind playing on the individual woman was not the part of the man to whose service she was humbling herself. He laid his hand on her bent head, and said :

" I ought to be a knight of the old times, Letty, to have a lady serve me so."

" You're just as good, Cousin Godfrey," she rejoined, rubbing away.

He turned from her, and left her at her work.

He had taken no real notice of the girl before—had felt next to no interest in her. Neither did he feel much now, save as owing her something beyond mere acknowledgment But was there anything now he could do for her—anything in her he could help ? He did not know. What she really was, he could not tell. She . . . . med to have just discovered ; and, as she sat polishing the stirrup, her hair shaken about her shoulders, she looked engaging ; but whether she was one he could do anything for that was worth doing, was hardly the less a question for those discoveries.

" There must be *something* in the girl ! " he said to himself —then suddenly reflected that he had never seen a book in her hand, except her prayer-book ; how *was* he to do anything for a girl like that ? For Godfrey knew no way of doing people good without the intervention of books. How could he get near one that had no taste for the quintessence of humanity ? How was he to offer her the only help he had, when she desired no such help ? " But," he continued, reflecting further, " she may have thirsted, may even now be athirst, without knowing that books are the bottles of the water of life ! " Perhaps, if he could make her drink once, she would drink again. The difficulty was, to find out what sort of spiritual drink would be most to her taste, and would most entice her to more. There must be some seeds lying cold and hard in her uncultured garden ; what water would soonest make them grow ? Not all the waters of Damascus will turn mere sand sifted of eternal winds into fruitful soil ; but Letty's soul could not be such. And then literature has seed to sow as well as water for the seed sown. Letty's foolish words about the hands that wrote poetry showed a shadow of respect for poetry—except, indeed, the girl had been but making game of him, which he was far from ready to believe, and for which, he said to himself, her face was at the time much too earnest, and her hands much too busy ; he must find out whether she had any instincts, any predilections, in the matter of poetry !

Thus pondering, he forgot all about his projected ride, and, going up to the study he had contrived for himself in the rambling roof of the ancient house, began looking along the backs of his books, in search of some suggestion of how to approach Letty ; his glance fell on a beautifully bound volume of verse —a selection of English lyrics, made with tolerable judgment— which he had bought to give, but the very color of which, every time his eye flitting along the book-shelves caught it, threw a

faint sickness over his heart, preluding the memory of old pain
and loss :

"It may as well serve some one," he said, and, taking it
down, carried it with him to the saddle-room.

Letty was not there, and the perfect order of the place
somehow made him feel she had been gone some time. He
went in search of her; she might be in the dairy.

That was the very picture of an old-fashioned English dairy
—green-shadowy, dark, dank, and cool—floored with great ir-
regular slabs, mostly of green serpentine, polished into smooth
hollows by the feet of generations of mistresses and dairy-
maids. Its only light came through a small window shaded
with shrubs and ivy, which stood open, and let in the scents of
bud and blossom, weaving a net of sweetness in the gloom,
through which, like a silver thread, shot the twittering song of
a bird, which had inherited the gathered carelessness and bliss
of a long ancestry in God's aviary.

Godfrey came softly to the door, which he found standing
ajar, and peeped in. There stood Letty, warm and bright in
the middle of the dusky coolness. She had changed her dress
since he saw her, and now, in a pink-rosebud print, with the
sleeves tucked above her elbows, was skimming the cream in a
great red-brown earthen pan. He pushed the door a little,
and, at its screech along the uneven floor, Letty's head turned
quickly on her lithe neck, and she saw Godfrey's brown face
and kind blue eyes where she had never seen them before. In
his hand glowed the book : some of the stronger light from
behind him fell on it, and it caught her eyes.

"Letty," he said, "I have just come upon this book in my
library : would you care to have it ?"

"You don't mean to keep for my own, Cousin Godfrey ?"
cried Letty, in sweet, childish fashion, letting the skimmer
dive like a coot to the bottom of the milk-pool, and hastily
wiping her hands in her apron. Her face had flushed rosy
with pleasure, and grew rosier and brighter still as she took
the rich morocco-bound thing from Godfrey's hand into her
own. Daintily she peeped within the boards, and the gilding
of the leaves responded in light to her smile.

"Poetry!" she cried, in a tone of delight. "Is it really for me, Cousin Godfrey? Do you think I shall be able to understand it?"

"You can soon settle that question for yourself," answered Godfrey, with a pleased smile—for he augured well from this reception of his gift—and turned to leave the dairy.

"But, Cousin Godfrey—please!" she called after him, "you don't give me time to thank you."

"That will do when you are certain you care for it," he returned.

"I care for it very *much!*" she replied.

"How can you say that, when you don't know yet whether you will understand it or not?" he rejoined, and closed the door.

Letty stood motionless, the book in her hand illuminating the dusk with its gold, and warming its coolness with its crimson boards and silken linings. One poem after another she read, nor knew how the time passed, until the voice of her aunt in her ears warned her to finish her skimming, and carry the jug to the pantry. But already Letty had taken a little cream off the book also, and already, between the time she entered and the time she left the dairy, had taken besides a fresh start in spiritual growth.

The next day Godfrey took an opportunity of asking her whether she had found in the book anything she liked. To his disappointment she mentioned one of the few commonplace things the collection contained—a last-century production, dull and respectable, which, surely, but for the glamour of some pleasant association, the editor would never have included. Happily, however, he bethought himself in time not to tell her the thing was worthless: such a word, instead of chipping the shell in which the girl's faculty lay dormant, would have smashed the whole egg into a miserable albuminous mass. And he was well rewarded; for, the same day, in the evening, he heard her singing gayly over her work, and listening discovered that she was singing verse after verse of one of the best ballads in the whole book. She had chosen with the fancy of pleasing Godfrey; she sang to please herself. After this discovery he set himself in earnest to the task of developing her intellectual life, and, daily almost, grew more interested in the endeavor. His main object was to make her think; and for the high purpose, chiefly but not exclusively, he employed verse.

The main obstacle to success he soon discovered to be Letty's exceeding distrust of herself. I would not be mistaken to mean that she had too little confidence in herself; of that no one can have too little. Self-distrust will only retard, while self-confidence will betray. The man ignorant in these things will answer me, "But you must have one or the other." "You must have neither," I reply. "You must follow the truth, and, in that pursuit, the less one thinks about himself, the pursuer, the better. Let him so hunger and thirst after the truth that the dim vision of it occupies all his being, and leaves no time to think of his hunger and his thirst. Self-forgetfulness in the reaching out after that which is essential to us is the healthiest of mental conditions. One has to look to his way, to his deeds, to his conduct—not to himself. In such losing of the false, or merely reflected, we find the true self. There is no harm in being stupid, so long as a man does not think himself clever; no good in being clever, if a man thinks himself so, for that is a short way to the worst stupidity. If you think yourself clever, set yourself to do something; then you will have a chance of humiliation.

With good faculties, and fine instincts, Letty was always thinking she must be wrong, just because it was she was in it —a lovely fault, no doubt, but a fault greatly impeditive to progress, and tormenting to a teacher. She got on very fairly in spite of it, however: and her devotion to Godfrey, as she felt herself growing in his sight, increased almost to a passion. Do not misunderstand me, my reader. If I say anything grows to a passion, I mean, of course, the passion of that thing, not of something else. Here I no more mean that her devotion became what in novels is commonly called love, than, if I said ambition or avarice had grown to a passion. I should mean those vices had changed to love. Godfrey Wardour was at least ten ~~~~~ ~~~~ ~~~~ ~~~~~ ~~~~~ ~~~~ ~~~~~ not a single male relative in this world—neither had she mother or sister on whom to let out her heart; while of Mrs. Wardour, who was more severe on her than on any one else, she was not a little afraid: from these causes it came that Cousin Godfrey grew and grew in Letty's imagination, until he was to her everything great and good—her idea of him naturally growing as she grew herself under his influences. To her he was the heart of wisdom, the head of knowledge, the arm of strength.

But her worship was quiet, as the worship of maiden, in whatever kind, ought to be. She knew nothing of what is called love except as a word, and from sympathy with the persons in the tales she read. Any remotest suggestion of its existence in her relation to Godfrey she would have resented as the most offensive impertinence—an accusation of impossible irreverence.

By degrees Godfrey came to understand, but then only in a measure, with what a self-refusing, impressionable nature he was dealing; and, as he saw, he became more generous toward her, more gentle and delicate in his ministration. Of necessity he grew more and more interested in her, especially after he had made the discovery that the moment she laid hold of a truth—the moment, that is, when it was no longer another's idea but her own perception—it began to sprout in her in all directions of practice. By nature she was not intellectually quick; but, because such was her character, the ratio of her progress was of necessity an increasing one.

If Godfrey had seen in his new relation to Letty a possibility of the revival of feelings he had supposed for ever extinguished, such a possibility would have borne to him purely the aspect of danger; at the mere idea of again falling in love he would have sickened with dismay; and whether or not he had any dread of such a catastrophe, certain it is that he behaved to her more as a pedagogue than a cousinly tutor, insisting on a precision in all she did that might have gone far to rouse resentment and recoil in the mind of a less childlike woman. Just as surely, notwithstanding all that, however, did the sweet girl grow into his heart: it *could* not be other-

wise. The idea of her was making a nest for itself in his soul
—what kind of a nest for long he did not know, and for long
did not think to inquire. Living thus, like an elder brother
with a much younger sister, he was more than satisfied, refusing, it may be, to regard the probability of intruding change.
But how far any man and woman may have been made capable
of loving without falling in love, can be answered only after
question has yielded to history. In the mean time, Mrs. Wardour, who would have been indignant at the notion of any
equal bond between her idolized son and her patronized cousin,
neither saw, nor heard, nor suspected anything to rouse uneasiness.

Things were thus in the old house, when the growing affection of Letty for Mary Marston took form one day in the request that she would make Thornwick the goal of her Sunday
walk. She repented, it is true, the moment she had said the
words, from dread of her aunt ; but they had been said, and
were accepted. Mary went, and the aunt difficulty had been
got over. The friendship of Godfrey also had now run into
that of the girls, and Mary's visits were continued with pleasure to all, and certainly with no little profit to herself ; for,
where the higher nature can not communicate the greater benefit, it will reap it. Her Sunday visit became to Mary the one
foraging expedition of the week—that which going to church
ought to be, and so seldom can be.

The beginning and main-stay of her spiritual life was, as
we have seen, her father, in whom she believed absolutely.
From books and sermons she had got little good ; for in neither
kind had the best come nigh her. She did very nearly her
best to obey, but without much perceiving the splendor of the
thing required, or much feeling its might upon her own eternal nature. She was as yet, in relation to the gospel, much as
the Jews were in relation to their law ; they had not yet
learned the gospel of their law, and she was yet only serving
the law of the gospel. But she was making progress, in simple
and pure virtue of her obedience. Show me the person ready
to step from any, let it be the narrowest, sect of Christian
Pharisees into a freer and holier air, and I shall look to find in

that person the one of that sect who, in the midst of its darkness and selfish worldliness, mistaken for holiness, has been living a life more obedient than the rest.

And now was sent Godfrey to her aid, a teacher himself far behind his pupil, inasmuch as he was more occupied with what he was, than what he had to become : the weakest may be sent to give the strongest saving help ; even the foolish may mediate between the wise and the wiser ; and Godfrey presented Mary to men greater than himself, whom in a short time she would understand even better than he.   Book after book he lent her —now and then gave her one of the best—introducing her, with no special intention, to much in the way of religion that was good in the way of literature as well.   Only where he delighted mainly in the literature, she delighted more in the religion.   Some of my readers will be able to imagine what it must have been to a capable, clear-thinking, warm-hearted, loving soul like Mary, hitherto in absolute ignorance of any better religious poetry than the chapel hymn-book afforded her, to make acquaintance with George Herbert, with Henry Vaughan, with Giles Fletcher, with Richard Crashaw, with old Mason, not to mention Milton, and afterward our own Father Newman and Father Faber.

But it was by no means chiefly upon such that Godfrey led the talk on the Sunday afternoons.   A lover of all truly imaginative literature, his knowledge of it was large, nor confined to that of his own country, although that alone was at present available for either of his pupils.   His seclusion from what is called the world had brought him into larger and closer contact with what is really the world.   The breakers upon reef and shore may be the ocean to some, but he who would know the ocean indeed must leave them afar, sinking into silence, and sail into wider and lonelier spaces.   Through Godfrey, Mary came to know of a land never promised, yet open—a land of whose nature even she had never dreamed—a land of the spirit, flowing with milk and honey—a land of which the fashionable world knows little more than the dwellers in the back slums, although it imagines it lying, with the kingdoms of the earth, at its feet.

As regards her feeling toward her new friend, this opener of unseen doors, the greatness of her obligation to him wrought against presumption and any possible folly. Besides, Mary was one who possessed power over her own spirit—rare gift, given to none but those who do something toward the taking of it. She was able in no small measure to order her own thoughts. Without any theory of self-rule, she yet ruled her Self. She was not one to slip about in the saddle, or let go the reins for a kick and a plunge or two. There was the thing that should be, and the thing that should not be: the thing that was reasonable, and the thing that was absurd. Add to all this, that she believed she saw in Mr. Wardour's behavior to his cousin, in the careful gentleness evident through all the severity of the schoolmaster, the presence of a deeper feeling, that might one day blossom to the bliss of her friend—and we need not wonder if Mary's heart remained calm in the very floods of its gratitude; while the truth she gathered by aid of the intercourse, enlarging her strength, enlarged likewise the composure that comes of strength. She did not even trouble herself much to show Godfrey her gratitude. We may spoil gratitude as we offer it, by insisting on its recognition. To receive honestly is the best thanks for a good thing.

Nor was Godfrey without payment for what he did: the revival of ancient benefits, a new spring-time of old flowers, and the fresh quickening of one's own soul, are the spiritual wages of every spiritual service. In giving, a man receives more than he gives, and the *more* is in proportion to the worth of the thing given.

Mary did not encourage Letty to call at the shop, because the rudeness of the Turnbulls was certain to break out on her departure, as it did one day that Godfrey, dismounting at the door, and entering the shop in quest of something for his mother, naturally shook hands with Mary over the counter. No remark was made so long as her father was in the shop, for, with all their professed contempt of him and his ways, the Turnbulls stood curiously in awe of him: no one could tell what he might or might not do, seeing they did not in the least understand him; and there were reasons for avoiding offense.

But the moment he retired, which he always did earlier than the rest, the small-arms of the enemy began to go off, causing Mary a burning cheek and indignant heart. Yet the great desire of Mr. Turnbull was a match between George and Mary, for that would, whatever might happen, secure the Marston money to the business. Their evil report Mary did not carry to her father. She scorned to trouble his lofty nature with her small annoyances ; neither could they long keep down the wellspring of her own peace, which, deeper than anger could reach, soon began to rise again fresh in her spirit, fed from that water of life which underlies all care. In a few moments it had cooled her cheek, stilled her heart, and washed the wounds of offense.

CHAPTER VI.

TOM HELMER.

When Tom Helmer's father died, his mother, who had never been able to manage him, sent him to school to get rid of him, lamented his absence till he returned, then writhed and fretted under his presence until again he went. Never thereafter did those two, mother and son, meet, whether from a separation of months or of hours, without at once tumbling into an obstinate difference. When the youth was at home, their sparring, to call it by a mild name, went on from morning to night, and sometimes almost from night to morning. Primarily, of course, the fault lay with the mother ; and things would have gone far worse, had not the youth, along with the self-will of his mother, inherited his father's good nature. At school he was a great favorite, and mostly had his own way, both with boys and masters, for, although a fool, he was a pleasant fool, clever, fond of popularity, and complaisant with everybody—except always his mother, the merest word from whom would at once rouse all the rebel in his blood. In person he was tall and loosely knit, with large joints and extremities. His face was handsome and vivacious, expressing far more than was in him to express, and giving ground for expectation such as he had never met. He was by no means an illintentioned fellow, preferred doing well and acting fairly, and neither at school nor at college had got into any serious scrape. But he had never found it imperative to reach out after his own ideal of duty. He had never been worthy the name of student, or cared much for anything beyond the amusements the universities provide so liberally, except dabbling in literature. Perhaps his only vice was self-satisfaction—which few will admit to be a vice; remonstrance never reached him : to himself he was ever in the right, judging himself only by his sentiments and vague intents, never by his actions ; that these had little correspondence never struck him, it had never even struck him that they ought to correspond. In his own eyes he did well enough, and a good deal better. (Gifted not only with fluency of speech, that crowning glory and ruin of a fool, but with plausibility of tone and demeanor, a confidence that imposed both on himself and on others, and a certain dropsical impressionableness of surface which made him seem and believe himself sympathetic, nobody could well help liking him, and it took some time to make one accept the disappointment he caused.)

He was now in his twenty-first year, at home, pretending that nothing should make him go back to Oxford, and enjoying more than ever the sport of plaguing his mother. A souldoctor might have prescribed for him a course of small-pox, to be followed by intermittent fever, with nobody to wait upon him but Mrs. Gamp : after that, his mother might have had a possible chance with him, and he with his mother. But, unhappily, he had the best of health—supreme blessing in the eyes of the fool whom it enables to be a worse fool still ; and was altogether the true son of his mother, who consoled herself for her absolute failure in his moral education with the reflection that she had reared him sound in wind and limb. Plaguing his mother, amusing himself as best he could, riding about the country on a good mare, of which he was proud, he was living in utter idleness, affording occasion for much wonder that he had never yet disgraced himself. He talked to everybody who would talk to him, and made acquaintance with anybody on the spur of the moment's whim.   He would sit on a log with a gypsy, and bamboozle him with lies made for the purpose, then thrash him for not believing them.   He called here and called there, made himself specially agreeable every-where, went to every ball and evening party to which he could get admittance in the neighborhood, and flirted with any girl who would let him.   He meant no harm, neither had done much, and was imagined by most incapable of doing any.   The strange thing to some was that he staid on in the country, and did not go to London and run up bills for his mother to pay; but the mare accounted for a good deal; and the fact that almost immediately on his late return he had seen Letty and fallen in love with her at first sight, accounted for a good deal more.   Not since then, however, had he yet been able to meet her so as only to speak to her; for Thornwick was one of the few houses of the middle class in the neighborhood where he was not encouraged to show himself.   He was constantly, therefore, on the watch for a chance of seeing her, and every Sunday went to church in that same hope and no other.   But Letty knew nothing of the favor in which she stood with him; for, although Tom had, as we have heard, confessed to her friend Mary Marston his admiration of her, Mary had far too much good sense to make herself his ally in the matter.

CHAPTER VII.

DURNMELLING.

IN the autumn, Mr. Mortimer of Durnmelling resolved to give a harvest-home to his tenants, and under the protection of the occasion to invite also a good many of his neighbors and of the townsfolk of Testbridge, whom he could not well ask to dinner: there happened to be a political expediency for some-thing of the sort: America is not the only country in which ambition opens the door to mean doings on the part of such as count themselves gentlemen. Not a few on whom Lady Margaret had never called, and whom she would never in any way acknowledge again, were invited, nor did the knowledge of what it meant cause many of them to decline the questionable honor—which fact carried in it the best justification of which the meanness and insult were capable. Mrs Wardour accepted for herself and Letty; but in their case Lady Margaret did call, and in person give the invitation. Godfrey positively refused to accompany them. He would not be patronized, he said; "—and by an inferior," he added to himself.

Mr. Mortimer was the illiterate son of a literary father who had reaped both money and fame. The son spent the former, on the strength of the latter married an earl's daughter, and thereupon began to embody in his own behavior his ideas of how a nobleman ought to carry himself; whence, from being only a small, he became an objectionable man, and failed of being amusing by making himself offensive. He had never manifested the least approach to neighborliness with Godfrey, although their houses were almost within a stone's throw of each other. Had Wardour been an ordinary farmer, of whose presuming on the acquaintance there could have been no danger, Mortimer would doubtless have behaved differently; but as Wardour had some pretensions—namely, old family, a small, though indeed *very* small, property of his own, a university education, good horses, and the habits and manners of a gentleman—the men scarcely even saluted when they met. The Mortimer ladies, indeed, had more than once remarked—but it was in solemn silence, each to herself only—how well the man sat, and how easily he handled the hunter he always rode; but not once until now had so much as a greeting passed between them and Mrs. Wardour. It was not therefore wonderful that Godfrey should not choose to accept their invitation. Finding, however, that his mother was distressed at having to go to the gathering without him, and far more exercised in her mind than was needful as to what would be thought of his absence, and what excuse it would be becoming to make, he resolved to go to London a day or two before the event, and pay a long-promised visit to a clerical friend

The relative situation of the houses—I mean the stone-and-lime houses—of Durnmelling and Thornwick, was curious; and that they had at one time formed part of the same property might have suggested itself to any beholder. Durnmelling was built by an ancestor of Godfrey's, who, forsaking the old nest for the new, had allowed Thornwick to sink into a mere farmhouse, in which condition it had afterward become the sole shelter of the withered fortunes of the Wardours. In the hands of Godfrey's father, by a continuity of judicious cares, and a succession of partial resurrections, it had been restored to something like its original modest dignity. Durnmelling, too, had in part sunk into ruin, and had been but partially recovered from it; still, it swelled important beside its antecedent Thornwick. Nothing but a deep ha-ha separated the two houses, of which the older and smaller occupied the higher ground. Between it and the ha-ha was nothing but grass—in front of the house fine enough and well enough kept to be called lawn, had not Godfrey's pride refused the word. On the lower, the Durnmelling side of the fence, were trees, shrubbery, and out-houses—the chimney of one of which, the laundry, gave great offense to Mrs. Wardour, when, as she said, wind and wash came together. But, although they stood so near, there was no lawful means of communication between the houses except the road; and the mile that implied was seldom indeed passed by any of the unneighborly neighbors.

The father of Lady Margaret would at one time have purchased Thornwick at twice its value; but the present owner could not have bought it at half its worth. He had of late been losing money heavily—whence, in part, arose that anxiety of Lady Margaret's not to keep Mr. Redmain fretting for his lunch.

The house of Durnmelling, new compared with that of Thornwick, was yet, as I have indicated, old enough to have passed also through vicissitudes, and a large portion of the original structure had for many years been nothing better than a ruin. Only a portion of one side of its huge square was occupied by the family, and the rest of that side was not habitable. Lady Margaret, of an ancient stock, had gathered

from it only pride, not reverence; therefore, while she valued
the old, she neglected it; and what money she and her husband at one time spent upon the house, was devoted to addition
and ornamentation, nowise to preservation or restoration. They
had enlarged both dining-room and drawing-rooms to twice
their former size, when half the expense, with a few trees from
a certain outlying oak-plantation of their own, would have
given them a room fit for a regal assembly. For, constituting
a portion of the same front in which they lived, lay roofless,
open to every wind that blew, its paved floor now and then in
winter covered with snow—an ancient hall, whose massy south
wall was pierced by three lovely windows, narrow and lofty,
with simple, gracious tracery in their pointed heads. This hall
connected the habitable portion of the house with another
part, less ruinous than itself, but containing only a few rooms
in occasional use for household purposes, or, upon necessity,
for quite inferior lodgment. It was a glorious ruin, of nearly
a hundred feet in length, and about half that in width, the
walls entire, and broad enough to walk round upon in safety.
Their top was accessible from a tower, which formed part of
the less ruinous portion, and contained the stair and some
small rooms.

Once, the hall was fair with portraits and armor and arms,
with fire and lights, and state and merriment; now the sculp-
tured chimney lay open to the weather, and the sweeping
winds had made its smooth hearthstone clean as if fire had
never been there. Its floor was covered with large flags, a
little broken: these, in prospect of the coming entertainment,
a few workmen were leveling, patching, replacing. For the
tables were to be set here, and here there was to be dancing
after the meal.

It was Miss Yolland's idea, and to her was committed the
responsibility of its preparation and adornment for the occasion, in which Hesper gave her active assistance. With colored
blankets, with carpets, with a few pieces of old tapestry, and
a quantity of old curtains, mostly of chintz, excellent in hues
and design, all cunningly arranged for as much of harmony as
could be had, they contrived to clothe the walls to the height

of six or eight feet, and so gave the weather-beaten skeleton an air of hospitable preparation and respectful reception.

The day and the hour arrived. It was a hot autumnal afternoon. Borne in all sorts of vehicles, from a carriage and pair to a taxed cart, the guests kept coming. As they came, they mostly scattered about the place. Some loitered on the lawn by the flower-beds and the fountain; some visited the stables and the home-farm, with its cow-houses and dairy and piggeries; some the neglected greenhouses, and some the equally neglected old-fashioned alleys, with their clipped yews and their moss-grown statues. No one belonging to the house was anywhere visible to receive them, until the great bell at length summoned them to the plentiful meal spread in the ruined hall. "The hospitality of some people has no roof to it," Godfrey said, when he heard of the preparations. "Ten people will give you a dinner, for one who will offer you a bed and a breakfast."

Then at last their host made his appearance, and took the head of the table : the ladies, he said, were to have the honor of joining the company afterward. They were at the time—but this he did not say—giving another stratum of society a less ponderous, but yet tolerably substantial, refreshment in the dining-room.

By the time the eating and drinking were nearly over, the shades of evening had gathered; but even then some few of the farmers, capable only of drinking, grumbled at having their potations interrupted for the dancers. These were presently joined by the company from the house, and the great hall was crowded.

Much to her chagrin, Mrs. Wardour had a severe headache, occasioned by her working half the night at her dress, and was compelled to remain at home. But she allowed Letty to go without her, which she would not have done had she not been so anxious to have news of what she could not lift her head to see : she sent her with an old servant—herself one of the invited guests—to gather and report. The dancing had begun before they reached the hall.

Tom Helmer had arrived among the first, and had joined

the tenants in their feast, faring well, and making friends, such as he knew how to make, with everybody in his vicinity. When the tables were removed, and the rest of the company began to come in, he went about searching anxiously for Letty's sweet face, but it did not appear; and, when she did arrive, she stole in without his seeing her, and stood mingled with the crowd about the door.

It was a pleasant sight that met her eyes The wide space was gayly illuminated with colored lamps, disposed on every shelf, and in every crevice of the walls, some of them gleaming like glow-worms out of mere holes; while candles in sconces, and lamps on the window-sills and wherever they could stand, gave a light the more pleasing that it was not brilliant. Over-head, the night-sky was spangled with clear pulsing stars, afloat in a limpid blue, vast even to awfulness in the eyes of such— were any such there ?—as say to themselves that to those worlds also were they born Outside, it was dark, save where the light streamed from the great windows far into the night. The moon was not yet up; she would rise in good time to see the scattering guests to their homes.

Tom's heart had been sinking, for he could see Letty no-where. Now at last, he had been saying to himself all the day, had come his chance! and his chance seemed but to mock him. More than any girl he had ever seen, had Letty moved him— perhaps because she was more unlike his mother He knew nothing, it is true, or next to nothing, of her nature; but that was of little consequence to one who knew nothing, and never troubled himself to know anything, of his own Was he doomed never to come near his idol ?—Ah, there she wa ! Yes; it was she—all but lost in a humble group near the door ' His foolish heart—not foolish in that—gave a great bound, as if it would leap to her where she stood. She was dressed in white muslin, from which her white throat rose warm and soft. Her head was bent forward, and a gentle dissolved smile was over all her face, as with loveliest eyes she watched eagerly the motions of the dance, and her ears drank in the music of the yeomanry band. He seized the first opportunity of getting nearer to l   that did not trouble Tom. Even in a more ceremonious assembly, that would never have abashed him ; and here there was little form, and much freedom. He had, besides, confidence in his own carriage and manners—which, indeed, were those of a gentleman—and knew himself not likely to repel by his approach.

Mr. Mortimer had opened the dancing by leading out the wife of his principal tenant, a handsome matron, whose behavior and expression were such as to give a safe, home-like feeling to the shy and doubtful of the company. But Tom knew better than injure his chance by precipitation : he would wait until the dancing was more general, and the impulse to movement stronger, and then offer himself. He stood therefore near Letty for some little time, talking to everybody, and making himself agreeable, as was his wont, all round ; then at last, as if he had just caught sight of her, walked up to her where she stood flushed and eager, and asked her to favor him with her hand in the next dance.

By this time Letty had got familiar with his presence, had recalled her former meeting with him, had heard his name spoken by not a few who evidently liked him, and was quite pleased when he asked her to dance with him.

In the dance, nothing but commonplaces passed between them ; but Tom had a certain pleasant way of his own in saying the commonest, emptiest things—an off-hand, glancing, skimming, swallow-like way of brushing and leaving a thing, as if he " could an' if he would," which made it seem for the moment as if he had said something : were his companion capable of discovering the illusion, there was no time ; Tom was instantly away, carrying him or her with him to something else. But there was better than this—there was poetry, more than one element of it, in Tom. In the presence of a girl that pleased him, there would rise in him a poetic atmosphere, full of a rainbow kind of glamour, which, first possessing himself, passed out from him and called up a similar atmosphere, a similar glamour, about many of the girls he talked to. This he could no more help than the grass can help smelling sweet after the rain.

Tom was a finely projected, well-built, unfinished, barely

furnished house, with its great central room empty, where the devil, coming and going at his pleasure, had not yet begun to make any great racket. There might be endless embryonic evil in him, but Letty was aware of no repellent atmosphere about him, and did not shrink from his advances. He pleased her, and why should she not be pleased with him? Was it a fault to be easily pleased? The truer and sweeter any human self, the readier is it to be pleased with another self—save, indeed, something in it grate on the moral sense: that jars through the whole harmonious hypostasy. To Tom, therefore, Letty responded with smiles and pleasant words, even grateful to such a fine youth for taking notice of her small self.

The sun had set in a bank of cloud, which, as if he had been a lump of leaven to it, immediately began to swell and rise, and now hung dark and thick over the still, warm night. Even the farmers were unobservant of the change: their crops were all in, they had eaten and drunk heartily, and were merry, looking on or sharing in the multiform movement, their eyes filled with light and color.

Suddenly came a torrent-sound in the air, heard of few and heeded by none, and straight into the hall rushed upon the gay company a deluge of rain, mingled with large, half-melted hailstones. In a moment or two scarce a light was left burning, except those in the holes and recesses of the walls. The merry-makers scattered like flies—into the house, into the tower, into the sheds and stables in the court behind, under the trees in front—anywhere out of the hall, where shelter was none from the perpendicular, abandoned down-pour.

At that moment, Letty was dancing with Tom, and her hand happened to be in his. He clasped it tight, and, as quickly as the crowd and the confusion of shelter-seeking would permit, led her to the door of the tower already mentioned. But many had run in the same direction, and already its lower story and stair were crowded with refugees—the elder bemoaning the sudden change, and folding tight around them what poor wraps they were fortunate enough to have retained; the younger merrier than ever, notwithstanding the colder's that now poked their spirit-arms hither and thither through the openings of the half-ruinous building : to them even the destruction of their finery was but added cause of laughter. But a few minutes before, its freshness had been a keen pleasure to them, brightening their consciousness with a rare feeling of perfection ; now crushed and rumpled, soiled and wet and torn, it was still fuel to the fire of gayety. But Tom did not stay among them. He knew the place well ; having a turn for scrambling, he had been all over it many a time. On through the crowd, he led Letty up the stair to the first floor. Even here were a few couples talking and laughing in the dark. With a warning, by no means unnecessary, to mind where they stepped, for the floors were bad, he passed on to the next stair.

"Let us stop here, Mr. Helmer," said Letty. "There is plenty of room here."

"I want to show you something," answered Tom. "You need not be frightened. I know every nook of the place."

"I am not frightened," said Letty, and made no further objection.

At the top of that stair they entered a straight passage, in the middle of which was a faint glimmer of light from an oval aperture in the side of it. Thither Tom led Letty, and told her to look through. She did so.

Beneath lay the great gulf, wide and deep, of the hall they had just left. This was the little window, high in its gable, through which, in far-away times, the lord or lady of the mansion could oversee at will whatever went on below.

The rain had ceased as suddenly as it came on, and already lights were moving about in the darkness of the abyss—one, and another, and another, was searching for something lost in the hurry of the scattering. It was a waste and dismal show. Neither of them had read Dante ; but Letty may have thought of the hall of Belshazzar, the night after the hand-haunted revel, when the Medes had had their will ; for she had but lately read the story. A strange fear came upon her, and she drew back with a shudder.

"Are you cold ?" said Tom. "Of course you must be,

with nothing but that thin muslin ! Shall I run down and get you a shawl ?"

"Oh, no ! do not leave me, please. It's not that." answered Letty. "I don't mind the wind a bit ; it's rather pleasant. It's only that the look of the place makes me miserable, I think. It looks as if no one had danced there for a hundred years."

"Neither any one has, I suppose, till to-night." said Tom. "What a fine place it would be if only it had a roof to it ! I can't think how any one can live beside it and leave it like that !"

But Tom lived a good deal closer to a worse ruin, and never spent a thought on it.

Letty shivered again.

"I'm quite ashamed of myself," she said, trying to speak cheerfully. "I can't think why I should feel like this—just as if something dreadful were watching me ! I'll go home, Mr. Helmer."

"It will be much the safest thing to do : I fear you have indeed caught cold." replied Tom, rejoiced at the chance of accompanying her. "I shall be delighted to see you safe."

"There is not the least occasion for that, thank you," answered Letty. "I have an old servant of my aunt's with me —somewhere about the place. The storm is quite over now : I will go and find her."

Tom made no objection, but helped her down the dark stair, hoping, however, the servant might not be found.

As they went, Letty seemed to herself to be walking in some old dream of change and desertion. The tower was empty as a monument, not a trace of the crowd left, which a few minutes before had thronged it. The wind had risen in earnest now, and was rushing about, like a cold wild ghost, through every cranny of the desolate place. Had Letty, when she reached the bottom of the stairs, found herself on the rocks of the seashore, with the waves dashing up against them, she would only have said to herself, "I knew I was in a dream !" But the wind having blown away the hail-cloud, the stars were again sh'   .   looking searchers were still there ; the rest had scattered like the gnats. A few were already at home ; some were harnessing their horses to go, nor would wait for the man in the moon to light his lantern ; some were already trudging on foot through the dark. Hesper and Miss Yolland were talking to two or three friends in the drawing-room ; Lady Margaret was in her boudoir, and Mr. Mortimer smoking a cigar in his study.

Nowhere could Letty find Susan. She was in the farmer's kitchen behind. Tom suspected as much, but was far from hinting the possibility. Letty found her cloak, which she had left in the hall, soaked with rain, and thought it prudent to go home at once, nor prosecute her search for Susan further. She accepted, therefore, Tom's renewed offer of his company.

They were just leaving the hall, when a thought came to Letty : the moon suddenly appearing above the horizon had put it in her head.

"Oh," she cried, "I know quite a short way home !" and, without waiting any response from her companion, she turned, and led him in an opposite direction, round, namely, by the back of the court, into a field. There she made for a huge oak, which gloomed in the moonlight by the sunk fence parting the grounds. In the slow strength of its growth, by the rounding of its bole, and the spreading of its roots, it had so rent and crumbled the wall as to make through it a little ravine, leading to the top of the ha-ha. When they reached it, before even Tom saw it, Letty turned from him, and was up in a moment. At the top she turned to bid him good night, but there he was, close behind her, insisting on seeing her safe to the house.

"Is this the way you always come ?" asked Tom.

"I never was on Durnmelling land before," answered Letty.

"How did you find the short-cut, then ?" he asked. "It certainly does not look as if it were much used."

"Of course not," replied Letty. "There is no communication between Durnmelling and Thornwick now. It was all ours once, though, Cousin Godfrey says. Did you notice how the great oak sends its biggest arm over our field ?"

"Yes."

"Well, I often sit there under it, when I want to learn my

lesson, and can't rest in the house; and that's how I know of the crack in the ha-ha."

She said it in absolute innocence, but Tom laid it up in his mind.

"Are you at lessons still?" he said. "Have you a governess?"

"No," she answered, in a tone of amusement. "But Cousin Godfrey teaches me many things."

This made Tom thoughtful; and little more had been said, when they reached the gate of the yard behind the house, and she would not let him go a step farther.

CHAPTER VIII.

THE OAK.

In the morning, as she narrated the events of the evening, she told her aunt of the acquaintance she had made, and that he had seen her home. This information did not please the old lady, as, indeed, without knowing any reason, Letty had expected. Mrs. Wardour knew all about Tom's mother, or thought she did, and knew little good, she knew also that, although her son was a general favorite, her own son had a very poor opinion of him. On these grounds, and without a thought of injustice to Letty, she sharply rebuked the poor girl for allowing such a fellow to pay her any attention, and declared that, if ever she permitted him so much as to speak to her again, she would do something which she left in a cloud of vaguest suggestion.

Letty made no reply. She was hurt. Nor was it any wonder if she judged this judgment of Tom by the injustice of the judge to herself. It was of no consequence to her, she said to herself, whether she spoke to him again or not; but had any one the right to compel another to behave rudely? Only what did it matter, since there was so little chance of her eve   nd disappointed, and, after the merrymaking of the night before, the household work was irksome. But she would soon have got over both weariness and tedium had her aunt been kind. It is true, she did not again refer to Tom, taking it for granted that he was done with ; but all day she kept driving Letty from one thing to another, nor was once satisfied with anything she did, called her even an ungrateful girl, and, before evening, had rendered her more tired, mortified, and dispirited, than she had ever been in her life.

But the tormentor was no demon ; she was only doing what all of us have often done, and ought to be heartily ashamed of : she was only emptying her fountain of bitter water. Oppressed with the dregs of her headache, wretched because of her son's absence, who had not been a night from home for years, annoyed that she had spent time and money in preparation for nothing, she had allowed the said cistern to fill to overflowing, and upon Letty it overflowed like a small deluge. Like some of the rest of us, she never reflected how balefully her evil mood might operate ; and that all things work for good in the end, will not cover those by whom come the offenses. Another night's rest, it is true, sent the evil mood to sleep again for a time, but did not exorcise it ; for there are demons that go not out without prayer, and a bad temper is one of them—a demon as contemptible, mean-spirited, and unjust, as any in the peerage of hell—much petted, nevertheless, and excused, by us poor lunatics who are possessed by him. Mrs. Wardour was a lady, as the ladies of this world go, but a poor lady for the kingdom of heaven : I should wonder much if she ranked as more than a very common woman there.

The next day all was quiet ; and a visit paid Mrs. Wardour by a favorite sister whom she had not seen for months, set Letty at such liberty as she seldom had. In the afternoon she took the book Godfrey had given her, in which he had set her one of Milton's smaller poems to study, and sought the shadow of the Durnmelling oak.

It was a lovely autumn day, the sun glorious as ever in the memory of Abraham, or the author of Job, or the builder

of the scaled pyramid at Sakkara. But there was a keen-
ness in the air notwithstanding, which made Letty feel a
little sad without knowing why, as she seated herself to the
task Cousin Godfrey had set her. She, as well as his mother,
heartily wished he were home. She was afraid of him, it is
true; but in how different a way from that in which she
was afraid of his mother! His absence did not make her feel
free, and to escape from his mother was sometimes the whole
desire of her day.

She was trying hard, not altogether successfully, to fix her
attention on her task, when a yellow leaf dropped on the very
line she was poring over. Thinking how soon the trees would
be bare once more, she brushed the leaf away, and resumed her
lesson.

"To fill thy odorous lamp with deeds of light,"

she had just read once more, when down fell a second tree-leaf
on the book-leaf. Again she brushed it away, and read to the
end of the sonnet:

"Hast gained thy entrance, virgin wise and pure."

What Letty's thoughts about the sonnet were, I can not
tell: how fix thought indefinite in words defined? But her
angel might well have thought what a weary road she had to
walk before she gained that entrance. But for all of us the
road *has* to be walked, every step, and the uttermost farthing
paid. The gate will open wide to welcome us, but it will not
come to meet us. Neither is it any use to turn aside; it only
makes the road longer and harder.

Down on the same spot fell the third leaf. Letty looked
up. There was a man in the tree over her head. She started
to her feet. At the same moment, he dropped on the ground
beside her, lifting his hat as coolly as if he had met her on the
road. Her heart seemed to stand still with fright. She stood
silent, with white lips parted.

"I hope I haven't frightened you," said Tom. "Do forgive me," he added, becoming more aware of the perturbation
he had caused her. "You were so kind to me the other

night, I could not help wanting to see you again. I had no idea the sight of me would terrify you so."

"You gave me such a start!" gasped Letty, with her hand pressed on her heart.

"I was afraid of it," answered Tom; "but what could I do? I was certain, if you saw me coming, you would run away."

"Why should you think that?" asked Letty, a faint color rising in her cheek.

"Because," answered Tom, "I was sure they would be telling you all manner of things against me. But there is no harm in me—really, Miss Lovel—nothing, that is, worth mentioning."

"I am sure there isn't," said Letty; and then there was a pause.

"What book are you reading, may I ask?" said Tom.

Letty had now remembered her aunt's injunctions and threats; but, partly from a kind of paralysis caused by his coolness, partly from its being impossible to her nature to be curt with any one with whom she was not angry, partly from mere lack of presence of mind, not knowing what to do, yet feeling she ought to run to the house, what should she do but drop down again on the very spot whence she had been scared! Instantly Tom threw himself on the grass at her feet, and there lay, looking up at her with eyes of humble admiration.

Confused and troubled, she began to turn over the leaves of her book. She supposed afterward she must have asked him why he stared at her so, for the next thing she remembered was hearing him say:

"I can't help it. You are so lovely!"

"Please don't talk such nonsense to me," she rejoined. "I am not lovely, and I know it. What is not true can not please anybody."

She spoke a little angrily now.

"I speak the truth," said Tom, quietly and earnestly. "Why should you think I do not?"

"Because nobody ever said so before."

"Then it is quite time somebody should say so," returned

Tom, changing his tone. "It may be a painful fact, but even ladies ought to be told the truth, and learn to bear it. To say you are not lovely would be a downright lie."

"I wish you wouldn't talk to me about myself!" said Letty, feeling confused and improper, but not altogether displeased that it was possible for such a mistake to be made. "I don't want to hear about myself. It makes me so uncomfortable! I am sure it isn't right: is it, now, Mr. Helmer?"

As she ended, the tears rose in her eyes, partly from unanalyzed uneasiness at the position in which she found herself and the turn the talk had taken, partly from the discomfort of conscious disobedience. But still she did not move.

"I am very sorry if I have vexed you," said Tom, seeing her evident trouble. "I can't think how I've done it. I know I didn't mean to; and I promise you not to say a word of the kind again—if I can help it. But tell me, Letty," he went on again, changing in tone and look and manner, and calling her by her name with such simplicity that she never even noticed it, "do tell me what you are reading, and that will keep me from *talking* about you—not from—the other thing, you know."

"There!" said Letty, almost crossly, handing him her book, and pointing to the sonnet, as she rose to go.

Tom took the book, and sprang to his feet. He had never read the poem, for Milton had not been one of his masters. He stood devouring it. He was doing his best to lay hold of it quickly, for there Letty stood, with her hand held out to take the book again, ready upon its restoration to go at once. Silent and motionless, to all appearance unhasting, he read and reread. Letty was restless, and growing quite impatient; but still Tom read, a smile slow-spreading from his eyes over his face; he was taking possession of the poem, he would have said. But the shades and kinds and degrees of possession are innumerable; and not until we downright love a thing, can we *know* we understand it, or rightly call it our own; Tom only admired this one; it was all he was capable of in regard to such at present. Had the whim for acquainting himself with it seized him ᵇ· · · ᵗ ᵇᵉ · · ᵗ ᵗⁱ·ᵉ ·ⁱᵗʰ a

far more superficial interview ; but the presence of the girl,
with those eyes fixed on him as he read—his mind's eye saw
them—was for the moment an enlargement of his being, whose
phase to himself was a consciousness of ignorance.

"It is a beautiful poem," he said at last, quite honestly ;
and, raising his eyes, he looked straight in hers.   There is
hardly a limit to the knowledge and sympathy a man may have
in respect of the finest things, and yet be a fool.   Sympathy is
not harmony.   A man may be a poet even, and speak with the
tongue of an angel, and yet be a very bad fool.

"I am sure it must be a beautiful poem," said Letty ; "but
I have hardly got a hold of it yet."   And she stretched her
hand a little farther, as if to proceed with its appropriation.

But Tom was not yet prepared to part with the book.   He
proceeded instead, in fluent speech and not inappropriate language, to set forth, not the power of the poem—that he both
took and left as a matter of course—but the beauty of those
phrases, and the turns of those expressions, which particularly
pleased him—nor failing to remark that, according to the strict
laws of English verse, there was in it one bad rhyme.

That point Letty begged him to explain, thus leading Tom
to an exposition of the laws of rhyme, in which, as far as English was concerned, he happened to be something of an expert,
partly from an early habit of scribbling in ladies' albums.
About these surface affairs, Godfrey, understanding them better and valuing them more than Tom, had yet taught Letty nothing, judging it premature to teach polishing before carving ;
and hence this little display of knowledge on the part of Tom
impressed Letty more than was adequate—so much, indeed,
that she began to regard him as a sage, and a compeer of her
cousin Godfrey.   Question followed question, and answer followed answer, Letty feeling all the time she *must* go, yet
standing and standing, like one in a dream, who thinks he can
not, and certainly does not break its spell—for in the act only
is the ability and the deed born.   Besides, was she to go away
and leave her beautiful book in his hand ?   What would Godfrey think if she did ?   Again and again she stretched out her
own to take it, but, although he saw the motion, he held on to

the book as to his best anchor, hurriedly turned its leaves by
fits, and searching for something more to his mind than anything of Milton's. Suddenly his face brightened.

"Ah !" he said—and remained a moment silent, reading.
"I don't wonder," he resumed, "at your admiration of Milton.
He's very grand, of course, and very musical, too ; but one can't
be listening to an organ always. Not that I prefer merry music ; that must be inferior, for the tone of all the beauty in
the world is sad." Much Tom Helmer knew of beauty or sadness either ! but ignorance is no reason with a fool for holding
his tongue. "But there is the violin, now !—that can be as
sad as any organ, without being so ponderous. Hear this, now !
This is the violin after the organ—played as only a master can '"

With this preamble, he read a song of Shelley's, and read it
well, for he had a good ear for rhythm and cadence, and prided
himself on his reading of poetry.

Now the path to Letty's heart through her intellect was
neither open nor well trodden ; but the song in question was a
winged one, and flew straight thither ; there was something in
the tone of it that suited the pitch of her spirit-chamber.
And, if Letty's heart was not easily found, it was the readier to
confess itself when found. Her eyes filled with tears, and
through those tears Tom looked large and injured. "He must
be a poet himself to read poetry like that !" she said to herself,
and felt thoroughly assured that her aunt had wronged him
greatly. "Some people scorn poetry like sin," she said again.
"I used myself to think it was only for children, until Cousin
Godfrey taught me differently."

As thus her thoughts went on interweaving themselves with
the music, all at once the song came to an end. Tom closed
the book, handed it to her, said, "Good morning, Miss Lovel,"
and ran down the rent in the ha-ha ; and, before Letty could
come to herself, she heard the soft thunder of hoofs on the
grass. She ran to the edge, and, looking over, saw Tom on his
bay mare, at full gallop across the field. She watched him as
he neared the hedge and ditch that bounded it, saw him go
flying over, and lost sight of him behind a hazel-copse. Slowly,
then, she turned, and slowly she went back to the house and

up to her room, vaguely aware that a wind had begun to blow in her atmosphere, although only the sound of it had yet reached her.

CHAPTER IX.

CONFUSION.

THEN first, and from that moment, Letty's troubles began. Up to this point neither she herself nor another could array troublous accusation or uneasy thought against her ; and now she began to feel like a very target, which exists but to receive the piercing of arrows. At first sight, and if we do not look a long way ahead of what people stupidly regard as the end when it is only an horizon, it seems hard that so much we call evil, and so much that *is* evil, should result from that unavoidable, blameless, foreordained, preconstituted, and essential attraction which is the law of nature, that is the will of God, between man and woman. Even if Letty had fallen in love with Tom at first sight, who dares have the assurance to blame her ? who will dare to say that Tom was blameworthy in seeking the society and friendship, even the love, of a woman whom in all sincerity he admired, or for using his wits to get into her presence, and detain her a little in his company ? Reasons there are, infinitely deeper than any philosopher has yet fathomed, or is likely to fathom, why a youth such as he—foolish, indeed, but not foolish in this—and a sweet and blameless girl such as Letty, should exchange regards of admiration and wonder. That which thus moves them, and goes on to draw them closer and closer, comes with them from the very source of their being, and is as reverend as it is lovely, rooted in all the gentle potencies and sweet glories of creation, and not unworthily watered with all the tears of agony and ecstasy shed by lovers since the creation of the world. What it is, I can not tell ; I only know it is *not* that which the young fool calls it, still less that which the old sinner thinks it.

As to Letty's disobedience of her aunt's extravagant orders concerning Tom, I must leave that to the judgment of the just, reminding them that she was taken by surprise, and that, besides, it was next to impossible to obey them. But Letty found herself very uncomfortable, because there now was that to be known of her, the knowledge of which would highly displease her aunt—for which very reason, if for no other, ought she not to tell her all? On the other hand, when she recalled how unkindly, how unjustly her aunt had spoken, when she confessed her new acquaintance, it became to her a question whether in very deed she *must* tell her all that had passed that afternoon. There was no smallest hope of any recognition of the act, surely more hard than incumbent, but severity and unreason; *must* she let the thing out of her hands, and yield herself a helpless prey—and that for good to none? Concerning Mrs. Wardour, she reasoned justly: she who is even once unjust can not complain if the like is expected of her again.

But, supposing it remained Letty's duty to acquaint her aunt with what had taken place, and not forgetting that, as one of the old people, I have to render account of the young that come after me, and must be careful over their lovely dignities and fair duties, I yet make haste to assert that the old people, who make it hard for the young people to do right, may be twice as much to blame as those whom they arraign for a concealment whose very heart is the dread of their known selfishness, fierceness, and injustice. If children have to obey their parents or guardians, those parents and guardians are over them in the name of God, and they must look to it: if in the name of God they act the devil, that will not prove a light thing for their answer. The causing of the little ones to offend hangs a fearful woe about the neck of the causer. It were a hard, as well as a needless task, seeing there is One who judges, to set forth how far the child is to blame as toward the parent, where the parent first of all is utterly wrong, yea out of true relation, toward the child. Not, therefore, is the child free; obligation remains—modified, it may be, but how difficult, alas, to fulfill! And, whether Letty and such as act like her are *excusable* or not in keeping attentions paid them a seeret, this sorrow for the good ones of them certainly remains, that, next to a crime, a secret is the heaviest as well as the most awkward of burdens to carry. It has to be carried always, and all about. From morning to night it hurts in tenderest parts, and from night to morning hurts everywhere. At any expense, let there be openness. Take courage, my child, and speak out. Dare to speak, I say, and that will give you strength to resist, should disobedience become a duty. Letty's first false step was here : she said to herself *I can not,* and did not. She lacked courage—a want in her case not much to be wondered at, but much to be deplored, for courage of the true sort is just as needful to the character of a woman as of a man. Had she spoken, she might have heard true things of Tom, sufficient so to alter her opinion of him as, at this early stage of their intercourse, to alter the *set* of her feelings, which now was straight for him. It may be such an exercise of courage would have rendered the troubles that were now to follow unnecessary to her development. For lack of it, she went about from that time with the haunting consciousness that she was one who might be found out ; that she was guilty of what would go a good way to justify the hard words she had so resented. Already the secret had begun to work conscious woe. She contrived, however, to quiet herself a little with the idea, rather than the resolve, that, as soon as Godfrey came home, she would tell him all, confessing, too, that she had not the courage to tell his mother. She was sure, she said to herself, he would forgive her, would set her at peace with herself, and be unfair neither to Mr. Helmer nor to her. In the mean time she would take care—and this was a real resolve, not a mere act contemplated in the future—not to go where she might meet him again. Nor was the resolve the less genuine that, with the very making of it, rose the memory of that delightful hour more enticing than ever. How beautifully, and with what feeling, he read the lovely song ! With what appreciation had he not expounded Milton's beautiful poem ! Not yet was she capable of bethinking herself that it was but on this phrase and on that he had dwelt, on this and on that line and rhythm, enforcing their loveliness of sound and shape ; while the poem, the really important thing, the drift of the whole—it was her own heart and conscience that revealed that to her, not the exposition of one who at best could understand it only with his brain. She kept to her resolve, nevertheless ; and, although Tom, leaving his horse now here now there, to avoid attracting attention, almost every day visited the oak, he looked in vain for the light of her approach. Disappointment increased his longing : what would he not have given to see once more one of those exquisite smiles break out in its perfect blossom ! He kept going and going—haunted the oak, sure of some blessed chance at last. It was the first time in his life he had followed one idea for a whole fortnight.

At length Godfrey came. But, although all the time he was away Letty had retained and contemplated with tolerable calmness the idea of making her confession to him, the moment she saw him she felt such confession impossible. It was a sad discovery to her. Hitherto Godfrey, and especially of late, had been the chief source of the peace and interest of her life, that portion of her life, namely, to which all the rest of it looked as its sky, its overhanging betterness—and now she felt before him like a culprit : she had done what he might be displeased with. Nay, would that were all ! for she felt like a hypocrite : she had done that which she could not confess. Again and again, while Godfrey was away, she had flattered herself that the help the objectionable Tom had given her with her task would at once recommend him to Godfrey's favorable regard ; but now that she looked in Godfrey's face, she was aware—she did not know why, but she was aware it would not be so. Besides, she plainly saw that the same fact would, almost of necessity, lead him to imagine there had been much more between them than was the case ; and she argued with herself, that, now there was nothing, now that everything was over, it would be a pity if, because of what she could not help, and what would never be again, there should arise anything, however small, of a misunderstanding between her cousin Godfrey and her.

The moment Godfrey saw her, he knew that something was the matter ; but there had been that going on in him which put him on a false track for the explanation. Scarcely had he, on his departure for London, turned his back on Thornwick, ere he found he was leaving one whom yet he could not leave behind him. Every hour of his absence he found his thoughts with the sweet face and ministering hands of his humble pupil. Therewith, however, it was nowise revealed to him that he was in love with her. He thought of her only as his younger sister, loving, clinging, obedient. So dear was she to him, he thought, that he would rejoice to secure her happiness at any cost to himself. *Any* cost? he asked—and reflected. Yes, he answered himself—even the cost of giving her to a better man. The thing was sure to come, he thought—nor thought without a keen pang, scarcely eased by the dignity of the self-denial that would yield her with a smile. But such a crisis was far away, and there was no necessity for now contemplating it. Indeed, there was no *certainty* it would ever arrive; it was only a possibility. The child was not beautiful, although to him she was lovely, and, being also penniless, was therefore not likely to attract attention; while, if her being unfolded under the genial influences he was doing his best to make powerful upon her, if she grew aware that by them her life was enlarging and being tenfold enriched, it was possible she might not be ready to fall in love, and leave Thornwick. He must be careful, however, he said to himself, quite plainly now, that his behavior should lead her into no error. He was not afraid she might fall in love with him; he was not so full of himself as that; but he recoiled from the idea, as from a humiliation, that she might imagine him in love with her. It was not merely that he had loved once for all, and, once deceived and forsaken, would love no more; but it was not for him, a man of thirty years, to bow beneath the yoke of a girl of eighteen— a child in everything except outward growth. Not for a moment would he be imagined by her a courtier for her favor.

Thus, even in the heart of one so far above ordinary men as Godfrey, and that in respect of the sweetest of child-maidens, pride had its evil place; and no good ever comes of pride, for it is the meanest of mean things, and no one but he who is full of it thinks it grand. For its sake this wise man was firmly resolved on caution ; and so, when at last they met, it was no more with that *abandon* of simple pleasure with which he had been wont to receive her when she came knocking at the door of his study, bearing clear question or formless perplexity ; and his restraint would of itself have been enough to make Letty, whose heart was now beating in a very thicket of nerves, at once feel it impossible to carry out her intent—impossible to confess to him any more than to his mother ; while Godfrey, on his part, perceiving her manifest shyness and unwonted embarrassment, attributed them altogether to his own wisely guarded behavior, and, seeing therein no sign of loss of influence, continued his caution. Thus the pride, which is of man, mingled with the love, which is of God, and polluted it. From that hour he began to lord it over the girl ; and this change in his behavior immediately reacted on himself, in the obscure perception that there might be danger to her in continued freedom of intercourse : he must, therefore, he concluded, order the way for both ; he must take care of her as well as of himself. But was it consistent with this resolve that he should, for a whole month, spend every leisure moment in working at a present for her—a written marvel of neatness and legibility ?

Again, by this meeting askance, as it were, another disintegrating force was called into operation : the moment Letty knew she could not tell Godfrey, and that therefore a wall had arisen between him and her, that moment woke in her the desire, as she had never felt it before, to see Tom Helmer. She could no longer bear to be shut up in herself ; she must see somebody, get near to somebody, talk to somebody ; her secret would choke her otherwise, would swell and break her heart ; and who was there to think of but Tom—and Mary Marston ?

She had never once gone to the oak again, but she had not altogether avoided a certain little cobwebbed gable-window in the garret, from which it was visible ; neither had she withheld her hands from cleaning a pane in that window, that through it she might see the oak ; and there, more than once or twice, now thick,   eath

it, she had descried a dark object, which could be nothing else
than Tom Helmer on the watch for herself. He must surely
be her friend, she reasoned, or how would he care, day after
day, to climb a tree to look if she were coming—she who was
the veriest nobody in all other eyes but his ? It was so good of
Tom ! She *would* call him Tom ; everybody else called him
Tom, and why shouldn't she—to herself, when nobody was
near ? As to Mary Marston, she treated her like a child ! When
she told her that she had met Tom at Durnmelling, and how
kind he had been, she looked as grave as if it had been wicked
to be civil to him ; and told her in return how he and his
mother were always quarreling : that must be his mother's
fault, she was sure—it could not be Tom's ; any one might see
that at a glance ! His mother must be something like her aunt !
But, after that, how could she tell Mary any more ? It would
not be fair to Tom, for, like the rest, she would certainly begin
to abuse him. What harm could come of it ? and, if harm did,
how could she help it ! If they had been kind to her, she would
have told them everything, but they all frightened her so, she
could not speak. It was not her fault if Tom was the only
friend she had ! She *would* ask his advice ; he was sure to advise her just the right thing. He had read that sonnet about
the wise virgin with such feeling and such force, he *must*
know what a girl ought to do, and how she ought to behave to
those who were unkind and would not trust her.

Poor Letty ! she had no stay, no root in herself yet. Well
do I know not one human being ought, even were it possible, to
be enough for himself ; each of us needs God and every human
soul he has made, before he has enough ; but we ought each to
be able, in the hope of what is one day to come, to endure for a
time, not having enough. Letty was unblamable that she desired the comfort of humanity around her soul, but I am not
sure that she was quite unblamable in not being fit to walk a
few steps alone, or even to sit still and expect. With all his
learning, Godfrey had not taught her what William Marston
had taught Mary ; and now her heart was like a child left
alone in a great room. She had not yet learned that we must
each bear his own burden, and so become able to bear each the

burden of the other. Poor friends we are, if we are capable only of leaning, and able never to support.

But the moment Letty's heart had thus cried out against Mary, came a shock, and something else cried out against herself, telling her that she was not fair to her friend, and that Mary, and no other, was the proper person to advise with in this emergency of her affairs. She had no right to turn from her because she was a little afraid of her. Perhaps Letty was on the point of discovering that to be unable to bear disapproval was an unworthy weakness. But in her case it came nowise of the pride which blame stirs to resentment, but altogether of the self-depreciation which disapproval rouses to yet greater dispiriting. Praise was to her a precious thing, in part because it made her feel as if she could go on ; blame, a misery, in part because it made her feel as if all was of no use, she never could do anything right. She had not yet learned that the right is the right, come of praise or blame what may. The right will produce more right and be its own reward—in the end a reward altogether infinite, for God will meet it with what is deeper than all right, namely, perfect love. But the more Letty thought, the more she was sure she must tell Mary ; and, disapprove as she might, Mary was a very different object of alarm from either her aunt or her cousin Godfrey.

The first afternoon, therefore, on which she thought her aunt could spare her, she begged leave to go and see Mary. Mrs. Wardour yielded it, but not very graciously. She had, indeed, granted that Miss Marston was not like other shopgirls, but she did not favor the growth of the intimacy, and liked Letty's going to her less than Mary's coming to Thornwick.

CHAPTER X.

THE HEATH AND THE HUT

LETTY seldom went into the shop, except to buy, for she knew Mr. Turnbull would not like it, and Mary did not encourage it, but now her misery made her bold. Mary saw the trouble in her eyes, and without a moment's hesitation drew her inside the counter, and thence into the house, where she led the way to her own room, up stairs and through passages which were indeed lanes through masses of merchandise, like those cut through deep-drifted snow. It was shop all over the house, till they came to the door of Mary's chamber, which, opening from such surroundings, had upon Letty much the effect of a chapel—and rightly, for it was a room not unused to having its door shut. It was small, and plainly but daintily furnished, with no foolish excess of the small refinements on which girls so often set value, spending large time on what it would be waste to buy : only they have to kill the weary captive they know not how to redeem, for he troubles them with his moans.

"Sit down, Letty dear, and tell me what is the matter," said Mary, placing her friend in a chintz-covered straw chair, and seating herself beside her.

Letty burst into tears, and sat sobbing.

"Come, dear, tell me all about it," insisted Mary. "If you don't make haste, they will be calling me."

Letty could not speak.

"Then I'll tell you what," said Mary; "you must stop with me to-night, that we may have time to talk it over. You sit here and amuse yourself as well as you can till the shop is shut, and then we shall have such a talk ! I will send your tea up here. Beenie will be good to you."

"Oh, but, indeed, I can't !" sobbed Letty; "my aunt would never forgive me."

"You silly child ! I never meant to keep you without sending to your aunt to let her know."

"She won't let me stop," persisted Letty.

"We will try her," said Mary, confidently ; and, without more ado, left Letty, and, going to her desk in the shop, wrote a note to Mrs. Wardour. This she gave to Beenie to send by special messenger to Thornwick ; after which, she told her, she must take up a nice tea to Miss Lovel in her bedroom. Mary then resumed her place in the shop, under the frowns and side-glances of Turnbull, and the smile of her father, pleased at her reappearance from even such a short absence.

But the return, in an hour or so, of the boy-messenger, whom Beenie had taken care not to pay beforehand, destroyed the hope of a pleasant evening; for he brought a note from Mrs. Wardour, absolutely refusing to allow Letty to spend the night from home: she must return immediately, so as to get in before dark.

The rare anger flushed Letty's cheek and flashed from her eyes as she read; for, in addition to the prime annoyance, her aunt's note was addressed to her and not to Mary, to whom it did not even allude. Mary only smiled inwardly at this, but Letty felt deeply hurt, and her displeasure with her aunt added yet a shade to the dimness of her judgment. She rose at once.

"Will you not tell me first what is troubling you, Letty?" said Mary.

"No, dear, not now," replied Letty, caring a good deal less about the right ordering of her way than when she entered the house. Why should she care, she said to herself—but it was her anger speaking in her—how she behaved, when she was treated so abominably?

"Then I will come and see you on Sunday," said Mary, "and then we shall manage to have our talk."

They kissed and parted—Letty unaware that she had given her friend a less warm kiss than usual. There can hardly be a plainer proof of the lowness of our nature, until we have laid hold of the higher nature that belongs to us by birthright, than this, that even a just anger tends to make us unjust and unkind: Letty was angry with every person and thing at Thornwick, and unkind to her best friend, for whose sake in part she was angry. With glowing cheeks, tear-filled eyes, and indignant heart she set out on her walk home.

It was a still evening, with a great cloud rising in the southwest; from which, as the sun drew near the horizon, a thin veil stretched over the sky between, and a few drops came scattering. This was in harmony with Letty's mood. Her soul was clouded, and her heaven was only a place for the rain to fall from. Annoyance, doubt, her new sense of constraint, and a wide-reaching, undefined feeling of homelessness, all wrought together to make her mind a chaos out of which mis-shapen things might rise, instead of an ordered world in which gracious and reasonable shapes appear. For as the place such will be the thoughts that spring there; when all in us is peace divine, then, and not till then, shall we think the absolutely reasonable. Alas, that by our thoughtlessness or unkindness we should so often be the cause of monster-births, and those even in the minds of the loved! that we should be, if but for a moment, the demons that deform a fair world that loves us! Such was Mrs. Wardour, with her worldly wisdom, that day to Letty.

About half-way to Thornwick, the path crossed a little heathy common; and just as Letty left the hedge-guarded field-side, and through a gate stepped, as it were, afresh out of doors on the open common, the wind came with a burst, and brought the rain in earnest. It was not yet very heavy, but heavy enough, with the wind at its back, and she with no defense but her parasol, to wet her thoroughly before she could reach any shelter, the nearest being a solitary, decrepit old hawthorn-tree, about half-way across the common. She bent her head to the blast, and walked on. She had no desire for shelter. She would like to get wet to the skin, take a violent cold, go into a consumption, and die in a fortnight. The wind whistled about her bonnet, dashed the rain-drops clanging on the drum-tight silk of her parasol, and made of her skirts fetters and chains. She could hardly get along, and was just going to take down her parasol, when suddenly, where was neither house nor hedge nor tree, came a lull. For from behind, over head and parasol, had come an umbrella, and now came a voice and an audible sigh of pleasure.

"I little thought when I left home this afternoon," said the voice, "that I should have such a happiness before night!"

At the sound of the voice Letty gave a cry, which ran through all the shapes of alarm, of surprise, of delight; and it was not much of a cry either.

"O Tom!" she said, and clasped the arm that held the

umbrella. How her foolish heart bounded! Here was help
when she had sought none, and where least she had hoped for
any! Her aunt would have her run from under the umbrella
at once, no doubt, but she would do as she pleased this time.
Here was Tom getting as wet as a spaniel for her sake, and
counting it a happiness! Oh, to have a friend like that—all to
herself! She would not reject such a friend for all the aunts
in creation. Besides, it was her aunt's own fault ; if she had
let her stay with Mary, she would not have met Tom. It was
not her doing ; she would take what was sent her, and enjoy
it! But, at the sound of her own voice calling him Tom, the
blood rushed to her cheeks, and she felt their glow in the heart
of the chill-beating rain.

"What a night for you to be out in, Letty," responded
Tom, taking instant advantage of the right she had given him.
"How lucky it was I chose the right place to watch in at last!
I was sure, if only I persevered long enough, I should be re-
warded."

"Have you been waiting for me long?" asked Letty, with
foolish acceptance.

"A fortnight and a day," answered Tom, with a laugh.
"But I would wait a long year for such another chance as
this." And he pressed to his side the hand upon his arm.
"Fate is indeed kind to-night."

"Hardly in the weather," said Letty, fast recovering her
spirits.

"Not?" said Tom, with seeming pretense of indignation.
"Let any one but yourself dare to say a word against the
weather of this night, and he will have me to reckon with.
It's the sweetest weather I ever walked in. I will write a
glorious song in praise of showery gusts and bare com-
mons."

"Do," said Letty, careful not to say Tom this time, but
unwilling to revert to Mr. Helmer, "and mind you bring in
the umbrella."

"That I will! See if I don't!" answered Tom.

"And make it real poetry too?" asked Letty, looking
archly r

"Thou shalt thyself be the lovely critic, fair maiden!" answered Tom.

And thus they were already on the footing of somewhere about a two years' acquaintance—thanks to the smart of ill-usage in Letty's bosom, the gayety in Tom's, the sudden wild weather, the quiet heath, the gathering shades, and the umbrella! The wind blew cold, the air was dank and chill, the west was a low gleam of wet yellow, and the rain shot stinging in their faces; but Letty cared quite as little for it all as Tom did, for her heart, growing warm with the comfort of the friendly presence, felt like a banished soul that has found a world; and a joy as of endless deliverance pervaded her being. And neither to her nor to Tom must we deny our sympathy in the pleasure which, walking over a bog, they drew from the flowers that mantled awful deeps; they will not sink until they stop, and begin to build their house upon it. Within that umbrella, hovered, and glided with them, an atmosphere of bliss and peace and rose-odors. In the midst of storm and coming darkness, it closed warm and genial around the pair. Tom meditated no guile, and Letty had no deceit in her. Yet was Tom no true man, or sweet Letty much of a woman. Neither of them was yet *of the truth.*

At the other side of the heath, almost upon the path, stood a deserted hut; door and window were gone, but the roof remained: just as they neared it, the wind fell, and the rain began to come down in earnest.

"Let us go in here for a moment," said Tom, "and get our breath for a new fight."

Letty said nothing, but Tom felt she was reluctant.

"Not a soul will pass to-night," he said. "We mustn't get wet to the skin."

Letty felt, or fancied, refusal would be more unmaidenly than consent, and allowed Tom to lead her in. And there, within those dismal walls, the twilight sinking into a cheerless night of rain, encouraged by the very dreariness and obscurity of the place, she told Tom the trouble of mind their interview at the oak was causing her, saying that now it would be worse than ever, for it was altogether impossible to confess that she had met him yet again that evening.

So now, indeed, Letty's foot was in the snare : she had a secret with Tom. Every time she saw him, liberty had withdrawn a pace. There was no room for confession now. If a secret held be a burden, a secret shared is a fetter. But Tom's heart rejoiced within him.

"Let me see !—How old are you, Letty ?" he asked gayly.

"Eighteen past," she answered.

"Then you are fit to judge for yourself. You ain't a child, and they are not your father and mother. What right have they to know everything you do ? I wouldn't let any such nonsense trouble me."

"But they give me everything, you know—food, and clothes, and all."

"Ah, just so !" returned Tom. "And what do you do for them ?"

"Nothing."

"Why ! what are you about all day ?"

Letty gave him a brief sketch of her day.

"And you call that nothing ?" exclaimed Tom. "Ain't that enough to pay for your food and your clothes ? Does it want your private affairs to make up the difference ? Or have you to pay for your food and clothes with your very thoughts ? —What pocket-money do they give you ?"

"Pocket-money ?" returned Letty, as if she did not quite know what he meant.

"Money to do what you like with," explained Tom.

Letty thought for a moment.

"Cousin Godfrey gave me a sovereign last Christmas," she answered. "I have got ten shillings of it yet."

Tom burst into a merry laugh.

"Oh, you dear creature !" he cried. "What a sweet slave you make ! The lowest servant on the farm gets wages, and you get none : yet you think yourself bound to tell them everything, because they give you food and clothes, and a sovereign last Christmas !"

Here   girl, hitherto so contented and grateful. She did not care about money, but she resented the claim her conscience made for them upon her confidence. She did not reflect that such claim had never been made by them ; nor that the fact that she felt the claim, proved that she had been treated, in some measure at least, like a daughter of the house.

"Why," continued Tom, "it is mere, downright, rank slavery ! You are walking to the sound of your own chains. Of course, you are not to do anything wrong, but you are not bound not to do anything they may happen not to like."

In this style he went on, believing he spoke the truth, and was teaching her to show a proper spirit. His heart, as well as Godfrey's, was uplifted, to think he had this lovely creature to direct and superintend : through her sweet confidence, he had to set her free from unjust oppression taking advantage of her simplicity. But in very truth he was giving her just the instruction that goes to make a slave—the slave in heart, who serves without devotion, and serves unworthily. Yet in this, and much more such poverty-stricken, swine-husk argument, Letty seemed to hear a gospel of liberty, and scarcely needed the following injunctions of Tom, to make a firm resolve not to utter a word concerning him. To do so would be treacherous to him, and would be to forfeit the liberty he had taught her ! Thus, from the neglect of a real duty, she became the slave of a false one.

"If you do," Tom had said, "I shall never see you again : they will set every one about the place to watch you, like so many cats after one poor little white mousey, and on the least suspicion, one way or another, you will be gobbled up, as sure as fate, before you can get to me to take care of you."

Letty looked up at him gratefully.

"But what could you do for me if I did ?" she asked. "If my aunt were to turn me out of the house, your mother would not take me in !"

Letty was not herself now ; she was herself and Tom—by no means a healthful combination.

"My mother won't be mistress long," answered Tom. "She will have to do as I bid her when I am one-and-twenty,

and that will be in a few months." Tom did not know the
terms of his father's will. "In the mean time we must keep
quiet, you know. I don't want a row—we have plenty of row
as it is. You may be sure *I* shall tell no one how I spent the
happiest hour of my life. How little circumstance has to do
with bliss!" he added, with a philosophical sigh. "Here we
are in a wretched hut, roared and rained upon by an equinoctial
tempest, and I am in paradise!"

"I must go home," said Letty, recalled to a sense of her
situation, yet set trembling with pleasure, by his words. "See,
it is getting quite dark!"

"Don't be afraid, my white bird," said Tom. "I will see
you home. But surely you are as well here as there anyhow!
Who knows when we shall meet again? Don't be alarmed,
I'm not going to ask you to meet me anywhere; I know your
sweet innocence would make you fancy it wrong, and then you
would be unhappy. But that is no reason why I should not
fall in with you when I have the chance. It is very hard that
two people who understand each other can not be friends without other people shoving in their ugly beaks! Where is the
harm to any one if we choose to have a few minutes' talk together now and then?"

"Where, indeed?" responded Letty shyly.

A tall shadow—no shadow either, but the very person of
Godfrey Wardour—passed the opening in the wall of the hut
where once had been a window, and the gloom it cast into the
dusk within was awful and ominous. The moment he saw it,
Tom threw himself flat on the clay floor of the hut. Godfrey
stopped at the doorless entrance, and stood on the threshold,
bending his head to clear the lintel as he looked in Letty's
heart seemed to vanish from her body. A strange feeling
shook her, as if some mysterious transformation were about to
pass upon her whole frame, and she were about to be changed
into some one of the lower animals. The question, where was
the harm, late so triumphantly put, seemed to have no heart
in it now. For a moment that had to Letty the air of an æon,
Godfrey stood peering.

Not ,   s mother of her refusal to grant Letty's request, and had set out in the hope of meeting and helping her home, for by that time it had begun to rain, and looked stormy.

In the darkness he saw something white, and, as he gazed, it grew to Letty's face. The strange, scared, ghastly expression of it bewildered him.

Letty became aware that Godfrey did not recognize her at first, and the hope sprung up in her heart that he might not see Tom at all; but she could not utter a word, and stood returning Godfrey's gaze like one fascinated with terror. Presently her heart began again to bear witness in violent piston-strokes.

"Is it really you, my child?" said Godfrey, in an uncertain voice—for, if it was indeed she, why did she not speak, and why did she look so scared at the sight of him?

"O Cousin Godfrey!" gasped Letty, then first finding a little voice, "you gave me such a start!"

"Why should you be so startled at seeing me, Letty?" he returned. "Am I such a monster of the darkness, then?"

"You came all at once," replied Letty, gathering courage from the playfulness of his tone, "and blocked up the door with your shoulders, so that not a ray of light fell on your face; and how was I to know it was you, Cousin Godfrey?"

From a paleness grayer than death, her face was now red as fire; it was the burning of the lie inside her. She felt all a lie now: there was the good that Tom had brought her! But the gloom was friendly. With a resolution new to herself, she went up to Godfrey and said:

"If you are going to the town, let me walk with you, Cousin Godfrey. It is getting so dark."

She felt as if an evil necessity—a thing in which man must not believe—were driving her. But the poor child was not half so deceitful inside as the words seemed to her issuing from her lips. It was such a relief to be assured Godfrey had not seen Tom, that she felt as if she could forego the sight of Tom for evermore. Her better feelings rushed back, her old confidence and reverence; and, in the altogether nebulo-chaotic condition of her mind, she felt as if, in his turn, Godfrey had just appeared for her deliverance.

"I am not going to the town, Letty," he answered. "I came to meet you, and we will go home together. It is no use waiting for the rain to stop, and about as little to put up an umbrella. I have brought your waterproof, and we must just take it as it comes."

The wind was up again, and the next moment Letty, on Godfrey's arm, was struggling with the same storm she had so lately encountered leaning on Tom's, while Tom was only too glad to be left alone on the floor of the dismal hut, whence he did not venture to rise for some time, lest any the most improbable thing should happen, to bring Mr. Wardour back. He was as mortally afraid of being discovered as any young thief in a farmer's orchard.

He had a dreary walk back to the public house where he had stabled his horse, but he trudged it cheerfully, brooding with delight on Letty's beauty, and her lovely confidence in Tom Helmer—a personage whom he had begun to feel nobody trusted as he deserved.

"Poor child!" he said to himself—he as well as Godfrey patronized her—"what a doleful walk home she will have with that stuck-up old bachelor fellow!"

Nor, indeed, was it a very comfortable walk home she had, although Godfrey talked all the way, as well as a head-wind, full of rain, would permit. A few weeks ago she would have thought the walk and the talk and everything delightful. But after Tom's airy converse on the same level with herself, Godfrey's sounded indeed wise—very wise—but dull, so dull! It is true the suspicion, hardly awake enough to be troublous, lay somewhere in her, that in Godfrey's talk there was a value of which in Tom's there was nothing; but then it was not wisdom Letty was in want of, she thought, but somebody to be kind to her—as kind as she should like; somebody, though she did not say this even to herself, to pet her a little, and humor her, and not require too much of her. Physically, Letty was not in the least lazy, but she did not enjoy being forced to   poor

purpose either, but as yet she had no hunger for the possible
results of thought, and how then could she care to think?
Seated on the edge of her bed, weary and wet and self-accused,
she recalled, and pondered, and, after her faculty, compared
the two scarce comparable men, until the voice of her aunt,
calling to her to make haste and come to tea, made her start
up, and in haste remove her drenched garments.   The old
lady imagined from her delay she was out of temper because
she had sent for her home; but, when she appeared, she was
so ready, so attentive, and so quick to help, that, a little repentant, she said to herself, "Really the girl is very good-na-
tured!" as if then first she discovered the fact.   But Thornwick could never more to Letty feel like a home!   Not at
peace with herself, she could not be in rhythmic relation with
her surroundings.

The next day, the old manner of life began again; but,
alas! it was only the old manner, it was not the old life; that
was gone for ever, like an old sunset, or an old song, and could
not be recalled from the dead.   We may have better, but we
can not have the same.   God only can have the same.   God
grant our new may inwrap our old!   Letty labored more than
ever to lay hold of the lessons, to his mind so genial, in hers
·bringing forth more labor than fruit, which Godfrey set before
her, but success seemed further from her than ever.   She was
now all the time aware of a weight, an oppression, which
seemed to belong to the task, but was in reality her self-dis-
satisfaction.   She was like a poor Hebrew set to make brick
without straw, but the Egyptian that had brought her into
bondage was the feebleness of her own will.   Now and then
would come a break—a glow of beauty, a gleam of truth; for
a moment she would forget herself; for a moment a shining
pool would flash on the clouded sea of her life; presently her
heart would send up a fresh mist, the light would fade and
vanish, and the sea lie dusky and sad.   Not seldom reproaching herself with having given Tom cause to think unjustly of
her guardians, she would try harder than ever to please her
aunt; and the small personal services she had been in the way
of rendering to Godfrey were now ministered with the care of

a devotee. Not once should he miss a button from a shirt or
find a sock insufficiently darned ! But even this conscience of
service did not make her happy. Duty itself could not, where
faith was wanting, where the heart was not at one with those
to whom the hands were servants. She would cry herself to
sleep, and rise early to be sad. She resolved at last, and seemed
to gain strength and some peace from the resolve, to do all in
her power to avoid Tom ; and certainly not once did she try
to meet him. Not with him, she could resist him.

Thus it went on. Her aunt saw that something was amiss,
and watched her, without attempt at concealment, which added
greatly to Letty's discomfort. But the only thing her keen-
ness discovered was, that the girl was forwardly eager to please
Godfrey, and the conviction began to grow that she was in-
dulging the impudent presumption of being in love with her
peerless cousin. Then maternal indignation misled her into
the folly of dropping hints that should put Godfrey on his
guard : men were so easily taken in by designing girls ! She
did not say much ; but she said a good deal too much for her
own ends, when she caused her fancy to present itself to the
mind of Godfrey.

He had not failed, no one could have failed, to observe the
dejection that had for some time ruled every feature and expression of the girl's countenance. Again and again he had
asked himself whether she might not be fancying him displeased
with her ; for he knew well that, becoming more and more
aware of what he counted his danger, he had kept of late stricter
guard than ever over his behavior ; but, watching her now with
the misleading light of his mother's lantern, nor quite unwilling, I am bound to confess, that the thing might be as she implied, he became by degrees convinced that she was right.

So far as this, perhaps, the man was pardonable—with a
mother to cause him to err. But, for what followed, punishment was inevitable. He had a true and strong affection for
the girl, but it was an affection as from conscious high to low ;
an affection, that is, not unmixed with patronage—a bad thing
—far worse than it can seem to the heart that indulges it. He
still recoiled, therefore, from the idea of such a leveling of him-

self as he counted it would be to show her anything like the love of a lover. All pride is more or less mean, but one pride may be grander than another, and Godfrey was not herein proud in any grand way. Good fellow as he was, he thought much too much of himself; and, unconsciously comparing it with Letty's, altogether overvalued his worth. Stranger than any bedfellow misery ever acquainted a man withal, are the heart-fellows he carries about with him. Noble as in many ways Wardour was, and kind as, to Letty, he thought he always was, he was not generous toward her; he was not Prince Arthur, "the Knight of Magnificence." Something may perhaps be allowed on the score of the early experience because of which he had resolved—pridefully, it is true—never again to come under the power of a woman; it was unworthy of any man, he said, to place his peace in a hand which could thenceforth wring his whole being with agony. But, had he now brought himself as severely to task as he ought, he would have discovered that he was making no objection to the little girl's loving him, only he would not love her in the same way in return; and where was the honor in that? Doubtless, had he thus examined himself, he would have thought he meant to take care that the child's love for him should not go too far—should not endanger her peace; and that, if the thing should give her trouble, it should be his business to comfort her in it; but descend he would not—would not *yet*—from his pedestal, to meet the silly thing on the level ground of humanity, and the relation of the man and the woman! Something like this, I say, he would have found in his heart, horrid as it reads. That heart's action was not even, was not healthy.

When in London he had ransacked Holywell Street for dainty editions of so many of his favorite authors as would make quite a little library for Letty; and on his return, had commissioned a cabinet-maker in Testbridge to put together a small set of book-shelves, after his own design, measured and fitted to receive them exactly; these shelves, now ready, he fastened to her wall one afternoon when she was out of the way, and filled them with the books. He never doubted that, the moment she saw them, she would rush to find him; and, when he had done, retreated, therefore, to his study, there to sit in readiness to receive her and her gratitude with gentle kindness; when he would express the hope that she would make real friends of the spirits whose quintessence he had thus stored to her hand; and would introduce her to what Milton says in his "Areopagitica" concerning good books. There, for her sake, then, he sat, in mental state, expectant; but sat in vain. When they met at tea, then, in the presence of his mother, with embarrassment and broken utterance, she did thank him.

"O Cousin Godfrey!" she said, and ceased; then, "It is so much more than I deserve, I dare hardly thank you." After another pause, with a shake of her pretty head, as if she would toss aside her hair, or the tears out of her eyes, "I don't know—I seem to have no right to thank you; I ought not to have such a splendid present. Indeed, I don't deserve it. You would not give it me if you knew how naughty I am."

These broken sentences were by both mother and son altogether misinterpreted. The mother, now hearing for the first time of Godfrey's present, was filled with jealousy, and began to revolve thoughts of dire disquietude—was the hussy actually beginning to gain her point, and steal from her the heart of her son? Was it in the girl's blood to wrong her? The father of her had wronged her: she would take care his daughter should not! She had taken a viper to her bosom! Who was *she*, to wriggle herself into an old family and property? Had *she* been born to such things? She would teach her who she was! When dependents began to presume, it was time they had a lesson.

Letty could not bear the sight of the books and their shelves; the very beauty of the bindings was a reproach to her. From the misery of this fresh burden, this new stirring of her sense of hypocrisy, she began to wish herself anywhere out of the house, and away from Thornwick. It was torture to her to think how she had deceived Cousin Godfrey at the hut; and throughout the night, across the darkness, she felt, though she could not see, the books gazing at her, like an embodied conscience from the wall of her chamber. Twenty times that night she started fiom her sleep, saying, "I will go where they shall never see me"; then rose with the dawn, and set herself to the hardest work she could find.

The next day was Sunday, and they all went to church. Letty felt that Tom was there, too, but she never raised her eyes to glance at him.

He had been looking out in vain for a sight of her—now from the oak-tree, now from his bay mare's back, as he haunted the roads about Thornwick, now from the window of the little public-house where the path across the fields joined the main road to Testbridge : but not once had he caught a glimpse of her.

He had seated himself where he could not fail to see her if she were in the Thornwick pew. How ill she looked! His heart swelled with indignation.

"They are cruel to her," he said ; "that is plain. Poor girl, they will kill her! She is a pearl in the oyster-maw of Thornwick. This will never do ; I *must* see her somehow!"

If at this crisis Letty had but had a real friend to strengthen and advise her, much suffering might have been spared her, for never was there a more teachable girl. She was, indeed, only too ready to be advised, too ready to accept for true whatever friendship offered itself. None but the friend who will strengthen us to stand, is worthy of the name. Such a friend Mary would have been, but Letty did not yet know what she needed. The unrest of her conscience made her shrink from one who was sure to side with that conscience, and help it to trouble her. It was sympathy Letty longed for, not strength, and therefore she was afraid of Mary. She came to see her, as she had promised, the Sunday after that disastrous visit; but the weather was still uncertain and gusty, and she found both her and Godfrey in the parlor ; nor did Letty give her a chance of speaking to her alone. The poor girl had now far more on her mind that needed help than then when she went in search of it, but she would seek it no more from her! For, the more she thought, the surer she felt that Mary would insist on her making a disclosure of the whole foolish business to Mrs. Wardour, and would admit neither

her own fear nor her aunt's harshness as reason sufficient to the contrary. "More than that," thought Letty, "I can't be sure she wouldn't go, in spite of me, and tell her all about it! and what would become of me then? I should be worse off a hundred times than if I had told her myself."

CHAPTER XI.

WILLIAM MARSTON.

THE clouds were gathering over Mary, too—deep and dark, but of altogether another kind from those that enveloped Letty: no troubles are for one moment to be compared with those that come of the wrongness, even if it be not wickedness, that is our own. Some clouds rise from stagnant bogs and fens; others from the wide, clean, large ocean. But either kind, thank God, will serve the angels to come down by. In the old stories of celestial visitants the clouds do much; and it is oftenest of all down the misty slope of griefs and pains and fears, that the most powerful joy slides into the hearts of men and women and children. Beautiful are the feet of the men of science on the dust-heaps of the world, but the patient heart will yield a myriad times greater thanks for the clouds that give foothold to the shining angels.

Few people were interested in William Marston. Of those who saw him in the shop, most turned from him to his jolly partner. But a few there were who, some by instinct, some from experience, did look for him behind the counter, and were disappointed if he were absent: most of them had a repugnance to the over-complaisant Turnbull. Yet Marston was the one whom the wise world of Testbridge called the hypocrite, and Turnbull was the plain-spoken, agreeable, honest man of the world, pretending to be no better either than himself or than other people. The few friends, however, that Marston had, loved him as not many are loved: they knew him, not ⏑ ⏑ ⏑ ⏑ ⏑ ⏑ ⏑ ⏑ ⏑ was.

Never did man do less either to conceal or to manifest himself. He was all taken up with what he loved, and that was neither himself nor his business. These friends knew that, when the far-away look was on him, when his face was paler, and he seemed unaware of person or thing about him, he was not indifferent to their presence, or careless of their existence; it was only that his thoughts were out, like heavenly bees, foraging; a word of direct address brought him back in a moment, and his soul would return to them with a smile. He stood as one on the keystone of a bridge, and held communion now with these, now with those : on this side the river and on that, both companies were his own.

He was not a man of much education, in the vulgar use of the word ; but he was a good way on in that education, for the sake of which, and for no other without it, we are here in our consciousness—the education which, once begun, will, soon or slow, lead knowledge captive, and teaches nothing that has to be unlearned again, because every flower of it scatters the seed of one better than itself. The main secret of his progress, the secret of all wisdom, was, that with him action was the beginning and end of thought. He was not one of that cloud of false witnesses, who, calling themselves Christians, take no trouble for the end for which Christ was born, namely, their salvation from unrighteousness—a class that may be divided into the insipid and the offensive, both regardless of obedience, the former indifferent to, the latter contentious for doctrine.

It may well seem strange that such a man should have gone into business with such another as John Turnbull ; but the latter had been growing more and more common, while Marston had been growing more and more refined. Still from the first it was an unequal yoking of believer with unbeliever —just as certainly, although not with quite such wretched results, as would have been the marriage of Mary Marston and George Turnbull. And it had been a great trial : punishment had not been spared—with best results in patience and purification ; for so are our false steps turned back to good by the evil to which they lead us.

Turnbull was ready to take every safe advantage to be gained from his partner's comparative carelessness about money. He drew a larger proportion of the profits than belonged to his share in the capital, justifying himself on the ground that he had a much larger family, did more of the business, and had to keep up the standing of the firm. He made him pay more than was reasonable for the small part of the house yielded from storage to the accommodation of him, his daughter, and their servant, notwithstanding that, if they had not lived there, some one must have been paid to do so. Far more than this, careless of his partner's rights, and insensible to his interests, he had for some time been risking the whole affair by private speculations. After all, Marston was the safer man of business, even from the worldly point of view. Alone, it is true, he would hardly have made money, but he would have got through, and would have left his daughter the means of getting through also : for he would have left her in possession of her own peace and the confidence of her friends, which will always prove enough for those who confess themselves to be strangers and pilgrims on the earth—those who regard it as a grand staircase they have to climb, not a plain on which to build their houses and plant their vineyards.

As to the peculiar doctrines of the sect to which he had joined himself, right or wrong in themselves, Marston, after having complied with what seemed to him the letter of the law concerning baptism, gave himself no further trouble. He had for a long time known—for, by the power of the life in him, he had gathered from the Scriptures the finest of the wheat, where so many of every sect, great church and little church, gather only the husks and chaff—that the only baptism of any avail is the washing of the fresh birth, and the making new by that breath of God, which, breathed into man's nostrils, first made of him a living soul. When a man *knows* this, potentially he knows all things. But, *just therefore*, he did not stand high with his sect any more than with his customers, though—a fact which Marston himself never suspected—the influence of his position had made them choose him for a deacon.

One evening George had had leave to go home early, because of a party at *the villa,* as the Turnbulls always called their house ; and, the boy having also for some cause got leave of absence, Mr. Marston was left to shut the shop himself, Mary, who was in some respects the stronger of the two, assisting him. When he had put up the last shutter, he dropped his arms with a weary sigh. Mary, who had been fastening the bolts inside, met him in the doorway.

"You look worn out, father," she said. "Come and lie down, and I will read to you."

"I will, my dear," he answered. "I don't feel quite myself to-night. The seasons tell upon me now. I suppose the stuff of my tabernacle is wearing thin."

Mary cast an anxious look at him, for, though never a strong man, he seldom complained. But she said nothing, and, hoping a good cup of tea would restore him, led the way through the dark shop to the door communicating with the house. Often as she had passed through it thus, the picture of it as she saw it that night was the only one almost that returned to her afterward : a few vague streaks of light, from the cracks of the shutters, fed the rich, warm gloom of the place ; one of them fell upon a piece of orange-colored cotton stuff, which blazed in the dark.

Arrived at their little sitting-room at the top of the stair, she hastened to shake up the pillows and make the sofa comfortable for him. He lay down, and she covered him with a rug ; then ran to her room for a book, and read to him while Beenie was getting the tea. She chose a poem with which Mr. Wardour had made her acquainted almost the last time she was at Thornwick—that was several weeks ago now, for plainly Letty was not so glad to see her as she used to be—it was Milton's little ode "On Time," written for inscription on a clock—one of the grandest of small poems. Her father knew next to nothing of literature ; having pondered his New Testament, however, for thirty years, he was capable of understanding Milton's best—to the childlike mind the best is always simplest and easiest—not unfrequently the *only* kind it can lay hold of. When she ended, he made her read it again, and then again ; not until she had read it six times did he seem content. And every time she read it, Mary found herself understanding it better. It was gradually growing very precious.

Her father had made no remark ; but, when she lifted her eyes from the sixth reading, she saw that his face shone, and, as the last words left her lips, he took up the line like a refrain, and repeated it after her :

    " ' Triumphing over death, and chance, and thee, O Time! ' "

"That will do now, Mary, I thank you." he said. "I have got a good hold of it, I think, and shall be able to comfort myself with it when I wake in the night. The man must have been very like the apostle Paul."

He said no more. The tea was brought, and he drank a cup of it, but could not eat ; and, as he could not, neither could Mary.

"I want a long sleep," he said ; and the words went to his child's heart—she dared not question herself why. When the tea-things were removed, he called her.

"Mary," he said, " come here. I want to speak to you."
She kneeled beside him.

"Mary," he said again, taking her little hand in his two long, bony ones. " I love you, my child, to that degree I can not say ; and I want you, I do want you, to be a Christian."

"So do I, father dear," answered Mary simply, the tears rushing into her eyes at the thought that perhaps she was not one ; "I want me to be a Christian."

"Yes, my love," he went on ; "but it is not that I do not think you a Christian ; it is that I want you to be a downright real Christian, not one that is but trying to feel as a Christian ought to feel. I have lost so much precious time in that way !"

"Tell me—tell me," cried Mary, clasping her other hand over his. "What would you have me do ? "

"I will tell you. I am just trying how," he responded. "A Christian is just one that does what the Lord Jesus tells him. Nei" . . . . It is not even understanding the Lord Jesus that makes one a Christian. That makes one dear to the Father; but it is being a Christian, that is, doing what he tells us, that makes us understand him. Peter says the Holy Spirit is given to them that obey him: what else is that but just actually, really, doing what he says—just as if I was to tell you to go and fetch me my Bible, and you would get up and go? Did you ever do anything, my child, just because Jesus told you to do it?"

Mary did not answer immediately. She thought awhile. Then she spoke.

"Yes, father," she said, "I think so. Two nights ago, George was very rude to me—I don't mean anything bad, but you know he is very rough."

"I know it, my child. And you must not think I don't care because I think it better not to interfere. I am with you all the time."

"Thank you, father; I know it. Well, when I was going to bed, I was angry with him still, so it was no wonder I found I could not say my prayers. Then I remembered how Jesus said we must forgive or we should not be forgiven. So I forgave him with all my heart, and kindly, too, and then I found I could pray."

The father stretched out his arms and drew her to his bosom, murmuring, "My child! my Christ's child!" After a little he began to talk again.

"It is a miserable thing to hear those who desire to believe themselves Christians, talking and talking about this question and that, the discussion of which is all for strife and nowise for unity—not a thought among them of the one command of Christ, to love one another. I fear some are hardly content with not hating those who differ from them."

"I am sure, father, I try—and I think I do love everybody that loves him," said Mary.

"Well, that is much—not enough though, my child. We must be like Jesus, and you know that it was while we were yet sinners that Christ died for us; therefore we must love all men, whether they are Christians or not."

"Tell me, then, what you want me to do, father dear. I will do whatever you tell me."

"I want you to be just like that to the Lord Christ, Mary. I want you to look out for his will, and find it, and do it. I want you not only to do it, though that is the main thing, when you think of it, but to look for it, that you may do it. I need not say to you that this is not a thing to be *talked* about much, for you don't do that. You may think me very silent, my love; but I do not talk always when I am inclined, for the fear I might let my feeling out that way, instead of doing something he wants of me with it. And how repulsive and full of offense those generally are who talk most! Our strength ought to go into conduct, not into talk—least of all, into talk about what they call the doctrines of the gospel. The man who does what God tells him, sits at his Father's feet, and looks up in his Father's face; and men had better leave him alone, for he can not greatly mistake his Father, and certainly will not displease him. Look for the lovely will, my child, that you may be its servant, its priest, its sister, its queen, its slave—as Paul calls himself. How that man did glory in his Master!"

"I will try, father," returned Mary, with a burst of tears. "I do want to be good. I do want to be one of his slaves, if I may."

"*May!* my child? You are bound to be. You have no choice but choose it. It is what we are made for—freedom, the divine nature, God's life, a grand, pure, open-eyed existence! It is what Christ died for. You must not talk about *may*: it is all *must*."

Mary had never heard her father talk like this, and, notwithstanding the endless interest of his words, it frightened her. An instinctive uneasiness crept up and laid hold of her. The unsealing hand of Death was opening the mouth of a dumb prophet.

A pause followed, and he spoke again.

"I will tell you one thing now that Jesus says: he is unchangeable; what he says once he says always; and I mention it now, 1   ecially called to mind it. It is this: ' *Let not your heart be trou-bled.*' "

"But he said that on one particular occasion, and to his disciples—did he not?" said Mary, willing, in her dread, to give the conversation a turn.

"Ah, Mary!" said her father, with a smile, "*will* you let the questioning spirit deafen you to the teaching one? Ask yourself, the first time you are alone, what the disciples were not to be troubled about, and why they were not to be troubled about it.—I am tired, and should like to go to bed."

He rose, and stood for a moment in front of the fire, winding his old double-cased silver watch. Mary took from her side the little gold one he had given her, and, as was her custom, handed it to him to wind for her. The next moment he had dropped it on the fender.

"Ah, my child!" he cried, and, stooping, gathered up a dying thing, whose watchfulness was all over. The glass was broken; the case was open; it lay in his hand a mangled creature. Mary heard the rush of its departing life, as the wheels went whirring, and the hands circled rapidly.

They stopped motionless. She looked up in her father's face with a smile. He was looking concerned.

"I am very sorry, Mary," he said; "but, if it is past repair, I will get you another.—You don't seem to mind it much!" he added, and smiled himself.

"Why should I, father dear?" she replied. "When one's father breaks one's watch, what is there to say but ' I am very glad it was you did it' ? I shall like the little thing the better for it."

He kissed her on the forehead.

"My child, say that to your Father in heaven, when he breaks something for you. He will do it from love, not from blundering. I don't often preach to you, my child—do I? but somehow it comes to me to-night."

"I will remember, father," said Mary; and she did remember.

She went with him to his bedroom, and saw that everything was right for him. When she went again, before going to her own, he felt more comfortable, he said, and expected to have a good night. Relieved, she left him; but her heart would be heavy. A shapeless sadness seemed pressing it down; it was being got ready for what it had to bear.

When she went to his room in the middle of the night, she found him slumbering peacefully, and went back to her own and slept better. When she went again in the morning, he lay white, motionless, and without a breath.

It was not in Mary's nature to give sudden vent to her feelings. For a time she was stunned. As if her life had rushed to overtake her departing parent, and beg a last embrace, she stood gazing motionless. The sorrow was too huge for entrance. The thing could not be! Not until she stooped and kissed the pale face, did the stone in her bosom break, and yield a torrent of grief. But, although she had left her father in that very spot the night before, already she not only knew but felt that was not he which lay where she had left him. He was gone, and she was alone. She tried to pray, but her heart seemed to lie dead in her bosom, and no prayer would rise from it. It was the time of all times when, if ever, prayer must be the one reasonable thing—and pray she could not. In her dull stupor she did not hear Beenie's knock. The old woman entered, and found her on her knees, with her forehead on one of the dead hands, while the white face of her master lay looking up to heaven, as if praying for the living not yet privileged to die. Then first was the peace of death broken. Beenie gave a loud cry, and turned and ran, as if to warn the neighbors that Death was loose in the town. Thereupon, as if Death were a wild beast yet lurking in it, the house was filled with noise and tumult; the sanctuary of the dead was invaded by unhallowed presence; and the poor girl, hearing behind her voices she did not love, raised herself from her knees, and, without lifting her eyes, crept from the room and away to her own.

"Follow her, George," said his father, in a loud, eager whisper. "You've got to comfort her now. That's your business, George. There's your chance!"

The last words he called from the bottom of the stair, as George sped up after her.

"Mary! Mary, dear," he called as he ran.

But Mary had the instinct—it was hardly more—to quicken her pace, and lock the door of her room the moment she entered. As she turned from it, her eye fell upon her watch—where it lay, silent and disfigured, on her dressing-table; and, with the sight, the last words of her father came back to her. She fell again on her knees with a fresh burst of weeping, and, while the foolish youth was knocking unheard at her door, cried, with a strange mixture of agony and comfort, "O my Father in heaven, give me back William Marston!" Never in his life had she thought of her father by his name; but death, while it made him dearer than ever, set him away from her so, that she began to see him in his larger individuality, as a man before the God of men, a son before the Father of many sons: Death turns a man's sons and daughters into his brothers and sisters. And while she kneeled, and, with exhausted heart, let her brain go on working of itself, as it seemed, came a dreamy vision of the Saviour with his disciples about him, reasoning with them that they should not give way to grief. "Let not your heart be troubled," he seemed to be saying, "although I die, and go out of your sight. It is all well. Take my word for it."

She rose, wiped her eyes, looked up, said, "I will try, Lord," and, going down, called Beenie, and sent her to ask Mr. Turnbull to speak with her. She knew her father's ideas, and must do her endeavor to have the funeral as simple as possible. It was a relief to have something, anything, to do in his name.

Mr. Turnbull came, and the coarse man was kind. It went not a little against the grain with him to order what he called a pauper's funeral for the junior partner in the firm; but, more desirous than ever to conciliate Mary, he promised all that she wished.

"Marston was but a poor-spirited fellow," he said to his wife when he told her; "the thing is a disgrace to the shop, but it's fit enough for him.—It will be so much money saved," he added in self-consolation, while his wife turned up her nose, as she always did at any mention of the shop.

Mary returned to her father's room, now silent again with

the air of that which is not. She took from the table the old
silver watch. It went on measuring the time by a scale now
useless to its owner. She placed it lovingly in her bosom, and
sat down by the bedside. Already, through love, sorrow, and
obedience, she began to find herself drawing nearer to him than
she had ever been before ; already she was able to recall his last
words, and strengthen her resolve to keep them. And, sitting
thus, holding vague companionship with the merely mortal,
the presence of that which was not her father, which was like
him only to remind her that it was not he, and which must so
soon cease to resemble him, there sprang, as in the very foot-
print of Death, yet another flower of rarest comfort—a strong
feeling, namely, of the briefness of time, and the certainty of
the messenger's return to fetch herself. Her soul did not sink
into peace, but a strange peace awoke in her spirit. She heard
the spring of the great clock that measures the years rushing
rapidly down with a feverous whir, and saw the hands that
measure the weeks and months careering around its face ;
while Death, like one of the white-robed angels in the tomb of
the Lord, sat watching, with patient smile, for the hour when
he should be wanted to go for her. Thus mingled her broken
watch, her father's death, and Jean Paul's dream ; and the
fancy might well comfort her.

I will not linger much more over the crumbling time. It
is good for those who are in it, specially good for those who
come out of it chastened and resolved ; but I doubt if any prolonged contemplation of death is desirable for those whose
business it now is to live, and whose fate it is ere long to die.
It is a closing of God's hand upon us to squeeze some of the
bad blood out of us, and, when it relaxes, we must live the more
diligently—not to get ready for death, but to get more life. I
will relate only one thing yet, belonging to this twilight time.

CHAPTER XII.

MARY'S DREAM.

THAT night, and every night until the dust was laid to the dust, Mary slept well; and through the days she had great composure; but, when the funeral was over, came a collapse and a change. The moment it became necessary to look on the world as unchanged, and resume former relations with it, then, first, a fuller sense of her lonely desolation declared itself. When she said good night to Beenie, and went to her chamber, over that where the loved parent and friend would fall asleep no more, she felt as if she went walking along to her tomb.

That night was the first herald of the coming winter, and blew a cold blast from his horn. All day the wind had been out. Wildly in the churchyard it had pulled at the long grass, as if it would tear it from its roots in the graves; it had struck vague sounds, as from a hollow world, out of the great bell overhead in the huge tower; and it had beat loud and fierce against the corner-buttresses which went stretching up out of the earth, like arms to hold steady and fast the lighthouse of the dead above the sea which held them drowned below; despairingly had the gray clouds drifted over the sky; and, like white clouds pinioned below, and shadows that could not escape, the surplice of the ministering priest and the garments of the mourners had flapped and fluttered as in captive terror; the only still things were the coffin and the church—and the soul which had risen above the region of storms in the might of Him who abolished death. At the time Mary had noted nothing of these things; now she saw them all, as for the first time, in minute detail, while slowly she went up the stair and through the narrowed ways, and heard the same wind that raved alike about the new grave and the old house, into which latter, for all the bales banked against the walls, it found many a chink of entrance. The smell of the linen, of the blue cloth, and of the brown paper—things no longer to be handled by those tender, faithful hands—was dismal and strange, and haunted her like things that intruded, things which she had done with, and which yet would not go away. Everything had gone dead, as it seemed, had exhaled the soul of it, and retained but the odor of its mortality. If for a moment a thing looked the same as before, she wondered vaguely, unconsciously, how it could be. The passages through the merchandise, left only wide enough for one, seemed like those she had read of in Egyptian tombs and pyramids : a sarcophagus ought to be waiting in her chamber. When she opened the door of it, the bright fire, which Beenie undesired had kindled there, startled her : the room looked unnatural, *uncanny,* because it was cheerful She stood for a moment on the hearth, and in sad, dreamy mood listened to the howling swoops of the wind, making the house quiver and shake. Now and then would come a greater gust, and rattle the window as if in fierce anger at its exclusion, then go shrieking and wailing through the dark heaven. Mechanically she took her New Testament, and, seating herself in a low chair by the fire, tried to read , but she could not fix her thoughts, or get the meaning of a sentence : when she had read it, there it lay, looking at her just the same, like an unanswered riddle.

The region of the senses is the unbelieving part of the human soul , and out of that now began to rise fumes of doubt and question into Mary's heart and brain Death was a fact. The loss, the evanishment, the ceasing, were incontrovertible —the only incontrovertible things : she was sure of them: could she be sure of anything else ? How could she ? She had not seen Christ rise : she had never looked upon one of the dead ; never heard a voice from the other bank : had received no certain testimony. These were not her thoughts , she was too weary to think ; they were but the thoughts that steamed up in her, and went floating about before her ; she looked on them calmly, coldly, as they came, and passed, or remained—saw them with indifference—there they were, and she could not help it—weariedly, believing none of them, unable to cope with and dispel them, hardly affected by their presence, save with a sense of dreariness and loneliness and wretched company At last she fe⁀   ⁀   ⁀   ⁀   ⁀   itly.

This was her dream, as nearly as she could recall it, when she came to herself after waking from it with a cry.

She was one of a large company at a house where she had never been before—a beautiful house with a large garden behind. It was a summer night, and the guests were wandering in and out at will, and through house and garden, amid lovely things of all colors and odors. The moon was shining, and the roses were in pale bloom. But she knew nobody, and wandered alone in the garden, oppressed with something she did not understand. Every now and then she came on a little group, or met a party of the guests, as she walked, but none spoke to her, or seemed to see her, and she spoke to none.

She found herself at length in an avenue of dark trees, the end of which was far off. Thither she went walking, the only living thing, crossing strange shadows from the moon. At the end of it she was in a place of tombs. Terror and a dismay indescribable seized her; she turned and fled back to the company of her kind. But for a long time she sought the house in vain; she could not reach it; the avenue seemed interminable to her feet returning. At last she was again upon the lawn, but neither man nor woman was there; and in the house only a light here and there was burning. Every guest was gone. She entered, and the servants, soft-footed and silent, were busy carrying away the vessels of hospitality, and restoring order, as if already they prepared for another company on the morrow. No one heeded her. She was out of place, and much unwelcome. She hastened to the door of entrance, for every moment there was a misery. She reached the hall. A strange, shadowy porter opened to her, and she stepped out into a wide street.

That, too, was silent. No carriage rolled along the center, no footfarer walked on the side. Not a light shone from window or door, save what they gave back of the yellow light of the moon. She was lost—lost utterly, with an eternal loss. She knew nothing of the place, had nowhere to go, nowhere she wanted to go, had not a thought to tell her what question to ask, if she met a living soul. But living soul there could be none to meet. She had nor home, nor direction, nor desire; she knew of nothing that she had lost, nor of anything she wished to gain ; she had nothing left but the sense that she was empty, that she needed some goal, and had none She sat down upon a stone between the wide street and the wide pavement, and saw the moon shining gray upon the stone houses. It was all deadness.

Presently, from somewhere in the moonlight, appeared, walking up to her, where she sat in eternal listlessness, the one only brother she had ever had. She had lost him years and years before, and now she saw him ; he was there, and she knew him. But not a throb went through her heart. He came to her side, and she gave him no greeting. " Why should I heed him ? " she said to herself. " He is dead. I am only in a dream. This is not he ; it is but his pitiful phantom that comes wandering hither—a ghost without a heart, made out of the moonlight. It is nothing. I am nothing. I am lost. Everything is an empty dream of loss. I know it, and there is no waking. If there were, surely the sight of him would give me some shimmer of delight. The old time was but a thicker dream, and this is truer because more shadowy." And, the form still standing by her, she felt it was ages away ; she was divided from it by a gulf of very nothingness. Her only life was, that she was lost. Her whole consciousness was merest, all but abstract, loss.

Then came the form of her mother, and bent over that of her brother from behind. " Another ghost of a ghost! another shadow of a phantom !" she said to herself. " She is nothing to me. If I speak to her, she is not there. Shall I pour out my soul into the ear of a mist, a fume from my own brain ? Oh, cold creatures, ye are not what ye seem, and I will none of you !"

With that, came her father, and stood beside the others, gazing upon her with still, cold eyes, expressing only a pale quiet. She bowed her face on her hands, and would not regard him. Even if he were alive, her heart was past being moved. It was settled into stone. The universe was sunk in one of the dreams that haunt the sleep of death ; and, if these were ghosts at all, they were ghosts walking in their sleep.

But the dead, one of them seized one of her hands, and

another the other. They raised her to her feet, and led her along, and her brother walked before. Thus was she borne away captive of her dead, neither willing nor unwilling, of life and death equally careless. Through the moonlight they led her from the city, and over fields, and through valleys, and across rivers and seas—a long journey; nor did she grow weary, for there was not life enough in her to be made weary. The dead never spoke to her, and she never spoke to them. Sometimes it seemed as if they spoke to each other, but, if it were so, it concerned some shadowy matter, no more to her than the talk of grasshoppers in the field, or of beetles that weave their much-involved dances on the face of the pool. Their voices were even too thin and remote to rouse her to listen.

They came at length to a great mountain, and, as they were going up the mountain, light began to grow, as if the sun were beginning to rise. But she cared as little for the sun that was to light the day as for the moon that had lighted the night, and closed her eyes, that she might cover her soul with her eyelids.

Of a sudden a great splendor burst upon her, and through her eyelids she was struck blind—blind with light and not with darkness, for all was radiance about her. She was like a fish in a sea of light. But she neither loved the light nor mourned the shadow.

Then were her ears invaded with a confused murmur, as of the mingling of all sweet sounds of the earth—of wind and water, of bird and voice, of string and metal—all afar and indistinct. Next arose about her a whispering, as of winged insects, talking with human voices; but she listened to nothing, and heard nothing of what was said: it was all a tiresome dream, out of which whether she waked or died it mattered not.

Suddenly she was taken between two hands, and lifted, and seated upon knees like a child, and she felt that some one was looking at her. Then came a voice, one that she never heard before, yet with which she was as familiar as with the sound of the blowing wind. And the voice said, "Poor child! something has closed the valve between her heart and mine." With that came a pang of intense pain. But it was her own cry of speechless delight that woke her from her dream.

CHAPTER XIII.

THE HUMAN SACRIFICE.

THE same wind that rushed about the funeral of William Marston in the old churchyard of Testbridge, howled in the roofless hall and ruined tower of Durnmelling, and dashed against the plate-glass windows of the dining-room, where the three ladies sat at lunch. Immediately it was over, Lady Malice rose, saying

"Hesper, I want a word with you. Come to my room."

Hesper obeyed, with calmness, but without a doubt that evil awaited her there. To that room she had never been summoned for anything she could call good. And indeed she knew well enough what evil it was that to-day played the Minotaur. When they reached the boudoir, rightly so called, for it was more in use for *sulking* than for anything else, Lady Margaret, with back as straight as the door she had just closed, led the way to the fire, and, seating herself, motioned Hesper to a chair. Hesper again obeyed, looking as unconcerned as if she cared for nothing in this world or in any other. Would we were all as strong to suppress hate and fear and anxiety as some ladies are to suppress all show of them! Such a woman looks to me like an automaton, in which a human soul, somewhere concealed, tries to play a good game of life, and makes a sad mess of it.

"Well, Hesper, what do you think?" said her mother, with a dull attempt at gayety, which could nowise impose upon the experience of her daughter.

"I think nothing, mamma," drawled Hesper.

"Mr. Redmain has come to the point at last, my dear child."

"What want, mamma?"

"He had a private interview with your father this morning."

"Indeed!"

"Foolish girl! you think to tease me by pretending indifference!"

"How can a fact be pretended, mamma? Why should I care what passes in the study? I was never welcome there. But, if you wish, I will pretend. What important matter was settled in the study this morning?"

"Hesper, you provoke me with your affectation!"

Hesper's eyes began to flash. Otherwise she was still—silent—not a feature moved. The eyes are more untamable than the tongue. When the wild beast can not get out at the door, nothing can keep him from the windows. The eyes flash when the will is yet lord even of the lines of the mouth. Not a nerve of Hesper's quivered. Though a mere child in the knowledge that concerned her own being, even the knowledge of what is commonly called the heart, she was yet a mistress of the art of self-defense, socially applied, and she would not now put herself at the disadvantage of taking anything for granted, or accept the clearest hint for a plain statement. She not merely continued silent, but looked so utterly void of interest, or desire to speak, that her mother, recognizing her own child, and quailing before the evil spirit she had herself sent on to the generations to come, yielded and spoke out.

"Mr. Redmain has proposed for your hand, Hesper," she said, in a tone as indifferent in her turn as if she were mentioning the appointment of a new clergyman to the family living.

For one moment, and one only, the repose of Hesper's faultless upper lip gave way; one writhing movement of scorn passed along its curves, and left them for a moment straightened out—to return presently to a grander bend than before. In a tone that emulated, and more than equaled, the indifference of her mother's, she answered:

"And papa?"

"Has referred him to you, of course," replied Lady Margaret.

" Meaning it ? "

" What else ? Why not ? Is he not a *bon parti?* "

" Then papa did not mean it ? "

" I do not understand you," elaborated the mother, with a mingled yawn, which she was far from attempting to suppress, seeing she simulated it.

"If Mr. Redmain is such a good match in papa's eyes," explained Hesper, " why does papa refer him to me ? "

" That you may accept him, of course "

" How much has the man promised to pay for me ? "

" *Hesper!* "

" I beg your pardon, mamma. I thought you approved of calling things by their right names ! "

" No girl can do better than follow her mother's example," said Lady Margaret, with vague sequence. " If *you* do, Hesper, you will accept Mr. Redmain."

Hesper fixed her eyes on her mother, but hers were too cold and clear to quail before them, let them flash and burn as they pleased.

" As you did papa ? " said Hesper.

" As I did Mr. Mortimer."

" That explains a good deal, mamma."

" We are *your* parents, anyhow, Hesper."

" I suppose so. I don't know which to be sorrier for— you or me. Tell me, mamma would *you* marry Mr. Redmain ? "

" That is a foolish question, and ought not to be put. It is one which, as a married woman, I could not consider without impropriety. Knowing the duty of a daughter, I did not put the question to *you*. You are yourself the offspring of duty."

" If you were in my place, mamma," reattempted Hesper, but her mother did not allow her to proceed.

" In any place, in every place, I should do my duty," she said.

It was not only born in Lady Malice's blood, but from earliest years had been impressed on her brain, that her first duty was to her family, and mainly consisted in getting well out of its   loch, that the rest might have good places in the Temple of Mammon. In her turn, she had trained her children to the bewildering conviction that it was duty to do a certain wrong, if it should be required. That wrong thing was now required of Hesper—a thing she scorned, hated, shuddered at; she must follow the rest; her turn to be sacrificed was come; she must henceforth be a living lie. She could recompense herself as the daughters who have sinned by yielding generally do when they are mothers, with the sin of compelling, and thus make the trespass round and full. There is in no language yet the word invented to fit the vileness of such mothers; but, as time flows and speech grows, it may be found, and, when it is found, it will have action retrospective. It is a frightful thing when ignorance of evil, so much to be desired where it can contribute to safety, is employed to smooth the way to the unholiest doom, in which love itself must ruthlessly perish, and those, who on the plea of virtue were kept ignorant, be perfected in the image of the mothers who gave them over to destruction. Some, doubtless, of the innocents thus immolated pass even through hideous fires of marital foulness to come out the purer and the sweeter; but whither must the stone about the neck of those that cause the little ones to offend sink those mothers? What company shall in the end be too low, too foul for them? Like to like it must always be.

Hesper was not so ignorant as some girls; she had for some time had one at her side capable of casting not a little light of the kind that is darkness.

"*Duty*, mamma!" she cried, her eyes flaming, and her cheek flushed with the shame of the thing that was but as yet the merest object in her thought; "can a woman be born for such things? How *could* I—mamma, how could any woman, with an atom of self-respect, consent to occupy the same—*room* with Mr. Redmain?"

"Hesper! I am shocked. *Where* did you learn to speak, not to say *think*, of such things? Have I taken such pains—good God! you strike me dumb! Have I watched my child like a very—angel, as anxious to keep her mind pure as her body fair, and is *this* the result?"

Upon what Lady Margaret founded her claim to a result more satisfactory to her maternal designs, it were hard to say. For one thing, she had known nothing of what went on in her nursery, positively nothing of the real character of the women to whom she gave the charge of it ; and—although, I dare say, for worldly women, Hesper's schoolmistresses were quite respectable—what did her mother, what could she know of the governesses or of the flock of sheep—all presumably, but how certainly *all* white ?—into which she had sent her ?

"Is *this* the result ?" said Lady Margaret.

"Was it your object, then, to keep me innocent, only that I might have the necessary lessons in wickedness first from my husband ?" said Hesper, with a rudeness for which, if an apology be necessary, I leave my reader to find it.

"Hesper, you are vulgar !" said Lady Margaret, with cold indignation, and an expression of unfeigned disgust. She was, indeed, genuinely shocked. That a young lady of Hesper's birth and position should talk like this, actually objecting to a man as her husband because she recoiled from his wickedness, of which she was not to be supposed to know, or to be capable of understanding, anything, was a thing unheard of in her world—a thing unmaidenly in the extreme ! What innocent girl would or could or dared allude to such matters ? She had no right to know an atom about them !

"You are a married woman, mamma," returned Hesper, "and therefore must know a great many things I neither know nor wish to know. For anything I know, you may be ever so much a better woman than I, for having learned not to mind things that are a horror to me. But there was a time when you shrunk from them as I do now. I appeal to you as a woman : for God's sake, save me from marrying that wretch !"

She spoke in a tone inconsistently calm.

"Girl ! is it possible you dare to call the man, whom your father and I have chosen for your husband, a wretch !"

"Is he not a wretch, mamma ?"

"If he were, how should I know it ? What has any lady got to do with a man's secrets ?"

"Not if he wants to marry her daughter ?"

"Certainly not. If he should not be altogether what he ought to be—and which of us is?—then you will have the honor of reclaiming him. But men settle down when they marry."

"And what comes of their wives?"

"What comes of women. You have your mother before you, Hesper."

"O mother!" cried Hesper, now at length losing the horrible affectation of calm which she had been taught to regard as *de rigueur,* "is it possible that you, so beautiful, so dignified, would send me on to meet things you dare not tell me—knowing they would turn me sick or mad? How dares a man like that even desire in his heart to touch an innocent girl?"

"Because he is tired of the other sort," said Lady Malice, half unconsciously, to herself. What she said to her daughter was ten times worse: the one was merely a fact concerning Redmain; the other revealed a horrible truth concerning herself. "He will settle three thousand a year on you, Hesper," she said with a sigh; "and you will find yourself mistress."

"I don't doubt it," answered Hesper, in bitter scorn. "Such a man is incapable of making any woman a wife."

Hesper meant an awful spiritual fact, of which, with all her ignorance of human nature, she had yet got a glimpse in her tortured reflections of late; but her mother's familiarity with evil misinterpreted her innocence, and caused herself utter dismay. What right had a girl to think at all for herself in such matters? These were things that must be done, not thought of!

> "These things must not be thought
> After these ways, so, they will drive us mad."

Yes, these things are hard to think about—harder yet to write about! The very persons who would send the white soul into arms whose mere touch is a dishonor will be the first to cry out with indignation against that writer as shameless who but utters the truth concerning the things they mean and do: they fear lest their innocent daughters, into whose hands his books might chance, by ill luck, to fall, should learn that it is *their* business to keep themselves pure.—Ah, sweet mothers! do not be afraid. You have brought them up so carefully, that they suspect you no more than they do the well-bred gentlemen you would have them marry. And have they not your blood in them? That will go far. Never heed the foolish puritan. Your mothers succeeded with you: you will succeed with your daughters.

But it is a shame to speak of those things that are done of you in secret, and I will forbear. Thank God, the day will come—it may be thousands of years away—when there shall be no such things for a man to think of, any more than for a girl to shudder at! There is a purification in progress, and the kingdom of heaven *will* come, thanks to the Man who was holy, harmless, undefiled, and separate from sinners. You have heard a little, probably only a little, about him at church sometimes. But, when that day comes, what part will you have had in causing evil to cease from the earth?

There had been a time in the mother's life when she herself regarded her approaching marriage, with a man she did not love, as a horror to which her natural maidenliness—a thing she could not help—had to be compelled and subjected: of the true maidenliness—that before which the angels make obeisance, and the lion cowers—she never had had any; for that must be gained by the pure will yielding itself to the power of the highest. Hence she had not merely got used to the horror, but in a measure satisfied with it: never suspecting, because never caring enough, that she had at the same time, and that not very gradually, been assimilating to the horror; had lost much of what purity she had once had, and become herself unclean, body and mind, in the contact with uncleanness. One thing she did know, and that swallowed up all the rest—that her husband's affairs were so involved as to threaten absolute poverty; and what woman of the world would not count damnation better than that?—while Mr. Redmain was rolling in money. Had she known everything bad of her daughter's suitor, short of legal crime, for her this would have covered it all.

In Hes

recognize the presence of Sepia, without whose knowledge of
the bad side of the world, Hesper, she believed, could not have
been awake to so much. But she was afraid of Sepia. Besides,
the thing was so far done; and she did not think she would
work to thwart the marriage. On that point she would speak
to her.

But it was a doubtful service that Sepia had rendered her
cousin—to rouse her indignation and not her strength; to
wake horror without hinting at remedy; to give knowledge
of impending doom, without poorest suggestion of hope, or
vaguest shadow of possible escape. It is one thing to see things
as they are; to be consumed with indignation at the wrong;
to shiver with aversion to the abominable; and quite another
to rouse the will to confront the devil, and resist him until he
flee. For this the whole education of Hesper had tended to
unfit her. What she had been taught—and that in a world
rendered possible only by the self-denial of a God—was to drift
with the stream, denying herself only that divine strength of
honest love, which would soonest help her to breast it.

For the earth, it is a blessed thing that those who arrogate
to themselves the holy name of society, and to whom so large
a portion of the foolish world willingly yields it, are in reality
so few and so ephemeral. Mere human froth are they, worked
up by the churning of the world-sea—rainbow-tinted froth,
lovely thinned water, weaker than the unstable itself out of
which it is blown. Great as their ordinance seems, it is evanescent as arbitrary: the arbitrary is but the slavish puffed up
—and is gone with the hour. The life of the people is below;
it ferments, and the scum is for ever being skimmed off, and
cast—God knows where. All is scum where will is not. They
leave behind them influences indeed, but few that keep their
vitality in shapes of art or literature. There they go—little
sparrows of the human world, chattering eagerly, darting on
every crumb and seed of supposed advantage! while from behind the great dustman's cart, the huge tiger-cat of an eternal
law is creeping upon them. Is it a spirit of insult that leads
me to such a comparison? Where human beings do not, will
not *will*, let them be ladies gracious as the graces, the com-

parison is to the disadvantage of the sparrows. Not time, but experience will show that, although indeed a simile. this is no hyperbole.

"I will leave your father to deal with you, Hesper," said her mother, and rose.

Up to this point, Mortimer children had often resisted their mother; beyond this point, never more than once.

"No, please, mamma!" returned Hesper, in a tone of expostulation. "I have spoken my mind, but that is no treason. As my father has referred Mr. Redmain to me, I would rather deal with him."

Lady Malice was herself afraid of her husband. There is many a woman, otherwise courageous enough, who will rather endure the worst and most degrading, than encounter articulate insult. The mere lack of conscience gives the scoundrel advantage incalculable over the honest man ; the lack of refinement gives a similar advantage to the cad over the gentleman ; the combination of the two lacks elevates the husband and father into an autocrat. Hesper was not one her world would have counted weak ; she had physical courage enough ; she rode well, and without fear, she sat calm in the dentist's chair ; she would have fought with knife and pistol against violence to the death ; and yet, rather than encounter the brutality of an evil-begotten race concentrated in her father, she would yield herself to a defilement eternally more defiling than that she would both kill and die to escape.

"Give me a few hours first, mamma," she begged. "Don't let him come to me just yet. For all your hardness, you feel a little for me—don't you ?"

"Duty is always hard, my child." said Lady Margaret. She entirely believed it, and looked on herself as a martyr, a pattern of self-devotion and womanly virtue. But, had she been certain of escaping discovery, she would have slipped the koh-i-noor into her belt-pouch. notwithstanding Never once in her life had she done or abstained from doing a thing *because* that thing was right or was wrong. Such a person. be she as old and as hard as the hills, is mere putty in the fingers of Beelzebub.

Hesper rose and went to her own room. There, for a long hour, she sat—with the skin of her fair face drawn tight over muscles rigid as marble—sat without moving, almost without thinking—in a mere hell of disgusted anticipation. She neither stormed nor wept; her life went smoldering on; she nerved herself to a brave endurance, instead of a far braver resistance.

I fancy Hesper would have been a little shocked if one had called her an atheist. She went to church most Sundays—when in the country; for, in the opinion of Lady Margaret, it was not decorous *there* to omit the ceremony : where you have influence you ought to set a good example—of hypocrisy, namely! But, if any one had suggested to Hesper a certain old-fashioned use of her chamber-door, she would have inwardly laughed at the absurdity. But, then, you see, her chamber was no closet, but a large and stately room ; and, besides, how, alas! *could* the child of Roger and Lady M. Alice Mortimer know that in the silence was hearing—that in the vacancy was a power waiting to be sought? Hesper was not much alone, and here was a chance it was a pity she should lose ; but, when she came to herself with a sigh, it was not to pray, and, when she rose, it was to ring the bell.

A good many minutes passed before it was answered. She paced the room—swiftly ; she could sit, but she could not walk slowly. With her hands to her head, she went sweeping up and down. Her maid's knock arrested her before her toilet-table, with her back to the door. In a voice of perfect composure, she desired the woman to ask Miss Yolland to come to her.

Entering with a slight stoop from the waist, Sepia, with a long, rapid, yet altogether graceful step, bore down upon Hesper like a fast-sailing cutter over broad waves, relaxing her speed as she approached her.

"Here I am, Hesper!" she said.

"Sepia," said Hesper, "I am sold."

Miss Yolland gave a little laugh, showing about the half of her splendid teeth—a laugh to which Hesper was accustomed, but the meaning of which she did not understand—nor would, without learning a good deal that were better left unlearned.

"To Mr. Redmain, of course!" she said.

Hesper nodded.

"When are you going to be—"—she was about to say "cut up," but there was a something occasionally visible in Hesper that now and then checked one of her less graceful coarsenesses. "When is the purchase to be completed?" she asked, instead.

"Good Heavens, Sepia! don't be so heartless!" cried Hesper. "Things are not quite so bad as that! I am not yet in the hell of knowing that. The day is not fixed for the great red dragon to make a meal of me."

"I see you were not asleep in church, as I thought, all the time of the sermon, last Sunday," said Sepia.

"I did my best, but I could not sleep: every time little Mowbray mentioned the beast, I thought of Mr. Redmain; and it made me too miserable to sleep."

"Poor Hesper!—Well! let us hope that, like the beast in the fairy-tale, he will turn out a man after all."

"My heart will break," cried Hesper, throwing herself into a chair. "Pity me, Sepia; *you* love me a little."

A slight shadow darkened yet more Sepia's shadowy brow.

"Hesper," she said, gravely, "you never told me there was anything of that sort! Who is it?"

"Mr. Redmain, of course!—I don't know what you mean, Sepia."

"You said your heart was breaking: who is it for?" asked Sepia, almost imperiously, and raising her voice a little.

"Sepia!" cried Hesper, in bewilderment.

"Why should your heart be breaking, except you loved somebody?"

"Because I hate *him*," answered Hesper.

"Pooh! is that all?" returned Miss Yolland. "If there were anybody you wanted—then I grant!"

"Sepia!" said Hesper, almost entreatingly, "I can not bear to be teased to-day. Do be open with me. You always puzzle me so! I don't understand you a bit better than the first day y   all.

Tell me—are you my friend, or are you in league with mamma? I have my doubts. I can't help it, Sepia."

She looked in her face pitifully. Miss Yolland looked at her calmly, as if waiting for her to finish.

"I thought you would—not help me," Hesper went on, "—that no one can except God—he could strike me dead; but I did think you would feel for me a little. I hate Mr. Redmain, and I loathe myself. If *you* laugh at me, I shall take poison."

"I wouldn't do that," returned Miss Yolland, quite gravely, and as if she had already contemplated the alternative; "—that is, not so long as there was a turn of the game left."

"The game!" echoed Hesper. "—Playing for love with the devil!—I wish the game were yours, as you call it!"

"Mine I'd make it, if I had it to play," returned Sepia. "I wish I were the other player instead of you, but the man hates me. Some men do.—Come," she went on, "I will be open with you, Hesper; you don't hang for thoughts in England. I will tell you what I would do with a man I hated—that is, if I was compelled to marry him; it would hardly be fair otherwise, and I have a weakness for fair play.—I would give him absolute fair play."

The last three words she spoke with a strange expression of mingled scorn and jest, then paused, and seemed to have said all she meant to say.

"Go on," sighed Hesper; "you amuse me." Her tone expressed anything but amusement. "What would a woman of your experience do in my place?"

Sepia fixed a momentary look on Hesper; the words seemed to have stung her. She knew well enough that, if Lady Malice came to know anything of her real history, she would have bare time to pack up her small belongings. She wanted Hesper married, that she might go with her into the world again; at the same time, she feared her marriage with Mr. Redmain would hardly favor her wishes. But she could not with prudence do anything expressly to prevent it; while she might even please Mr. Redmain a little, if she were supposed to have used influence on his side. That, however, must not seem to

Hesper. Sepia did not yet know in fact upon what ground she had to build.

For some time she had been trying to get nearer to Hesper, but—much like Hesper's experience with her—had found herself strangely baffled, she could not tell how—the barrier being simply the half innocence, half ignorance, of Hesper. When minds are not the same, words do not convey between them.

She gave a ringing laugh, throwing back her head, and showing all her fine teeth.

"You want to know what I would do with a man I hated, as you *say* you hate Mr. Redmain?—I would send for him at once—not wait for him to come to me—and entreat him, *as he loved me*, to deliver me from the dire necessity of obeying my father. If he were a gentleman, as I hope he may be, he would manage to get me out of it somehow, and wouldn't compromise me a hair's breadth. But, that is, *if I were you*. If I were *myself* in your circumstances, and hated him as you do, that would not serve my turn. I would ask him all the same to set me free, but I would behave myself so that he could not do it. While I begged him, I mean, I should make him feel that he could not—should make him absolutely determined to marry me, at any price to him, and at whatever cost to me. He should say to himself that I did not mean what I said—as, indeed, for the sake of my revenge, I should not. For that I would give anything—supposing always, don't you know? that I hated him as you do Mr. Redmain. He should declare to me it was impossible; that he would die rather than give up the most precious desire of his life—and all that rot, you know. I would tell him I hated him—only so that he should not believe me. I would say to him, 'Release me, Mr. Redmain, or I will make you repent it. I have given you fair warning. I have told you I hated you.' He should persist, should marry me, and then I *would*."

"Would what?"

"Do as I said."

"But what?"

"Make him repent it."

With the words, Miss Yolland broke into a second fit of

laughter, and, turning from Hesper, went, with a kind of loitering, strolling pace toward the door, glancing round more than once, each time with a fresh bubble rather than ripple in her laughter. Whether it was all nonsensical merriment, or whether the author of laughter without fun, Beelzebub himself, was at the moment stirring in her, Hesper could not have told ; as it was, she sat staring after her, unable even to think. Just as she reached the door, however, she turned quickly, and, with the smile of a hearty, innocent child, or something very like it, ran back to Hesper, threw her arms round her, and said :

"There, now ! I've done for you what I could : I have made you forget the odious man for a moment. I was curious to know whether I could not make a bride forget her bridegroom. The other thing is too easy."

"What other thing ?"

"To make a bridegroom forget his bride, of course, you silly child !—But there I am, off again ! when really it is time to be serious, and come to the only important point in the matter.—In what shade of purity do you think of ascending the funeral pyre ?—In absolute white ?—or rose-tinged ?—or cream-colored !—or gold-suspect ?—Eh, happy bride ?"

As she ceased, she turned her head away, pulled out her handkerchief, and whimpered a little.

"Sepia !" said Hesper, annoyed, "you are a worse goose than I thought you ! What have *you* got to cry about ? *You* have not got to marry him !"

"No ; I wish I had !" returned Sepia, wiping her eyes. "Then I shouldn't lose you. I should take care of that."

"And am I likely to gain such a friend in Mr. Redmain as to afford the loss of the only *other* friend I have ?" said Hesper, calmly.

"Ah, Hesper ! a sad experience has taught me differently. The moment you are married to the man—as married you will be —you all are—bluster as you may—that moment you will begin to change into a wife—a domesticated animal, that is—a tame tabby. Unwilling a woman must be to confess herself only the better half of a low-bred brute, with a high varnish—or not, as the case may be ; and there is nothing left her to do but set herself to find out the wretch's virtues, or, as he hasn't got any, to invent for him the least unlikely ones. She wants for her own sake to believe in him, don't you know ? Then she begins to repent having said hard words of the poor gentleman. The next thing, of course, will be, that you begin to hate the person. to whom you said them, and to persuade yourself she drew them out of you ; and so you break off all communication with the obnoxious person , who being, in the present instance, that black-faced sheep, Sepia Yolland, she is very sorry before-hand, and hates Mr. Redmain with all her heart ; first, because Hesper Mortimer hates him, and next, but twice as much, be-cause she is going to love him. It is a great pity *you* should have him, Hesper I wish you would hand him over to me. *I* shouldn't mind what he was. I should soon tame him."

"You ought to be ashamed of yourself," said Hesper, with righteous indignation. " *You would not mind what he was !* "

Sepia laughed—this time her curious half-laugh.

"If I did, I wouldn't marry him, Hesper," she said. "Which is worse—not to mind, and marry him ; or to mind, and marry him all the same ? Eh, Cousin Hesper Mortimer ?"

"I *can't* make you out, Sepia !" said Hesper. " I believe I never shall "

" Very likely. Give it up ? "

" Quite."

" The best thing you could do. I can't always make my-self out. But, then, I always give it up directly, and so it does me no harm. But it's ten times worse to worry your poor lit-tle heart to rags about such a man as that ; he's not worth a thought from a grand creature like you. Where's the use, be-sides ? Would you stand staring at your medicine a whole day before the time for taking it comes ? I wouldn't have my right leg cut off because that is the side my dog walks on, and dogs go mad ! Slip, cup, and lip—don't you know ? The man may be underground long before the wedding-day : he's anything but sound, they tell me. But it would be far better soon after it, of course. Think only—a young widow, rich, and not a straw the worse ! "

"Sepia, I can't for the life of me tell whether you are a Job's comforter or the devil's advocate."

"Not the latter, my child; for I want to see you emerge a saint from the miseries of matrimony. But, whatever you do, Hesper, don't break your heart, for you will find it hard to mend. I broke mine once, and have been mad ever since."

"What is the use of saying that to me, when you know I have to marry the man?"

"I never said you were not to marry him; I said you were not to break your heart. Marriage is nothing so long as you do not make a heart affair of it; that hurts; and, as you are not in love, there is no occasion for it at all."

"Marriage is nothing, Sepia! Is it nothing to be tied to a man—to *any* man—for all your life?"

"That's as you take it. Nobody makes so much of it now-adays as they used. The clergy themselves, who are at the bottom of all the business, don't fuss about every trifle in the prayer-book. They sign the articles, and have done with it—meaning, of course, to break them, if they stand in their way."

Hesper rose in anger.

"How dare you—" she began.

"Good gracious!" cried Sepia, "you don't imagine I meant anything so wicked! How could you let such a thing come into your head? I declare you are quite dangerous to talk to!"

"It's such a horrible business," said Hesper, "it seems to make one capable of anything wicked, only to think about it. I would rather not say another word on the subject."

A shudder ran through her, as if at the sight of some hid-eously offensive object.

"That would be the best thing," said Sepia, "if it meant not think more about it. Everything is better for not being thought about. I would do anything to comfort you, dear. I would marry him for you, if that would do; but I fear it would scarcely meet the views of Herr Papa. If I could please the beast as well—and I think I should in time—I would willingly hand him the purchase-money. But, of course, he would scorn to touch it, except as the proceeds of the *bona-fide* sale of his own flesh and blood."

CHAPTER XIV.

UNGENEROUS BENEVOLENCE.

As the time went on, and Letty saw nothing more of Tom, she began to revive a little, and feel as if she were growing safe again. The tide of temptation was ebbing away : there would be no more deceit ; never again would she place herself in circumstances whence might arise any necessity for concealment. She began, much too soon, alas ! to feel as if she were new-born ; nothing worthy of being called a new birth can take place anywhere but in the will, and poor Letty's will was not yet old enough to give birth to anything ; it scarcely, indeed, existed. The past was rapidly receding, that was all, and had begun to look dead, and as if it wanted only to be buried out of her sight. For what is done is done, in small faults as well as in murders ; and, as nothing can recall it, or make it not be, where can be the good in thinking about it ?—a reasoning worse than dangerous, before one has left off being capable of the same thing over again. Still, in the mere absence of renewed offense, it is well that some shadow of peace should return ; else how should men remember the face of innocence ? or how should they live long enough to learn to repent ? But for such breaks, would not some grow worse at full gallop ?

That the idea of Tom's friendship was very pleasant to her, who can blame her ? He had never said he loved her , he had only said she was lovely was she therefore bound to persuade herself he meant nothing at all ? Was it not as much as could be required of her, that, in her modesty, she took him for no more than a true, kind friend, who would gladly be of service to her ? Ah ! if Tom had but been that ! If he was not, he did not know it, which is something to say both for and against him. It could not be other than pleasant to Letty to have one, in her eyes so superior, who would talk to her as an equal. It was not that ever she resented being taught ; but she did get tired of lessons only, beautiful as they were. A kiss from Mrs. Wardour on a little teasing from C——— C——— If ———'d have done far more than all his intellectual labor upon her to lift her feet above such snares as she was now walking amid. She needed some play—a thing far more important to life than a great deal of what is called business and acquirement. Many a matter, over which grown people look important, long-faced, and consequential, is folly, compared with the merest child's frolic, in relation to the true affairs of existence.

All the time, Letty had not in the least neglected her house-duties; and, again, her readings with her cousin Godfrey, since Tom's apparent recession, had begun to revive in interest. He grew kinder and kinder to her, more and more fatherly.

But the mother, once disquieted, had lost no time in taking measures. In every direction, secretly, through friends, she was inquiring after some situation suitable for Letty : she owed it to herself, she said, to find for the girl the right thing, before sending her from the house. In the true spirit of benevolent tyranny, she said not a word to Letty of her design. She had the chronic distemper of concealment, where Letty had but a feverish attack. Much false surmise might have been corrected, and much evil avoided, had she put it in Letty's power to show how gladly she would leave Thornwick. In the mean time the old lady kept her lynx-eye upon the young people.

But Godfrey, having caught a certain expression in the said eye, came to the resolution that thenceforth their schoolroom should be the common sitting-room. This would aid him in carrying out his resolve of a cautious and staid demeanor toward his pupil. To preserve his freedom, he must keep himself thoroughly in hand. Experience had taught him that, were he once to give way and show his affection, there would from that moment be an end of teaching and learning. And yet so much was he drawn to the girl, that, at this very time, he gave her the manuscript of his own verses to which I have referred —a volume exquisitely written, and containing, certainly, the outcome of the best that was in him : he did not tell her that he had copied them all with such care and neatness, and had the book so lovelily bound, expressly and only for her eyes.

News of something that seemed likely to suit her ideas for Letty at length came to Mrs. Wardour's ears, whereupon she thought it time to prepare the girl for the impending change. One day, therefore, as she herself sat knitting one sock for Godfrey, and Letty darning another, she opened the matter.

"I am getting old, Letty," she said, "and you can't be here always. You are a thoughtless creature, but I suppose you have the sense to see that?"

"Yes, indeed, aunt," answered Letty.

"It is high time you should be thinking," Mrs. Wardour went on, "how you are to earn your bread. If you left it till I was gone, you would find it very awkward, for you would have to leave Thornwick at once, and I don't know who would take you while you were looking out. I must see you comfortably settled before I go."

"Yes, aunt."

"There are not many things you could do."

"No, aunt; very few. But I should make a better housemaid than most—I do believe that."

"I am glad to find you willing to work; but we shall be able, I trust, to do a little better for you than that. A situation as housemaid would reflect little credit on my pains for you—would hardly correspond to the education you have had."

Mrs. Wardour referred to the fact that Letty was for about a year a day-boarder at a ladies' school in Testbridge, where no immortal soul, save that of a genius, which can provide its own sauce, could have taken the least interest in the chaff and chopped straw that composed the provender.

"It is true," her aunt went on, "you might have made a good deal more of it, if you had cared to do your best; but, such as you are, I trust we shall find you a very tolerable situation as governess."

At the word, Letty's heart ran half-way up her throat. A more dreadful proposal she could not have imagined. She felt, and was, utterly insufficient for—indeed, incapable of such an office. She felt she knew nothing: how was she to teach anything? Her heart seemed to grow gray within her. By nature, from lack of variety of experience, yet more from daily repression of her natural joyousness, she was exceptionally apprehen   it she understood, she encountered willingly and bravely ; but, the simplest thing that seemed to involve any element of obscurity, she dreaded like a dragon in his den.

"You don't seem to relish the proposal, Letty," said Mrs. Wardour. "I hope you had not taken it in your head that I meant to leave you independent. What I have done for you, I have done purely for your father's sake. I was under no obligation to take the least trouble about you. But I have more regard to your welfare than I fear you give me credit for."

"O aunt ! it's only that I'm not fit for being a governess. I shouldn't a bit mind being dairymaid or housemaid. I would go to such a place to-morrow, if you liked."

"Letty, your tastes may be vulgar, but you owe it to your family to look at least like a lady."

"But I am not scholar enough for a governess, aunt."

"That is not my fault. I sent you to a good school. Now, I will find you a good situation, and you must contrive to keep it."

"O aunt ! let me stay here—just as I am. Call me your dairymaid or your housemaid. It is all one—I do the work now."

"Do you mean to reflect on me that I have required menial offices of you ? I have been to you in the place of a mother ; and it is for me, not for you, to make choice of your path in life."

"Do you want me to go at once ? " asked Letty, her heart sinking again, and her voice trembling with a pathos her aunt quite misunderstood.

"As soon as I have secured for you a desirable situation— not before," answered Mrs. Wardour, in a tone generously protective.

Her affection for the girl had never been deep ; and, the moment she fancied she and her son were drawing toward each other, she became to her the thawed adder : she wished the adder well, but was she bound to harbor it after it had begun to bite ? There are who never learn to see anything except in its relation to themselves, nor that relation except as fancied by themselves ; and, this being a withering habit of mind, they keep growing drier, and older, and smaller, and deader, the longer they live—thinking less of other people, and more of themselves and their past experience, all the time as they go on withering.

But Mrs. Wardour was in some dread of what her son would say when he came to know what she had been doing; for, when we are not at ease with ourselves, when conscience keeps moving as if about to speak, then we dread the disapproval of the lowliest, and Godfrey was the only one before whom his mother felt any kind of awe. Toward him, therefore, she kept silence for the present. If she had spoken then, things might have gone very differently: it might have brought Godfrey to the point of righteous resolve or of passionate utterance. He could not well have opposed his mother's design without going further and declaring that, if Letty would, she should remain where she was, the mistress of the house. If not the feeling of what was due to her, the dread of the house without her might well have brought him to this.

Letty, for her part, believed her cousin Godfrey regarded her with pity, and showed her kindness from a generous sense of duty; she was a poor, dull creature for whom her cousin must do what he could: one word of genuine love from him, one word even of such love as was in him, would have caused her nature to shoot heavenward and spread out earthward with a rapidity that would have astonished him; she would thereby have come into her spiritual property at once, and heaven would have opened to her—a little way at least—probably to close again for a time. Now she felt crushed. The idea of undertaking that for which she knew herself so ill fitted was not merely odious but frightful to her. She was ready enough to work, but it must be real, not sham work. She must see and consult Mary! This was quite another affair from Tom! She would take the first opportunity. In the mean time there was nothing to be done or said; and with a heavy heart she held her peace—only longed for her own room, that she might have a cry. To her comfort the clock struck ten and all that now lay between her and that refuge was the usual round of the house with Mrs. Wardour, to see all safe for the night. That done, they parted, and Letty went slowly and sadly up the stair. It was a dark prospect before her. At best, she had to leave the only home she remembered, and go among strangers.

CHAPTER XV.

THE MOONLIGHT.

It was a still, frosty night, with a full moon. When she reached her chamber, Letty walked mechanically to the window, and there stood, with the candle in her hand, looking carelessly out, nor taking any pleasure in the great night. The window looked on an open, grassy yard, where were a few large ricks of wheat, shining yellow in the cold, far-off moon. Between the moon and the earth hung a faint mist, which the thin clouds of her breath seemed to mingle with and augment. There lay her life—out of doors—dank and dull; all the summer faded from it—all its atmosphere a growing fog! She would never see Tom again! It was six weeks since she saw him last! He must have ceased to think of her by this time! And, if he did think of her again, she would be far off, nobody knew where.

Something struck the window with a slight, sharp clang. It was winter, and there were no moths or other insects flying. What could it be? She put her face close to the pane, and looked out. There was a man in the shadow of one of the ricks! He had his hat off, and was beckoning to her. It could be nobody but Tom! The thought sent to her heart a pang of mingled pleasure and pain. Clearly he wanted to speak to her! How gladly she would! but then would come again all the trouble of conscious deceit : how was she to bear that all over again! Still, if she was going to be turned out of the house so soon, what would it matter ? If her aunt was going to compel her to be her own mistress, where was the harm if she began it a few days sooner? What did it matter anyhow what she did? But she dared not speak to him! Mrs Wardour's ears were as sharp as her eyes. The very sound of her own voice in the moonlight would terrify her. She opened the lattice softly, and gently shaking her head— she dared not shake it vigorously—was on the point of closing it again, when, making frantic signs of entreaty, the man stepped into the moonlight, and it was plainly Tom. It was too dreadful! He might be seen any moment! She shook her head again, in a way she meant, and he understood, to mean she dared not. He fell on his knees and laid his hands together like one praying. Her heart interpreted the gesture as indicating that he was in trouble, and that, therefore, he begged her to go to him. With sudden resolve she nodded acquiescence, and left the window.

Her room was in a little wing, projecting from the back of the house, over the kitchen. The servants' rooms were in another part, but Letty forgot a tiny window in one of them, which looked also upon the ricks. There was a back stair to the kitchen, and in the kitchen a door to the farm-yard She stole down the stair, and opened the door with absolute noiselessness. In a moment more she had stolen on tiptoe round the corner, and was creeping like a ghost among the ricks. Not even a rustle betrayed her as she came up to Tom from behind. He still knelt where she had left him, looking up to her window, which gleamed like a dead eye in the moonlight. She stood for a moment, afraid to move, lest she should startle him, and he should call out, for the slightest noise about the place would bring Godfrey down. The next moment, however, Tom, aware of her presence, sprang to his feet, and, turning, bounded to her, and took her in his arms. Still possessed by the one terror of making a noise, she did not object even by a contrary motion, and, when he took her hand to lead her away out of sight of the house, she yielded at once.

When they were safe in the field behind the hedge—

"Why did you make me come down, Tom?" she whispered, half choked with fear, looking up in his face, which was radiant in the moonshine

"Because I could not bear it one day longer," he answered. "All this time I have been breaking my heart to get a word with you, and never seeing you except at church, and there you would never even look at me. It is cruel of you, Letty. I know you could manage it, if you liked, well enough. Why should you try me so?"

"Do speak a little lower, Tom: sound goes so far at night!—I didn't know you would want to see me like that," she answered, looking up in his face with a pleased smile.

"Didn't know!" repeated Tom. "I want nothing else, think of nothing else, dream of nothing else. Oh, the delight of having you here all alone to myself at last! You darling Letty!"

"But I must go directly, Tom. I have no business to be out of the house at this time of the night. If you hadn't made me think you were in some trouble, I daredn't have come."

"And ain't I in trouble enough—trouble that nothing but your coming could get me out of? To love your very shadow, and not be able to get a peep even of that, except in church, where all the time of the service I'm raging inside like a wild beast in a cage—ain't that trouble enough to make you come to me?"

Letty's heart leaped up. He loved her, then! Love, real love, was what it meant! It was paradise! Anything might come that would! She would be afraid of nothing any more. They might say or do to her what they pleased—she did not care a straw, if he loved her—really loved her! And he did! he did! She was going to have him all to her own self, and nobody was to have any right to meddle with her more!

"I didn't know you loved me, Tom!" she said, simply, with a little gasp.

"And I don't know yet whether you love me," returned Tom.

"Of course, if you love *me*," answered Letty, as if everybody must give back love for love.

Tom took her again in his arms, and Letty was in greater bliss than she had ever dreamed possible. From being a nobody in the world, she might now queen it to the top of her modest bent; from being looked down on by everybody, she had the whole earth under her feet; from being utterly friend-less, she had the heart of Tom Helmer for her own! Yet even then, eluding the barriers of Tom's arms, shot to her heart, sharp as an arrow, the thought that she was forsaking Cousin Godfrey. She did not attempt to explain it to herself; she was in too great confusion, even if she had been capable of the necessary analysis. It came, probably, of what her aunt had told her concerning her cousin's opinion of Tom. Often and often since, she had said to herself that, of course, Cousin God-frey was mistaken and quite wrong in not liking Tom; she was sure he would like him if he knew him as she did!—and yet to act against his opinion, and that never uttered to her-self, cost her this sharp pang, and not a few that followed! To soften it for the moment, however, came the vaguely, sadly reproachful feeling, that, seeing they were about to send her out into the world to earn her bread, they had no more any right to make such demands upon her loyalty to them as should ex-clude the closest and only satisfying friend she had—one who would not turn her away, but wanted to have her for ever. That Godfrey knew nothing of his mother's design, she did not once suspect

"Now, Tom, you have seen me, and spoken to me, and I must go," said Letty.

"O Letty!" cried Tom, reproachfully, "now when we understand each other? Would you leave me in the very mo-ment of my supremest bliss? That would be mockery, Letty! That is the way my dreams serve me always. But, surely, you are no dream! Perhaps I *am* dreaming, and shall wake to find myself alone! I never was so happy in my life, and you want to leave me all alone in the midnight, with the moon to comfort me! Do as you like, Letty!—I won't leave the place till the morning. I will go back to the rick-yard, and lie under your window all night."

The idea of Tom out on the cold ground, while she was warm in bed, was too much for Letty's childish heart. Had she known Tom better, she would not have been afraid: she would have known that he would indeed do as he had said—so far ; that he would lie down under her window, and there remain, even to the very moment when he began to feel miserable, and a moment longer, but not more than two ; that then he would get up, and, with a last look, start home for bed.

"I will stop a little while, Tom," she offered, "if you will promise to go home as soon as I leave you."

Tom promised.

They went wandering along the farm-lanes, and Tom made love to her, as the phrase is—in his case, alas ! a phrase only too correct. I do not say, or wish understood, that he did not love her—with such love as lay in the immediate power of his development ; but, being a sort of a poet, such as a man may be who loves the form of beauty, but not the indwelling power of it, that is, the truth, he *made* love to her—fashioned forms of love, and offered them to her ; and she accepted them, and found the words of them very dear and very lovely. For neither had she got far enough, with all Godfrey's endeavors for her development, to love aright the ring of the true gold, and therefore was not able to distinguish the dull sound of the gilt brass Tom offered her. Poor fellow ! it was all he had. But compassion itself can hardly urge that as a reason for accepting it for genuine. What rubbish most girls will take for poetry, and with it heap up impassably their door to the garden of delights ! what French polish they will take for refinement ! what merest French gallantry for love ! what French sentiment for passion ! what commonest passion they will take for devotion !—passion that has little to do with their beauty even, still less with the individuality of it, and nothing at all with their loveliness !

In justice to Tom, I must add, however, that he also took not a little rubbish for poetry, much sentiment for pathos, and all passion for love. He was no intentional deceiver ; he was so self-deceived, that, being himself a deception, he could be nothing but a deceiver—at once the most complete and the most pardonable, and perhaps the most dangerous of deceivers.

With all his fine talk of love, to which he now gave full flow, it was characteristic of him that, although he saw Letty without hat or cloak, just because he was himself warmly clad, he never thought of her being cold, until the arm he had thrown round her waist felt her shiver. Thereupon he was kind, and would have insisted that she should go in and get a shawl, had she not positively refused to go in and come out again. Then he would have had her put on his coat, that she might be able to stay a little longer; but she prevailed on him to let her go. He brought her to the nearest point not within sight of any of the windows, and, there leaving her, set out at a rapid pace for the inn where he had put up his mare

When Tom was gone, and the bare night, a diffused conscience, all about her, Letty, with a strange fear at her heart, like one in a churchyard, with the ghost-hour at hand, and feeling like "a guilty thing surprised," although she had done nothing wrong in its mere self, stole back to the door of the kitchen, longing for the shelter of her own room, as never exile for his fatherland.

She had left the door an inch ajar, that he might run the less risk of making a noise in opening it; but ere she reached it, the moon shining full upon it, she saw plainly, and her heart turned sick when she saw, that it was closed. Between cold and terror she shuddered from head to foot, and stood staring.

Recovering a little, she said to herself some draught must have blown it to. If so, there was much danger that the noise had been heard; but, in any case, there was no time to lose. She glided swiftly to it. She lifted the latch softly—but, horror of horrors! in vain. The door was locked. She was shut out. She must lie or confess! And what he would serve? Poor Letty! And yet, for all her dismay, her terror, her despair that night, in her innocence, she never once thought of the worst danger in which she stood!

The least perilous, where no safe way was left, would now have been to let the simple truth appear; Letty ought immediately to have knocked at the door, and, should that have proved unavailing, to have broken her aunt's window even, to gain hearing and admittance. But that was just the kind of action of which, truthful as was her nature, poor Letty, both by constitution and training, was incapable; human opposition, superior anger, condemnation, she dared not encounter.　She sank, more than half fainting, upon the door-step.

The moment she came to herself, apprehension changed into active dread, rushed into uncontrollable terror.　She sprang to her feet, and, the worst thing she could do, fled like the wind after Tom—now, indeed, she imagined, her only refuge !　She knew where he had put up his horse, and knew he could hardly take any other way than the foot-path to Testbridge.　He could not be more than a few yards ahead of her, she thought. Presently she heard him whistling, she was sure, as he walked leisurely along, but she could not see him.　The way was mostly between hedges until it reached the common : there she would catch sight of him, for, notwithstanding the gauzy mist, the moon gave plenty of light.　On she went swiftly, still fancying at intervals she heard in front of her his whistle, and even his step on the hard, frozen path.　In her eager anxiety to overtake him, she felt neither the chilling air nor the fear of the night and the loneliness.　Dismay was behind her, and hope before her.　On and on she ran.　But when, with now failing breath, she reached the common, and saw it lie so bare and wide in the moonlight, with the little hut standing on its edge, like a ghastly lodge to nowhere, with gaping black holes for door and window, then, indeed, the horror of her deserted condition and the terrors of the night began to crush their way into her soul.　What might not be lurking in that ruin, ready to wake at the lightest rustle, and, at sight of a fleeing girl, start out in pursuit, and catch her by the hair that now streamed behind her !　And there was the hawthorn, so old and grotesquely contorted, always bringing to her mind a frightful German print at the head of a poem called "The Haunted Heath," in one of her cousin Godfrey's books !　It was like an old miser, decrepit with age, pursued and unable to run !　Miserable as was her real condition, it was rendered yet more pitiable by these terrors of the imagination.　The distant howl of a dog which the moon would not let sleep, the muffled low of a cow from a shippen, and a certain strange sound, coming again and again, which she could not account for, all turned to things unnatural, therefore frightful. Faintly, once or twice, she tried to persuade herself that it was only a horrible dream, from which she would wake in safety; but it would not do ; it was, alas ! all too real—hard, killing fact ! Anyhow, dream or fact, there was no turning ; on to the end she must go More frightful than all possible dangers. most frightful thing of all, was the old house she had left, standing silent in the mist, holding her room inside it empty, the candle burning away in the face of the moon ! Across the common she glided like a swift wraith, and again into the shadow of the hedges.

There seems to be a hope as well as a courage born of despair : immortal. yet inconstant children of a death-doomed sire, both were now departing. If Tom had come this way, she must, she thought, have overtaken him long before now ! But, perhaps, she had fainted outright, and lain longer than she knew at the kitchen-door ; and when she started to follow him, Tom was already at home ! Alas, alas ! she was lost utterly !

The footpath came to an end, and she was on the high-road. There was the inn where Tom generally put up ' It was silent as the grave. The clang of a horse-shoe striking a stone came through the frosty air from far along the road. Her heart sank into the depths of the infinite sea that encircles the soul, and, for the second time that night, Death passing by gave her an alms of comfort. and she lay insensible on the border of the same highway along which Tom, on his bay mare, went singing home.

CHAPTER XVI.

THE MORNING.

AT Thornwick, Tom had been descried in the yard, by the spying organs of one of the servants—a woman not very young, and not altogether innocent of nightly interviews. Through the small window of her closet she had seen. and having seen she watched—not without hope she might be herself the object of the male presence, which she recognized as that of Tom Helmer, whom almost everybody knew. T   ites,

however, Letty appeared behind him, and therewith a throb of
evil joy shot through her bosom : what a chance ! what a good
joke ! what a thing for her to find out Miss Letty ; to surprise
her naughty secret ! to have her in her power ! She would
have no choice but tell her everything—and then what privileges
would be hers ! and what larks they two would have together,
helping each other ! She had not a thought of betraying her :
there would be no fun in that ! not the less would she encourage a little the fear that she might, for it would be as a charm
in her bosom to work her will withal !—To make sure of Letty
and her secret, partly also in pure delight of mischief, and enjoyment of the power to tease, she stole down stairs, and locked
the kitchen door—the bolt of which, for reasons of her own,
she kept well oiled ; then sat down in an old rocking-chair, and
waited—I can not say watched, for she fell fast asleep. Letty
lifted the latch almost too softly for her to have heard had she
been awake ; but on the door-step Letty, had she been capable
of listening, might have heard her snoring.

When the young woman awoke in the cold gray of the
morning, and came to herself, compunction seized her. Opening the door softly, she went out and searched everywhere ;
then, having discovered no trace of Letty, left the door unlocked, and went to bed, hoping she might yet find her way
into the house before Mrs. Wardour was down.

When that lady awoke at the usual hour, and heard no
sound of stir, she put on her dressing-gown, and went, in the
anger of a housekeeper, to Letty's room : there, to her amazement and horror, she saw the bed had lain all the night expectant. She hurried thence to the room occupied by the girl who
was the cause of the mischief. Roused suddenly by the voice
of her mistress, she got up half awake, and sleepy-headed ;
and, assailed by a torrent of questions, answered so, in her confusion, as to give the initiative to others : before she was well
awake, she had told all she had seen from the window, but
nothing of what she had herself done. Mrs. Wardour hurried
to the kitchen, found the door on the latch, believed everything and much more, went straight to her son's room, and, in
a calm rage, woke him up, and poured into his unwilling ears

a torrent of mingled fact and fiction, wherein floated side by
side with Letty's name every bad adjective she could bring the
lips of propriety to utter. Before he quite came to himself the
news had wellnigh driven him mad. There stood his mother,
dashing her cold hailstorm of contemptuous wrath on the girl
he loved, whom he had gone to bed believing the sweetest creature in creation, and loving himself more than she dared show!
He had been dreaming of her with the utmost tenderness, when
his mother woke him with the news that she had gone in the
night with Tom Helmer, the poorest creature in the neighborhood.

"For God's sake, mother," he cried, "go away, and let me
get up!"

"What can you do, Godfrey? What is there to be done?
Let the jade go to her ruin!" cried Mrs. Wardour, alarmed in
the midst of her wrath. "You *can* do nothing now. As she
has made her bed, so she must lie."

Her words were torture to him. He sprang from his bed,
and proceeded to pull on his clothes. Terrified at the wildness
of his looks, his mother fled from the room, but only to watch
at the door.

Scarcely could Godfrey dress himself for agitation; brain
and heart seemed to mingle in chaotic confusion. Anger strove
with unbelief, and indignation at his mother with the sense of
bitter wrong from Letty. It was all incredible and shameful,
yet not the less utterly miserable. The girl whose Idea lay in
the innermost chamber of his heart like the sleeping beauty in
her palace! while he loved and ministered to her outward
dream-shape which flitted before the eyes of his sense, in the
hope that at last the Idea would awake, and come forth and
inform it!—he dared not follow the thought! it was madness
and suicide! He had been silently worshiping an angel with
wings not yet matured to the spreading of themselves to the
winds of truth; those wings were a little maimed, and he had
been tending them with precious balms, and odors, and oint-
ments: all at once she had turned into a bat, a skin-winged
creature that flies by night, and had disappeared in the darkness! Of all possible mockeries, for Letty to steal out at night

to the embraces of a fool ! a wretched, weak-headed, idle fellow, whom every clown called by his Christian name ! an ass that did nothing but ride the country on a horse too good for him, and quarrel with his mother from Sunday to Saturday ! For such a man she had left him, Godfrey Wardour ! a man who would have lifted her to the height of her nature ! whereas the fool Helmer would sink her to the depth of his own merest nothingness ! The thing was inconceivable ! yet it was ! He knew it ; they were all the same ! Never woman worthy of true man ! The poorest show would take them captive, would draw them from reason !

He knew *now* that he loved the girl. Gnashing his teeth with fellest rage, he caught from the wall his heaviest hunting-whip, rushed heedless past his mother where she waited on the landing, and out of the house.

In common with many, he thought worse of Tom Helmer than he yet deserved. He was a characterless fool, a trifler, a poetic babbler, a good-for-nothing good sort of fellow ; that was the worst that as yet was true of him ; and better things might with equal truth have been said of him, had there been any one that loved him enough to know them.

Godfrey ran to the stable, and to the stall of his fastest horse. As he threw the saddle over his back, he almost wept in the midst of his passion at the sight of the bright stirrups. His hands trembled so that he failed repeatedly in passing the straps through the buckles of the girths. But the moment he felt the horse under him, he was stronger, set his head straight for the village of Warrender, where Tom's mother lived, and went away over everything. His crow-flight led him across the back of the house of Durnmelling. Hesper, who had not slept well, and found the early morning even a worse time to live in than the evening, saw him from her window, going straight as an arrow. The sight arrested her. She called Sepia, who for a few nights had slept in her room, to the window.

" There, now !" she said, " there is a man who looks a man ! Good Heavens ! how recklessly he rides ! I don't believe Mr. Redmain could keep on a horse's back if he tried !"

Sepia looked, half asleep. Her eyes grew wider. Her sleepiness vanished.

"Something is wrong with the proud yeoman!" she said. "He is either mad or in love, probably both! We shall hear more of this morning's ride, Hesper, as I hope to die a maid! —That's a man I should like to know now," she added, carelessly. "There is some go in him! I have a weakness for the kind of man that *could* shake the life out of me if I offended him."

"Are you so anxious, then, to make a good, submissive wife?" said Hesper.

"I should take the very first opportunity of offending him —mortally, as they call it. It would be worth one's while with a man like that."

"Why? How? For what good?"

"Just to see him look. There is nothing on earth so scrumptious as having a grand burst of passion all to yourself." She drew in her breath like one in pain. "My God!" she said, "to see it come and go! the white and the red! the tugging at the hair! the tears and the oaths, and the cries and the curses! To know that you have the man's heart-strings stretched on your violin, and that with one dash of your bow, one tiniest twist of a peg, you can make him shriek!"

"Sepia!" said Hesper, "I think Darwin must be right, and some of us at least are come from—"

"Tiger-cats? or perhaps the Tasmanian devil?" suggested Sepia, with one of her scornful half-laughs.

But the same instant she turned white as death, and sat softly down on the nearest chair.

"Good Heavens, Sepia! what is the matter? I did not mean it," said Hesper, remorsefully, thinking she had wounded her, and that she had broken down in the attempt to conceal the pain.

"It's not that, Hesper, dear. Nothing you could say would hurt me," replied Sepia, drawing breath sharply. "It's a pain that comes sometimes—a sort of picture drawn in pains —something I saw once."

"A picture?"

"Oh! well!—picture, or what you will!—Where's the difference, once it's gone and done with? Yet it will get the better of me now and then for a moment! Some day, when you are married, and a little more used to men and their ways, I will tell you. My little cousin is much too innocent now"

"But you have not been married, Sepia! What should you know about disgraceful things?"

"I will tell you when you are married, and not until then, Hesper. There's a bribe to make you a good child, and do as you must—that is, as your father and mother and Mr. Redmain would have you!"

While they talked, Godfrey, now seen, now vanishing, had become a speck in the distance. Crossing a wide field, he was now no longer to be distinguished from the grazing cattle, and so was lost to the eyes of the ladies.

By this time he had collected his thoughts a little, and it had grown plain to him that the last and only thing left for him to do for Letty was to compel Tom to marry her at once. "My mother will then have half her own way!" he said to himself bitterly. But, instead of reproaching himself that he had not drawn the poor girl's heart to his own, and saved her by letting her know that he loved her, he tried to congratulate himself on the pride and self-important delay which had preserved him from yielding his love to one who counted herself of so little value. He did not reflect that, if the value a woman places upon herself be the true estimate of her worth, the world is tolerably provided with utterly inestimable treasures of womankind; yet is it the meek who shall inherit it; and they who make least of themselves are those who shall be led up to the dais at last.

"But the wretch shall marry her at once!" he swore. "Her character is nothing now but a withered flower in the hands of that woman. Even were she capable of holding her tongue, by this time a score must have seen them together."

Godfrey hardly knew what he was to gain by riding to Warrender, for how could he expect to find Tom there? and what could any one do with the mother? Only, where else could he go first to learn anything about him? Some hint he might there get, suggesting in what direction to seek them. And he must be doing something, however useless : inaction at such a moment would be hell itself !

Arrived at the house—a well-appointed cottage, with out-houses larger than itself—he gave his horse to a boy to lead up and down, while he went through the gate and rang the bell in a porch covered with ivy. The old woman who opened the door said Master Tom was not up yet, but she would take his message. Returning presently, she asked him to walk in. He declined the hospitality, and remained in front of the house.

Tom was no coward, in the ordinary sense of the word : there was in him a good deal of what goes to the making of a gentleman : but he confessed to being " in a bit of a funk " when he heard who was below : there was but one thing it could mean, he thought—that Letty had been found out, and here was her cousin come to make a row. But what did it matter, so long as Letty was true to him ? The world should know that Wardour nor Pat—her mother's maiden name !—nor any power on earth should keep from him the woman of his choice ! As soon as he was of age, he would marry her, in spite of them all. But he could not help being a little afraid of Godfrey Wardour, for he almost hated him.

For Godfrey, he would have rather liked Tom Helmer, had he ever seen down into the best of him ; but Tom's carelessness had so often misrepresented him, that Godfrey had too huge a contempt for him. And now the miserable creature had not merely grown dangerous, but had of a sudden done him the greatest possible hurt ! It was all Godfrey could do to keep his contempt and hate within what he would have called the bounds of reason, as he waited for " the miserable mongrel." He kept walking up and down the little lawn, which a high shrubbery protected from the road, making a futile attempt, as often as he thought of the policy of it, to look unconcerned, and the next moment striking fierce, objectless blows with his whip. Catching sight of him from a window on the stair, Tom was so little reassured by his demeanor, that, crossing the hall, he chose from the stand a thick oak stick—poor odds against a hunting-whip in the hands of one like Godfrey, with the steel of ten years of manhood in him.

Tom's long legs came doubling carelessly down the two steps from the door, as, with a gracious wave of the hand, and swinging his cudgel as if he were just going out for a stroll, he coolly greeted his visitor. But the other, instead of returning the salutation, stepped quickly up to him.

"Mr. Helmer, where is Miss Lovel?" he said, in a low voice.

Tom turned pale, for a pang of undefined fear shot through him, and his voice betrayed genuine anxiety as he answered:

"I do not know. What has happened?"

Wardour's fingers gripped convulsively his whip-handle, and the word *liar* had almost escaped his lips; but, through the darkness of the tempest raging in him, he yet read truth in Tom's scared face and trembling words.

"You were with her last night," he said, grinding it out between his teeth.

"I was," answered Tom, looking more scared still.

"Where is she now?" demanded Godfrey again.

"I hope to God you know," answered Tom, "for I don't."

"Where did you leave her?" asked Wardour, in the tone of an avenger rather than a judge.

Tom, without a moment's hesitation, described the place with precision—a spot not more than a hundred yards from the house.

"What right had you to come sneaking about the place?" hissed Godfrey, a vain attempt to master an involuntary movement of the muscles of his face at once clinching and showing his teeth. At the same moment he raised his whip unconsciously.

Tom instinctively stepped back, and raised his stick in attitude of defense. Godfrey burst into a scornful laugh.

"You fool!" he said; "you need not be afraid; I can see you are speaking the truth. You dare not tell me a lie!"

"It is enough," returned Tom with dignity, "that I do not tell lies. I am not afraid of you, Mr. Wardour. What I dare or dare not do, is neither for you nor me to say. You are the older and stronger and every way better man, but that gives you no right to bully me."

This answer brought Godfrey to a better sense of what became himself, if not of what Helmer could claim of him. Using positive violence over himself, he spoke next in a tone calm even to iciness.

"Mr. Helmer," he said, "I will gladly address you as a gentleman, if you will show me how it can be the part of a gentleman to go prowling about his neighbor's property after nightfall."

"Love acknowledges no law but itself, Mr. Wardour," answered Tom, inspired by the dignity of his honest affection for Letty. "Miss Lovel is not your property. I love her, and she loves me. I would do my best to see her, if Thornwick were the castle of Giant Blunderbore."

"Why not walk up to the house, like a man, in the daylight, and say you wanted to see her?"

"Should I have been welcome, Mr. Wardour?" said Tom, significantly. "You know very well what my reception would have been; and I know better than throw difficulties in my own path. To do as you say would have been to make it next to impossible to see her."

"Well, we must find her now anyhow; and you must marry her off-hand."

"Must!" echoed Tom, his eyes flashing, at once with anger at the word and with pleasure at the proposal. "Must?" he repeated, "when there is nothing in the world I desire or care for but to marry her? Tell me what it all means, Mr. Wardour; for, by Heaven! I am utterly in the dark."

"It means just this—and I don't know but I am making a fool of myself to tell you—that the girl was seen in your company late last night, and has been neither seen nor heard of since."

"My God!" cried Tom, now first laying hold of the fact; and with the word he turned and started for the stable. His run, however, broke down, and with a look of scared bewilderment he came back to Godfrey.

"Mr. Wardour," he said, "what am I to do? Please advise

me. If we raise a hue and cry, it will set people saying all manner of things, pleasant neither for you nor for us."

"That is your business, Mr. Helmer," answered Godfrey, bitterly. "It is you who have brought this shame on her."

"You are a cold-hearted man," said Tom. "But there is no shame in the matter. I will soon make that clear—if only I know where to go after her. The thing is to me utterly mysterious: there are neither robbers nor wild beasts about Thornwick. What *can* have happened to her?"

He turned his back on Godfrey for a moment, then, suddenly wheeling, broke out:

"I will tell you what it is; I see it all now; she found out that she had been seen, and was too terrified to go into the house again!—Mr. Wardour," he continued, with a new look in his eyes, "I have more reason to be suspicious of you and your mother than you have to suspect me. Your treatment of Letty has not been of the kindest."

So Letty had been accusing him of unkindness! Ready as he now was to hear anything to her disadvantage, it was yet a fresh stab to the heart of him. Was this the girl for whom, in all honesty and affection, he had sought to do so much! How could she say he was unkind to her?—and say it to a fellow like this? It was humiliating, indeed! But he would not defend himself. Not to Tom, not to his mother, not to any living soul, would he utter a word even resembling blame of the girl! He, at least, would carry himself generously! Everything, though she had plunged his heart in a pitcher of gall, should be done for her sake! She should go to her lover, and leave blame behind her with him! His sole care should be that the wind-bag should not collapse and slip out of it, that he should actually marry her; and, as soon as he had handed him over to her in safety, he would have done with her and with all women for ever, except his mother! Not once more would he speak to one of them in tone of friendship!

He looked at Tom full in the eyes, and made him no answer.

"If I don't find Letty this very morning," said Tom, "I

shall apply for a warrant to search your house : my uncle Rendall will give me one."

Godfrey smiled a smile of scorn, turned from him as a wise man turns from a fool, and went out of the gate.

He had just taken his horse from the boy and sent him off, when he saw a young woman coming hurriedly across the road, from the direction of Testbridge. Plainly she was on business of pressing import. She came nearer, and he saw it was Mary Marston. The moment she recognized Godfrey, she began to run to him ; but, when she came near enough to take notice of his mien, as he stood with his foot in the stirrup, with no word of greeting or look of reception, and inquiry only in every feature, her haste suddenly dropped, her flushed face turned pale, and she stood still, panting. Not a word could she utter, and was but just able to force a faint smile, with intent to reassure him.

CHAPTER XVII.

THE RESULT.

LETTY would never perhaps have come to herself in the cold of this world, under the shifting tent of the winter night, but for an outcast mongrel dog, which, wandering masterless and hungry, but not selfish, along the road, came upon her where she lay seemingly lifeless, and, recognizing with pity his neighbor in misfortune, began at once to give her—it was all he had that was separable—what help and healing might lie in a warm, honest tongue. Diligently he set himself to lick her face and hands.

By slow degrees her misery returned, and she sat up. Rejoiced at his success, the dog kept dodging about her, catching a lick here and a lick there, wherever he saw a spot of bare within his reach. By slow degrees, next, the knowledge of herself joined on to the knowledge of her misery, and she knew who it was that was miserable. She threw her arms round the dog, laid her head on his, and wept. This relieved her a little :

weeping is good, even to such as Alberigo in an ice-pot of hell. But she was cold to the very marrow, almost too cold to feel it ; and, when she rose, could scarcely put one foot before the other.

Not once, for all her misery, did she imagine a return to Thornwick. Without a thought of whither, she moved on, unaware even that it was in the direction of the town. The dog, delighted to believe that he had raised up to himself a mistress, followed humbly at her heel : but always when she stopped, as she did every few paces, ran round in front of her, and looked up in her face, as much as to say, "Here I am, mistress ! shall I lick again ?" If a dog could create, he would make masters and mistresses. Gladly would she then have fondled him, but feared the venture ; for, it seemed, were she to stoop, she must fall flat on the road, and never rise more.

Slowly the two went on, with motion scarce enough to keep the blood moving in their veins. Had she not been, for all her late depression, in fine health and strength, Letty could hardly have escaped death from the cold of that night. For many months after, some portion of every night she passed in dreaming over again this dreariest wandering ; and in her after life people would be puzzled to think why Mrs. Helmer looked so angry when any one spoke as if the animals died outright.

But, although she never forgot this part of the terrible night, she never dreamed of any rescue from it ; memory could not join it on to the next part, for again she lost consciousness, and could recall nothing between feeling the dog once more licking her face and finding herself in bed.

When Beenie opened her kitchen-door in the morning to let in the fresh air, she found seated on the step, and leaning against the wall, what she took first for a young woman asleep, and then for the dead body of one ; for, when she gave her a little shake, she fell sideways off the door-step. Beenie's heart smote her ; for during the last hours of her morning's sleep she had been disturbed by the howling of a dog, apparently in their own yard, but had paid no further attention to it than that of repeated mental objurgation : there stood the offender, looking up at her pitifully—ugly, disreputable, of breed unknown, one of the *canaille!* When the girl fell down, he darted at her, licked her cold face for a moment, then stretching out a long, gaunt neck, uttered from the depth of his hidebound frame the most melancholy appeal, not to Beenie, at whom he would not even look again, but to the open door. But, when Beenie, in whom, as in most of us, curiosity had the start of service, stooped, and, peering more closely into the face of the girl, recognized, though uncertainly, a known face, she too uttered a kind of howl, and straightway raising Letty's head drew her into the house. It is the mark of an imperfect humanity, that personal knowledge should spur the sides of hospitable intent : what difference does our knowing or not knowing make to the fact of human need ? The good Samaritan would never have been mentioned by the mouth of the True, had he been even an old acquaintance of the "certain man." But it is thus we learn ; and, from loving this one and that, we come to love all at last, and then is our humanity complete.

Letty moved not one frozen muscle, and Beenie, growing terrified, flew up the stair to her mistress. Mary sprang from her bed and hurried down. There, on the kitchen-floor, in front of the yet fireless grate, lay the body of Letty Lovel. A hideous dog was sitting on his haunches at her head The moment she entered, again the animal stretched out a long, bony neck, and sent forth a howl that rang penetrative through the house. It sounded in Mary's ears like the cry of the whole animal creation over the absence of their Maker. They raised her and carried her to Mary's room. There they laid her in the still warm bed, and proceeded to use all possible means for the restoration of heat and the renewal of circulation.

Here I am sorry to have to mention that Beenie, returning, unsuccessful, from their first efforts, to the kitchen, to get hot water, and finding the dog sitting there motionless, with his face turned toward the door by which they had carried Letty out, peevish with disappointment and dread, drove him from the kitchen, and from the court, into the street, where that same day he was seen wildly running with a pan at

his tail, and the next was found lying dead in a bit of waste
ground among stones and shards.   God rest all such !

But, as far as Letty was concerned, happily Beenie was not
an old woman for nothing.   With a woman's sympathy, Mary
hesitated to run for the doctor : who could tell what might be
involved in so strange an event ?   If they could but bring her
to, first, and learn something to guide them !   She pushed
delay to the very verge of danger.   But, soon after, thanks to
Beenie's persistence, indications of success appeared, and Letty
began to breathe.   It was then resolved between the nurses
that, for the present, they would keep the affair to themselves,
a conclusion affording much satisfaction to Beenie, in the consciousness that therein she had the better of the Turnbulls,
against whom she cherished an ever-renewed indignation.

But, when Mary set herself at length to find out from Letty
what had happened, without which she could not tell what to
do next, she found her mind so far gone that she understood
nothing said to her, or, at least, could return no rational response, although occasionally an individual word would seem
to influence the current of her ideas.   She kept murmuring
almost inarticulately ; but, to Mary's uneasiness, every now
and then plainly uttered the name Tom.   What was she to
make of it ?   In terror lest she should betray her, she must
yet do something.   Matters could not have gone wrong so far
that nothing could be done to set them at least a little straight !
If only she knew what !   A single false step might do no end
of mischief !   She must see Tom Helmer : without betraying
Letty, she might get from him some enlightenment.   She
knew his open nature, had a better opinion of him than many
had, and was a little nearer the right of him.   The doctor
must be called ; but she would, if possible, see Tom first.

It was not more than half an hour's walk to Warrender, and
she set out in haste.   She must get back before George Turnbull came to open the shop.

When she got near enough to see Mr. Wardour's face, she
read in it at once that he was there from the same cause as herself ; but there was no good omen to be drawn from its expression : she read there not only keen anxiety and bitter disap-

pointment, but lowering anger ; nor was that absent which she felt to be distrust of herself. The sole acknowledgment he made of her approach was to withdraw his foot from the stirrup and stand waiting.

"You know something," he said, looking cold and hard in her face.

"About what?" returned Mary, recovering herself; she was careful, for Letty's sake, to feel her way.

"I hope to goodness," returned Godfrey, almost fiercely, yet with a dash of rude indifference, "*you* are not concerned in this—business !"—he was about to use a bad adjective, but suppressed it.

"I *am* concerned in it," said Mary, with perfect quietness.

"You knew what was going on?" cried Wardour. "You knew that fellow there came prowling about Thornwick like a fox about a hen-roost? By Heaven! if I had but suspected it—"

"No, Mr. Wardour," interrupted Mary, already catching a glimpse of light, "I knew nothing of that."

"Then what do you mean by saying you are concerned in the matter?"

Mary thought he was behaving so unlike himself that a shock might be of service.

"Only this," she answered, "—that Letty is now lying in my room, whether dead or alive I am in doubt. She must have spent the night in the open air—and that without cloak or bonnet."

"Good God!" cried Godfrey. "And you could leave her like that!"

"She is attended to," replied Mary, with dignity. "There are worse evils to be warded than death, else I should not be here ; there are hard judgments and evil tongues.—Will you come and see her, Mr. Wardour?"

"No," answered Godfrey, gruffly.

"Shall I send a note to Mrs. Wardour, then?"

"I will tell her myself."

"What would you have me do about her?"

"I have no concern in the matter, but I suppose you had

better send for a doctor. Talk to that fellow there," he added, pointing with his whip toward the cottage, and again putting his foot in the stirrup. "Tell him he has brought her to disgrace—"

"I don't believe it," interrupted Mary, her face flushing with indignant shame. But Godfrey went on without heeding her :

"A—nd get him to marry her off-hand, if you can—for, by God ! he *shall* marry her, or I will kill him."

He spoke looking round at her over his shoulder, a scowl on his face, his foot in the stirrup, one hand twisted in the mane of his horse, and the other with the whip stretched out as if threatening the universe. Mary stood white but calm, and made no answer. He swung himself into the saddle, and rode away. She turned to the gate.

From behind the shrubbery, Tom had heard all that passed between them, and, meeting her as she entered, led the way to a side-walk, unseen from the house.

"O Miss Marston ! what is to be done ?" he said. "This is a terrible business ! But I am so glad you have got her, poor girl ! I heard all you said to that brute, Wardour. Thank you, thank you a thousand times, for taking her part. Indeed, you spoke but the truth for her. Let me tell you all I know."

He had not much to tell, however, beyond what Mary knew already.

"She keeps calling out for you, Mr. Helmer," she said, when he had ended.

"I will go with you. Come, come," he answered.

"You will leave a message for your mother ?"

"Never mind my mother. She's good at finding out for herself."

"She ought to be told," said Mary ; "but I can't stop to argue it with you. Certainly your first duty is to Letty now. Oh, if people only wouldn't hide things !"

"Come along," cried Tom, hurrying before her ; "I will soon set everything right."

"How shall we manage with the doctor ?" said Mary, as

they went. "We can not do without him, for I am sure she is in danger."

"Oh, no!" said Tom. "She will be all right when she sees me. But we will take the doctor on our way, and prepare him."

When they came to the doctor's house, Mary walked on, and Tom told the doctor he had met Miss Marston on her way to him, and had come instead : she wanted to let him know that Miss Lovel had come to her quite unexpected that morning; that she was delirious, and had apparently wandered from home under an attack of brain-fever, or something of the sort.

CHAPTER XVIII.

MARY AND GODFREY.

EVERYTHING went very tolerably, so far as concerned the world of talk, in the matter of Letty's misfortunes. Rumors, it is true—and more than one of them strange enough—did for a time go floating about the country ; but none of them came to the ears of Tom or of Mary, and Letty was safe from hearing anything ; and the engagement between her and Tom soon became generally known.

Mrs. Helmer was very angry, and did all she could to make Tom break it off—it was so much below him ! But in nothing could the folly of the woman have been more apparent than in her fancying, with the experience of her life before her, that any opposition of hers could be effectual otherwise than to the confirmation of her son's will. So short-sighted was she as to originate most of the reports to Letty's disadvantage ; but Tom's behavior, on the other hand, was strong to put them down ; for the man is seldom found so faithful where such reports are facts.

Mrs. Wardour took care to say nothing unkind of Letty. She was of her own family ; and, besides, not only was Tom a better match than she could have expected for her, but she was more than satisfied to have Godfrey's dangerous toy thus drawn away beyond his reach. As soon as ever the doctor gave his permission, she went to see her; but, although, dismayed at sight of her suffering face, she did not utter one unkind word, her visit was so plainly injurious in its effects, that it was long before Mary would consent to a repetition of it.

Letty's recovery was very slow. The spring was close at hand before the bloom began to reappear—and then it was but fitfully—in Letty's cheek. Neither her gayety nor her usual excess of timorousness returned. A certain sad seriousness had taken the place of both, and she seemed to look out from deeper eyes. I can not think that Letty had begun to perceive that there actually is a Nature shaping us to its own ends; but I think she had begun to feel that Mary lived in the conscious presence of such a power. To Tom she behaved very sweetly, but more like a tender sister than a lover, and Mary began to doubt whether her heart was altogether Tom's. From mention of approaching marriage, she turned with a nervous, uneasy haste. Had the insight which the enforced calmness of suffering sometimes brings opened her eyes to anything in Tom? The doubt filled Mary with anxiety. She thought and thought, until—delicate matter as it was to meddle with, and small encouragement as Godfrey Wardour had given her to expect sympathy—she yet made up her mind to speak to him on the subject—and the rather that she was troubled at the unworthiness of his behavior to Letty: gladly would she have him treat her with the generosity essential to the idea she had formed of him.

She went, therefore, one Sunday evening, to Thornwick, and requested to see Mr. Wardour.

It was plainly an unwilling interview he granted her, but she was not thereby deterred from opening her mind to him.

"I fear, Mr. Wardour," she said, "—I come altogether without authority—but I fear Letty has been rather hurried in her engagement with Mr. Helmer. I think she dreads being married—at least so soon."

"You would have her break it off?" said Godfrey, with cold restraint.

up Tom, satisfied that she did not love him, she could be
nothing more to him, even in the relation in which he had
allowed her to think she stood to him. She had behaved too
deceitfully, too heartlessly, too ungratefully, too *vulgarly* for
that! Yet was his heart torn every time the vision of the
gentle girl rose before "that inward eye," which, for long,
could no more be to him "the bliss of solitude"; when he saw
those hazel depths looking half anxious, half sorrowful in his
face, as, with sadly comic sense of her stupidity, she listened
while he explained or read something he loved. But no; nothing else would do than act the mere honest guardian, compelling them to marry, no matter how slight or transient the
shadow the man had cast over her reputation!

Mary returned with a sense of utter failure.

But before long she came to the conclusion that all was
right between Tom and Letty, and that the cause of her anxiety
had lain merely in Letty's loss of animal spirits.

Now and then Mary tried to turn Tom's attention a little
toward the duty of religion: Tom received the attempt with
gentle amusement and a little *badinage*. It was all very well
for girls! Indeed, he had made the observation that girls who
had no religion were "strong-minded," and that he could not
endure! Like most men, he was so well satisfied with himself,
that he saw no occasion to take trouble to be anything better
than he was. Never suspecting what a noble creature he was
meant to be, he never saw what a poor creature he was. In
his own eyes he was a man any girl might be proud to marry.
He had not yet, however, sunk to the depth of those who, having caught a glimpse of nobility, confess wretchedness, excuse
it, and decline to allow that the noble they see they are bound
to be; or, worse still, perhaps, admit the obligation, but move
no inch to fulfill it. It seems to me that such must one day
make acquaintance with *essential* misery—a thing of which they
have no conception.

Day after day Tom passed through Turnbull and Marston's
shop to see Letty. Tom cared for nobody, else he would have
gone in by the kitchen-door, which was the only other entrance
to the house; but I do not know whether it is a pity or not

that he did not hear the remarks which rose like the dust of his passage behind him. In the same little sitting-room, where for so many years Mary had listened to the slow, tender wisdom of her father, a clever young man was now making love to an ignorant girl, whom he did not half understand or half appreciate, all the time he feeling himself the greater and wiser and more valuable of the two. He was unaware, however, that he did feel so, for he had never yet become conscious of any *fact* concerning himself.

The whole Turnbull family, from the beginnings of things self-constituted judges of the two Marstons, were not the less critical of the daughter, that the father had been taken from her. There was grumbling in the shop every time she ran up to see Letty, every one regarding her and speaking of her as a servant neglecting her duty. Yet all knew well enough that she was co-proprietor of business and stock, and the elder Turnbull knew besides that, if the lawyer to whose care William Marston had committed his daughter were at that moment to go into the affairs of the partnership, he would find that Mary had a much larger amount of money actually in the business than he.

Of all matters connected with the business, except those of her own department, Mary was ignorant. Her father had never neglected his duty, but he had so far neglected what the world calls a man's interests as to leave his affairs much too exclusively in the hands of his partner; he had been too much interested in life itself to look sharply after anything less than life. He acknowledged no *worldly* interests at all: either God cared for his interests or he himself did not. Whether he might not have been more attentive to the state of his affairs without danger of deeper loss, I do not care to examine or determine; the result of his life in the world was a grand success. Now, Mary's feeling and judgment in regard to *things* being identical with her father's, Turnbull, instructed by his greed, both natural and acquired, argued thus—unconsciously almost, but not the less argued—that what Mary valued so little, and he valued so much, must, by necessary deduction, be more his than hers—and *logically* ought to be *legally*. So servants begin to steal, arguing that such and such things are only lying about, and nobody cares for them.

But Turnbull, knowing that, notwithstanding the reason on his side, it was not safe to act on such a conclusion, had for some time felt no little anxiety to secure himself from investigation and possible disaster by the marriage of Mary to his son George.

Tom Helmer had now to learn that, by his father's will, made doubtless under the influence of his mother, he was to have but a small annuity so long as she lived. Upon this he determined nevertheless to marry, confident in his literary faculty, which, he never doubted, would soon raise it to a very sufficient income. Nor did Mary attempt to dissuade him : for what could be better for a disposition like his than care for the things of this life, occasioned by the needs of others dependent upon him ! Besides, there seemed to be nothing else now possible for Letty. So, in the early summer, they were married, no relative present except Mrs. Wardour, Mr. Helmer and Godfrey having both declined their invitation : and no friend, except Mary for bridesmaid, and Mr. Pycroft, a school and college friend of Tom's, who was now making a bohemian livelihood in London by writing for the weekly press, as he called certain journals of no high standing, for groom's man. After the ceremony, and a breakfast provided by Mary, the young couple took the train for London.

CHAPTER XIX.

MARY IN THE SHOP.

MORE than a year had now passed from the opening of my narrative. It was full summer again at Testbridge, and things, to the careless eye, were unchanged, and, to the careless mind, would never change, although, in fact, nothing was the same, and nothing could continue as it now was. For were not the earth and the sun a little colder ? Had not the moon crumbled a little ? And had not the eternal warmth, unperceived save of a few, drawn a little nearer—the clock that measures the eternal day ticked one tick more to the hour when the Son of Man will come ? But the greed and the fawning did go on unchanged, save it were for the worse, in the shop of Turnbull and Marston, seasoned only with the heavenly salt of Mary's good ministration.

She was very lonely. Letty was gone ; and the link between Mr. Wardour and her not only broken, but a gulf of separation in its place. Not the less remained the good he had given her. No good is ever lost. The heavenly porter was departed, but had left the door wide. She had seen him but once since Letty's marriage, and then his salutation was like that of a dead man in a dream ; for in his sore heart he still imagined her the confidante of Letty's deception.

But the shadow of her father's absence swallowed all the other shadows. The air of warmth and peace and conscious safety which had hitherto surrounded her was gone, and in its place cold, exposure, and annoyance. Between them her father and she had originated a mutually protective atmosphere of love ; when that failed, the atmosphere of earthly relation rushed in and enveloped her. The moment of her father's departure, malign influences, inimical to the very springs of her life, concentrated themselves upon her : it was the design of John Turnbull that she should not be comfortable so long as she did not irrevocably cast in her lot with his family ; and, the rest in the shop being mostly creatures of his own choice, by a sort of implicit understanding they proceeded to make her uncomfortable. So long as they confined themselves to silence, neglect, and general exclusion, Mary heeded little their behavior, for no intercourse with them, beyond that of external good offices, could be better than indifferent to her ; but, when they advanced to positive interference, her position became indeed hard to endure. They would, for instance, keep watch on her serving, and, as soon as the customer was gone, would find open fault with this or that she had said or done. But even this was comparatively endurable : when they advanced to the insolence of doing the same in the presence of

the customer, she found it more than she could bear with even
a show of equanimity. She did her best, however ; and for
some time things went on without any symptom of approaching crisis. But it was impossible this should continue : for,
had she been capable of endless endurance, her persecutors
would only have gone on to worse. But Mary was naturally
quick-tempered, and the chief trouble they caused her was the
control of her temper ; for, although she had early come to
recognize the imperative duty of this branch of self-govern-
ment, she was not yet perfect in it. Not every one who can serve
unboundedly can endure patiently : and the more gentle some
natures, the more they resent the rudeness which springs from
an opposite nature ; absolutely courteous, they flame at discourtesy, and thus lack of the perfection to which patience
would and must raise them. When Turnbull, in the narrow
space behind the counter, would push his way past her without
other pretense of apology than something like a sneer, she did
feel for a moment as if evil were about to have the victory over
her ; and when Mrs. Turnbull came in, which happily was but
seldom, she felt as if from some sepulchre in her mind a very
demon sprang to meet her. For she behaved to her worst of
all. She would heave herself in with the air and look of a vulgar duchess , for, from the height of her small consciousness,
she looked down upon the shop, and never entered it save as a
customer. The daughter of a small country attorney, who,
notwithstanding his unneglected opportunities, had not been
too successful to accept as a husband for his daughter such a
tradesman as John Turnbull, she arrogated position from her
idea of her father's position : and, while bitterly cherishing
the feeling that she had married beneath her, obstinately excluded the fact that therein she had descended to her husband's level, regarding herself much in the light of a prin-
cess whose disguise takes nothing from her rank. She was
like those ladies who, having set their seal to the death of
their first husbands by marrying again, yet cling to the title
they gave them, and continue to call themselves by their name.

Mrs. Turnbull never bought a dress at the shop. No one
should say of her, it was easy for a snail to live in a castle !

She took pains to let her precious public know that she went to London to make her purchases. If she did not mention also that she made them at the warehouses where her husband was a customer, procuring them at the same price he would have paid, it was because she saw no occasion. It was indeed only for some small occasional necessity she ever crossed the threshold of the place whence came all the money she had to spend. When she did, she entered it with such airs as she imagined to represent the consciousness of the scion of a county family : there is one show of breeding vulgarity seldom assumes — simplicity. No sign of recognition would pass between her husband and herself : by one stern refusal to acknowledge his advances, she had from the first taught him that in the shop they were strangers : he saw the rock of ridicule ahead, and required no second lesson : when she was present, he never knew it. George had learned the lesson before he went into the business, and Mary had never required it. The others behaved to her as to any customer known to stand upon her dignity, but she made them no return in politeness ; and the way she would order Mary, now there was no father to offend, would have been amusing enough but for the irritation its extreme rudeness caused her. She did, however, manage sometimes to be at once both a little angry and much amused. Small idea had Mrs. Turnbull of the diversion which on such occasions she afforded the customers present.

One day, a short time before her marriage, delayed by the illness of Mr. Redmain, Miss Mortimer happened to be in the shop, and was being served by Mary, when Mrs. Turnbull entered. Careless of the customer, she walked straight up to her as if she saw none, and in a tone that would be dignified, and was haughty, desired her to bring her a reel of marking-cotton. Now it had been a principle with Mary's father, and she had thoroughly learned it, that whatever would be counted a rudeness by *any* customer, must be shown to *none*. " If all are equal in the sight of God," he would say, " how dare I leave a poor woman to serve a rich ? Would I leave one countess to serve another ? My business is to sell in the name of

Christ. To respect persons in the shop would be just the
same as to do it in the chapel, and would be to deny him."

" Excuse me, ma'am," said Mary, " I am waiting on Miss
Mortimer," and went on with what she was about. Mrs.
Turnbull flounced away, a little abashed, not by Mary, but by
finding who the customer was, and carried her commands
across the shop. After a moment or two, however, imagining,
in the blindness of her surging anger, that Miss Mortimer was
gone, whereas she had only moved a little farther on to look at
something, she walked up to Mary in a fury.

"Miss Marston," she said, her voice half choked with rage,
" I am at a loss to understand what you mean by your impertinence."

"I am sorry you should think me impertinent," answered
Mary. " You saw yourself I was engaged with a customer,
and could not attend to you."

" Your tone was insufferable, miss!" cried the grand lady ;
but what more she would have said I can not tell, for just then
Miss Mortimer resumed her place in front of Mary. She had
no idea of her position in the shop, neither suspected who her
assailant was, and, fearing the woman's accusation might do her
an injury, felt compelled to interfere.

" Miss Marston," she said—she had just heard Mrs. Turnbull
use her name—" if you should be called to account by your em-
ployer, will you, please, refer to me ? You were perfectly civil
both to me and to this—" she hesitated a perceptible moment,
but ended with the word "*lady,*" peculiarly toned.

" Thank you, ma'am," said Mary, with a smile, " but it is
of no consequence."

This answer would have almost driven the woman out of
her reason—already, between annoyance with herself and anger
with Mary, her hue was purple : something she called her constitution required a nightly glass of brandy-and-water—but she
was so dumfounded by Miss Mortimer's defense of Mary, which
she looked upon as an assault on herself, so painfully aware
that all hands were arrested and all eyes fixed on herself, and
so mortified with the conviction that her husband was enjoying
her discomfiture, that, with what haughtiness she could extem-

porize from consuming offense, she made a sudden vortical gyration, and walked from the vile place.

Now, George never lost a chance of recommending himself to Mary by siding with her—but only after the battle. He came up to her now with a mean, unpleasant look, intended to represent sympathy, and, approaching his face to hers, said, confidentially :

"What made my mother speak to you like that, Mary ?"

"You must ask herself," she answered.

"There you are, as usual, Mary !" he protested ; "you will never let a fellow take your part !"

"If you wanted to take my part, you should have done so when there would have been some good in it."

"How could I, before Miss Mortimer, you know !"

"Then why do it now ?"

"Well, you see—it's hard to bear hearing you ill used ! What did you say to Miss Mortimer that angered my mother ?"

His father heard him, and, taking the cue, called out in the rudest fashion :

"If you think, Mary, you're going to take liberties with customers because you've got no one over you, the sooner you find you're mistaken the better."

Mary made him no answer.

On her way to "the villa," Mrs. Turnbull, spurred by spite, had got hold of the same idea as George, only that she invented where he had but imagined it ; and when her husband came home in the evening fell out upon him for allowing Mary to be impertinent to his customers, in whom for the first time she condescended to show an interest :

"There she was, talking away to that Miss Mortimer as if she was Beenie in the kitchen ! County people won't stand being treated as if one was just as good as another, I can tell you ! She'll be the ruin of the business, with her fine-lady-airs ! Who's *she*, I should like to know ?"

"I shall speak to her," said the husband. "But," he went on, "I fear you will no longer approve of marrying her to George, if you think she's an injury to the business !"

"You know, as well as I do, that is the readiest way to get

her out of it. Make her marry George, and she will fall into my hands. If I don't make her repent her impudence then, you may call me the fool you think me."

Mary knew well enough what they wanted of her; but of the real cause at the root of their desire she had no suspicion. Recoiling altogether from Mr. Turnbull's theories of business, which were in flat repudiation of the laws of Him who alone understands either man or his business, she yet had not a doubt of his honesty as the trades and professions count honesty. Her father had left the money affairs of the firm to Mr. Turnbull, and she did the same. It was for no other reason than that her position had become almost intolerable, that she now began to wonder if she was bound to this mode of life, and whether it might not be possible to forsake it.

Greed is the soul's thieving; where there is greed, there can not be honesty. John Turnbull, it is true, was not only proud of his reputation for honesty, but prided himself on being an honest man; yet not the less was he dishonest—and that with a dishonesty such as few of those called thieves have attained to.

Like most of his kind, he had been neither so vulgar nor so dishonest from the first. In the prime of youth he had had what the people about him called high notions, and counted quixotic fancies. But it was not their mockery of his tall talk that turned him aside; opposition invariably confirmed Turnbull. He had never set his face in the right direction. The seducing influence lay in himself. It was not the truth he had loved; it was the show of fine sentiment he had enjoyed. The distinction of holding loftier opinions than his neighbors was the ground of his advocacy of them. Something of the beauty of the truth he must have seen—who does not?—else he could not have been thus moved at all; but he had never denied himself even a whim for the carrying out of one of his ideas; he had never set himself to be better; and the whole mountain-chain, therefore, of his notions sank and sank, until at length their loftiest peak was the maxim, *Honesty is the best policy*— a maxim which, true enough in fact, will no more make a man honest than the economic aphorism, *The supply equals the demand*, will makes policy the ground of his honesty will discover more and more exceptions to the rule. The career, therefore, of Turnbull of the high notions had been a gradual descent to the level of his present dishonesty and vulgarity; nothing is so vulgarizing as dishonesty. I do not care to follow the history of any man downward. Let him who desires to look on such a panorama, faithfully and thoroughly depicted, read Auerbach's "Diethelm von Buchenberg."

Things went a little more quietly in the shop after this for a while: Turnbull probably was afraid of precipitating matters, and driving Mary to seek counsel—from which much injury might arise to his condition and prospects. As if to make amends for past rudeness, he even took some pains to be polite, putting on something of the manners with which he favored his "best customers," of all mankind in his eyes the most to be honored. This, of course, rendered him odious in the eyes of Mary, and ripened the desire to free herself from circumstances which from garments seemed to have grown cerements. She was, however, too much her father's daughter to do anything in haste.

She might have been less willing to abandon them, had she had any friends like-minded with herself, but, while they were all kindly disposed to her, none of the religious associates of her father, who knew, or might have known her well, approved of her. They spoke of her generally with a shake of the head, and an unquestioned feeling that God was not pleased with her. There are few of the so-called religious who seem able to trust either God or their neighbor in matters that concern those two and no other. Nor had she had opportunity of making acquaintance with any who believed and lived like her father, in other of the Christian communities of the town. But she had her Bible, and, when that troubled her, as it did not a little sometimes, she had the Eternal Wisdom to cry to for such wisdom as she could receive; and one of the things she learned was, that nowhere in the Bible was she called on to believe in the Bible, but in the living God, in whom is no darkness, and who alone can give light to understand his own intent. All her troubles she carried to him.

It was not always the solitude of her room that Mary sought to get out of the wind of the world. Her love of nature had been growing stronger, notably, from her father's death. If the world is God's, every true man ought to feel at home in it. Something is wrong if the calm of the summer night does not sink into the heart, for the peace of God is there embodied. Something is wrong in the man to whom the sunrise is not a divine glory, for therein are embodied the truth, the simplicity, the might of the Maker. When all is true in us, we shall feel the visible presence of the Watchful and Loving : for the thing that he works is its sign and symbol, its clothing fact. In the gentle conference of earth and sky, in the witnessing colors of the west, in the wind that so gently visited her cheek, in the great burst of a new morning, Mary saw the sordid affairs of Mammon, to whose worship the shop seemed to become more and more of a temple, sink to the bottom of things, as the mud, which, during the day, the feet of the drinking cattle have stirred, sinks in the silent night to the bottom of the clear pool ; and she saw that the sordid is all in the soul, and not in the shop. The service of Christ is help. The service of Mammon is greed.

Letty was no good correspondent : after one letter in which she declared herself perfectly happy, and another in which she said almost nothing, her communication ceased. Mrs. Wardour had been in the shop again and again, but on each occasion had sought the service of another ; and once, indeed, when Mary alone was disengaged, had waited until another was at liberty. While Letty was in her house, she had been civil, but, as soon as she was gone, seemed to show that she held her concerned in the scandal that had befallen Thornwick. Once, as I have said, she met Godfrey. It was in the fields. He was walking hurriedly, as usual, but with his head bent, and a gloomy gaze fixed upon nothing visible. He started when he saw her, took his hat off, and, with his eyes seeming to look far away beyond her, passed without a word. Yet had she been to him a true pupil ; for, although neither of them knew it, Mary had learned more from Godfrey than Godfrey was capable of teaching. She had turned thought and feeling into life, into reality, into creation. They speak of the *creations* of the human intellect, of the human imagination! there is nothing man can do comes half so near the making of the Maker as the ordering of his way—except one thing: the highest creation of which man is capable, is to will the will of the Father. That *has* in it an element of the purely creative, and then is man likest God. But simply to do what we ought, is an altogether higher, diviner, more potent, more creative thing, than to write the grandest poem, paint the most beautiful picture, carve the mightiest statue, build the most worshiping temple, dream out the most enchanting commotion of melody and harmony. If Godfrey could have seen the soul of the maiden into whose face his discourtesy called the hot blood, he would have beheld there simply what God made the earth for; as it was, he saw a shop-girl, to whom in happier circumstances he had shown kindness, in whom he was now no longer interested. But the sight of his troubled face called up all the mother in her; a rush of tenderness, born of gratitude, flooded her heart. He was sad, and she could do nothing to comfort him! He had been royally good to her, and no return was in her power. She could not even let him know how she had profited by his gifts! She could come near him with no ministration! The bond between them was an eternal one, yet were they separated by a gulf of unrelation. Not a mountain-range, but a stayless nothingness parted them. She built many a castle, with walls of gratitude and floors of service to entertain Godfrey Wardour; but they stood on no foundation of imagined possibility.

CHAPTER XX.

THE WEDDING-DRESS.

For all her troubles, however, Mary had her pleasures, even in the shop. It was a delight to receive the friendly greetings of such as had known and honored her father. She had the pleasure, as real as it was simple, of pure service, reaping the fruit of the earth in the joy of the work that was given her to do ; there is no true work that does not carry its reward, though there are few that do not drop it and lose it. She gathered also the pleasure of seeing and talking with people whose manners and speech were of finer grain and tone than those about her. When Hesper Mortimer entered the shop, she brought with her delight : her carriage was like the gait of an ode ; her motions were rhythm ; and her speech was music. Her smile was light, and her whole presence an enchantment to Mary. The reading aloud which Wardour had led her to practice had taught her much, not only in respect of the delicacies of speech and utterance, but in the deeper matters of motion, relation, and harmony. Hesper's clear-cut but not too sharply defined consonants, her soft but full-bodied vowels ; above all, her slow cadences that hovered on the verge of song, as her walk on the verge of a slow aerial dance ; the carriage of her head, the movements of her lips, her arms, her hands ; the self-possession that seemed the very embodiment of law—these formed together a whole of inexpressible delight, inextricably for Mary associated with music and verse : she would hasten to serve her as if she had been an angel come to do a little earthly shopping, and return with the next heavenward tide. Hesper, in response all but unconscious, would be waited on by no other than Mary ; and always between them passed some sweet, gentle nothings, which afforded Hesper more pleasure than she could have accounted for.

Her wedding-day was now for the third time fixed, when one morning she entered the shop to make some purchases. Not happy in the prospect before her, she was yet inclined to make the best of it so far as clothes were concerned—the more so, perhaps, that she had seldom yet been dressed to her satisfaction : she was now brooding over a certain idea for her wedding-dress, which she had altogether failed in the attempt to convey to her London *couturière;* and it had come into her head to try whether Mary might not grasp her idea, and help her to make it intelligible.

Mary listened and thought, questioned, and desired explanations—at length, begged she would allow her to ponder the thing a little : she could hardly at once venture to say anything. Hesper laughed, and said she was taking a small matter too seriously—concluding from Mary's hesitation that she had but perplexed her, and that she could be of no use to her in the difficulty.

"A small matter ? Your wedding-dress !" exclaimed Mary, in a tone of expostulation.

Hesper did not laugh again, but gave a little sigh instead, which struck sadly on Mary's sympathetic heart. She cast a quick look in her face. Hesper caught the look, and understood it. For one passing moment she felt as if, amid the poor pleasure of adorning herself for a hated marriage, she had found a precious thing of which she had once or twice dreamed, never thought as a possible existence—a friend, namely, to love her : the next, she saw the absurdity of imagining a friend in a shop-girl.

"But I must make up my mind so soon !" she answered. "Madame Crepine gave me her idea, in answer to mine, but nothing like it, two days ago ; and, as I have not written again, I fear she may be taking her own way with the thing. I am certain to hate it."

"I will talk to you about it as early as you please to-morrow, if that will do," returned Mary.

She knew nothing about dressmaking beyond what came of a true taste, and the experience gained in cutting out and making her own garments, which she had never yet found a dressmaker to do to her mind ; and, indeed, Hesper had been led to ask her advice mainly from observing how neat the design of her dresses was, and how faithfully they fitted her. Dress is a sort of freemasonry between girls.

"But I can not have the horses to-morrow," said Hesper.

"I might," pondered Mary aloud, after a moment's silence, " walk out to Durnmelling this evening after the shop is shut. By that time I shall have been able to think ; I find it impossible, with you before me."

Hesper acknowledged the compliment with a very pleasant

smile. If it be true, as I may not doubt, that women, in dressing, have the fear of women and not of men before their eyes,
then a compliment from some women must be more acceptable
to some than a compliment from any man but the specially
favored.

"Thank you a thousand times," she drawled, sweetly.
"Then I shall expect you. Ask for my maid. She will take
you to my room. Good-by for the present."

As soon as she was gone, Mary, her mind's eye full of her
figure, her look, her style, her motion, gave herself to the important question of the dress conceived by Hesper; and during
her dinner-hour contrived to cut out and fit to her own person
the pattern of a garment such as she supposed intended in the
not very lucid description she had given her. When she was
free, she set out with it for Durnmelling.

It was rather a long walk, the earlier part of it full of sad
reminders of the pleasure with which, greater than ever accompanied her to church, she went to pay her Sunday visit at
Thornwick; but the latter part, although the places were so
near, almost new to her: she had never been within the gate
of Durnmelling, and felt curious to see the house of which she
had so often heard.

The butler opened the door to her—an elderly man, of conscious dignity rather than pride, who received the "young person" graciously, and, leaving her in the entrance-hall, went to
find "Miss Mortimer's maid," he said, though there was but
one lady's-maid in the establishment.

The few moments she had to wait far more than repaid her
for the trouble she had taken: through a side-door she looked
into the great roofless hall, the one grand thing about the house.
Its majesty laid hold upon her, and the shopkeeper's daughter
felt the power of the ancient dignity and ineffaceable beauty
far more than any of the family to which it had for centuries
belonged.

She was standing lost in delight, when a rude voice called
to her from half-way up a stair:

"You're to come this way, miss."

With a start, she turned and went.

It was a large room to which she was led. There was no one in it, and she walked to an open window, which had a wide outlook across the fields. A little to the right, over some trees, were the chimneys of Thornwick. She almost started to see them—so near, and yet so far—like the memory of a sweet, sad story.

"Do you like my prospect?" asked the voice of Hesper behind her. "It is flat."

"I like it much, Miss Mortimer," answered Mary, turning quickly with a bright face. "Flatness has its own beauty. I sometimes feel as if room was all I wanted; and of that there is so much there! You see over the tree-tops, too, and that is good—sometimes—don't you think?"

Miss Mortimer gave no other reply than a gentle stare, which expressed no curiosity, although she had a vague feeling that Mary's words meant something. Most girls of her class would hardly have got so far.

The summer was backward, but the day had been fine and warm, and the evening was dewy and soft, and full of evasive odor. The window looked westward, and the setting sun threw long shadows toward the house. A gentle wind was moving in the tree-tops. The spirit of the evening had laid hold of Mary. The peace of faithfulness filled the air. The day's business vanished, molten in the rest of the coming night. Even Hesper's wedding-dress was gone from her thoughts. She was in her own world, and ready, for very quietness of spirit, to go to sleep. But she had not forgotten the delight of Hesper's presence; it was only that all relation between them was gone except such as was purely human.

"This reminds me so of some beautiful verses of Henry Vaughan!" she said, half dreamily.

"What do they say?" drawled Hesper.

Mary repeated as follows:

> "'The frosts are past, the storms are gone,
> And backward life at last comes on.
> And here in dust and dirt, O here,
> The Lilies of His love appear!'"

"Whose did you say the lines were?' asked Hesper, with merest automatic response.

"Henry Vaughan's," answered Mary, with a little spiritual shiver, as of one who had dropped a pearl in the miry way

"I never heard of him," rejoined Hesper, with entire indifference.

For anything she knew, he might be an occasional writer in "The Belgrave Magazine," or "The Fireside Herald." Ignorance is one of the many things of which a lady of position is never ashamed; wherein she is, it may be, more right than most of my readers will be inclined to allow; for ignorance is not the thing to be ashamed of, but neglect of knowledge. That a young person in Mary's position should know a certain thing, was, on the other hand, a reason why a lady in Hesper's position should not know it! Was it possible a shop-girl should know anything that Hesper ought to know and did not? It was foolish of Mary, perhaps, but she had vaguely felt that a beautiful lady like Miss Mortimer, and with such a name as Hesper, must know all the lovely things she knew, and many more besides.

"He lived in the time of the Charleses," she said, with a tremble in her voice, for she was ashamed to show her knowledge against the other's ignorance.

"Ah!" drawled Hesper, with a confused feeling that people who kept shops read stupid old books that lay about, because they could not subscribe to a circulating library —"Are you fond of poetry?" she added: for the slight, shadowy shyness, into which her venture had thrown Mary, drew her heart a little, though she hardly knew it, and inclined her to say something.

"Yes," answered Mary, who felt like a child questioned by a stranger in the road; "—when it is good," she added, hesitatingly.

"What do you mean by good?" asked Hesper—out of her knowledge, Mary thought, but it was not even out of her ignorance, only out of her indifference People must say something, lest life should stop.

"That is a question difficult to answer," replied Mary.

"I have often asked it of myself, but never got any plain answer."

"I do not see why you should find any difficulty in it," returned Hesper, with a shadow of interest. "You know what you mean when you say to yourself you like this, or you do not like that."

"How clever she is, too!" thought Mary; but she answered: "I don't think I ever say anything to myself about the poetry I read—not at the time, I mean. If I like it, it drowns me; and, if I don't like it, it is as the Dead Sea to me, in which you know you can't sink, if you try ever so."

Hesper saw nothing in the words, and began to fear that Mary was so stupid as to imagine herself clever; whereupon the fancy she had taken to her began to sink like water in sand. The two were still on their feet, near the window—Mary, in her bonnet, with her back to it, and Hesper, in evening attire, with her face to the sunset, so that the one was like a darkling worshiper, the other like the radiant goddess. But the truth was, that Hesper was a mere earthly woman, and Mary a heavenly messenger to her. Neither of them knew it, but so it was; for the angels are essentially humble, and Hesper would have condescended to any angel out of her own class.

"I think I know good poetry by what it does to me," resumed Mary, thoughtfully, just as Hesper was about to pass to the business of the hour.

"Indeed!" rejoined Hesper, not less puzzled than before, if the word should be used where there was no effort to understand. Poetry had never done anything to her, and Mary's words conveyed no shadow of an idea.

The tone of her *indeed* checked Mary. She hesitated a moment, but went on.

"Sometimes," she said, "it makes me feel as if my heart were too big for my body; sometimes as if all the grand things in heaven and earth were trying to get into me at once; sometimes as if I had discovered something nobody else knew; sometimes as if—no, not *as if*, for then I *must* go and pray to God. But I am trying to tell you what I don't know how to tell. I am not talking nonsense, I hope, only ashamed of myself that I can't talk sense.—I will show you what I have been doing about your dress."

Far more to Hesper's surprise and admiration than any of her half-foiled attempts at the utterance of her thoughts, Mary, taking from her pocket the shape she had prepared, put it on herself, and, slowly revolving before Hesper, revealed what in her eyes was a masterpiece.

"But how clever of you!" she cried.—Her own fingers had not been quite innocent of the labor of the needle, for money had long been scarce at Durnmelling, and in the paper shape she recognized the hand of an artist.—"Why," she continued, "you are nothing less than an accomplished dress-maker!"

"That I dare not think myself," returned Mary, "seeing I never had a lesson."

"I wish you would make my wedding-dress," said Hesper.

"I could not venture, even if I had the time," answered Mary. "The moment I began to cut into the stuff, I should be terrified, and lose my self-possession. I never made a dress for anybody but myself."

"You are a little witch!" said Hesper; while Mary, who had roughly prepared a larger shape, proceeded to fit it to her person.

She was busy pinning and unpinning, shifting and pinning again, when suddenly Hesper said:

"I suppose you know I am going to marry money?"

"Oh! don't say that. It's too dreadful!" cried Mary, stopping her work, and looking up in Hesper's face.

"What! you supposed I was going to marry a man like Mr. Redmain for love?" rejoined Hesper, with a hard laugh.

"I can not bear to think of it!" said Mary. "But you do not really mean it! You are only—making fun of me! Do say you are."

"Indeed, I am not. I wish I could say I was! It is very horrid, I know, but where's the good of mincing matters? If I did not call the thing by its name, the thing would be just the same. You know, people in our world have to do as they must; they can't pick and choose like you happy creatures. I dare say, now, you are engaged to a young man you love with all your heart, one you would rather marry than any other in the whole universe."

"Oh, dear, no!" returned Mary, with a smile most plainly fancy-free. "I am not engaged, nor in the least likely to be."

"And not in love either?" said Hesper—with such coolness that Mary looked up in her face to know if she had really said so.

"No," she replied.

"No more am I," echoed Hesper; "that is the one good thing in the business: I sha'n't break my heart, as some girls do. At least, so they say—I don't believe it: how could a girl be so indecent? It is bad enough to marry a man: that one can't avoid; but to die of a broken heart is to be a traitor to your sex. As if women couldn't live without men!"

Mary smiled, and was silent. She had read a good deal, and thought she understood such things better than Miss Mortimer. But she caught herself smiling, and felt as if she had sinned. For that a young woman should speak of love and marriage as Miss Mortimer did, was too horrible to be understood—and she had smiled! She would have been less shocked with Hesper, however, had she known that she forced an indifference she could not feel—her last poor rampart of sand against the sea of horror rising around her. But from her heart she pitied her, almost as one of the lost.

"Don't fix your eyes like that," said Hesper, angrily, "or I shall cry. Look the other way, and listen.—I am marrying money, I tell you—and for money; therefore, I ought to get the good of it. Mr. Mortimer will be father enough to see to that! So I shall be able to do what I please. I have fallen in love with you; and why shouldn't I have you for my—"

She paused, hesitating: what was it she was about to propose to the little lady standing before her? She had been going to say *maid*: what was it that checked her? The feeling was to herself shapeless and nameless; but, however some of my readers may smile at the notion of a girl who served behind a counter being a lady, and however ready Hesper Mortimer would have been to join them, it was yet a vague sense of the fact that was now embarrassing her, for she was not half lady enough to deal with it. In very truth, Mary Marston was already immeasurably more of a lady than Hesper Mortimer was ever likely to be in this world. What was the stateliness and pride of the one compared to the fact that the other would have died in the workhouse or the street rather than let a man she did not love embrace her—yes, if all her ancestors in hell had required the sacrifice! To be a martyr to a lie is but false ladyhood She only is a lady who witnesses to the truth, come of it what may.

"—For my—my companion, or something of the sort," concluded Hesper; "and then I should be sure of being always dressed to my mind."

"That *would* be nice!" responded Mary, thinking only of the kindness in the speech

"Would you really like it?" asked Hesper, in her turn pleased.

"I should like it very much," replied Mary, not imagining the proposal had in it a shadow of seriousness. "I wish it were possible."

"Why not, then? Why shouldn't it be possible? I don't suppose you would mind using your needle a little?"

"Not in the least," answered Mary, amused. "Only what would they do in the shop without me?"

"They could get somebody else, couldn't they?"

"Hardly, to take my place. My father was Mr. Turnbull's partner."

"Oh!" said Hesper, not much instructed. "I thought you had only to give warning."

There the matter dropped, and Mary thought no more about it.

"You will let me keep this pattern?" said Hesper.

"It was made for you," answered Mary.

While Hesper was lazily thinking whether that meant she was to pay for it. Mary made her a pretty obeisance, and bade her good night. Hesper returned her adieu kindly, but neither shook hands with her nor rang the bell to have her shown out. Mary found her own way, however, and presently was breathing the fresh air of the twilight fields on her way home to her piano and her books.

For some time after she was gone, Hesper was entirely occupied with the excogitation of certain harmonies of the toilet that must minister effect to the dress she had now so plainly before her mind's eye; but by and by the dress began to melt away, and like a dissolving view disappeared, leaving in its place the form of "that singular shop-girl." There was nothing striking about her; she made no such sharp impression on the mind as compelled one to think of her again; yet always, when one had been long enough in her company to feel the charm of her individuality, the very quiet of any quiet moment was enough to bring back the sweetness of Mary's twilight presence. For this girl, who spent her days behind a counter, was one of the spiritual forces at work for the conservation and recovery of the universe.

Not only had Hesper Mortimer never had a friend worthy of the name, but no idea of pure friendship had as yet been generated in her. Sepia was the nearest to her intimacy: how far friendship could have place between two such I need not inquire; but in her fits of misery Hesper had no other to go to. Those fits, alas! grew less and less frequent; for Hesper was on the downward incline; but, when the next came, after this interview, she found herself haunted, at a little distance, as it were, by a strange sense of dumb, invisible tending. It did not once come close to her; it did not once offer her the smallest positive consolation; the thing was only this, that the essence of Mary's being was so purely ministration, that her form could not recur to any memory without bringing with it a dreamy sense of help. Most powerful of all powers in its holy insinuation is *being.* *To be* is more powerful than even *to do.* Action *may* be hypocrisy, but being is the thing itself, and is the parent of action. Had anything that Mary *said* recurred to Hesper, she would have thought of it only as the poor sentimentality of a low education.

But Hesper did not think of Mary's position as low; that would have been to measure it; and it did not once suggest itself as having any relation to any life in which she was interested. She saw no difference of level between Mary and the lawyer who came about her marriage settlements : they were together beyond her social horizon. In like manner, moral differences—and that in her own class—were almost equally beyond recognition. If by neglect of its wings, an eagle should sink to a dodo, it would then recognize only the laws of dodo life. For the dodos of humanity, did not one believe in a consuming fire and an outer darkness, what would be left us but an ever-renewed *alas!* It is truth and not imperturbability that a man's nature requires of him ; it is help, not the leaving of cards at doors, that will be recognized as the test ; it is love, and no amount of flattery that will prosper ; differences wide as that between a gentleman and a cad will contract to a hair's breadth in that day ; the customs of the trade and the picking of pockets will go together, with the greater excuse for the greater need and the less knowledge ; liars the most gentleman-like and the most rowdy will go as liars ; the first shall be last, and the last first.

Hesper's day drew on. She had many things to think about —things very different from any that concerned Mary Marston. She was married ; found life in London somewhat absorbing ; and forgot Mary.

CHAPTER XXI.

MR. REDMAIN.

A LIFE of comparatively innocent gayety could not be attractive to Mr. Redmain, but at first he accompanied his wife everywhere. No one knew better than he that not an atom of love had mingled with her motives in marrying him ; but for a time he seemed bent on showing her that she needed not have been so averse to him. Whether this was indeed his design or not, I imagine he enjoyed the admiration she roused : for why should not a man take pride in the possession of a fine woman as well as in that of a fine horse ? To be sure, Mrs. Redmain was not quite in the same way, nor quite so much his, as his

horses were, and might one day be a good deal less his than
she was now ; but in the mean time she was, I fancy, a pleasant break in the gathering monotony of his existence. As he
got more accustomed to the sight of her in a crowd, however,
and at the same time to her not very interesting company in
private, when she took not the smallest pains to please him, he
gradually lapsed into his former ways, and soon came to spend
his evenings in company that made him forget his wife. He
had loved her in a sort of a way, better left undefined, and had
also, almost from the first, hated her a little ; for, following
her cousin's advice, she had appealed to him to save her, and,
when he evaded her prayer, had addressed him in certain terms
too appropriate to be agreeable, and too forcible to be forgotten. His hatred, however, if that be not much too strong a
name, was neither virulent nor hot, for it had no inverted love
to feed and embitter it. It was more a thing of his head than
his heart, revealing itself mainly in short, acrid speeches, meant
to be clever, and indubitably disagreeable. Nor did Hesper
prove an unworthy antagonist in their encounters of polite
Billingsgate : what she lacked in experience she made up in
breeding. The common remark, generally false, about no love
being lost, was in their case true enough, for there never had
been any between them to lose. The withered rose-leaves have
their sweetness yet, but what of the rotted peony ? It was
generally when Redmain had been longer than usual without
seeing his wife that he said the worst things to her, as if spite
had grown in absence ; but that he should then be capable of
saying such things as he did say, could be understood only by
those who knew the man and his history.

Ferdinand Goldberg Redmain—parents with mean surroundings often give grand names to their children—was the
son of an intellectually gifted laborer, who, rising first to be
boss of a gang, began to take portions of contracts, and
arrived at last, through one lucky venture after another, at
having his estimate accepted and the contract given him for a
rather large affair. The result was that, through his minute
knowledge of details, his faculty for getting work out of his
laborers, a toughness of heart and will that enabled him to

screw wages to the lowest mark, and the judicious employment of inferior material, the contract paid him much too well for any good to come out of it. From that time, what he called his life was a continuous course of what he called success, and he died one of the richest dirt-beetles of the age, bequeathing great wealth to his son, and leaving a reputation for substantial worth behind him ; hardly leaving it, I fancy, for surely he found it waiting him where he went. He had been guilty of a thousand meannesses, oppressions, rapacities, and some quiet rogueries, but none of them worse than those of many a man whose ultimate failure has been the sole cause of his excommunication by the society which all the time knew well enough what he was. Often had he been held up by would-be teachers as a pattern to aspiring youth of what might be achieved by unwavering attention to *the main chance*, combined with unassailable honesty, from his experience they would once more prove to a gaping world the truth of the maxim, the highest intelligible to a base soul, that " honesty is the best policy." With his money he left to his son the seeds of a varied meanness, which bore weeds enough, but curiously, neither avarice nor, within the bounds of a modest prudence, any unwillingness to part with money—a fact which will probably appear the stranger when I have told the following anecdote concerning a brother of the father, of whom few indeed mentioned in my narrative ever heard.

This man was a joiner, or working cabinet-maker, or something of the sort. Having one day been set by his master to repair for an old lady an escritoire which had been in her possession for a long time, he came to her house in the evening with a five-pound note of a country bank, which he had found in a secret drawer of the same, handing it to her with the remark that he had always found honesty the best policy. She gave him half a sovereign, and he took his leave well satisfied. *He had been first to make inquiry, and had learned that the bank stopped payment many years ago.* I can not help wondering, curious in the statistics of honesty, how many of my readers will be more amused than disgusted with the story.

It is a great thing to come of decent people, and Ferdinand Goldberg Redmain must not be judged like one who, of honorable parentage, whether noble or peasant, takes himself across to the shady side of the road. Much had been against Redmain. I do not know of what sort his mother was, but from certain embryonic virtues in him, which could hardly have been his father's, I should think she must have been better than her husband. She died, however, while he was a mere child ; and his father married, some said did not *marry* again. The boy was sent to a certain public school, which at that time, whatever it may or may not be now, was simply a hot-bed of the lowest vices, and in devil-matters Redmain was an apt pupil. There is fresh help for the world every time a youth starts clean upon manhood's race ; his very being is a hope of cleansing : this one started as foul as youth could well be, and had not yet begun to repent. His character was well known to his associates, for he was no hypocrite, and Hesper's father knew it perfectly, and was therefore worse than he. Had Redmain had a daughter, he would never have given her to a man like himself. But, then, Mortimer was so poor, and Redmain was so *very* rich ! Alas for the man who degrades his poverty by worshiping wealth ! there is no abyss in hell too deep for him to find its bottom.

Mr. Redmain had no profession, and knew nothing of business beyond what was necessary for understanding whether his factor or steward, or whatever he called him, was doing well with his money—to that he gave heed. Also, wiser than many, he took some little care not to spend at full speed what life he had. With this view he laid down and observed certain rules in the ordering of his pleasures, which enabled him to keep ahead of the vice-constable for some time longer than would otherwise have been the case. But he is one who can never finally be outrun, and now, as Mr. Redmain was approaching the end of middle age, he heard plainly enough the approach of the wool-footed avenger behind him. Horrible was the inevitable to him, as horrible as to any ; but it had not yet looked frightful enough to arrest his downward rush. In his better conditions—physical, I mean—whether he had any better moral conditions, I can not tell—he would laugh and say, "*Gather the*

roses while you may"—heaven and earth ! what roses !—but, in
his worse, he maledicted everything, and was horribly afraid
of hell. When in tolerable health, he laughed at the notion of
such an out-of-the-way place, repudiating its very existence,
and, calling in all the arguments urged by good men against
the idea of an eternity of aimless suffering, used them against
the idea of any punishment after death. Himself a bad man,
he reasoned that God was too good to punish sin ; himself a
proud man, he reasoned that God was too high to take heed of
him. He forgot the best argument he could have adduced—
namely, that the punishment he had had in this life had done
him no good ; from which he might have been glad to argue
that none would, and therefore none would be tried. But I
suppose his mother believed there was a hell, for at such times,
when from weariness he was less of an evil beast than usual,
the old-fashioned horror would inevitably raise its deinosaurian
head afresh above the slime of his consciousness ; and then even
his wife, could she have seen how the soul of the man shuddered and recoiled, would have let his brutality pass unheeded,
though it was then at its worst, his temper at such times being
altogether furious. There was no grace in him when he was
ill, nor at any time, beyond a certain cold grace of manner,
which he kept for ceremony, or where he wanted to please

Happily, Mr. Redmain had one intellectual passion, which,
poor thing as it was, and in its motive, most of its aspects, and
almost all its tendencies, evil exceedingly, yet did something
to delay that corruption of his being which, at the same time,
it powerfully aided to complete : it was for the understanding
and analysis of human evil—not in the abstract, but alive and
operative. For the appeasement of this passion, he must render intelligible to himself, and that on his own exclusive theory
of human vileness, the aims and workings of every fresh specimen of what he called human nature that seemed bad enough,
or was peculiar enough to interest him. In this region of darkness he ranged like a discoverer—prowled rather, like an unclean
beast of prey—ever and always on the outlook for the false and
foul ; acknowledging, it is true, that he was no better himself,
but arrogating on that ground a correctness of judgment be-

yond the reach of such as, desiring to be better, were unwilling to believe in the utter badness of anything human. Like a lover, he would watch for the appearance of the vile motive, the self-interest, that "must be," *he knew*, at the heart of this or that deed or proceeding of apparent benevolence or generosity. Often, alas! the thing was provable; and, where he did not find, he was quick to invent; and, where he failed in finding or inventing, he not the less believed the bad motive was there, and followed the slightest seeming trail of the cunning demon only the more eagerly. What a smile was his when he heard, which truly he was not in the way to hear often, the praise of some good deed, or an ascription of high end to some endeavor of one of the vile race to which he belonged! Do those who abuse their kind actually believe they are of it? Do they hold themselves exceptions? Do they never reflect that it must be because such is their own nature, whether their accusation be true or false, that they know how to attribute such motives to their fellows? Or is it that, actually and immediately rejoicing in iniquity, they delight in believing it universal?

Quiet as a panther, Redmain was, I say, always in pursuit, if not of something sensual for himself, then of something evil in another. He would sit at his club, silent and watching, day after day, night after night, waiting for the chance that should cast light on some idea of detection, on some doubt, bewilderment, or conjecture. He would ask the farthest-off questions: who could tell what might send him into the track of discovery? He would give to the talk the strangest turns, laying trap after trap to ensnare the most miserable of facts, elevated into a desirable secret only by his hope to learn through it something equally valueless beyond it. Especially he delighted in discovering, or flattering himself he had discovered, the hollow full of dead men's bones under the flowery lawn of seeming goodness. Nor as yet had he, so far as he knew, or at least was prepared to allow, ever failed. And this he called the study of human nature, and quoted Pope. Truly, next to God, the proper study of mankind is man; but how shall a man that knows only the evil in himself, nor sees it hateful, read the thousandfold-compounded heart of his neighbor? To rake over the contents of an ash-pit, is not to study geology. There were motives in Redmain's own being, which he was not merely incapable of understanding, but incapable of seeing, incapable of suspecting.

The game had for him all the pleasure of keenest speculation; nor that alone, for, in the supposed discovery of the evil of another, he felt himself vaguely righteous.

One more point in his character I may not in fairness omit: he had naturally a strong sense of justice, and, if he exercised it but little in some of the relations of his life, he was none the less keenly alive to his own claims on its score: for chiefly he cried out for fair play on behalf of those who were wicked in similar fashion to himself. But, in truth, no one dealt so hardly with Redmain as his own conscience at such times when suffering and fear had awaked it.

So much for a portrait-sketch of the man to whom Mortimer had sold his daughter—such was the man whom Hesper, entirely aware that none could compel her to marry against her will, had, partly from fear of her father, partly from moral laziness, partly from reverence for the Moloch of society, whose priestess was her mother, vowed to love, honor, and obey! In justice to her, it must be remembered, however, that she did not and could not know of him what her father knew.

CHAPTER XXII.

MRS. REDMAIN.

In the autumn the Redmains went to Durnmelling: why they did so, I should find it hard to say. If, when a child, Hesper loved either of her parents, the experiences of later years had so heaped that filial affection with the fallen leaves of dead hopes and vanished dreams, that there was now nothing in her heart recognizable to herself as love to father or mother. She always behaved to them, of course, with perfect propriety; never refused any small request; never showed

resentment when blamed—never felt any, for she did not care
enough to be angry or sorry that father or mother should disapprove.

On the other hand, Lady Margaret saw great improvement
in her daughter. To the maternal eye, jealous for perfection,
Hesper's carriage was at length satisfactory. It was cold, and
the same to her mother as to every one else, but the mother
did not find it too cold. It was haughty, even repellent, but
by no means in the mother's eyes repulsive. Her voice came
from her in well-balanced sentences, sounding as if they had
been secretly constructed for extempore use, like the points of
a parliamentary orator. " Marriage has done everything for
her !" said Lady Malice to herself with a dignified chuckle,
and dismissed the last shadowy remnant of maternal regret for
her part in the transaction of her marriage.

She never saw herself in the wrong, and never gave herself
the least trouble to be in the right. She was in good health,
ate, and liked to eat ; drank her glass of champagne, and
would have drunk a second, but for her complexion, and that
it sometimes made her feel ill, which was the only thing, after
marrying Mr. Redmain, she ever felt degrading. Of her own
worth she had never had a doubt, and she had none yet : how
was she to generate one, courted wherever she went, both for
her own beauty and her husband's wealth ?

To her father she was as stiff and proud as if she had been
a maiden aunt, bent on destroying what expectations from her
he might be cherishing. Who will blame her ? He had done
her all the ill he could, and by his own deed she was beyond
his reach. Nor can I see that the debt she owed him for being her father was of the heaviest.

Her husband was again out of health—certain attacks to
which he was subject were now coming more frequently. I do
not imagine his wife offered many prayers for his restoration.
Indeed, she never prayed for the thing she desired ; and, while
he and she occupied separate rooms, the one solitary thing she
now regarded as a privilege, how *could* she pray for his recovery ?

Greatly contrary to Mr. Redmain's unexpressed desire,

Miss Yolland had been installed as Hesper's cousin-companion.
After the marriage, she ventured to unfold a little, as she had
promised, but what there was yet of womanhood in Hesper
had shrunk from further acquaintance with the dimly shadowed
mysteries of Sepia's story ; and Sepia, than whom none more
sensitive to change of atmosphere, had instantly closed again ;
and now not unfrequently looked and spoke like one feeling
her way. The only life-principle she had, so far as I know,
was to get from the moment the greatest possible enjoyment
that would leave the way clear for more to follow. She had
not been in his house a week before Mr. Redmain hated her.
He was something given to hating people who came near him,
and she came much too near. She was by no means so different in character as to be repulsive to him ; neither was she so
much alike as to be tiresome ; their designs could not well
clash, for she was a woman and he was a man ; if she had not
been his wife's friend, they might, perhaps, have got on together better than well ; but the two were such as must either
be hand in glove or hate each other. There had not, however, been the least approach to rupture between them. Mr.
Redmain, indeed, took no trouble to avoid such a catastrophe,
but Sepia was far too wise to allow even the dawn of such a
risk. When he was ill, he was, if possible, more rude to her
than to every one else, but she did not seem to mind it a straw.
Perhaps she knew something of the ways of such *gentlemen* as
lose their manners the moment they are ailing, and seem to
consider a headache or an attack of indigestion excuse sufficient for behaving like the cad they scorn. It was not long,
however, before he began to take in her a very real interest,
though not of a sort it would have made her comfortable with
him to know.

Every time Mr. Redmain had an attack, the baldness on
the top of his head widened, and the skin of his face tightened
on his small, neat features ; his long arms looked longer ; his
formerly flat back rounded yet a little ; and his temper grew
yet more curiously spiteful. Long after he had begun to recover, he was by no means an agreeable companion. Nevertheless, as if at last, though late in the day, she must begin to

teach her daughter the duty of a married woman, from the moment he arrived, taken ill on the way, Lady Malice, regardless of the brusqueness with which he treated her from the first, devoted herself to him with an attention she had never shown her husband. She was the only one who manifested any appearance of affection for him, and the only one of the family for whom, in return, he came to show the least consideration. Rough he was, even to her, but never, except when in absolute pain, rude as to everybody in the house besides. At times, one might have almost thought he stood in some little awe of her. Every night, after his man was gone, she would visit him to see that he was left comfortable, would tuck him up as his mother might have done, and satisfy herself that the night-light was shaded from his eyes. With her own hands she always arranged his breakfast on the tray, nor never omitted taking him a basin of soup before he got up; and, whatever he may have concluded concerning *her* motives, he gave no sign of imagining them other than generous. Perhaps the part in him which had never had the opportunity of behaving ill to his mother, and so had not choked up its channels with wrong, remained, in middle age and illness, capable of receiving kindness.

Hesper saw the relation between them, but without the least pleasure or the least curiosity. She seemed to care for nothing—except the keeping of her back straight. What could it be, inside that lovely form, that gave itself pleasure to be, were a difficult question indeed. The bear as he lies in his winter nest, sucking his paw, has no doubt his rudimentary theories of life, and those will coincide with a desire for its continuance; but whether what either the lady or the bear counts the good of life, be really that which makes either desire its continuance, is another question. Mere life without suffering seems enough for most people, but I do not think it could go on so for ever. I can not help fancying that, but for death, utter dreariness would at length master the healthiest in whom the true life has not begun to shine. But so satisfying is the mere earthly existence to some at present, that this remark must sound to them bare insanity.

Partly out of compliment to Mr. Redmain, the Mortimers had scarcely a visitor ; for he would not come out of his room when he knew there was a stranger in the house Fond of company of a certain kind when he was well, he could not endure an unknown face when he was ill. He told Lady Malice that at such times a stranger always looked a devil to him. Hence the time was dull for everybody—dullest, perhaps, for Sepia, who, as well as Redmain, had a few things that required forgetting. It was no wonder, then, that Hesper, after a fortnight of it, should think once more of the young woman in the draper's shop of Testbridge. One morning, in consequence, she ordered her brougham, and drove to the town.

CHAPTER XXIII.

THE MENIAL.

THINGS had been going nowise really better with Mary, though there was now more lull and less storm around her. The position was becoming less and less endurable to her, and she had as yet no glimmer of a way out of it. Breath of genial air never blew in the shop, except when this and that customer entered it. But how dear the dull old chapel had grown ! Not that she heard anything more to her mind, or that she paid any more attention to what was said ; but the memory of her father filled the place, and when the Bible was read, or some favorite hymn sung, he seemed to her actually present. And might not love, she thought, even love to her, be strong enough to bring him from the gracious freedom of the new life, back to the house of bondage, to share it for an hour with his daughter ?

When Hesper entered, she was disappointed to see Mary so much changed. But when, at sight of her, the pale face brightened, and a faint, rosy flush overspread it from brow to chin, Mary was herself again as Hesper had known her ; and the radiance of her own presence, reflected from Mary, cast a reflex of sunshine into the February of Hesper's heart : had Mary known how long it was since such a smile had lighted the face she so much admired, hers would have flushed with a profounder pleasure. Hesper was human after all, though her humanity was only molluscous as yet, and it is not in the power of humanity in any stage of development to hold itself indifferent to the pleasure of being loved. Also, poor as is the feeling comparatively, it is yet a reflex of love itself—the shine of the sun in a rain-pool.

She walked up to Mary, holding out her hand.

"O ma'am, I am so glad to see you!" exclaimed Mary, forgetting her manners in her love.

"I, too, am glad," drawled Hesper, genuinely, though with condescension. "I hope you are well. I can not say you look so."

"I am pretty well, thank you, ma'am," answered Mary, flushing afresh : not much anxiety was anywhere expressed about her health now, except by Beenie, who mourned over the loss of her plumpness, and told her if she did not eat she would soon follow her poor father.

"Come and have a drive with me," said Hesper, moved by a sudden impulse : through some hidden motion of sympathy, she felt, as she looked at her, that the place was stuffy. "It will do you good," she went on. "You are too much in-doors.—And the ceiling is low," she added, looking up.

"It is very kind of you," replied Mary, "but—I don't think I could quite manage it to-day."

She looked round as she spoke. There were not many customers ; but for conscience' sake she was trying hard to give as little ground for offense as possible.

"Why not ?—If I were to ask Mr.—"

"If you really wish it, ma'am, I will venture to go for half an hour. There is no occasion to speak to Mr. Turnbull. Besides, it is almost dinner-time."

"Do, then. I am sure you will eat a better dinner for having had a little fresh air first. It is a lovely morning. We will drive to the Roman camp on the top of Clover-down."

"I shall be ready in two minutes," said Mary. and ran from the shop.

As she passed along the outside of his counter coming back, she stopped and told Mr. Turnbull where she was going. Instead of answering her, he turned himself toward Mrs. Redmain, and went through a series of bows and smiles recognizant of favor, which she did not choose to see. She turned and walked from the shop, got into the brougham, and made room for Mary at her side.

But, although the drive was a lovely one, and the view from either window delightful, and to Mary it was like getting out of a tomb to leave the shop in the middle of the day, she saw little of the sweet country on any side, so much occupied was she with Hesper. Ere they stopped again at the shop-door, the two young women were nearer being friends than Hesper had ever been with any one. The sleepy heart in her was not yet dead, but capable still of the pleasure of showing sweet condescension and gentle patronage to one who admired her, and was herself agreeable. To herself she justified her kindness to Mary with the remark that *the young woman deserved encouragement*—whatever that might mean—*because she was so anxious to improve herself!*—a duty Hesper could recognize in another.

As they went, Mary told her something of her miserable relations with the Turnbulls; and, as they returned, Hesper actually—this time with perfect seriousness—proposed that she should give up business, and live with her

Nor was this the ridiculous thing it may at first sight appear to not a few of my readers. It arose from what was almost the first movement in the direction of genuine friendship Hesper had ever felt. She had been familiar in her time with a good many, but familiarity is not friendship, and may or may not exist along with it. Some, who would scorn the idea of a *friendship* with such as Mary, will be familiar enough with maids as selfish as themselves, and part from them—no—part *with* them, the next day, or the next hour, with never a twinge of regret. Of this, Hesper was as capable as any; but friendship is its own justification, and she felt no horror at the new

motion of her heart. At the same time she did not recognize
it as friendship, and, had she suspected Mary of regarding
their possible relation in that light, she would have dismissed
her pride, perhaps contempt. Nevertheless the sorely whelmed
divine thing in her had uttered a feeble sigh of incipient longing after the real ; Mary had begun to draw out the love in
her ; while her conventional judgment justified the proposed
extraordinary proceeding with the argument of the endless
advantages to result from having in the house, devoted to her
wishes, a young woman with an absolute genius for dressmaking ; one capable not only of originating in that foremost
of arts, but, no doubt, with a little experience, of carrying
out also with her own hands the ideas of her mistress. No
more would she have to send for the dressmaker on every
smallest necessity ! No more must she postpone confidence in
her appearance, that was, in herself, until Sepia, dressed,
should be at leisure to look her over ! Never yet had she found
herself the best dressed in a room : now there would be hope !

Nothing, however, was clear in her mind as to the position
she would have Mary occupy. She had a vague feeling that
one like her ought not to be expected to undertake things be-
fitting such women as her maid Folter ; for between Mary and
Folter there was, she saw, less room for comparison than between Folter and a naked Hottentot. She was incapable, at
the same time, of seeing that, in the eyes of certain courtiers
of a high kingdom, not much known to the world of fashion,
but not the less judges of the beautiful, there was a far greater
difference between Mary and herself than between herself and
her maid, or between her maid and the Hottentot. For, while
the said beholders could hardly have been astonished at Hesper's marrying Mr. Redmain, there would, had Mary done such
a thing, have been dismay and a hanging of the head before
the face of her Father in heaven.

"Come and live with me, Miss Marston," said Hesper ; but
it was with a laugh, and that light touch of the tongue which
suggests but a flying fancy spoken but for the sake of the pre-
posterous ; while Mary, not forgetting she had heard the same
thing once before, heard it with a smile, and had no rejoinder

ready ; whereupon Hesper, who was, in reality, feeling her way, ventured a little more seriousness.

"I should never ask you to do anything you would not like," she said.

"I don't think you could," answered Mary. "There are more things I should like to do for you than you would think to ask. — In fact," she added, looking round with a loving smile, "I don't know what I shouldn't like to do for you."

"My meaning was, that, as a thing of course, I should never ask you to do anything menial," explained Hesper, venturing a little further still, and now speaking in a tone perfectly matter-of-fact.

"I don't know what you intend by *menial*," returned Mary.

Hesper thought it not unnatural she should not be familiar with the word, and proceeded to explain it as well as she could. That seeming ignorance may be the consequence of more knowledge, she had yet to learn

"*Menial*, don't you know ?" she said, "is what you give servants to do."

But therewith she remembered that Mary's help in certain things wherein her maid's incapacity was harrowing, was one of the hopes she mainly cherished in making her proposal : that definition of *menial* would hardly do.

"I mean—I mean," she resumed, with a little embarrassment, a rare thing with her, "—things like—like—cleaning one's shoes, don't you know ?—or brushing your hair."

Mary burst out laughing.

"Let me come to you to-morrow morning," she said, "and I will brush your hair that you will want me to come again the next day. You beautiful creature ! whose hands would not be honored to handle such stuff as that ?"

As she spoke, she took in her fingers a little stray drift from the masses of golden twilight that crowned one of the loveliest temples in which the Holy Ghost had not yet come to dwell.

"If cleaning your shoes be menial, brushing your hair must be royal," she added.

Hesper's heart was touched ; and if at the same time her

self was flattered, the flattery was mingled with its best antidote—love.

"Do you really mean," she said, "you would not mind
doing such things for me ?—Of course I should not be exacting."

She laughed again, afraid of showing herself too much in
earnest before she was sure of Mary.

"You would not ask me to do anything *menial?*" said Mary,
archly.

"I dare not promise," said Hesper, in tone responsive.
"How could I help it, if I saw you longing to do what I was
longing to have you do ?" she added, growing more and more
natural.

"I would no more mind cleaning your boots than my own,"
said Mary.

"But I should not like to clean my own boots," rejoined
Hesper.

"No more should I, except it had to be done. Even then
I would much rather not," returned Mary, "for cleaning my
own would not interest me. To clean yours would. Still I
would rather not, for the time might be put to better use—
except always it were necessary, and then, of course, it couldn't.
But as to anything degrading in it, I scorn the idea. I heard
my father once say that, to look down on those who have to do
such things may be to despise them for just the one honorable
thing about them.—Shall I tell you what I understand by the
word *menial?* You know it has come to have a disagreeable
taste about it, though at first it only meant, as you say, something that fell to the duty of attendants."

"Do tell me," answered Hesper, with careless permission.

"I did not find it out myself," said Mary. "My father
taught me. He was a wise as well as a good man, Mrs. Redmain."

"Oh !" said Hesper, with the ordinary indifference of fashionable people to what an inferior may imagine worth telling
them.

"He said," persisted Mary, notwithstanding, "that it is
menial to undertake anything you think beneath you for the

sake of money; and still more menial, having undertaken it, not to do it as well as possible."

"That would make out a good deal more of the menial in the world than is commonly supposed," laughed Hesper. "I wonder who would do anything for you if you didn't pay them —one way or another!"

"I've taken my father's shoes out of Beenie's hands many a time," said Mary, "and finished them myself, just for the pleasure of making them shine for *him*."

"Re-a-ally!" drawled Hesper, and set out for the conclusion that after all it was no such great compliment the young woman had paid her in wanting to brush her hair. Evidently she had a taste for low things!—was naturally menial!—would do as much for her own father as for a lady like her! But the light in Mary's eyes checked her.

"Any service done without love, whatever it be," resumed Mary, "is slavery—neither more nor less. It can not be anything else. So, you see, most slaves are made slaves by themselves; and that is what makes me doubtful whether I ought to go on serving in the shop; for, as far as the Turnbulls are concerned, I have no pleasure in it; I am only helping them to make money, not doing them any good."

"Why do you not give it up at once then?" asked Hesper.

"Because I like serving the customers. They were my father's customers; and I have learned so much from having to wait on them!"

"Well, now," said Hesper, with a rush for the goal, "if you will come to me, I will make you comfortable; and you shall do just as much or as little as you please."

"What will your maid think?" suggested Mary. "If I am to do what I please, she will soon find me trespassing on her domain."

"I never trouble myself about what my servants think," said Hesper.

"But it might hurt her, you know—to be paid to do a thing, and then not allowed to do it."

"She . . . . ght of

parting with her, but I should not be at all sorry if she went. She would be no loss to me."

"Why should you keep her, then ?"

"Because one is just as good—and as bad as another. She knows my ways, and I prefer not having to break in a new one. It is a bore to have to say how you like everything done."

"But you are speaking now as if you meant it," said Mary, waking up to the fact that Hesper's tone was of business, and she no longer seemed half playing with the proposal. "*Do* you mean you want me to come and live with you ?"

"Indeed, I do," answered Hesper, emphatically. "You shall have a room close to my bedroom, and there you shall do as you like all day long ; and, when I want you, I dare say you will come."

"Fast enough," said Mary, cheerily, as if all was settled. In contrast with her present surroundings, the prospect was more than attractive. "—But would you let me have my piano ?" she asked, with sudden apprehension.

"You shall have my grand piano always when I am out, which will be every night in the season, I dare say. That will give you plenty of practice ; and you will be able to have the best of lessons. And think of the concerts and oratorios you will go to !"

As she spoke, the carriage drew up at the door of the shop, and Mary took her leave. Hesper accepted her acknowledgments in the proper style of a benefactress, and returned her good-by kindly. But not yet did she shake hands with her.

Some of my readers may wonder that Mary should for a moment dream of giving up what they would call her independence ; for was she not on her own ground in the shop of which she was a proprietor ? and was the change proposed, by whatever name it might be called, anything other than *service?* But they are outside it, and Mary was in it, and knew how little such an independence was worth the name. Almost everything about the shop had altered in its aspect to her. The very air she breathed in it seemed slavish. Nor was the change in her. The whole thing was growing more and more sordid, for now—save for her part—the one spirit ruled it entirely.

The work had therefore more or less grown a drudgery to her.
The spirit of gain was in full blast, and whoever did not trim
his sails to it was in danger of finding it rough weather. No
longer could she, without offense, and consequent disturbance
of spirit, arrange her attendance as she pleased, or have the
same time for reading as before. She could encounter black
looks, but she could not well live with them ; and how was she
to continue the servant of such ends as were now exclusively
acknowledged in the place ? The proposal of Mrs. Redmain
stood in advantageous contrast to this treadmill-work. In her
house she would be called only to the ministrations of love,
and would have plenty of time for books and music, with a
thousand means of growth unapproachable in Testbridge. All
the slavery lay in the shop, all the freedom in the personal service. But she strove hard to suppress anxiety, for she saw
that, of all poverty-stricken contradictions, a Christian with
little faith is the worst.

The chief attraction to her, however, was simply Hesper
herself. She had fallen in love with her—I hardly know how
otherwise to describe the current with which her being set
toward her. Few hearts are capable of loving as she loved.
It was not merely that she saw in Hesper a grand creature, and
lovely to look upon, or that one so much her superior in position showed such a liking for herself : she saw in her one she
could help, one at least who sorely needed help, for she seemed
to know nothing of what made life worth having—one who
had done, and must yet be capable of doing, things degrading
to the humanity of womanhood. Without the hope of helping
in the highest sense, Mary could not have taken up her abode
in such a house as Mrs. Redmain's. No outward service of any
kind, even to the sick, was to her service enough to *choose* :
were it laid upon her, she would hasten to it ; for necessity is
the push, gentle or strong, as the man is more or less obedient,
by which God sends him into the path he would have him
take. But to help to the birth of a beautiful Psyche, enveloped all in the gummy cerecloths of its chrysalis, not yet
aware, even, that it must get out of them, and spread great
wings to the sunny wind of God—that was a thing for which

the holiest of saints might well take a servant's place—the
thing for which the Lord of life had done it before him.   To
help out such a lovely sister—how Hesper would have drawn
herself up at the word! it is mine, not Mary's—as she would
be when no longer holden of death, but her real self, the self
God meant her to be when he began making her, would indeed
be a thing worth having lived for!   Between the ordinarily
benevolent woman and Mary Marston, there was about as great
a difference as between the fashionable church-goer and Cath-
erine of Siena.   She would be Hesper's servant that she
might gain Hesper.   I would not have her therefore wondered
at as a marvel of humility.   She was simply a young woman
who believed that the man called Jesus Christ is a real person,
such as those represent him who profess to have known him ;
and she therefore believed the man himself—believed that,
when he said a thing, he entirely meant it, knowing it to be
true ; believed, therefore, that she had no choice but do as he
told her.   That man was the servant of all ; therefore, to regard *any* honest service as degrading would be, she saw, to
deny Christ, to call the life of creation's hero a disgrace.   Nor
was he the first servant ; he did not of himself choose his life ;
the Father gave it him to live—sent him to be a servant, because he, the Father, is the first and greatest servant of all.
He gives it to one to serve as the rich can, to another as the
poor must.   The only disgrace, whether of the counting-house,
the shop, or the family, is to think the service degrading.   If
it be such, why not sit down and starve rather than do it ?
No man has a right to disgrace himself. Starve, I say ; the world
will lose nothing in you, for you are its disgrace, who count
service degrading.   You are much too grand people for what
your Maker requires of you, and does himself, and yet you do
it after a fashion, because you like to eat and go warm.   You
would take rank in the kingdom of hell, not the kingdom of
heaven.   But obedient love, learned by the meanest Abigail,
will make of her an angel of ministration, such a one as he who
came to Peter in the prison, at whose touch the fetters fell
from the limbs of the apostle.

"What forced, overdriven, Utopian stuff ! A kingdom always coming, and never come ! I hold by what *is*. This solid, plowable earth will serve my turn. My business is what I can find in the oyster."

I hear you, friend. Your answer will come whence you do not look for it. For some, their only answer will be the coming of that which they deny ; and the *Presence* will be a very different thing to those who desire it and those who do not. In the mean time, if we are not yet able to serve like God from pure love, let us do it because it is his way ; so shall we come to do it from pure love also.

The very next morning, as she called it—that is, at four o'clock in the afternoon—Hesper again entered the shop, and, to the surprise and annoyance of the master of it, was taken by Mary through the counter and into the house. "What a false impression," thought the great man, "will it give of the way *we* live, to see the Marstons' shabby parlor in a warehouse !" But he would have been more astonished and more annoyed still, had the deafening masses of soft goods that filled the house permitted him to hear through them what passed between the two. Before they came down, Mary had accepted a position in Mrs. Redmain's house, if that may be called a position which was so undefined ; and Hesper had promised that she would not mention the matter. For Mary judged Mr. Turnbull would be too glad to get rid of her to mind how brief the notice she gave him, and she would rather not undergo the remarks that were sure to be made in contempt of her scheme. She counted it only fair, however, to let him know that she intended giving up her place behind the counter, hinting that, as she meant to leave when it suited her without further warning, it would be well to look out at once for one to take her place.

As to her money in the business, she scarcely thought of it, and said nothing about it, believing it as safe as in the bank It was in the power of a dishonest man who prided himself on his honesty—the worst kind of rogue in the creation ; but she had not yet learned to think of him as a dishonest man—only as a greedy one—and the money had been there ever since she had heard of money.

Mr. Turnbull was so astonished by her communication that, not seeing at once how the change was likely to affect him, he held his peace—with the cunning pretense that his silence arose from anger. His first feeling was of pleasure, but the man of business must take care how he shows himself pleased. On reflection, he continued pleased; for, as they did not seem likely to succeed in securing Mary in the way they had wished, the next best thing certainly would be to get rid of her. Perhaps, indeed, it was the very best thing; for it would be easy to get George a wife more suitable to the position of his family than a little canting dissenter, and her money would be in their hands all the same; while, once clear of her haunting cat-eyes, ready to pounce upon whatever her soft-headed father had taught her was wicked, he could do twice the business. But, while he continued pleased, he continued careful not to show his satisfaction, for she would then go smelling about for the cause! During three whole days, therefore, he never spoke to her. On the fourth, he spoke as if nothing had ever been amiss between them, and showed some interest in her further intentions. But Mary, in the straightforward manner peculiar to herself, told him she preferred not speaking of them at present; whereupon the cunning man concluded that she wanted a place in another shop, and was on the outlook—prepared to leave the moment one should turn up.

She asked him one day whether he had yet found a person to take her place.

"Time enough for that," he answered. "You're not gone yet."

"As you please, Mr. Turnbull," said Mary. "It was merely that I should be sorry to leave you without sufficient help in the shop."

"And *I* should be sorry," rejoined Turnbull, "that Miss Marston should fancy herself indispensable to the business she turned her back upon."

From that moment, the restraint he had for the last week or two laid upon himself thus broken through, he never spoke to her except with such rudeness that she no longer ventured to address him even on shop-business; and all the people in

the place, George included, following the example so plainly
set them, she felt, when, at last, in the month of November, a
letter from Hesper heralded the hour of her deliverance, that
to take any formal leave would be but to expose herself to in-
dignity. She therefore merely told Turnbull, one evening as
he left the shop, that she would not be there in the morning,
and was gone from Testbridge before it was opened the next
day.

CHAPTER XXIV.

MRS. REDMAIN'S DRAWING-ROOM.

A FEW years ago, a London drawing-room was seldom
beautiful ; but size is always something, and, if Mrs. Redmain's
had not harmony, it had gilding—a regular upholsterer's drawing-room it was, on which about as much taste had been ex-
pended as on the fattening of a prize-pig. Happily there is as
little need as temptation to give any description of it, with its
sheets of glass and steel, its lace curtains, crude-colored walls
and floor and couches, and glittering chandeliers of a thousand
prisms. Everybody knows the kind of room—a huddle of the
chimera ambition wallowing in the chaos of the commonplace
—no miniature world of harmonious abiding. The only interesting thing in it was, that on all sides were doors, which
must lead out of it, and might lead to a better place.

It was about eleven o'clock of a November morning—more
like one in March. There might be a thick fog before the
evening, but now the sun was shining like a brilliant lump of
ice—so inimical to heat, apparently, that a servant had just
dropped the venetian blind of one of the windows to shut his
basilisk-gaze from the sickening fire, which was now rapidly
recovering. Betwixt the cold sun and the hard earth, a dust-
befogged wind, plainly borrowed from March, was sweeping
the street.

Mr. and Mrs. Redmain had returned to town thus early
because ʼ   C   e Mr.

Redmain was too far from his physician. He was now considerably better, however, and had begun to go about again, for the weather did not yet affect him much. He was now in his study, as it was called, where he generally had his breakfast alone. Mrs. Redmain always had hers in bed, as often with a new novel as she could, of which her maid cut the leaves, and skimmed the cream. But now she was descending the stair, straight as a Greek goddess, and about as cold as the marble she is made of—mentally rigid, morally imperturbable, and vacant of countenance to a degree hardly equaled by the most ordinary of goddesses. She entered the drawing-room with a slow, careless, yet stately step, which belonged to her, I can not say by nature, for it was not natural, but by ancestry. She walked to the chimney, seated herself in a low, soft, shiny chair almost on the hearth-rug, and gazed listlessly into the fire. In a minute she rose and rang the bell.

"Send my maid, and shut the door," she said.

The woman came.

"Has Miss Yolland left her room yet?" she asked.

"No, ma'am."

"Let her know I am in the drawing-room."

This said, she resumed her fire-gazing.

There was not much to see in the fire, for the fire is but a reflector, and there was not much behind the eyes that looked into it for that fire to reflect. Hesper was no dreamer—the more was the pity, for dreams are often the stuff out of which actions are made. Had she been a truer woman, she might have been a dreamer, but where was the space for dreaming in a life like hers, without heaven, therefore without horizon, with so much room for desiring, and so little room for hope? The buz that greeted her entrance of a drawing-room, was the chief joy she knew; to inhabit her well-dressed body in the presence of other well-dressed bodies, her highest notion of existence. And even upon these hung ever as an abating fog the consciousness of having a husband. I can not say she was tired of marriage, for she had loathed her marriage from the first, and had not found it at all better than her expectation: she had been too ignorant to forebode half its horrors.

Education she had had but little that was worth the name, for she had never been set growing; and now, although well endowed by nature, she was gradually becoming stupid. People who have plenty of money, and neither hope nor aspiration, must become stupid, except indeed they hate, and then for a time the devil in them will make them a sort of clever.

Miss Yolland came undulating. No kiss, no greeting whatever passed between the ladies. Sepia began at once to rearrange a few hot-house flowers on the mantel-piece, looking herself much like some dark flower painted in an old missal.

"This day twelve months!" said Hesper.

"I know," returned Sepia.

"If one could die without pain, and there was nothing to come after!" said Hesper. "What a tiresome dream it is!"

"Dream, or nightmare, or what you will, you had better get all you can out of it before you break it," said Sepia.

"You seem to think it worth keeping!" yawned Hesper.

Sepia smiled, with her face to the glass, in which she saw the face of her cousin with her eyes on the fire; but she made no answer. Hesper went on.

"Ah!" she said, "your story is not mine. You are free; I am a slave. You are alive; I am in my coffin."

"That's marriage," said Sepia, dryly.

"It would not matter much," continued Hesper, "if you could have your coffin to yourself; but when you have to share it—ugh!"

"If I were you, then," said Sepia, "I would not lie still; I would get up and bite—I mean, be a vampire."

Hesper did not answer. Sepia turned from the mirror, looked at her, and burst into a laugh—at least, the sound she made had all the elements of a laugh—except the merriment.

"Now really, Hesper, you ought to be ashamed of yourself," she cried. "You to put on the pelican and the sparrow, with all the world before you, and all the men in it at your feet!"

"A pack of fools!" remarked Hesper, with a calmness which in itself was scorn

"I don't deny it—but amusing fools—you must allow that!"

"They don't amuse me."

"That's your fault : you won't be amused. The more foolish they are, the more amusing I find them."

"I am sick of it all. Nothing amuses me. How can it, when there is nothing behind it? You can't live on amusement. It is the froth on water an inch deep, and then the mud!"

"I declare, misery makes a poetess of you! But as to the mud, I don't mind a little mud. It is only dirt, and has its part in the inevitable peck, I hope."

"*I* don't mind mud so long as you can keep out of it. But when one is over head and ears in it, I should like to know what life is worth," said Hesper, heedless that the mud was of her own making. "I declare, Sepia," she went on, drawling the declaration, "if I were to be asked whether I would go on or not—"

"You would ask a little time to make up your mind, Hesper, I fancy," suggested Sepia, for Hesper had paused. As she did not reply, Sepia resumed.

"Which is your favorite poison, Hesper?" she said.

"When I choose, it will be to use," replied Hesper.

"Rhyming, at last!" said Sepia.

But Hesper would not laugh, and her perfect calmness checked the laughter which would have been Sepia's natural response : she was careful not to go too far.

"Do you know, Hesper," she said, with seriousness, "what is the matter with you?"

"Tolerably well," answered Hesper.

"You do not—let me tell you. You are nothing but a baby yet. You have no heart."

"If you mean that I have never been in love, you are right. But you talk foolishly ; for you know that love is no more within my reach than if I were the corpse I feel."

Sepia pressed her lips together, and nodded knowingly ; then, after a moment's pause, said :

"When your hour is come, you will understand. Every

woman's hour comes, one time or another—whether she will or not."

"Sepia, if you think that, because I hate my husband, I would allow another man to make love to me, you do not know me yet."

"I know you very well : you do not know yourself, Hesper ; you do not know the heart of a woman—because your own has never come awake yet."

"God forbid it ever should, then—so long as—as the man I hate is alive !"

Sepia laughed.

"A good prayer," she said , "for who can tell what you might do to him !"

"Sepia, I sometimes think you are a devil."

"And I sometimes think you are a saint."

"What do you take me for the other times ?"

"A hypocrite. What do *you* take *me* for the other times ?"

"No hypocrite," answered Hesper.

With a light, mocking laugh, Sepia turned away, and left the room.

Hesper did not move. If stillness indicates thought, then Hesper was thinking ; and surely of late she had suffered what might have waked something like thought in what would then have been something like a mind : all the machinery of thought was there—sorely clogged, and rusty ; but for a woman to hate her husband is hardly enough to make a thinking creature of her. True as it was, there was no little affectation in her saying what she did about the worthlessness of her life. She was plump and fresh ; her eye was clear, her hand firm and cool : suffering would have to go a good deal deeper before it touched in her the issues of life, or the love of it. What set her talking so, was in great part the *ennui* of endeavor after enjoyment, and the reaction from success in the pursuit Her low moods were, however, far more frequent than, even with such fatigue and reaction to explain them, belonged to her years, her health, or her temperament.

The fire grew hot. Hesper thought of her complexion, and pushed her chair back. Then she rose, and having taken

a hand-screen from the chimney-piece, was fanning herself
with it, when the door opened, and a servant asked if she were
at home to Mr. Helmer. She hesitated a moment : what an
unearthly hour for a caller !

"Show him up," she answered : anything was better than
her own company.

Tom Helmer entered—much the same—a little paler and
thinner. He made his approach with a certain loose grace natural to him, and seated himself on the chair, at some distance
from her own, to which Mrs. Redmain motioned him.

Tom seldom failed of pleasing. He was well dressed, and
not too much ; and, to the natural confidence of his shallow
character, added the assurance born of a certain small degree
of success in his profession, which he took for the pledge of approaching supremacy. He carried himself better than he used,
and his legs therefore did not look so long. His hair continued
to curl soft and silky about his head, for he protested against
the fashionable convict-style. His hat was new, and he bore
it in front of him like a ready apology.

It was to no presentableness of person, however, any more
than to previous acquaintance, that Tom now owed his admittance. True, he had been to Durnmelling not unfrequently,
but that was in the other world of the country, and even there
Hesper had taken no interest in the self-satisfied though not
ill-bred youth who went galloping about the country, showing
off to rustic girls. It was merely, as I have said, that she
could no longer endure a *tête-à-tête* with one she knew so little as herself, and whose acquaintance she was so little desirous
of cultivating.

Tom had been to a small party at the house a few evenings
before, brought thither by the well-known leader of a certain
literary clique, who, in return for homage, not seldom took
younger aspirants under a wing destined never to be itself more
than half-fledged. It was, notwithstanding, broad enough
already so to cover Tom with its shadow that under it he was
able to creep into several houses of a sort of distinction, and
among them into Mrs. Redmain's.

Nothing of less potency than the presumption attendant on

self-satisfaction could have emboldened him to call thus early, and that in the hope not merely of finding Mrs. Redmain at home, but of finding her alone ; and, with the not unusual reward of unworthy daring, he had succeeded. He was ambitious of making himself acceptable to ladies of social influence, and of being known to stand well with such. In the case of Mrs. Redmain he was the more anxious, because she had not received him on any footing of former acquaintance.

At the gathering to which I have referred, a certain song was sung by a lady, not without previous manœuvre on the part of Tom, with which Mrs. Redmain had languidly expressed herself pleased : that song he had now brought her— for, concerning words and music both, he might have said with Touchstone, "An ill-favored thing, but mine own." He did not quote Touchstone because he believed both words and music superexcellent, the former being in truth not quite bad, and the latter nearly as good. Appreciation was the very hunger of Tom's small life, and here was a chance !

"I ought to apologize," he said, airily. "and I will, if you will allow me."

Mrs. Redmain said nothing, only waited with her eyes. They were calm, reposeful eyes, not fixed, scarcely lying upon Tom. It was chilling, but he was not easily chilled when self was in the question—as it generally was with Tom. He felt, however, that he must talk or be lost.

"I have taken the liberty," he said, "of bringing you the song I had the pleasure—a greater pleasure than you will readily imagine—of hearing you admire the other evening."

"I forget," said Hesper.

"I would not have ventured," continued Tom, "had it not happened that both air and words were my own."

"Ah !—indeed !—I did not know you were a poet, Mr.—"

She had forgotten his name.

"That or nothing," answered Tom, boldly.

"And a musician, too ?"

"At your service, Mrs. Redmain."

"I . . . . musician either," she said, with just enough of a smile to turn the rudeness into what Tom accepted as a flattering familiarity.

"Nor am I in want of a place," he replied, with spirit; "a bird can sing on any branch. Will you allow me to sing this song on yours? Mrs. Downport scarcely gave the expression I could have desired.—May I read the voices before I sing them?"

Without either intimacy or encouragement, Tom was capable of offering to read his own verses! Such fools self-partisanship makes of us.

Mrs. Redmain was, for her, not a little amused with the young man; he was not just like every other that came to the house.

"I should li-i-ike," she said.

Tom laid himself back a little in his chair, with the sheet of music in his hand, closed his eyes, and repeated as follows— he knew all his own verses by heart:

"Lovely lady, sweet disdain!
    Prithee keep thy Love at home;
Bind him with a tressèd chain;
    Do not let the mischief roam.

"In the jewel-cave, thine eye,
    In the tangles of thy hair,
It is well the imp should lie—
    There his home, his heaven is there.

"But for pity's sake, forbid
    Beauty's wasp at me to fly;
Sure the child should not be chid,
    And his mother standing by.

"For if once the villain came
    To my house, too well I know
He would set it all aflame—
    To the winds its ashes blow.

"Prithee keep thy Love at home;
    Net him up or he will start;
And if once the mischief roam,
    Straight he'll wing him to my heart."

What there might be in verse like this to touch with faintest emotion, let him say who cultivates art for art's sake. Doubtless there is that in rhythm and rhyme and cadence which will touch the pericardium when the heart itself is not to be reached by divinest harmony ; but, whether such women as Hesper feel this touch or only admire a song as they admire the church-prayers and Shakespeare, or whether, imagining in it some *tour de force* of which they are themselves incapable, they therefore look upon it as a mighty thing, I am at a loss to determine. All I know is that a gleam as from some far-off mirror of admiration did certainly, to Tom's great satisfaction, appear on Hesper's countenance. As, however, she said nothing, he, to waive aside a threatening awkwardness, lightly subjoined :

"Queen Anne is all the rage now, you see."

Mrs. Redmain knew that Queen-Anne houses were in fashion, and was even able to recognize one by its flush window-frames, while she had felt something odd, which might be old-fashioned, in the song ; between the two, she was led to the conclusion that the fashion of Queen Anne's time had been revived in the making of verses also.

"Can you, then, make a song to any pattern you please ?" she asked.

"I fancy so," answered Tom, indifferently, as if it were nothing to him to do whatever he chose to attempt. And in fact he could imitate almost anything—and well, too—the easier that he had nothing of his own pressing for utterance ; for he had yet made no response to the first demand made on every man, the only demand for originality made on any man —that he should order his own way aright.

"How clever you must be !" drawled Hesper ; and, notwithstanding the tone, the words were pleasant in the ears of goose Tom. He rose, opened the piano, and, with not a little cheap facility, began to accompany a sweet tenor voice in the song he had just read.

The door opened, and Mr. Redmain came in. He gave a glance at Tom as he sang, and went up to his wife where she still sat, with her face to the fire, and her back to the piano.

"New singing-master, eh?" he said.

"No," answered his wife.

"Who the deuce is he?"

"I forget his name," replied Hesper, in the tone of one bored by question. "He used to come to Durnmelling."

"That is no reason why he should not have a name to him."

Hesper did not reply. Tom went on playing. The moment he struck the last chord, she called to him in a clear, soft, cold voice:

"Will you tell Mr. Redmain your name? I happen to have forgotten it."

Tom picked up his hat, rose, came forward, and, mentioning his name, held out his hand.

"I don't know you," said Mr. Redmain, touching his palm with two fingers that felt like small fishes.

"It is of no consequence," said his wife; "Mr. Aylmer is an old acquaintance of our family."

"Only you don't quite remember his name!"

"It is not my *friends'* names only I have an unhappy trick of forgetting. I often forget yours, Mr. Redmain!"

"My *good* name, you must mean."

"I never heard that."

Neither had raised the voice, or spoken with the least apparent anger.

Mr. Redmain gave a grin instead of a retort. He appreciated her sharpness too much to get one ready in time. Turning away, he left the room with a quiet, steady step, taking his grin with him: it had drawn the clear, scanty skin yet tighter on his face, and remained fixed; so that he vanished with something of the look of a hairless tiger.

The moment he disappeared, Tom's gaze, which had been fascinated, sought Hesper. Her lips were shaping the word *brute!*—Tom heard it with his eyes; her eyes were flashing, and her face was flushed. But the same instant, in a voice perfectly calm—

"Is there anything else you would like to sing, Mr. Helmer?" she said. "Or—"

Here she ceased, with the slightest possible choking—it was only of anger—in the throat

Tom's was a sympathetic nature, especially where a pretty woman was in question. He forgot entirely that she had given quite as good, or as bad, as she received, and was hastening to say something foolish, imagining he had looked upon the sorrows of a lovely and unhappy wife and was almost in her confidence, when Sepia entered the room, with a dark glow that flashed into dusky radiance at sight of the handsome Tom. She had noted him on the night of the party, and remembered having seen him at the merrymaking in the old hall of Durnmelling, but he had not been introduced to her. A minute more, and they were sitting together in a bay-window, blazing away at each other like two corvettes, though their cartridges were often blank enough, while Hesper, never heeding them, kept her place by the chimney, her gaze transferred from the fire to the novel she had sent for from her bedroom.

— — —

CHAPTER XXV

MARY'S RECEPTION.

In the afternoon of the same day, now dreary enough, with the dreariness naturally belonging to the dreariest month of the year, Mary arrived in the city preferred to all cities by those who live in it, but the most uninviting, I should imagine, to a stranger, of all cities on the face of the earth. Cold seemed to have taken to itself a visible form in the thin, gray fog that filled the huge station from the platform to the glass roof. The latter had vanished, indistinguishable from sky invisible, and from the brooding darkness, in which the lamps innumerable served only to make spots of thinness. It was a mist, not a November fog, properly so called ; but every breath breathed by every porter, as he ran along by the side of the slowly halting train, was adding to its mass, which seemed to Mary to grow in bulk and density as she gazed. Her quiet, simple, decided manner at once secured her attention, and she was among the first who had their boxes on cabs and were driving away.

But the drive seemed interminable, and she had grown anxious and again calmed herself many times, before it came to an end. The house at which the cab drew up was large, and looked as dreary as large, but scarcely drearier than any other house in London on that same night of November. The cabman rang the bell, but it was not until they had waited a time altogether unreasonable that the door at length opened, and a lofty, well-built footman in livery appeared framed in it.

Mary got out, and, going up the steps, said she hoped the driver had brought her to the right house: it was Mrs. Redmain's she wanted.

"Mrs. Redmain is not at home, miss," answered the man. "I didn't hear as how she was expecting of any one," he added, with a glance at the boxes, formlessly visible on the cab, through the now thicker darkness.

"She is expecting me, I know," returned Mary; "but of course she would not stay at home to receive me," she remarked, with a smile.

"Oh!" returned the man, in a peculiar tone, and adding, "I'll see," went away, leaving her on the top of the steps, with the cabman behind her, at the bottom of them, waiting orders to get her boxes down.

"It don't appear as you was overwelcome, miss!" he remarked: with his comrades on the stand he passed for a wit; "—leastways, it don't seem as your sheets was quite done hairing."

"It's all right," said Mary, cheerfully.

She was not ready to imagine her dignity in danger, therefore did not provoke assault upon it by anxiety for its safety.

"I'm sorry to hear it, miss," the man rejoined.

"Why?" she asked.

"'Cause I should ha' liked to ha' taken *you* farther."

"But why?" said Mary, the second time, not understanding him, and not unwilling to cover the awkwardness of that slow minute of waiting.

"Because it gives a poor man with a whole family o' provo-
cations some'at of a chance, to 'ave a affable young lady like
you, miss, behind him in his cab. once a year, or thereabouts.
It's not by no means as I'd have you go farther and fare worse.
which it's a sayin' as I've heerd said, miss. So, if you're sure
o' the place, I may as well be a-gettin' down of *your* boxes."

So saying, he got on the cab, and proceeded to unfasten the
chain that secured the luggage.

"Wait a bit, cabbie. Don't you be in such a 'urry as if you
was a 'ansom, now," cried the footman, reappearing at the
farther end of the hall. "I should be sorry if there was a mistake, and you wasn't man enough to put your boxes up again
without assistance." Then, turning to Mary, "Mrs. Perkin
says, miss—that's the housekeeper, miss," he went on. "—that,
if as you're the young woman from the country—and I'm sure
I beg your pardon if I make a mistake—it ain't my fault, miss
—Mrs. Perkin says she did hear Mrs. Redmain make mention
of one, but she didn't have any instructions concerning her.—
But, as there you are," he continued more familiarly, gathering
courage from Mary's nodded assent, "you can put your boxes
in the hall, and sit down. she says, till Mrs. R. comes 'ome."

"Do you think she will be long?" asked Mary.

"Well, that's what no fellow can't say, seein' its a new play
as she's gone to. They call it Doomsday, an' there's no tellin'
when parties is likely to come 'ome from that," said the man,
with a grin of satisfaction at his own wit.

Was London such a happy place that everybody in it was
given to joking, thought Mary.

"'Ere, mister! gi' me a 'and wi' this 'ere luggage," cried
the cabman, finding the box he was getting down too much for
him. "Yah wouldn't see me break my back, an' my poor
'orse standin' there a lookin' on—would ye now?"

"Why don't you bring a man with you?" objected the
footman, as he descended the steps notwithstanding, to give
the required assistance. "I ain't paid as a crane.—By Juppi-
ter! what a weight the new party's boxes is!"

"Only that one," said Mary, apologetically. "It is full of
books. The other is not half so heavy."

"Oh, it ain't the weight, miss!" returned the footman, who had not intended she should hear the remark. "I believe Mr. Cabman and myself will prove equal to the occasion."

With that the book-box came down a great bump on the pavement, and presently both were in the hall, the one on the top of the other. Mary paid the cabman, who asked not a penny more than his fare; he departed with thanks; the facetious footman closed the door, told her to take a seat, and went away full of laughter, to report that the young person had brought a large library with her to enliven the dullness of her new situation.

Mrs. Perkin smiled crookedly, and, in a tone of pleasant reproof, desired her laughter-compressing inferior not to forget his manners.

"Please, ma'am, am I to leave the young woman sittin' up there all by herself in the cold?" he asked, straightening himself up. "She do look a rayther superior sort of young person," he added, "and the 'all-stove is dead out."

"For the present, Castle," replied Mrs. Perkin.

She judged it wise to let the young woman have a lesson at once in subjection and inferiority.

Mrs. Perkin was a rather tall, rather thin, quite straight, and very dark-complexioned woman. She always threw her head back on one side and her chin out on the other when she spoke, and had about her a great deal of the authoritative, which she mingled with such consideration toward her subordinates as to secure their obedience to her, while she cultivated antagonism to her mistress. She had had a better education than most persons of her class, but was morally not an atom their superior in consequence. She never went into a new place but with the feeling that she was of more importance by far than her untried mistress, and the worthier person of the two. She entered her service, therefore, as one whose work it was to take care of herself against a woman whose mistress she ought to have been, had Providence but started her with her natural rights. At the same time, she would have been *almost* as much offended by a hint that she was not a Christian, as she would have been by a doubt whether she was a lady.

For, indeed, she was both, if a great opinion of herself consti-
tuted the latter, and a great opinion of going to church con-
stituted the former.

She had not been taken into Hesper's confidence with regard to Mary, had discovered that "a young person" was expected, but had learned nothing of what her position in the
house was to be. She welcomed, therefore, this opportunity
both of teaching Mrs. Redmain—she never called her her *mistress*, while severely she insisted on the other servants' speaking of her so—the propriety of taking counsel with her housekeeper and of letting the young person know in time that
Mrs. Perkin was in reality her mistress.

The relation of the upper servants of the house to their
employers was more like that of the managers of an hotel to
their guests. The butler, the lady's-maid, and Mr. Redmain's
body-servant, who had been with him before his marriage, and
was supposed to be deep in his master's confidence, ate with
the housekeeper in her room, waited upon by the livery and
maid-servants, except the second cook : the first cook only
came to superintend the cooking of the dinner, and went away
after. To all these Mrs. Perkin was careful to be just ; and, if
she was precise even to severity with them, she was herself
obedient to the system she had established—the main feature
of which was punctuality. She not only regarded punctuality
as the foremost of virtues, but, in righteous moral sequence,
made it the first of her duties : and the benefit everybody
reaped. For nothing oils the household wheels so well as this
same punctuality. In a family, love, if it be strong, genuine,
and patent, will make up for anything ; but, where there is no
family and no love, the loss of punctuality will soon turn a
house into the mere pouch of a social *inferno*. Here the master and mistress came and went, regardless of each other, and
of all household polity ; but their meals were ready for them
to the minute, when they chose to be there to eat them : the
carriage came round like one of the puppets on the Strasburg
clock ; the house was quiet as a hospital ; the bells were answered—all except the door-bell outside of calling hours—with
swiftness ; you could not soil your fingers anywhere—not even

if the sweep had been that same morning; the manners of the servants—*when serving*—were unexceptionable; but the house was scarcely more of a home than one of the huge hotels characteristic of the age.

In the hall of it sat Mary for the space of an hour, not exactly learning the lesson Mrs. Perkin had intended to teach her, but learning more than one thing Mrs. Perkin was not yet capable of learning. I can not say she was comfortable, for she was both cold and hungry; but she was far from miserable. She had no small gift of patience, and had taught herself to look upon the less troubles of life as on a bad dream. There are children, though not yet many, capable, through faith in their parents, of learning not a little by their experience, and Mary was one of such : from the first she received her father's lessons like one whose business it was to learn them, and had thereby come to learn where he had himself learned. Hence she was not one to say *our Father in heaven,* and act as if there were no such Father, or as if he cared but little for his children. She was even foolish enough to believe that that Father both knew and cared that she was hungry and cold and wearily uncomfortable ; and thence she was weak enough to take the hunger and cold and discomfort as mere passing trifles, which could not last a moment longer than they ought. From her sore-tried endeavors after patience, had grown the power of active waiting—and a genuinely waiting child is one of the loveliest sights the earth has to show.

This was not the reception she had pictured to herself, as the train came rushing from Testbridge to London ; she had not, indeed, imagined a warm one, but she had not expected to be forgotten—for so she interpreted her abandonment in the hall, which seemed to grow colder every minute. She saw no means of reminding the household of her neglected presence, and indeed would rather have remained where she was till the morning than encounter the growing familiarity of the man who had admitted her. She did think once—if Mrs. Redmain were to hear of her reception, how she would resent it ! and would have found it difficult to believe how far people like her are from troubling themselves about the behavior of their servants to other people ; for they have no idea of an obligation to rule their own house, neither seem to have a notion of being accountable for what goes on in it.

She had grown very weary, and began to long for a floor on which she might stretch herself ; there was not a sound in the house but the ticking of a clock somewhere ; and she was now wondering whether everybody had gone to bed, when she heard a step approaching, and presently Castle, who was the only man at home, stood up before her, and, with the ease of perfect self-satisfaction, and as if there was nothing in the neglect of her but the custom of the house to cool people well in the hall before admitting them to its penetralia, said, "Step this way—miss" ; the last word added after a pause of pretended hesitation, for the man had taken his cue from the housekeeper.

Mary rose, and followed him to the basement story, into a comfortable room, where sat Mrs. Perkin, embroidering large sunflowers on a piece of coarse stuff. She was *artistic*, and despised the whole style of the house.

"You may sit down," she said, and pointed to a chair near the door.

Mary, not a little amused, for all her discomfort, did as she was permitted, and awaited what should come next.

"What part of the country are you from ?" asked Mrs. Perkin, with her usual diagonal upward toss of the chin, but without lifting her eyes from her work.

"From Testbridge," answered Mary.

"The servants in this house are in the habit of saying *ma'am* to their superiors : it is required of them," remarked Mrs. Perkin. But, although her tone was one of rebuke, she said the words lightly, tossed the last of them off, indeed, almost playfully, as if the lesson was meant for one who could hardly have been expected to know better. "And what place did you apply for in the house ?" she went on to ask.

"I can hardly say, ma'am," answered Mary, avoiding both inflection and emphasis, and by her compliance satisfying Mrs. Perkin that she had been right in requiring the *kotou.*

10

"It is not usual for young persons to be engaged without knowing for what purpose."

"I suppose not, ma'am."

"What wages were you to have?" next inquired Mrs. Perkin, gradually assuming a more decided drawl as she became more assured of her position with the stranger. She would gladly get some light on the affair. "You need not object to mentioning them," she went on, for she imagined Mary hesitated, whereas she was only a little troubled to keep from laughing; "I always pay the wages myself."

"There was nothing said about wages, ma'am," answered Mary.

"Indeed! Neither work nor wages specified? Excuse me if I say it seems rather peculiar.—We must be content to wait a little, then—until we learn what Mrs. Redmain expected of you, *and whether or not you are capable of it.* We can go no further now."

"Certainly not, ma'am," assented Mary.

"Can you use your needle?"

"Yes, ma'am."

"Have you done any embroidery?"

"I understand it a little, but I am not particularly fond of it."

"You mistake: I did not ask you whether you were fond of it," said Mrs. Perkin; "I asked you if you had ever done any"; and she smiled severely, but ludicrously, for a diagonal smile is apt to have a comic effect. "Here!—take off your gloves," she continued, "and let me see you do one of these loose-worked sunflowers. They are the fashion now, though, I dare say, you will not be able to see the beauty of them."

"Please, ma'am," returned Mary, "if you will excuse me, I would rather go to my room. I have had a long journey, and am very tired."

"There is no room yours.—I have had no character with you.—Nothing can be done till Mrs. Redmain comes home, and she and I have had a little talk about you. But you can go to the housemaid's—the second housemaid's room, I mean —and make yourself tidy. There is a spare bed in it, I believe, which you can have for the night ; only mind you don't keep the girl awake talking to her, or she will be late in the morning, and that I never put up with. I think you will do. You seem willing to learn, and that is half the battle."

Therewith Mrs. Perkin, believing she had laid in awe the foundation of a rightful authority over the young person, gave her a nod of dismissal, which she intended to be friendly.

"Please, ma'am," said Mary, "could I have one of my boxes taken up stairs ?"

"Certainly not. I can not have two movings of them ; I must take care of my men. And your boxes, I understand, are heavy, quite absurdly so. It would *look* better in a young person not to have so much to carry about with her."

"I have but two boxes, ma'am," said Mary.

"Full of *books*, I am told."

"One of them only."

"You must do your best without them to-night. When I have made up my mind what is to be done with you, I shall let you have the one with your clothes ; the other shall be put away in the box-room. I give my people what books I think fit. For light reading, the " Fireside Herald " is quite enough for the room.—There—good night !"

Mary courtesied, and left her. At the door she glanced this way and that to find some indication to guide her steps. A door was open at the end of a passage, and from the odor that met her, it seemed likely to be that of the kitchen. She approached, and peeped in.

"Who is that ?" cried a voice irate.

It was the voice of the second cook, who was there supreme except when the *chef* was present. Mary stepped in, and the woman advanced to meet her.

"May I ask to what I am indebted for the honner of this unexpected visit ?" said the second cook, whose head its over-charge of self-importance jerked hither and thither upon her neck, as she seized the opportunity of turning to her own use a sentence she had just read in the " Fireside Herald " which had taken her fancy—spoken by Lady Blanche Rivington Delaware to a detested lover disinclined to be dismissed.

"Would you please tell me where to find the second house-maid," said Mary. "Mrs. Perkin has sent me to her room."

"Why don't Mrs. Perkin show you the way, then ?" returned the woman. "There ain't nobody else in the house as I knows on fit to send to the top o' them stairs with you. A nice way Jemim' 'ill be in when *she* comes 'ome, to find a stranger in her room !"

The same instant, however, the woman bethought herself that, if what she had said in her haste were reported, it would be as much as her place was worth ; and at once thereupon she assumed a more complaisant tone. Casting a look at her saucepans, as if to warn them concerning their behavior in her absence, she turned again to Mary, saying :

"I believe I better show you the way myself. It's easier to take you than find a girl to do it. Them hussies is never where they oughto be ! *You* follow *me.*"

She led the way along two passages, and up a back stair-case of stone—up and up, till Mary, unused to such heights, began to be aware of knees. Plainly at last in the regions of the roof, she thought her hill Difficulty surmounted ; but the cook turned a sharp corner, and Mary following found herself once more at the foot of a stair—very narrow and steep, leading up to one of those old-fashioned roof-turrets which had begun to appear in the new houses of that part of London.

"Are you taking me to the clouds, cook ?" she said, willing to be cheerful, and to acknowledge her obligation for laborious guidance.

"Not yet a bit, I hope," answered the cook ; "we'll get there soon enough, anyhow—excep' you belong to them peculiars as wants to be saints afore their time. If that's your sort, don't you come here ; for a wickeder 'ouse, or an 'ouse as you got to work harder in o' Sundays, no one won't easily find in this here west end."

With these words she panted up the last few steps, immediately at the top of which was the room sought. It was a very small one, scarcely more than holding the two beds. Having lighted the gas, the cook left her ; and Mary, noting that one of the beds was not made up, was glad to throw herself upon it. Covering herself with her cloak, her traveling-rug, and the woolen counterpane, she was soon fast asleep.

She was roused by a cry, half of terror, half of surprise. There stood the second housemaid, who, having been told nothing of her room-fellow, stared and gasped.

"I am sorry to have startled you," said Mary, who had half risen, leaning on her elbow. "They ought to have told you there was a stranger in your room."

The girl was not long from the country, and, in the midst of the worst vulgarity in the world, namely, among the servants of the selfish, her manners had not yet ceased to be simple. For a moment, however, she seemed capable only of panting, and pressing her hand on her heart.

"I am very sorry," said Mary, again : "but you see 1 won't hurt you ! I don't look dangerous, do I ?"

"No, miss," answered the girl, with an hysterical laugh. "I been to the play, and there was a man in it was a thief, you know, miss !" And with that she burst out crying.

It was some time before Mary got her quieted, but, when she did, the girl was quite reasonable. She deplored that the bed was not made up, and would willingly have yielded hers ; she was sorry she had not a clean night-gown to offer her—"not that it would be fit for the likes of *you*, miss !"—and showed herself full of friendly ministration. Mary being now without her traveling-cloak, Jemima judged from her dress she must be some grand visitor's maid, vastly her superior in the social scale : if she had taken her for an inferior, she would doubtless, like most, have had some airs handy.

CHAPTER XXVI.

HER POSITION.

Mary seemed to have but just got to sleep again, when she was startled awake by the violent ringing of a bell, almost at her ear.

"Oh, you needn't trouble yet a long while, miss !" said the girl, who was already dressing. "I've got ever so many fires to light, ere the' 'll be a thought of you !"

Mary lay down again, and once more fell fast asleep.

She was waked the third time by the girl telling her that breakfast was ready ; whereupon she rose, and made herself as tidy as she could, while Jemima *cleaned herself up a bit,* and was not a little improved in the process.

"I thought," she said, "as Mrs. Perkin would 'a' as't you to your first meal with her ; but she told me, when I as't what were to be done with you, as how you must go to the room, and eat your breakfast with the rest of us."

"As Mrs. Perkin pleases," said Mary.

She had before this come to understand the word of her Master, that not what enters into a man defiles him, but only what comes out of him ; hence, that no man's dignity is affected by what another does to him, but only by what he does, or would like to do, himself.

She did, however, feel a little shy on entering "the room," where all the livery and most of the women servants were already seated at breakfast. Two of the men, with a word to each other, made room for her between them, and laughed ; but she took no notice, and seated herself at the bottom of the table with her companion. Everything was as clean and tidy as heart could wish, and Mary was glad enough to make a good meal.

For a few minutes there was loud talking—from a general impulse to show off before the stranger ; then fell a silence, as if some feeling of doubt had got among them. The least affected by it was the footman who had opened the door to her : he had witnessed her reception by Mrs. Perkin. Addressing her boldly, he expressed a hope that she was not too much fatigued by her journey. Mary thanked him in her own natural, straightforward way, and the consequence was, that, when he spoke to her next, he spoke like a gentleman—in the tone natural to him, that is, and in the language of the parlor, without any mock-politeness. And, although the way they talked among themselves made Mary feel as if she were in a strange country, with strange modes, not of living merely, but of feeling and of regarding, she received not the smallest annoyance during the rest of the meal—which did not last long: Mrs. Perkin took care of that.

For an hour or more, after the rest had scattered to their respective duties, she was left alone. Then Mrs. Perkin sent for her.

When she entered her room, she found her occupied with the cook, and was allowed to stand unnoticed.

" When shall I be able to see Mrs. Redmain, ma'am ?" she asked, when the cook at length turned to go.

" Wait," rejoined Mrs. Perkin, with a quiet dignity, well copied, "until you are addressed, young woman.'—Then first casting a glance at her, and perhaps perceiving on her countenance a glimmer of the amusement Mary felt, she began to gather a more correct suspicion of the sort of being she might possibly be, and hastily added, " Pray, take a seat."

The idea of making a blunder was unendurable to Mrs. Perkin, and she was most unwilling to believe she had done so ; but, even if she had, to show that she knew it would only be to render it the more difficult to recover her pride of place. An involuntary twinkle about the corners of Mary's mouth made her hasten to answer her question.

" I am sorry," she said, " that I can give you no prospect of an interview with Mrs. Redmain before three o'clock. She will very likely not be out of her room before one.—I suppose you saw her at Durnmelling ?"

" Yes, ma'am," answered Mary, "—and at Testbridge."

It kept growing on the housekeeper that she had made a mistake—though to what extent she sought in vain to determine.

" You will find it rather wearisome waiting," she said next ; "—would you not like to help me with my work ?"

Already she had the sunflowers under her creative hands. ·

" I should be very glad—if I can do it well enough to please you, ma'am," answered Mary. " But," she added, " would you kindly see that Mrs. Redmain is told, as soon as she wakes, that I am here ?"

"Oblige me by ringing the bell," said Mrs. Perkin.—
"Send Mrs. Folter here."

A rather cross-looking, red-faced, thin woman appeared,
whom she requested to let her mistress know, as soon as
was proper, that there was a young person in the house
who said she had come from Testbridge by appointment to
see her.

"Yes, ma'am," said Folter, with a supercilious yet familiar nod to Mary ; "I'll take care she knows."

Mary passed what would have been a dreary morning to
one dependent on her company. It was quite three o'clock
when she was at length summoned to Mrs. Redmain's boudoir.
Folter, who was her guide thither, lingered, in the soft closing
of the door, long enough to learn that her mistress received the
young person with a kiss—almost as much to Mary's surprise
as Folter's annoyance, which annoyance partly to relieve,
partly to pass on to Mrs. Perkin, whose reception of Mary she
had learned, Folter hastened to report the fact, and succeeded
thereby in occasioning no small uneasiness in the bosom of the
housekeeper, who was almost as much afraid of her mistress as
the other servants were of herself. Some time she spent in
expectant trepidation, but gradually, as nothing came of it,
calmed her fears, and concluded that her behavior to Mary
had been quite correct, seeing the girl had made it no ground
of complaint.

But, although Hesper, being at the moment in tolerable
spirits, in reaction from her depression of the day before, received Mary with a kiss, she did not ask her a question about
her journey, or as to how she had spent the night. She was
there, and looking all right, and that was enough. On the
other hand, she did proceed to have her at once properly settled.

The little room appointed her looked upon a small court or
yard, and was dark, but otherwise very comfortable. As soon
as she was left to herself, she opened her boxes, put her things
away in drawers and wardrobe, arranged her books within easy
reach of the low chair Hesper had sent for from the drawing-
room for her, and sat down to read a little, brood a little, and

build a few castles in the air, more lovely than evanescent: no other house is so like its builder as this sort of castle.

About eight o'clock, Folter summoned her to go to Mrs. Redmain. By this time she was tired: she was accustomed to tea in the afternoon, and since her dinner with the house-keeper she had had nothing.

She found Mrs. Redmain dressed for the evening. As soon as Mary entered, she dismissed Folter.

"I am going out to dinner," she said. "Are you quite comfortable?"

"I am rather cold, and should like some tea," said Mary.

"My poor girl! have you had no tea?" said Hesper, with some concern, and more annoyance. "You are looking quite pale, I see! When did you have anything to eat?"

"I had a good dinner at one o'clock," replied Mary, with a rather weary smile.

"This is dreadful!" said Hesper. "What can the servants be about!"

"And, please, may I have a little fire?" begged Mary.

"Certainly," replied Hesper, knitting her brows with a look of slight anguish. "Is it possible you have been sitting all day without one? Why did you not ring the bell?" She took one of her hands. "You are frozen!" she said.

"Oh, no!" answered Mary; "I am far from that. You see nobody knows yet what to do with me.—You hardly know yourself," she added, with a merry look. "But, if you wouldn't mind telling Mrs. Perkin where you wish me to have my meals, that would put it all right, I think."

"Very well," said Hesper, in a tone that for her was sharp. "Will you ring the bell?"

She sent for the housekeeper, who presently appeared—lank and tall, with her head on one side like a lamp-post in distress, but calm and prepared—a dumb fortress, with a live garri-son.

"I wish you, Mrs. Perkin, to arrange with Miss Marston about her meals."

"Yes, ma'am," answered Mrs. Perkin, with sedatest utter-ance.

"Mrs. Perkin," said Mary, "I don't want to be trouble-
some ; tell me what will suit you best."

But Mrs. Perkin did not even look at her ; standing straight
as a rush, she kept her eyes on her mistress.

"Do you desire, ma'am, that Miss Marston should have her
meals in the housekeeper's room ?" she asked.

"That must be as Miss Marston pleases," answered Hesper.
"If she prefer them in her own, you will see they are properly
sent up."

"Very well, ma'am !—Then I wait Miss Marston's orders,"
said Mrs. Perkin, and turned to leave the room.   But, when
her mistress spoke again, she turned again and stood.   It was
Mary, however, whom Hesper addressed.

"Mary," she said, apparently foreboding worse from the
tone of the housekeeper's obedience than from her occurred
neglect, "when I am alone, you shall take your meals with
me ; and when I have any one with me, Mrs. Perkin will see
that they are sent to your room.   We will settle it so."

"Thank you," said Mary.

"Very well, ma'am," said Mrs. Perkin.

"Send Miss Marston some tea directly," said Hesper.

Scarcely was Mrs. Perkin gone when the brougham was announced.   Mary returned to her room, and in a little while tea,
with thin bread and butter in limited quantity, was brought her.
But it was brought by Jemima, whose face wore a cheerful
smile over the tray she carried : she, at least, did not grudge
Mary her superior place in the household.

"Do you think, Jemima," asked Mary, "you could manage to answer my bell when I ring ?"

"I should only be too glad, miss ; it would be nothing but
a pleasure to me ; and I'd jump to it if I was in the way ; but
if I was up stairs, which this house ain't a place to hear bells
in, sure I am nobody would let me know as you was a-ringin' ;
and if you was to think as how I was giving of myself airs,
like some people not far out of this square, I should be both
sorry and ashamed—an' that's more'n I'd say for my place to
Mrs. Perkin, miss."

"You needn't be afraid of that, Jemima," returned Mary.

"If you don't answer when I ring, I shall know, as well as if you told me, that you either don't hear or can't come at the moment. I sha'n't be exacting."

"Don't you be afeared to ring, miss; I'll answer your bell as often as I hear it."

"Could you bring me a loaf? I have had nothing since Mrs. Perkin's dinner; and this bread and butter is rather too delicately cut," said Mary.

"Laws, miss, you must be nigh clemmed!" said the girl; and, hastening away, she soon returned with a loaf, and butter, and a pot of marmalade sent by the cook, who was only too glad to open a safety-valve to her pleasure at the discomfiture of Mrs. Perkin.

"When would you like your breakfast, miss?" asked Jemima, as she removed the tea-things.

"Any time convenient," replied Mary.

"It's much the same to me, miss, so it's not before there's bilin' water. You'll have it in bed, miss?"

"No, thank you. I never do."

"You'd better, miss."

"I could not think of it."

"It makes no more trouble—less, miss, than if I had to get it when the room-breakfast was on. I've got to get the things together anyhow; and why shouldn't you have it as well as Mrs. Perkin, or that ill-tempered cockatoo, Mrs. Folter? You're a lady, and that's more'n can be said for either of them —justly, that is."

"You don't mean," said Mary, surprised out of her discretion, "that the housekeeper and the lady's-maid have breakfast in bed?"

"It's every blessed mornin' as I've got to take it up to 'em, miss, upon my word of honor, with a soft-biled egg, or a box o' sardines, new-opened, or a slice o' breakfast bacon, streaky. An' I do *not* think as it belongs proper to my place; only you see, miss, the kitchen-maid has got to do it for the cook, an' if I don't, who is there? It's not them would let the scullery-maid come near them in their beds."

"Does Mrs. Perkin know that the cook and the lady's-maid have it as well as herself?"

"Not she, miss; she'd soon make their coffee too 'ot! She's the only lady down stairs—she is! No more don't Mrs. Folter know as the cook has hers, only, if she did, it wouldn't make no differ, for she daren't tell. And cook, to be sure, it ain't her breakfast, only a cup o' tea an' a bit o' toast, to get her heart up first."

"Well," said Mary, "I certainly shall not add another to the breakfasts in bed. But I must trouble you all the same to bring it me here. I will make my bed, and do out the room myself, if you will come and finish it off for me."

"Oh, no, indeed, miss, you mustn't do that! Think what they'd say of you down stairs! They'd despise you down-right!"

"I shall do it, Jemima. If they were servants of the right sort, I should like to have their good opinion, and they would think all the more of me for doing my share ; as it is, I should count it a disgrace to care a straw what they thought. We must do our work, and not mind what people say."

"Yes, miss, that's what my mother used to say to my father, when he wouldn't be reasonable. But I must go, miss, or I shall catch it for gossiping with you—that's what *she'll* call it.

When Jemima was gone, Mary fell a-thinking afresh. It was all very well, she said to herself, to talk about doing her work, but here she was with scarce a shadow of an idea what her work was! Had *any* work been given her to do in this house? Had she presumed in coming—anticipated the guidance of Providence, and was she therefore now where she had no right to be? She could not tell ; but, anyhow, here she was, and no one could be anywhere without the fact involving its own duty. Even if she had put herself there, and was to blame for being there, that did not free her from the obligations of the position, and she was willing to do whatever should *now* be given her to do. God was not a hard master ; if she had made a mistake, he would pardon her, and either give her work here, where she found herself, or send her elsewhere. I need not say that thinking was not all her care; for she thought in the presence of Him who, because he is always setting our wrong things right, is called God our Saviour.

CHAPTER XXVII.

MR. AND MRS. HELMER.

THE next morning, Mary set out to find Letty, from whom, as I have said, she had heard but twice since her marriage. Mary had written again about a month ago, but had had no reply. The sad fact was, that, ever since she left Testbridge, Letty, for a long time, without knowing it, had been going down hill. There have been many whose earnestness has vanished with the presence of those whose influence awoke it. Letty's better self seemed to have remained behind with Mary; and not even if he had been as good as she thought him, could Tom himself have made up to her for the loss of such a friend.

But Letty had not found marriage at all the grand thing she had expected. With the faithfulness of a woman, however, she attributed her disappointment to something inherent in marriage, nowise affecting the man whom marriage had made her husband.

That he might be near the center to which what little work he did gravitated, Tom had taken a lodging in a noisy street, as unlike all that Letty had been accustomed to as anything London, except in its viler parts, could afford. Never a green thing was to be looked upon in any direction. Not a sweet sound was to be heard. The sun, at this time of the year, was seldom to be seen in London anywhere; and in Lydgate Street, even when there was no fog, it was but askance, and for a brief portion of the day, that he shone upon that side where stood their dusty windows. And then the noise!—a ceaseless torrent of sounds, of stony sounds, of iron sounds, of grinding sounds, of clashing sounds, of yells and cries—of all deafening and unpoetic discords! Letty had not much poetry in her, and

needed what could be had from the outside so much the more.
It is the people of a land without springs that must have cis-
terns. It is the poetic people without poetry that pant and
pine for the country. When such get hold of a poet, they
expect him to talk poetry, or, at least, to talk about poetry ! I
fancy poets do not read much poetry, and except to their peers
do not often care to talk about it. But to one like Letty, however little she may understand or even be aware of the need,
the poetic is as necessary as rain in summer; while, to one so
little skilled in the finding of it, there was none visible, audible, or perceptible about her—except, indeed, what, of poorest
sort for her uses, she might discover bottled in some circulating
library : there was one—blessed proximity !—within ten minutes' walk of her.

Once a week or so, some weeks oftener, Tom would take
her to the play, and that was, indeed, a happiness—not because
of the pleasure of the play only or chiefly, though that was
great, but in the main because she had Tom beside her all the
time, and mixed up Tom with the play, and the play with
Tom.

Alas ! Tom was not half so dependent upon her, neither
derived half so much pleasure from her company. Some of
his evenings every week he spent at houses where those who
received him had not the faintest idea whether he had a wife
or not, and cared as little, for it would have made no difference : they would not have invited her. Small, silly, conceited
Tom, regarding himself as a somebody, was more than content
to be asked to such people's houses. He thought he went as a
lion, whereas it was merely as a jackal : so great is the love of
some for wild beasts in general, that they even think something
of jackals. He was aware of no insult to himself in asking him
whether as a lion or any other wild beast, nor of any to his wife
and himself together in not asking her with him. While she
sat in her dreary lodging, dingily clad and lonely, Tom, dressed
in the height of the fashion, would be strolling about grand
rooms, now exchanging a flying shot of recognition, now paus-
ing to pay a compliment to this lady on her singing, to that on
her verses, to a third, where he dared, on her dress; for good-

natured Tom was profuse of compliments, not without a degree and kind of honesty in them ; now singing one of his own
songs to the accompaniment of some gracious goddess, now accompanying the same or some other gracious goddess as she
sang—for Tom could do that well enough for people without a
conscience in their music ; now in the corner of a conservatory,
now in a cozy little third room behind a back drawing-room,
talking nonsense with some lady foolish enough to be amused
with his folly.   Tom meant no harm and did not do much—
was only a human butterfly, amusing himself with other creatures of a day, who have no notion that death can not kill
them, or they might perhaps be more miserable than they are.
They think, if they think at all, that it is life, strong in them,
that makes them forget death ; whereas, in truth, it is death,
strong in them, that makes them forget life.   Like a humming-
bird, all sparkle and flash, Tom flitted through the tropical
delights of such society as his "uncommon good luck" had
gained him admission to, forming many an evanescent friendship, and taking many a graceful liberty for which his pleasant
looks, confident manners, and free carriage were his indemnity
—for Tom seemed to have been born to show what a nice sort
of a person a fool, well put together, may be—with his high-
bred air, and his ready replies, for he had also a little of that
social element, once highly valued, now less countenanced, and
rare—I mean wit.

He had, indeed, plenty of all sorts of brains ; but no amount
of talent could reveal to him the reason or the meaning of the
fact that wedded life was less interesting than courtship ; for
the former, the reason lay in himself, and of himself proper
he knew, as I have said, next to nothing ; while the latter, the
meaning of the fact, is profound as eternity.   He had no notion that, when he married, his life was thereby, in a lofty and
blessed sense, forfeit : that, to save his wife's life, he must yield
his own, she doing the same for him—for God himself can save
no other way.   But the notion of any saving, or the need of it,
was far from Tom ; nor had Letty, for her part, any thought
of it either, except from the tyranny of her aunt.   Not the
less, in truth, did they both want saving, very much saving—

before life could be to either of them a good thing. It is only
its inborn possibility of and divine tendency toward blossom-
ing that constitute life a good thing. Life's blossom is its
salvation, its redemption, the justification of its existence—
and is a thing far off with most of us. For Tom, his highest
notion of life was to be recognized by the world for that which
he had chosen as his idea of himself—to have the reviews allow
him a poet, not grudgingly, nor with abatement of any sort,
but recognizing him as the genius he must contrive to believe
himself, or "perish in" his "self-contempt." Then would he
live and die in the blessed assurance that his name would be for
ever on the lips and in the hearts of that idol of fools they call
posterity—divinity as vague as the old gray Fate, and less noble,
inasmuch as it is but the supposed concave whence is to rebound
the man's own opinion of himself.

While jewelly Tom was idling away time which yet could
hardly be called precious, his little brown wife, as I have said,
sat at home—such home as a lodging can be for a wife whose
husband finds his interest mainly outside of it—inquired after
by nobody, thought of by nobody, hardly even taken up by her
own poor, weary self; now trying in vain after interest in the
feeble trash she was reading; now getting into the story for
the last half of a chapter, to find herself, when the scene
changed at the next, as far out and away and lost as ever;
now dropping the book on her knee, to sit musing—if, indeed,
such poor mental vagaries as hers can be called even musing!—
ignorant what was the matter with her, hardly knowing that
anything was the matter, and yet pining morally, spiritually,
and psychically; now wondering when Tom would be home;
now trying to congratulate herself on his being such a favorite,
and thinking what an honor it was to a poor country girl like
her to be the wife of a man so much courted by the best society
—for she never doubted that the people to whose houses Tom
went desired his company from admiration of his writings.
She had not an idea that never a soul of them or of their guests
cared a straw about what he wrote—except, indeed, here and
there, a young lady in her first season, who thought it a grand
thing to know an author, as poor Letty thought it a grand

thing to be the wife of one. Hail to the coming time when, those who write books outnumbering those who do not, a man will be thought no more of because he can write than because he can sit a horse or brew beer! In that happy time the true writer will be neither an atom the more regarded nor disregarded; he will only be less troubled with birthday books, requests for autographs, and such-like irritating attentions. From that time, also, it may be, the number of writers will begin to diminish; for then, it is to be hoped, men will begin to see that it is better to do the inferior thing well than the superior thing after a middling fashion. The man who would not rather be a good shoemaker than a middling author would be no honor to the shoemakers, and can hardly be any to the authors. I have the comfort that in this all authors will agree with me, for which of us is now able to see himself *middling?* Honorable above all honor that authorship can give is he who can.

It was through some of his old college friends that Tom had thus easily stepped into the literary profession. They were young men with money and friends to back them, who, having taken to literature as soon as they chipped the university shell, were already in the full swing of periodical production, when Tom, to quote two rather contradictory utterances of his mother, ruined his own prospects and made Letty's fortune by marrying her. I can not say, however, that they had found him remunerative employment. The best they had done for him was to bring him into such a half sort of connection with a certain weekly paper that now and then he got something printed in it, and now and then, with the joke of acknowledging an obligation irremunerable, the editor would hand him what he called an honorarium, but what in reality was a five-pound note. When such an event occurred, Tom would feel his bosom swell with the imagined dignity of supporting a family by literary labor, and, forgetful of the sparseness of his mother's doles, who delighted to make the young couple feel the bitterness of dependence, would immediately, on the strength of it, invite his friends to supper—not at the lodging where Letty sat lonely, but at some tavern frequented by people of the craft. It was at such times, and in the company of men certainly not better than himself, that Tom's hopes were brightest, and his confidence greatest: therefore such seasons were those of his highest bliss. Especially, when his sensitive but poor imagination was stimulated from the nerve-side of the brain, was Tom in his glory; and it was not the "few glasses of champagne," of which he talked so airily, that had all the honor of crowning him king of fate and poet of the world. Long after midnight, upon such and many other occasions, would he and his companions sit laughing and jesting and drinking, some saying witty things, and all of them foolish things and worse; inventing stories apropos of the foibles of friends, and relating anecdotes which grew more and more irreverent to God and women as the night advanced, and the wine gained power, and the shame-faced angels of their true selves, made in the image of God, withdrew into the dark; until at last, between night and morning, Tom would reel gracefully home, using all the power of his will—the best use to which it ever was put—to subdue the drunkenness of which, even in its embrace, he had the lingering honor to be ashamed, that he might face his wife with the appearance of the gentleman he was anxious she should continue to consider him.

It was an unhappy thing for Tom that his mother, having persuaded her dying husband, "for Tom's sake," to leave the money in her power, should not now have carried her tyranny further, and refused him money altogether. He would then have been compelled to work harder, and to use what he made in procuring the necessaries of life. There might have been some hope for him then. As it was, his profession was the mere grasping after the honor of a workman without the doing of the work; while the little he gained by it was, at the same time, more than enough to foster the self-deception that he did something in the world. With the money he gave her, which was never more than a part of what his mother sent him, Letty had much ado to make both ends meet; and, while he ran in debt to his tailor and bootmaker, she never had anything new to wear. She did sometimes wish he would take her out with him a little oftener of an evening; for sometimes she felt so lonely as to be quite unable to amuse herself. her resources were not many in her position, and fewer still in herself : but she always reflected that he could not afford it. and it was long ere she began to have any doubt or uneasiness about him—long before she began even to imagine it might be well if he spent his evenings with her, or, at least, in other ways and other company than he did. When first such a thought presented itself, she banished it as a disgrace to herself and an insult to him. But it was no wonder if she found marriage dull. poor child ! —after such expectations, too, from her Tom !

What a pity it seems to our purblind eyes that so many girls should be married before they are women ! The woman comes at length, and finds she is forestalled—that the prostrate and mutilated Dagon of a girl's divinity is all that is left her to do the best with she can ! But. thank God, in the faithfully accepted and encountered responsibility, the woman must at length become aware that she has under her feet an ascending stair by which to climb to the woman of the divine ideal.

There was at present, however, nothing to be called thought in the mind of Letty. She had even lost much of what faculty of thinking had been developed in her by the care of Cousin Godfrey. That had speedily followed the decay of the aspiration kindled in her by Mary. Her whole life now—as much of it, that is, as was awake—was Tom, and only Tom. Her whole day was but the continuous and little varied hope of his presence. Most of the time she had a book in her hands. but ever again book and hands would sink into her lap, and she would sit staring before her at nothing. She was not unhappy, she was only not happy. At first it was a speechless delight to have as many novels as she pleased. and she thought Tom the very prince of bounty in not merely permitting her to read them, but bringing them to her, one after the other, sometimes two at once, in spendthrift profusion. The first thing that made her aware she was not quite happy was the discovery that novels were losing their charm, that they were not sufficient to make her day pass, that they were only dessert, and she had no dinner. When it came to difficulty in going on with a new one long enough to get interested in it, she sighed heavily, and began to think that perhaps life was rather a dreary thing—at least considerably diluted with the unsatisfactory. How many of my readers feel the same! How few of them will recognize that the state of things would indeed be desperate were it otherwise! How many would go on and on being only butterflies, but for life's dismay! And who would choose to be a butterfly, even if life and summer and the flowers were to last for ever!

"I would," I fancy this and that reader saying.

"Then," I answer, "the only argument you are equal to, is the fact that life nor summer nor the flowers do last for ever."

"I suppose I am made a butterfly," do you say? "seeing I prefer to be one."

"Ah! do you say so, indeed? Then you begin to excuse yourself, and what does that mean? It means that you are no butterfly, for a butterfly—no, nor an angel in heaven—could never begin excusing the law of its existence. Butterfly-brother, the hail will be upon you."

I may not then pity Letty that she had to discover that novels taken alone serve one much as sweetmeats *ad libitum* do children, nor that she had to prove that life has in it that spiritual quinine, precious because bitter, whose part it is to wake the higher hunger.

Tom talked of himself as on the staff of "The Firefly"—such was the name of the newspaper whose editor sometimes paid him—a weekly of great pretense, which took upon itself the mystery of things, as if it were God's spy. It was popular in a way, chiefly in fashionable circles. As regarded the opinions it promulgated, I never heard one, who understood the particular question at any time handled, say it was correct. Its writers were mostly young men, and their passion was to say clever things. If a friend's book came in their way, it was treated worse or better than that of a stranger, but with impartial disregard for truth in either case; yet many were the authors who would go up endless back stairs to secure from that paper a flattering criticism, and then be as proud of it as if it had been the genuine and unsought utterance of a true man's conviction; and many were the men, immeasurably the

superiors of the reviewers, and in a general way acquainted
with their character, who would accept as conclusive upon the
merits of a book the opinions they gave, nor ever question a
mode of quotation by which a book was made to show itself
whatever the reviewer chose to call it. A scandalous rumor
of any kind, especially from the region styled " high life,"
often false, and always incorrect, was the delight both of the
paper and of its readers; and the interest it thus awoke,
united to the fear it thus caused, was mainly what procured
for such as were known to be employed upon it the *entrée* of
houses where, if they had had a private existence only, their
faces would never have been seen. But, to do Tom justice, he
wrote nothing of this sort: he was neither ill-natured nor
experienced enough for that department; what he did write
was clever, shallow sketches of that same society into whose
charmed precincts he was but so lately a comer that much was
to him interesting which had long ceased to be observed by
eyes turned horny with the glare of the world's footlights; and,
while these sketches pleased the young people especially, even
their jaded elders enjoyed the sparkling reflex of what they
called life, as seen by an outsider; for they were thereby enabled to feel for a moment a slight interest in themselves
objectively, along with a galvanized sense of existence as the
producers of history These sketches did more for the paper
than the editor was willing to know or acknowledge.

But " The Firefly " produced also a little art on its own account—not always very original, but, at least, not a sucking of
life from the labor of others, as is most of that parasitic thing
miscalled criticism. In this branch Tom had a share, in the
shape of verse. A ready faculty was his, but one seldom
roused by immediate interest, and never by insight. It was
not things themselves, but the reflection of things in the art
of others, that moved him to produce. Coleridge, I think,
says of Dryden, that he took fire with the running of his own
wheels: so did Tom; but it was the running of the wheels of
others that set his wheels running. He was like some young
preachers who spend a part of the Saturday in reading this or
that author, in order to *get up* the mental condition favorable

to preaching on the Sunday. He was really fond of poetry; delighted in the study of its external elements for the sake of his craft; possessed not only a good but cultivated ear for verse, which is a rare thing out of the craft; had true pleasure in a fine phrase, in a strong or brilliant word; last and chief, had a special faculty for imitation; from which gifts, graces, and acquirements, it came, that he could write almost in any style that moved him—so far, at least, as to remind one who knew it, of that style; and that every now and then appeared verses of his in "The Firefly."

As often as this took place, Letty was in the third heaven of delight. For was not Tom's poetry unquestionably superior to anything else the age could produce? was the poetry Cousin Godfrey made her read once to be compared to Tom's? and was not Tom her own husband? Happy woman she!

But, by the time at which my narrative has arrived, the first mist of a coming fog had begun to gather faintly dim in her heart. When Tom would come home happy, but talk perplexingly; when he would drop asleep in the middle of a story she could make nothing of; when he would burst out and go on laughing, and refuse to explain the motive—how was she to avoid the conclusion forced upon her, that he had taken too much strong drink? and, when she noted that this condition reappeared at shorter and shorter intervals, might she not well begin to be frightened, and to feel, what she dared not allow, that she was being gradually left alone—that Tom had struck into a diverging path, and they were slowing parting miles from each other?

* * *

CHAPTER XXVIII.

MARY AND LETTY.

WHEN her landlady announced a visitor, Letty, not having yet one friend in London, could not think who it should be. When Mary entered, she sprang to her feet and stood staring: what with being so much in the house, and seeing so few people, the poor girl had, I think, grown a little stupid. But, when the fact of Mary's presence cleared itself to her, she rushed forward with a cry, fell into her arms, and burst out weeping. Mary held her fast until she had a little come to herself, then, pushing her gently away to the length of her arms, looked at her.

She was not a sight to make one happy. She was no longer the plump, fresh girl that used to go singing about; nor was she merely thin and pale, she looked unhealthy. Things could not be going well with her. Had her dress been only disordered, that might have been accidental, but it looked neglected —was not merely dingy, but plainly shabby, and, to Mary's country eyes, appeared on the wrong side of clean. Presently, as those eyes got accustomed to the miserable light, they spied in the skirt of her gown a perfunctory darn, revealing but too evidently that to Letty there no longer seemed occasion for being particular. The sadness of it all sunk to Mary's heart: Letty had not found marriage a grand affair!

But Mary had not come into the world to be sad or to help another to be sad. Sorrowful we may often have to be, but to indulge in sorrow is either not to know or to deny God our Saviour. True, her heart ached for Letty, and the ache immediately laid itself as close to Letty's ache as it could lie; but that was only the advance-guard of her army of salvation, the light cavalry of sympathy: the next division was help; and behind that lay patience, and strength, and hope, and faith, and joy. This last, modern teachers, having failed to regard it as a virtue, may well decline to regard as a duty; but he is a poor Christian indeed in whom joy has not at least a growing share, and Mary was not a poor Christian—at least, for the time she had been learning, and as Christians go in the present æon of their history. Her whole nature drew itself together, confronting the destroyer, whatever he might be, in possession of Letty. How to help she could not yet tell, but sympathy was already at its work.

"You are not looking your best, Letty," she said, clasping her again in her arms.

With a little choking, Letty assured her she was quite well, only rather overcome with the pleasure of seeing her so unexpectedly.

"How is Mr. Helmer?" asked Mary.

"Quite well—and very busy," answered Letty—a little hurriedly, Mary thought. "—But," she added, in a tone of disappointment, "you always used to call him Tom!"

"Oh!" answered Mary, with a smile, "one must be careful how one takes liberties with married people. A certain mysterious change seems to pass over some of them; they are not the same somehow, and you have to make your acquaintance with them all over again from the beginning."

"I shouldn't think such people's acquaintance worth making over again," said Letty.

"How can you tell what it may be worth?" said Mary, "—they are so different from what they were? Their friendship may now be one that won't change so easily."

"Ah! don't be hard on me, Mary. I have never ceased to love you."

"I am *so* glad!" answered Mary. "People don't generally take much to me—at least, not to come *near* me. But you can *be* friends without *having* friends," she added, with a sententiousness she had inherited.

"I don't quite understand you," said Letty, sadly; "but, then, I never could quite, you know. Tom finds me very stupid."

These words strengthened Mary's suspicion, from the first a probability, that all was not going well between the two; but she shrunk from any approach to confidences with *one* of a married pair. To have such, she felt instinctively, would be a breach of unity, except, indeed, that were already, and irreparably, broken. To encourage in any married friend the placing of a confidence that excludes the other, is to encourage that friend's self-degradation. But neither was this a fault to which Letty could have been tempted; she loved her Tom too much for it: with all her feebleness, there was in Letty not a little of childlike greatness, born of faith.

But, although Mary would make Letty tell nothing, she was not the less anxious to discover, that she might, if possible, help. She would observe : side-lights often reveal more than direct illumination. It might be for Letty, and not for Mrs. Redmain, she had been sent. He who made time in time would show.

"Are you going to be long in London, Mary?" asked Letty.

"Oh, a long time!" answered Mary, with a loving glance.

Letty's eyes fell, and she looked troubled.

"I am so sorry, Mary," she said, "that I can not ask you to come here! We have only these two rooms, and—and—you see—Mrs. Helmer is not very liberal to Tom, and—because they—don't get on together very well—as I suppose everybody knows—Tom won't—he won't consent to—to—"

"You little goose!" cried Mary; "you don't think I would come down on you like a devouring dragon, without even letting you know, and finding whether it would suit you !—I have got a situation in London."

"A situation !" echoed Letty. "What can you mean, Mary? You haven't left your own shop, and gone into somebody else's ?"

"No, not exactly that," replied Mary, laughing; "but I have no doubt most people would think that by far the more prudent thing to have done."

"Then I don't," said Letty, with a little flash of her old enthusiasm. "Whatever you do, Mary, I am sure will always be the best."

"I am glad I have so much of your good opinion, Letty; but I am not sure I shall have it still, when I have told you what I have done. Indeed, I am not quite sure myself that I have done wisely; but, if I have made a mistake, it is from having listened to love more than to prudence."

"What!" cried Letty; "you're married, Mary?"

And here a strange thing, yet the commonest in the world, appeared; had her own marriage proved to Letty the most blessed of fates, she could not have shown more delight at the idea of Mary's. I think men find women a little incomprehensible in this matter of their friends' marriage; in their largerheartedness, I presume, women are able to hope for their friends, even when they have lost all hope for themselves.

"No," replied Mary, amused at having thus misled her. "It is neither so bad nor so good as that. But I was far from comfortable in the shop without my father, and kept thinking how to find a life more suitable for me. It was not plain to me that my lot was cast there any longer, and one has no right to choose difficulty; for, even if difficulty be the right thing for you, the difficulty you choose can't be the right difficulty. Those that are given to choosing, my father said, are given to regretting. Then it happened that I fell in love—not with a gentleman—don't look like that, Letty—but with a lady; and, as the lady took a small fancy to me at the same time, and wanted to have me about her, here I am."

"But, surely, that is not a situation fit for one like you, Mary!" cried Letty, almost in consternation; for, notwithstanding her opposition to her aunt's judgment in the individual case of her friend, Letty's own judgments, where she had any, were mostly of this world. "I suppose you are a kind of —of—companion to your lady-friend?"

"Or a kind of lady's-maid, or a kind of dressmaker, or a kind of humble friend—something like a dog, perhaps—only not to be quite so much loved and petted! In truth, Letty, I do not know what I am, or what I am going to be; but I shall find out before long, and where's the use of knowing, any more than anything else before it's wanted?"

"You take my breath away, Mary! The thing doesn't seem at all like you! It's not consistent!—Mary Marston in a menial position! I can't get a hold of it!"

"You remind me," said Mary, laughing, "of what my father said to Mr. Turnbull once. They were nearer quarreling then than ever I saw them. You remember my father's way, Letty—how he would say a thing too quietly even to smile with it? I can't tell you what a delight it is to me to talk to anybody that knew him!—Mr. Turnbull imagined he did not know what he was about, for the thoughts my father was thinking could not have lived a moment in Mr. Turnbull. 'You see, John Turnbull,' my father said, 'no man can look so inconsistent as one whose principles are not understood ; for hardly in anything will that man do as his friend must have thought he would.'—I suppose you think, Letty." Mary went on, with a merry air, "that, for the sake of consistency, I should never do anything but sell behind a counter ?"

"In that case," said Letty, "I ought to have married a milkman, for a dairy is the only thing I understand I can't help Tom ever so little !—But I suppose it wouldn't be possible for two to write poetry together, even if they were husband and wife, and both of them clever !"

"Something like it has been tried, I believe," answered Mary, "but not with much success. I suppose, when a man sets himself to make anything, he must have it all his own way, or he can't do it."

"I suppose that's it. I know Tom is very angry with the editor when he wants to alter anything he has written. I'm sure Tom's right, too. You can't think how much better Tom's way always is !—He makes that quite clear, even to poor, stupid me. But then, you know, Tom's a genius ; that's one thing there's *no* doubt of !—But you haven't told me yet where you are."

"You remember Miss Mortimer, of Durnmelling ?"

"Quite well, of course."

"She is Mrs. Redmain now I am with her."

"You don't mean it ! Why, Tom knows her very well ! He has been several times to parties at her house."

"And not you, too ?" asked Mary.

"Oh, dear, no !" answered Letty, laughing, superior at Mary's ignorance. "It's not the fashion in London, at least for distinguished persons like my Tom, to take their wives to parties."

"Are there no ladies at those parties, then ?"

"Oh, yes !" replied Letty, smiling again at Mary's ignorance of the world, "the grandest of ladies—duchesses and all. You don't know what a favorite Tom is in the highest circles !"

Now Mary could believe almost anything bearing on Tom's being a favorite, for she herself had li   d   more

than she approved of him ; but she could not see the sense of
his going to parties without his wife, neither could she see that
the *height* of the circle in which he was a favorite made any
difference.　She had old-fashioned notions of a man and his
wife being one flesh, and felt a breach of the law where they
were separated, whatever the custom—reason there could be
none.　But Letty seemed much too satisfied to give her any
light on the matter.　Did it seem to her so natural that she
could not understand Mary's difficulty ?　She could not help
suspecting, however, that there might be something in this
recurrence of a separation absolute as death—for was it not a
passing of one into a region where the other could not follow ?
—to account for the change in her.—The same moment, as
if Letty divined what was passing in Mary's thought, and were
not altogether content with the thing herself, but would gladly
justify what she could not explain, she added, in the tone of
an unanswerable argument :

"Besides, Mary, how could I get a dress fit to wear at such
parties ?　You wouldn't have me go and look like a beggar !
That would be to disgrace Tom.　Everybody in London judges
everybody by the clothes she wears.　You should hear Tom's
descriptions of the ladies' dresses when he comes home !"

Mary was on the verge of crying out indignantly, "Then,
if he can't take you, why doesn't he stop at home with you ?"
but she bethought herself in time to hold her peace.　She
settled it with herself, however, that Tom must have less heart
or yet more muddled brains than she had thought.

"So, then," reverted Letty, as if willing to turn definitively
from the subject, "you are actually living with the beautiful
Mrs. Redmain !　What a lucky girl you are !　You will see no
end of grand people !　You will see my Tom sometimes—when
I can't !" she added, with a sigh that went to Mary's heart.

"Poor thing !" she said to herself, "it isn't anything
much out of the way she wants—only a little more of a foolish
husband's company !"

It was no wonder that Tom found Letty dull, for he had
just as little of his own in him as she, and thought he had a
great store—which is what sends a man most swiftly along the

road to that final poverty in which even that which he has shall be taken from him.

Mary did not stay so long with Letty as both would have liked, for she did not yet know enough of Hesper's ways. When she got home, she learned that she had a headache, and had not yet made her appearance.

CHAPTER XXIX.

THE EVENING STAR.

NOTWITHSTANDING her headache, however, Mrs. Redmain was going in the evening to a small fancy-ball, meant for a sort of rehearsal to a great one when the season should arrive. The part and costume she had chosen were the suggestion of her own name : she would represent the Evening Star, clothed in the early twilight : and neither was she unfit for the part, nor was the dress she had designed altogether unsuitable either to herself or to the part. But she had sufficient confidence neither in herself nor her maid to forestall a desire for Mary's opinion. After luncheon, therefore, she sent for Miss Marston to her bedroom.

Mary found her half dressed, Folter in attendance, a great heap of pink lying on the bed.

"Sit down, Mary," said Hesper, pointing to a chair ; "I want your advice. But I must first explain. Where I am going this evening, nobody is to be herself except me. I am not to be Mrs. Redmain, though, but Hesper. You know what Hesper means ?"

Mary said she knew, and waited—a little anxious ; for sideways in her eyes glowed the pink of the chosen Hesperian clouds, and, if she should not like it, what could be done at that late hour.

"There is my dress," continued the Evening Star, with a glance of her eyes, for Folter was busied with her hair ; "I want to know your opinion of it."

Folter gave a toss of her head that seemed to say, "Have not *I* spoken ?" but what it really did mean, how should other mortal know ? for the main obstructions to understanding are profundity and shallowness, and the latter is far the more perplexing of the two.

"1 should like to see it on first," said Mary : she was in doubt whether the color—bright, to suggest the brightest of sunset-clouds—would suit Hesper's complexion. Then, again, she had always associated the name *Hesper* with a later, a solemnly lovely period of twilight, having little in common with the color so voluminous in the background.

Hesper had a good deal of appreciative faculty, and knew therefore when she liked and when she did not like a thing ; but she had very little originative faculty—so little that, when anything was wrong, she could do next to nothing to set it right. There was small originality in taking a suggestion for her part from her name, and less in the idea, following by concatenation, of adopting for her costume sunset colors upon a flimsy material, which might more than hint at clouds. She had herself, with the assistance of Sepia and Folter, made choice of the particular pink ; but, although it continued altogether delightful in the eyes of her maid, it had, upon nearer and prolonged acquaintance, become doubtful in hers ; and she now waited, with no little anxiety, the judgment of Mary, who sat silently thinking.

"Have you nothing to say ?" she asked, at length, impatiently.

"Please, ma'am," replied Mary, "I must think, if I am to be of any use. I am doing my best, but you must let me be quiet."

Half annoyed, half pleased, Hesper was silent, and Mary went on thinking. All was still, save for the slight noises Folter made, as, like a machine, she went on heartlessly brushing her mistress's hair, which kept emitting little crackles, as of dissatisfaction with her handling. Mary would now take a good gaze at the lovely creature, now abstract herself from the visible, and try to call up the vision of her as the real Hesper, not a Hesper dressed up—a process which had in it hope for the lady, but not much for the dress upon the bed.

At last Folter had done her part.

"I suppose you *must* see it on!" said Hesper, and she rose up.

Folter jerked herself to the bed, took the dress, arranged it on her arms, got up on a chair, dropped it over her mistress's head, got down, and, having pulled it this way and that for a while, fastened it here, undone it there, and fastened it again, several times, exclaimed, in a tone whose confidence was meant to forestall the critical impertinence she dreaded:

"There, ma'am! If you don't look the loveliest woman in the room, I shall never trust my eyes again."

Mary held her peace, for the commonplace style of the dress but added to her dissatisfaction with the color. It was all puffed and bubbled and blown about, here and there and everywhere, so that the form of the woman was lost in the frolic shapelessness of the cloud. The whole, if whole it could be called, was a miserable attempt at combining fancy and fashion, and, in result, an ugly nothing.

"I see you don't like it!" said Hesper, with a mingling of displeasure and dismay. "I wish you had come a few days sooner! It is much too late to do anything now. I might just as well have gone without showing it to you!—Here, Folter!"

With a look almost of disgust, she began to pull off the dress, in which, a few hours later, she would yet make the attempt to enchant an assembly.

"O ma'am!" cried Mary, "I wish you had told me yesterday. There would have been time then.—And I don't know," she added, seeing disgust change to mortification on Hesper's countenance, "but something might be done yet."

"Oh, indeed!" dropped from Folter's lips with an indescribable expression.

"What can be done?" said Hesper, angrily. "There can be no time for anything."

"If only we had the stuff!" said Mary. "That shade doesn't suit your complexion. It ought to be much, much darker—in fact, a different color altogether."

Folter was furious, but restrained herself sufficiently to pre-

serve some calmness of tone, although her face turned almost
blue with the effort, as she said :

"Miss Marston is not long from the country, ma'am, and
don't know what's suitable to a London drawing-room."

Her mistress was too dejected to snub her impertinence.

"What color were you thinking of, Miss Marston ?" Hesper asked, with a stiffness that would have been more in place
had Mary volunteered the opinion she had been asked to give.
She was out of temper with Mary from feeling certain she was
right, and believing there was no remedy.

"I could not describe it," answered Mary. "And, indeed,
the color I have in my mind may not be to be had. I have
seen it somewhere, but, whether in a stuff or only in nature, I
can not at this moment be certain."

"Where's the good of talking like that—excuse me, ma'am
—it's more than I can bear—when the ball comes off in a few
hours ?" cried Folter, ending with eyes of murder on Mary.

"If you would allow me, ma'am," said Mary, "I should
like much to try whether I could not find something that would
suit you and your idea too. However well you might look in
that, you would owe it no thanks. The worst is, I know nothing of the London shops."

"I should think not !" remarked Folter, with emphasis.

"I would send you in the brougham, if I thought it was
of any use," said Hesper. "Folter could take you to the
proper places."

"Folter would be of no use to me," said Mary. "If your
coachman knows the best shops, that will be enough."

"But there's no time to make up anything," objected Hesper, despondingly, not the less with a glimmer of hope in her
heart.

"Not like that," answered Mary ; "but there is much there
as unnecessary as it is ugly. If Folter is good at her needle—"

"I won't take up a single stitch. It would be mere waste
of labor," cried Folter.

"Then, please, ma'am," said Mary, "let Folter have that
dress ready, and, if I don't succeed, you have something to wear."

"I hate it. I won't go if you don't find me another."

" Some people may like it, though I don't," said Mary.

" Not a doubt of that !" said Folter.

" Ring the bell," said her mistress.

The woman obeyed, and the moment afterward repented she had not given warning on the spot, instead. The brougham was ordered immediately, and in a few minutes Mary was standing at a counter in a large shop, looking at various stuffs, of which the young man waiting on her soon perceived she knew the qualities and capabilities better than he.

She had set her heart on carrying out Hesper's idea, but in better fashion ; and after great pains taken, and no little trouble given, left the shop well satisfied with her success. And now for the greater difficulty !

She drove straight to Letty's lodging, and, there dismissing the brougham, presented herself, with a great parcel in her arms, for the second time that day, at the door of her room, as unexpected as the first, and even more to the joy of her solitary friend.

She knew that Letty was good at her needle. And Letty was, indeed, even now, by, fits, fond of using it ; and on several occasions, when her supply of novels had for a day run short, had asked a dressmaker who lived above to let her help her for an hour or two : before Mary had finished her story, she was untying the parcel, and preparing to receive her instructions. Nor had they been at work many minutes, when Letty bethought her of calling in the help of the said dressmaker ; so that presently there were three of them busy as bees—one with genius, one with experience, and all with faculty. The notions of the first were quickly taken up by the other two, and, the design of the dress being simplicity itself, Mary got all done she wanted in shorter time than she had thought possible. The landlady sent for a cab, and Mary was home with the improbability in more than time for Mrs. Redmain's toilet. It was with some triumph, tempered with some trepidation, that she carried it to her room.

There Folter was in the act of persuading her mistress of the necessity of beginning to dress : Miss Marston, she said, knew nothing of what she had undertaken : and even if she

arrived in time, it would be with something too ridiculous for
any lady to appear in—when Mary entered, and was received
with a cry of delight from Hesper ; in proportion to whose increasing disgust for the pink robe, was her pleasure when she
caught sight of Mary's colors, as she undid the parcel : when
she lifted the dress on her arm for a first effect, she was enrap-
tured with it—aërial in texture, of the hue of a smoky rose,
deep, and cloudy with overlying folds, yet diaphanous, a darkness dilute with red.

Silent as a torture-maiden, and as grim, Folter approached
to try the filmy thing, scornfully confident that the first sight
of it on would prove it unwearable. But Mary judged her
scarcely in a mood to be trusted with anything so ethereal ;
and begged therefore that, as the dress had, of necessity, been
in many places little more than run together, and she knew
its weak points, she might, for that evening, be allowed the
privilege of dressing Mrs. Redmain. Hesper gladly consented ;
Folter left the room ; Mary, now at her case, took her place ;
and presently, more to Hesper's pleasure than Mary's surprise,
for she had made and fixed in her mind the results of minute
observation before she went, it was found that the dress fitted
quite sufficiently well. and, having confined it round the waist
with a cincture of thin pale gold, she advanced to her chief
anxiety—the head-dress.

For this she had chosen such a doubtful green as the sky
appears through yellowish smoke—a sad, lovely color—the fair
past clouded with the present—youth not forgotten, but filmed
with age. They were all colors of the evening, as it strives to
keep its hold of the heavens, with the night pressing upon it
from behind. In front, above the lunar forehead, among the
coronal masses, darkly fair, she fixed a diamond star, and over
it wound the smoky green like a turbaned vapor, wind-ruffled,
through which the diamonds gleamed faintly by fits. Not
once would she, while at her work, allow Hesper to look, and
the self-willed lady had been submissive in her hands as a
child of the chosen ; but the moment she had succeeded—for
her expectations were more than realized—she led her to the
cheval-glass.

Hesper gazed for an instant, then, turning, threw her arms about Mary, and kissed her.

"I don't believe you're a human creature at all!" she cried. "You are a fairy godmother, come to look after your poor Cinderella, the sport of stupid lady's-maids and dressmakers!"

The door opened, and Folter entered.

"If you please, ma'am, I wish to leave this day month," she said, quietly.

"Then," answered her mistress, with equal calmness, "oblige me by going at once to Mrs. Perkin, and telling her that I desire her to pay you a month's wages, and let you leave the house to-morrow morning.—You won't mind helping me to dress till I get another maid—will you, Mary?" she added; and Folter left the room, chagrined at her inability to cause annoyance.

"I do not see why you should have another maid so long as I am with you, ma'am," said Mary. "It should not need many days' apprenticeship to make one woman able to dress another."

"Not when she is like you, Mary," said Hesper. "It is well the wretch has done my hair for to-night, though! That will be the main difficulty."

"It will not be a great one," said Mary, "if you will allow me to undo it when you come home."

"I begin almost to believe in a special providence," said Hesper. "What a blessed thing for me that you came to drive away that woman! She has been getting worse and worse."

"If I have driven her away," answered Mary, "I am bound to supply her place."

As they talked, she was giving her final touches of arrangement to the head-dress—with which she found it least easy to satisfy herself. It swept round from behind in a misty cloak, the two colors mingling with and gently obscuring each other; while, between them, the palest memory of light, in the golden cincture, helped to bring out the somber richness, the delicate darkness of the whole

Searching now again Hesper's jewel-case, Mary found a fine bracelet of the true, the Oriental topaz, the old chrysolite—of

that clear yellow of the sunset-sky that looks like the 'scaped
spirit of miser-smothered gold : this she clasped upon one arm ;
and when she had fastened a pair of some ancient Mortimer's
garnet buckles in her shoes, which she had insisted should be
black, and taken off all the rings that Hesper had just put on,
except a certain glorious sapphire, she led her again to the mirror ; and, if there Hesper was far more pleased with herself
than was reasonable or lovely, my reader needs not therefore
fear a sermon from the text, " Beauty is only skin-deep," for
that text is out of the devil's Bible. No Baal or Astarte is the
maker of beauty, but the same who made the seven stars and
Orion, and His works are past finding out. If only the woman
herself and her worshipers knew how deep it is ! But the
woman's share in her own beauty may be infinitely less than
skin-deep ; and there is but one greater fool than the man who
worships that beauty—the woman who prides herself upon it,
as if she were the fashioner and not the thing fashioned.

But poor Hesper had much excuse, though no justification.
She had had many of the disadvantages and scarce one of the
benefits of poverty. She had heard constantly from childhood
the most worldly and greedy talk, the commonest expression
of abject dependence on the favors of Mammon, and thus had
from the first been in preparation for *marrying money.* She
had been taught no other way of doing her part to procure the
things of which the Father knows we have need. She had
never earned a dinner ; had never done or thought of doing a
day's work—of offering the world anything for the sake of
which the world might offer her a shilling to do it again ; she
had never dreamed of being of any use, even to herself ; she
had learned to long for money, but had never been hungry,
never been cold : she had sometimes felt shabby. Out of it all
she had brought but the knowledge that this matter of beauty,
with which, by some blessed chance, she was endowed, was
worth much precious money in the world's market—worth all
the dresses she could ever desire, worth jewels and horses and
servants, adoration and adulation — everything, in fact, the
world calls fine, and the devil offers to those who, unscared
by his inherent ugliness, will fall down and worship him.

CHAPTER XXX.

A SCOLDING.

THE Evening Star found herself a success—that is, much followed by the men and much complimented by the women. Her triumph, however, did not culminate until the next appearance of "The Firefly," containing a song "To the Evening Star," which *everybody* knew to stand for Mrs. Redmain. The chaos of the uninitiated, indeed, exoteric and despicable, remained in ignorance, nor dreamed that the verses meant anybody of note ; to them they seemed but the calf-sigh of some young writer so deep in his first devotion that he jumbled up his lady-love, Hesper, and Aphrodite, in the same poetic bundle—of which he left the string-ends hanging a little loose, while, upon the whole, it remained a not altogether unsightly bit of prentice-work. Tom had not been at the party, but had gathered fire enough from what he heard of Hesper's appearance there to write the verses. Here they are, as nearly as I can recall them. They are in themselves not worth writing out for the printers, but, in their surroundings, they serve to show Tom, and are the last with which I shall trouble the readers of this narrative.

"TO THE EVENING STAR.

" From the buried sunlight springing,
  Through flame-darkened, rosy loud,
Native sea-hues with thee bringing,
  In the sky thou reignest proud!

" Who is like thee, lordly lady,
  Star-choragus of the night!
Color worships, fainting fady,
  Night grows darker with delight!

" Dusky-radiant, far, and somber,
  In the coolness of thy state,
From my eyelids chasing slumber,
  Thou dost smile upon my fate :

" Calmly shinest; not a whisper
 Of my songs can reach thine ear;
 What is it to thee, O Hesper,
 That a heart should long or fear? "

Tom did not care to show Letty this poem—not that there
was anything more in his mind than an artistic admiration of
Hesper, and a desire to make himself agreeable in her eyes;
but, when Letty, having read it, betrayed no shadow of annoyance with its folly, he was a little relieved. The fact was,
the simple creature took it as a pardon to herself.

"I am glad you have forgiven me, Tom," she said.

"What do you mean?" asked Tom.

"For working for Mrs. Redmain with *your* hands," she
said, and, breaking into a little laugh, caught his cheeks between those same hands, and reaching up gave him a kiss that
made him ashamed of himself—a little, that is, and for the
moment, that is: Tom was used to being this or that a little
for the moment.

For this same dress, which Tom had thus glorified in song,
had been the cause of bitter tears to Letty. He came home
too late the day of Mary's visit, but the next morning she told
him all about both the first and the second surprise she had
had—not, however, with much success in interesting the lordly
youth.

"And then," she went on, "what do you think we were
doing all the afternoon, Tom?"

" How should I know?" said Tom, indifferently.

"We were working hard at a dress—a dress for a fancy-
ball!"

"A fancy-ball, Letty? What do you mean? You going
to a fancy-ball!"

" Me!" cried Letty, with merry laugh; "no, not quite
me. Who do you think it was for?"

" How should I know?" said Tom again, but not quite so
indifferently; he was prepared to be annoyed.

"For Mrs. Redmain!" said Letty, triumphantly, clapping
her hands with delight at what she thought the fun of the
thing, for was not Mrs. Redmain Tom's friend?—then stooping

a little—it was an unconscious, pretty trick she had—and holding them out, palm pressed to palm, with the fingers toward his face.

"Letty," said Tom, frowning—and the frown deepened and deepened; for had he not from the first, if in nothing else, taken trouble to instruct her in what became the wife of Thomas Helmer, Esq.?—"Letty, this won't do!"

Letty was frightened, but tried to think he was only pretending to be displeased.

"Ah! don't frighten me, Tom," she said, with her merry hands now changed to pleading ones, though their position and attitude remained the same.

But he caught them by the wrists in both of his, and held them tight.

"Letty," he said once more, and with increased severity, "this won't do. I tell you, it won't do."

"What won't do, Tom?" she returned, growing white. "There's no harm done."

"Yes, there is," said Tom, with solemnity; "there is harm done, when *my* wife goes and does like that. What would people say of *me*, if they were to come to know—God forbid they should!—that your husband was talking all the evening to ladies at whose dresses his wife had been working all the afternoon!—You don't know what you are doing, Letty. What do you suppose the ladies would think if they were to hear of it?"

Poor, foolish Tom, ignorant in his folly, did not know how little those grand ladies would have cared if his wife had been a char-woman: the eyes of such are not discerning of fine social distinctions in women who are not of their set, neither are the family relations of the bohemians they invite of the smallest consequence to them.

"But, Tom," pleaded his wife, "such a grand lady as that! one you go and read your poetry to! What harm can there be in your poor little wife helping to make a dress for a lady like that?"

"I tell you, Letty, I don't choose *my* wife to do such a thing for the greatest lady in the land! Good Heavens! if it were to come to the ears of the staff ! It would be the ruin of me ! I should never hold up my head again !"

By this time Letty's head was hanging low, like a flower half broken from its stem, and two big tears were slowly rolling down her cheeks. But there was a gleam of satisfaction in her heart notwithstanding. Tom thought so much of his little wife that he would not have her work for the greatest lady in the land ! She did not see that it was not pride in her, but pride in himself, that made him indignant at the idea. It was not "my *wife*," but "*my* wife" with Tom. She looked again up timidly in his face, and said, her voice trembling, and her cheeks wet, for she could not wipe away the tears, because Tom still held her hands as one might those of a naughty child :

"But, Tom ! I don't exactly see how you can make so much of it, when you don't think me—when you know I am not fit to go among such people."

To this Tom had no reply at hand : he was not yet far enough down the devil's turnpike to be able to tell his wife that he had spoken the truth—that he did not think her fit for such company ; that he would be ashamed of her in it ; that she had no style ; that, instead of carrying herself as if she knew herself somebody—as good as anybody there, indeed, being the wife of Tom Helmer—she had the meek look of one who knew herself nobody, and did not know her husband to be anybody. He did not think how little he had done to give the unassuming creature that quiet confidence which a woman ought to gather from the assurance of her husband's satisfaction in her, and the consciousness of being, in dress and everything else, pleasing in his eyes, therefore of occupying the only place in the world she desires to have. But he did think that Letty's next question might naturally be, "Why do you not take me with you ?" No doubt he could have answered, no one had ever asked her ; but then she might rejoin, had he ever put it in any one's way to ask her ? It might even occur to her to inquire whether he had told Mrs. Redmain that he had a wife ! and he had heart enough left to imagine it might mortally hurt her to find he lived a life so utterly apart from hers—that she had so little of the relations though all the rights of wifehood.

It was no wonder, therefore, if he was more than willing to change the subject. He let the poor, imprisoned hands drop so abruptly that, in their abandonment, they fell straight from her shoulders to her sides.

"Well, well, child!" he said, "put on your bonnet, and we shall be in time for the first piece at the Lyceum."

Letty flew, and was ready in five minutes. She could dress the more quickly that she was delayed by little doubt as to what she had better wear : she had scarcely a choice. Tom, looking after his own comforts, left her to look after her necessities ; and she, having a conscience, and not much spirit, went even shabbier than she yet needed.

CHAPTER XXXI.

SEPIA.

As naturally as if she had been born to that very duty and no other, Mary slid into the office of lady's-maid to Mrs. Redmain, feeling in it, although for reasons very different, no more degradation than her mistress saw in it. If Hesper was occasionally a little rude to her, Mary was not one to *accept* a rudeness—that is, to wrap it up in resentment, and put it away safe in the pocket of memory. She could not help feeling things of the kind—sometimes with indignation and anger ; but she made haste to send them from her, and shut the doors against them. She knew herself a far more blessed creature than Hesper, and felt the obligation, from the Master himself, of so enduring as to keep every channel of service open between Hesper and her. To Hesper, the change from the vulgar service of Folter to the ministration of Mary was like passing from a shallow purgatory to a gentle paradise. Mary's service was full of live and near presence, as that of dew or summer wind ; Folter handled her as if she were dressing a doll, Mary as if she were dressing a baby ; her hands were deft as an angel's, her feet as noiseless as swift. And to have Mary near was not only to have a ministering spirit at hand, but to have a good atmosphere all around—an air, a heaven, out of which good things must momently come. Few could be closely associated with her and not become aware at least of the capacity of being better, if not of the desire to be better.

In the matter of immediate result, it was a transition from decoration to dress. If in any sense Hesper was well dressed before, she was in every sense well dressed now—dressed so, that is, as to reveal the nature, the analogies, and the associations of her beauty : no manner of dressing can make a woman look more beautiful than she is, though many a mode may make her look less so.

There was one in the house, however, who was not pleased at the change from Folter to Mary . Sepia found herself in consequence less necessary to Hesper. Hitherto Hesper had never been satisfied without Sepia's opinion and final approval in that weightiest of affairs, the matter of dress ; but she found in Mary such a faculty as rendered appeal to Sepia unnecessary ; for she not only satisfied her idea of herself, and how she would choose to look, but showed her taste as much surer than Sepia's as Sepia's was readier than Hesper's own. Sepia was equal to the dressing of herself—she never blundered there ; but there was little dependence to be placed upon her in dressing another. She cared for herself, not for another ; and to dress another, love is needful—love, the only true artist —love, the only opener of eyes. She cared nothing to minister to the comfort or beautification of her cousin, and her displeasure did not arise from the jealousy that is born of affection. So far as Hesper's self was concerned, Sepia did not care a straw whether she was well or ill dressed ; but, if the link between them of dress was severed, what other so strong would be left ? And to find herself in any way a less object in Hesper's eyes, would be to find herself on the inclined plane of loss, and probable ruin.

Another, though a smaller, point was, that hitherto she had generally been able so to dress Hesper as to make of her more or less a foil to herself. My reader may remember that there was between Hesper and Sepia, if not a resemblance, yet a re-

lation of appearance, like, vaguely, that between the twilight
and the night ; seen in certain positions and circumstances, the
one would recall the other ; and it was therefore a matter of no
small consequence to Sepia that the relation of her dress to
Hesper's should be such as to give herself any advantage to be
derived in it from the relation of their looks. This was far
more difficult, of course, when she had no longer a voice in the
matter of Hesper's dress, and when the loving skill of the new
maid presented her rival to her individual best. Mary would
have been glad to help her as well, but Sepia drew back as from
a hostile nature, and they made no approximation. This was
more loss to Sepia than she knew, for Mary would have assist-
ed her in doing the best when she had no money, a condition
which often made it the more trying that she had now so little
influence over her cousin's adornment. To dress was a far more
difficult, though not more important, affair with Sepia than
with Hesper, for she had nothing of her own, and from her
cousin no fixed allowance. Any arrangement of the kind had
been impossible at Durnmelling, where there was no money ;
and here, where it would have been easy enough, she judged it
better to give no hint in its direction, although plainly it had
never suggested itself to Hesper. There was nothing of the
money-mean in her, any more than in her husband. They were
of course, as became people of fashion, regular and unwearied
attendants of the church of Mammon, ordering all their judgments and ways in accordance with the precepts there delivered ; but they were none of Mammon's priests or pew-openers,
money-grubs, or accumulators. They gave liberally where they
gave, and scraped no inferior to spend either on themselves or
their charities. They had plenty, it is true ; but so have many
who withhold more than is meet, and take the ewe-lamb to add
to their flock. For one thing, they had no time for that sort
of wickedness, and took no interest in it. So Hesper, although
it had not come into her mind to give her the ease of a stated
allowance, behaved generously to Sepia—when she thought of
it ; but she did not love her enough to be love-watchful, and
seldom thought how her money must be going, or questioned
whether she might not at the moment be in want of more.

There are many who will give freely, who do not care to understand need and anticipate want. Hence at times Sepia's
purse would be long empty before the giving-thought would
wake in the mind of Hesper. When it woke, it was gracious
and free.

Had Sepia ventured to run up bills with the tradespeople,
Hesper would have taken it as a thing of course, and settled
them with her own. But Sepia had a certain politic pride in
spending only what was given her ; also she saw or thought she
saw serious reason for avoiding all appearances of taking liberties ; from the first of Mr. Redman's visits to Durnmelling,
she had been aware, with an instinct keen in respect of its objects, though blind as to its own nature, that he did not like
her, and soon satisfied herself that any overt attempt to please
him would but ripen his dislike to repugnance ; and her dread
was that he might make it a condition with Mr. Mortimer that
Hesper's intimacy with her should cease ; whereas, if once they
were married, the husband's disfavor would, she believed, only
strengthen the wife's predilection. Having so far gained her
end, it remained, however, almost as desirable as before that
she should do nothing to fix or increase his dislike—nay, that,
if within the possible, she should become pleasing to him. Did
not even hate turn sometimes to its mighty opposite ? But
she understood so little of the man with whom she had to deal
that her calculations were ill-founded.

She was right in believing that Mr. Redman disliked her,
but she was wrong in imagining that he had therefore any objection to her being for the present in the house. He certainly
did not relish the idea of her continuing to be his wife's insep-
arable companion, but there would be time enough to get rid
of her after he had found her out. For she had not long been
one of his *family*, before he knew, with insight unerring, that
she had to be found out, and was therefore an interesting subject for the exercise of his faculty of moral analysis. He was
certain her history was composed mainly of secrets. As yet,
however, he had discovered nothing.

I must just remind my reader of the intellectual passion I
have already mentioned as characterizing Mr. Redman's men-

tal constitution. His faults and vices were by no means peculiar; but the bent to which I refer, certainly no virtue, and springing originally from predominant evil, was in no small degree peculiar, especially in the degree to which, derived as it was from his father, he had in his own being developed it. Most men, he judged with himself, were such fools as well as rogues, that there was not the least occasion to ask what they were after : they did but turn themselves inside out before you ! But, on the other hand, there were not a few who took pains, more or less successful, to conceal their game of life : and such it was the delight of his being to lay bare to his own eyes—not to those of other people ; that, he said, would be to spoil his game ! Men were his library, he said—his history, his novels, his sermons, his philosophy, his poetry, his whole literature— and he did not like to have his books thumbed by other people. Human nature, in its countless aspects, was all about him, he said, every mask crying to him to take it off. Unhappily, it was but the morbid anatomy of human nature he cared to study. For all his abuse of it, he did not yet recognize it as morbid, but took it as normal, and the best to be had No doubt, he therein judged and condemned himself, but that he never thought of—nor, perceived, would it have been a point of any consequence to him.

From the first, he saw through Mr. Mortimer, and all belonging to him, except Miss Yolland : she soon began to puzzle—and, so far, to please him, though, as I have said, he did not like her. Had he been a younger man, she would have captivated him ; as it was, she would have repelled him entirely, but that she offered him a good subject. He said to himself that she was a bad lot, but what sort of a bad lot was not so clear as to make her devoid of interest to him ; he must discover how she played her life-game ; she had a history, and he would fain know it. As I have said, however, so far it had come to nothing, for, upon the surface, Sepia showed herself merely like any other worldly girl who knows "on which side her bread is buttered."

The moment he had found, or believed he had found, what there was to know about her, he was sure to hate her heartily.

For some time after his marriage, he appeared at his wife's parties oftener than he otherwise would have done, just for the sake of having an eye upon Sepia ; but had seen nothing, nor the shadow of anything—until one night, by the merest chance, happening to enter his wife's drawing-room, he caught a peculiar glance between Sepia and a young man—not very young—who had just entered, and whom he had not seen before.

To not a few it seemed strange that, with her unquestioned powers of fascination, she had not yet married ; but London is not the only place in which poverty is as repellent as beauty is attractive. At the same time it must be confessed there was something about her which made not a few men shy of her. Some found that, if her eyes drew them within a certain distance, there they began to repel them, they could not tell why. Others felt strangely uncomfortable in her presence from the first. Not only much that a person has done, but much of what a person is capable of, is, I suspect, written on the bodily presence ; and, although no human eye is capable of reading more than here and there a scattered hint of the twilight of history, which is the aurora of prophecy, the soul may yet shudder with an instinctive foreboding it can not explain, and feel the presence, without recognizing the nature, of the hostile.

Sepia's eyes were her great power. She knew the laws of mortar-practice in that kind as well as any officer of engineers those of projectiles. There was something about her engines which it were vain to attempt to describe. Their lightest glance was a thing not to be trifled with, and their gaze a thing hardly to be withstood. Sustained and without hurt defied, it could hardly be by man of woman born. They were large, but no fool would be taken with mere size. They were as dark as ever eyes of woman, but our older poets delighted in eyes as gray as glass : certainly not in their darkness lay their peculiar witchery. They were grandly proportioned, neither almond-shaped nor round, neither prominent nor deep-set ; but even shape by itself is not much. If I go on to say they were luminous, plainly there the danger begins. Sepia's eyes, I confess, were not lords of the deepest light—for she was not true ; but neither was theirs a surface light, generated of merely physical causes: through them, concentrating h will upon their utterance she could establish a psychical contact with *almost* any man she chose. Their power was an evil, selfish shadow of original, universal love. By them she could produce at once, in the man on whom she turned their play, a sense as it were of some primordial, fatal affinity between her and him—of an aboriginal understanding, the rare possession of but a few of the pairs made male and female. Into those eyes she would call up her soul, and there make it sit, flashing light, in gleams and sparkles, shoots and coruscations—not from great, black pupils alone—to whose size there were who said the suicidal belladonna lent its aid—but from great, dark irids as well— nay, from eyeballs, eyelashes, and eyelids, as from spiritual catapult or culverin, would she dart the lightnings of her present soul, invading with influence as irresistible as subtile the soul of the man she chose to assail, who, thenceforward, for a season, if he were such as she took him for, scarce had choice but be her slave. She seldom exerted their full force, however, without some further motive than mere desire to captivate There are women who fly their falcons at any game, little birds and all; but Sepia did not so waste herself: her quarry must be worth her hunt: she must either love him or need him. *Love!* did I say? Alas! if ever holy word was put to unholy use, *love* is that word! When Diana goes to hell, her name changes to Hecate, but love among the devils is called love still!

In more than one other country, whatever might be the cause, Sepia had found *the men* less shy of her than here: and she had almost begun to think her style was not generally pleasing to English eyes. Whether this had anything to do with the fact that now in London she began to amuse herself with Tom Helmer, I can not say with certainty; but almost if not quite the first time they met, that morning, namely, when first he called, and they sat in the bay-window of the drawing-room in Glammis Square, she brought her eyes to play upon him; and, although he addressed "The Firefly" poem to Hesper in the ⸳⸳⸳⸳⸳ ⸳⸳⸳ ⸳ ⸳⸳ ⸳ ⸳⸳ ⸳ Sepia chiefly that he desired the door of her house to be an open one to him. Whether at that time she knew he was a married man, it is hardly necessary to inquire, seeing it would have made no difference whatever to one like her, whose design was only to amuse herself with the youth, and possibly to make of him a screen. She went so far, however, as to allow him, when there was opportunity, to draw her into quiet corners, and even to linger when the other guests were gone, and he had had his full share of champagne. Once, indeed, they remained together so long in the little conservatory, lighted only by an alabaster lamp, pale as the moon in the dawning, that she had to unbolt the door to let him out. This did not take place without coming to the knowledge of both Mr. and Mrs. Redmain; but the former was only afraid there was nothing in it, and was far from any wish to control her; and Sepia herself was the informant of the latter. To her she would make game of her foolish admirer, telling how, on this and that occasion, it was all she could do to get rid of him.

CHAPTER XXXII.

HONOR.

HAVING now gained a partial insight into Letty's new position, Mary pondered what she could do to make life more of life to her. Not many knew better than she that the only true way to help a human heart is to lift it up; but she knew also that every kind of loving aid tends more or less to that uplifting; and that, if we can not do the great thing, we must be ready to do the small: if we do not help in little things, how shall we be judged fit to help in greater? We must help where we can, that we may help where we can not. The first and the only thing she could for a time think of, was, to secure for Letty, if possible, a share in her husband's pleasures.

Quietly, yet swiftly, a certain peaceful familiarity had estab-

lished itself between Hesper and Mary, to which the perfect
balance of the latter and her sense of the only true foundation
of her position contributed far more than the undefined par-
tiality of the former. The possibility of such a conversation
as I am now going to set down was one of the results.

"Do you like Mr. Helmer, ma'am?" asked Mary one morning, as she was brushing her hair.

"Very well. How do you know anything of him?"

"Not many people within ten miles of Testbridge do not
know Mr. Helmer," answered Mary.

"Yes, yes, I remember," said Hesper. "He used to ride
about on a long-legged horse, and talked to anybody that would
listen to him. But there was always something pleasing about
him, and he is much improved. Do you know, he is considered
really very clever?"

"I am not surprised," rejoined Mary. "He used to be
rather foolish, and that is a sign of cleverness—at least, many
clever people are foolish, I think."

"*You* can't have had much opportunity for making the
observation, Mary!"

"Clever people think as much of themselves in the country
as they do in London, and that is what makes them foolish,"
returned Mary. "But I used to think Mr. Helmer had very
good points, and was worth doing something for—if one only
knew what."

"He does not seem to want anything done for him," said
Hesper

"I know one thing *you* could do for him, and it would be
no trouble," said Mary.

"I will do anything for anybody that is no trouble," answered Hesper. "I should like to know something that is no
trouble."

"It is only, the next time you ask him, to ask his wife,"
said Mary.

"He is married, then?" returned Hesper with indifference.
"Is the woman presentable? Some shopkeeper's daughter, I
suppose!"

Mary l.. .' ¹

"You don't imagine the son of a lawyer would be likely to marry a shopkeeper's daughter!" she said.

"Why not?" returned Hesper, with a look of non-intelligence.

"Because a professional man is so far above a tradesman."

"Oh!" said Hesper. "—But he should have told me if he wanted to bring his wife with him. I don't care who she is, so long as she dresses decently and holds her tongue. What are you laughing at, Mary?"

Hesper called it laughing, but Mary was only smiling.

"I can't help being amused," answered Mary, "that you should think it such an out-of-the-way thing to be a shopkeeper's daughter, and here am I all the time, feeling quite comfortable, and proud of the shopkeeper whose daughter I am."

"Oh! I beg your pardon," exclaimed Hesper, growing hot for, I almost believe, the first time in her life, and therein, I fear, showing a drop of bad blood from somewhere, probably her father's side of the creation; for not even the sense of having hurt the feelings of an inferior can make the thorough-bred woman of the world aware of the least discomfort; and here was Hesper, not only feeling like a woman of God's making, but actually showing it!—"How cruel of me!" she went on. "But, you see, I never think of you—when I am talking to you—as—as one of that class!"

Mary laughed outright this time: she was amused, and thought it better to show it, for that would show also she was not hurt. Hesper, however, put it down to insensibility.

"Surely, dear Mrs. Redmain," said Mary, "you can not think the class to which I belong in itself so objectionable that it is rude to refer to it in my hearing!"

"I am very sorry," repeated Hesper, but in a tone of some offense: it was one thing to confess a fault; another to be regarded as actually guilty of the fault. "Nothing was further from my intention than to offend you. I have not a doubt that shopkeepers are a most respectable class in their way—"

"Excuse me, dear Mrs. Redmain," said Mary again, "but you quite mistake me. I am not in the least offended. I don't care what you think of the class. There are a great many shopkeepers who are anything but respectable—as bad, indeed, as any of the nobility."

"I was not thinking of morals," answered Hesper. "In that, I dare say, all classes are pretty much alike. But, of course, there are differences."

"Perhaps one of them is, that, in our class, we make respectability more a question of the individual than you do in yours."

"That may be very true," returned Hesper. "So long as a man behaves himself, we ask no questions."

"Will you let me tell you how the thing looks to me?" said Mary.

"Certainly. You do not suppose I care for the opinions of the people about me! I, too, have my way of looking at things."

So said Hesper; yet it was just the opinions of the people about her that ruled all those of her actions that could be said to be ruled at all. No one boasts of freedom except the willing slave—the man so utterly a slave that he feels nothing irksome in his fetters. Yet, perhaps, but for the opinions of those about her, Hesper would have been worse than she was.

"Am I right, then, in thinking," began Mary, "that people of your class care only that a man should wear the look of a gentleman, and carry himself like one?—that, whether his appearance be a reality or a mask, you do not care, so long as no mask is removed in your company?—that he may be the lowest of men, but, so long as other people receive him, you will, too, counting him good enough?"

Hesper held her peace. She had by this time learned some facts concerning the man she had married which, beside Mary's question, were embarrassing.

"It is interesting," she said at length, "to know how the different classes in a country regard each other." But she spoke wearily: it was interesting in the abstract, not interesting to her.

"The way to try a man," said Mary, "would be to turn him the other way, as I saw the gentleman who is taking your portrait do yesterday turning a square—change — — — quite,

I mean, and mark how far he continued to look a true man.
He would show something of his real self then, I think. Make
a nobleman a shopkeeper, for instance, and see what kind of a
shopkeeper he made. If he showed himself just as honorable
when a shopkeeper as he had seemed when a nobleman, there
would be good reason for counting him an honorable man."

"What odd fancies you have, Mary!" said Hesper, yawning.

"I know my father would have been as honorable as a nobleman as he was when a shopkeeper," persisted Mary.

"That I can well believe—he was your father," said Hesper,
kindly, meaning what she said, too, so far as her poor understanding of the honorable reached.

"Would you mind telling me," asked Mary, "how you would
define the difference between a nobleman and a shopkeeper?"

Hesper thought a little. The question to her was a stupid
one. She had never had interest enough in humanity to care
a straw what any shopkeeper ever thought or felt. Such people inhabited a region so far below her as to be practically out
of her sight. They were not of her kind. It had never occurred to her that life must look to them much as it looked to
her; that, like Shylock, they had feelings, and would bleed if
cut with a knife. But, although she was not interested, she
peered about sleepily for an answer. Her thoughts, in a lazy
fashion, tumbled in her, like waves without wind—which, indeed, was all the sort of thinking she knew. At last, with the
decision of conscious superiority, and the judicial air afforded
by the precision of utterance belonging to her class—a precision so strangely conjoined with the lack of truth and logic
both—she said, in a tone that gave to the merest puerility the
consequence of a judgment between contending sages:

"The difference is, that the nobleman is born to ease and
dignity and affluence, and the—shopkeeper to buy and sell for
his living."

"Many a nobleman," suggested Mary, "buys and sells without the necessity of making a living."

"That is the difference," said Hesper.

"Then the nobleman buys and sells to make money, and
the shopkeeper to make a living?"

" Yes," granted Hesper, lazily.

" Which is the nobler end—to live, or to make money ? "

But this question was too far beyond Hesper. She did not even choose to hear it.

" *And*," she said, resuming her definition instead, " the nobleman deals with great things, the shopkeeper with small."

" When things are finally settled," said Mary—

" Gracious, Mary ! " cried Hesper, " what do you mean ? Are not things settled for good this many a century ? I am afraid I have been harboring an awful radical !—a—what do they call it ?—a communist ! "

She would have turned the whole matter out of doors, for she was tired of it.

" Things hardly look as if they were going to remain just as they are at this precise moment," said Mary. " How could they, when, from the very making of the world, they have been going on changing and changing, hardly ever even seeming to stand still ? "

" You frighten me, Mary ! You will do something terrible in my house, and I shall get the blame of it ! " said Hesper, laughing.

But she did in truth feel a little uncomfortable. The shadow of dismay, a formless apprehension overclouded her. Mary's words recalled sentiments which at home she had heard alluded to with horror : and, however little parents may be loved or respected by their children, their opinions will yet settle, and, until they are driven out by better or worse, will cling.

" When I tell you what I was really thinking of, you will not be alarmed at my opinions," said Mary, not laughing now, but smiling a deep, sweet smile : " I do not believe there ever will be any settlement of things but one ; they can not and must not stop changing, until the kingdom of heaven is come. Into that they must change, and rest."

" You are leaving politics for religion now, Mary. That is the one fault I have to find with you—you won't keep things in their own places ! You are always mixing them up—like that Mrs.   I love in her novels, though everybody tells her they have nothing to do with each other! It is so irreverent!"

"Is it irreverent to believe that God rules the world he made, and that he is bringing things to his own mind in it?"

"You can't persuade me religion means turning things upside down."

"It means that a good deal more than people think. Did not our Lord say that many that are first shall be last, and the last first?"

"What has that to do with this nineteenth century?"

"Perhaps that the honorable shopkeeper and the mean nobleman will one day change places."

"Oh," thought Hesper, "that is why the lower classes take so to religion!" But what she said was: "Oh, yes, I dare say! But everything then will be so different that it won't signify. When we are all angels, nobody will care who is first, and who is last. I'm sure, for one, it won't be anything to me."

Hesper was a tolerable attendant at church—I will not say whether high or low church, because I should be supposed to care.

"In the kingdom of heaven," answered Mary, "things will always look what they are. My father used to say people will grow their own dresses there, as surely as a leopard his spots. He had to do with dresses, you know. There, not only will an honorable man look honorable, but a mean or less honorable man must look what he is."

"There will be nobody mean there."

"Then a good many won't be there who are called honorable here."

"I have no doubt there will be a good deal of allowance made for some people," said Hesper. "Society makes such demands!"

CHAPTER XXXIII.

THE INVITATION.

WHEN Letty received Mrs. Redmain's card, inviting her with her husband to an evening party, it raised in her a bewildered flutter—of pleasure, of fear, of pride, of shyness, of dismay: how dared she show her face in such a grand assembly? She would not know a bit how to behave herself! But it was impossible, for she had no dress fit to go anywhere! What would Tom say if she looked a dowdy? He would be ashamed of her, and she dared not think what might come of it!

But close upon the postman came Mary, and a long talk followed. Letty was full of trembling delight, but Mary was not a little anxious with herself how Tom would take it.

The first matter, however, was Letty's dress. She had no money, and seemed afraid to ask for any. The distance between her and her husband had been widening.

Their council of ways and means lasted a good while, including many digressions. At last, though unwillingly, Letty accepted Mary's proposal that a certain dress, her best indeed, though she did not say so, which she had scarcely worn, and was not likely to miss, should be made to fit Letty. It was a lovely black silk, the best her father had been able to choose for her the last time he was in London. A little pang did shoot through her heart at the thought of parting with it, but she had too much of that father in her not to know that the greatest honor that can be shown any *thing*, is to make it serve a *person*; that the dearest gift of love, withheld from human necessity, is handed over to the moth and the rust. But little idea had Letty, much as she appreciated her kindness, what a sacrifice Mary was making for her that she might look her own sweet self, and worthy of her renowned Tom!

When Tom came home that night, however, the look of the world and all that is in it changed speedily for Letty, and terribly. He arrived in great good humor—somebody had been praising his verses, and the joy of the praise overflowed on his wife. But when, pleased as any little girl with the prospect of a party and a new frock, she told him, with gleeful gratitude, of the invitation and the heavenly kindness which had rendered it possible for her to accept it, the countenance of the great man changed. He rejected the idea of her going with him to any gathering of his grand friends—objected most of all to her going to Mrs. Redmain's. Alas! he had begun to allow to himself that he had married in too great haste—and beneath him. Wherever he went, his wife could be no credit to him, and her presence would take from him all sense of liberty! Not choosing, however, to acknowledge either of these objections, and not willing, besides, to appear selfish in the eyes of the woman who had given herself to him, he was only too glad to put all upon another, to him equally genuine ground. Controlling his irritation for the moment, he set forth with lordly kindness the absolute impossibility of accepting such an offer as Mary's. Could she for a moment imagine, he said, that he would degrade himself by taking his wife out in a dress that was not her own?

Here Letty interrupted him.

"Mary has given me the dress," she sobbed, "—for my very own."

"A second-hand dress! A dress that has been worn!" cried Tom. "How could you dream of insulting me so? The thing is absolutely impossible. Why, Letty, just think!— There should I be, going about as if the house were my own, and there would be my wife in the next room, or perhaps at my elbow, dressed in the finery of the lady's-maid of the house! It won't bear thinking of! I declare it makes me so ashamed, as I lie here, that I feel my face quite hot in the dark! To have to reason about such a thing—with my own wife, too!"

"It's not finery," sobbed Letty, laying hold of the one fact within her reach; "it's a beautiful black silk."

"It matters not a straw what it is," persisted Tom, adding humbug to cruelty. "You would be nothing but a sham!— A live dishonesty! A jackdaw in peacock's feathers!—I am sorry, Letty, your own sense of truth and uprightness should not prevent even the passing desire to act such a lie. Your fine dress would be just a fine fib—yourself would be but a walking fib. I have been taking too much for granted with you : I must bring you no more novels. A volume or two of Carlyle is what *you* want."

This was too much. To lose her novels and her new dress together, and be threatened with nasty moral medicine—for she had never read a word of Carlyle beyond his translation of that dream of Richter's, and imagined him dry as a sand-pit—was bad enough, but to be so reproved by her husband was more than she could bear. If she was a silly and ignorant creature, she had the heart of a woman-child ; and that precious thing in the sight of God, wounded and bruised by the husband in whom lay all her pride, went on beating laboriously for him only. She did not blame him. Anything was better than that. The dear, simple soul had a horror of rebuke. It would break hedges and climb stone walls to get out of the path of judgment—ten times more eagerly if her husband were the judge. She wept and wailed like a sick child, until at length the hard heart of selfish Tom was touched, and he sought, after the fashion of a foolish mother, to read the inconsolable a lesson of wisdom. But the truer a heart, the harder it is to console with the false. By and by, however, sleep, the truest of things, did for her what even the blandishments of her husband could not

When she woke in the morning, he was gone . he had thought of an emendation in a poem that had been *set up* the day before, and made haste to the office, lest it should be printed without the precious betterment.

Mary came before noon, and found sadness where she had left joy. When she had heard as much as Letty thought proper to tell her, she was filled with indignation, and her first thought was to compass the tyrant's own exclusion from the paradise whose gates he closed against his wife. But second thoughts are sometimes best, and she saw the next moment not only that punishment did not belong to her, but that the weight of such would fall on Letty. The sole thing she could think of to comfort her was, to ask her to spend the same evening wi͏   Letty

up at once : some time or other in the course of the evening
she would, she fancied, see, or at least catch a glimpse of Tom
in his glory !

The evening came, and with beating heart Letty went up
the back stairs to Mary's room. She was dressing her mistress,
but did not keep her waiting long. She had provided tea beforehand, and, when Mrs. Redmain had gone down, the two
friends had a pleasant while together. Mary took Letty to
Mrs. Redmain's room while she put away her things, and there
showed her many splendors, which, moving no envy in her
simple heart, yet made her sad, thinking of Tom. As she
passed to the drawing-room, Sepia looked in, and saw them
together.

But, as the company kept arriving, Letty grew very restless.
She could not talk of anything for two minutes together, but
kept creeping out of the room and half-way down the stair, to
look over the banister-rail, and have a bird's-eye peep of a portion of the great landing, where indeed she caught many a
glimpse of beauty and state, but never a glimpse of her Tom.
Alas ! she could not even imagine herself near him. What she
saw made her feel as if her idol were miles away, and she could
never draw nigh him again. How should the familiar associate
of such splendid creatures care a pin's point for his humdrum
wife ?

Worn out at last, and thoroughly disappointed, she wanted
to go home. It was then past midnight. Mary went with
her, and saw her safe in bed before she left her.

As she went up to her room on her return, she saw, through
the door by which the gardener entered the conservatory, Sepia
standing there, and Tom, with flushed face, talking to her eagerly.

Letty cried herself to sleep, and dreamed that Tom had
disowned her before a great company of grand ladies, who
mocked her from their sight.

Tom came home while she slept, and in the morning was
cross and miserable—in part, because he had been so abominably selfish to her. But the moment that, half frightened,
half hopeful, she told him where she was the night before, he

broke into the worst anger he had ever yet shown her. His shameful pride could not brook the idea that, where he was a guest, his wife was entertained by one of the domestics!

"How dare you be guilty of such a disgraceful thing!" he cried.

"Oh, don't, Tom—dear Tom!" pleaded Letty in terror. "It was you I wanted to see—not the great people, Tom! I don't care if I never see one of them again."

"Why should you ever see one of them again, I should like to know! What are they to you, or you to them?"

"But you know I was asked to go, Tom!"

"You're not such a fool as to fancy they cared about you! Everybody knows they are the most heartless set of people in the world!"

"Then why do you go, Tom?" said Letty, innocently.

"That's quite another thing! A man has to cultivate connections his wife need not know anything about. It is one of the necessities laid on my position."

Letty supposed it all truer than it was either intelligible or pleasant, and said no more, but let poor, self-abused, fine-fellow Tom scold and argue and reason away till he was tired. She was not sullen, but bewildered and worn out. He got up, and left her without a word.

Even at the risk of hurt to his dignity, of which there was no danger from the presence of his sweet, modest little wife in the best of company, it had been well for Tom to have allowed Letty the pleasure within her reach; for that night Sepia's artillery played on him ruthlessly. It may have been merely for her amusement—time, you see, moves so slowly with such as have no necessities they must themselves supply, and recognize no duties they must perform: without those two main pillars of life, necessity and duty, how shall the temple stand, when the huge, weary Samson comes tugging at it? The wonder is, there is not a great deal more wickedness in the world. For listlessness and boredness and nothing-to-do-ness are the best of soils for the breeding of the worms that never stop gnawing. Anyhow, Sepia had flashed on Tom, the tinder of Tom's heart had responded, and one day when Sepia chose, she might blow up a wicked as well as foolish flame ; nor, if it should suit her purpose, was Sepia one to hesitate in the use of the fire-fan. All the way home, her eyes haunted him, and it is a more dreadful thing than most are aware to be haunted by anything, good or bad, except the being who is our life. And those eyes, though not good, were beautiful. Evil, it is true, has neither part nor lot in beauty ; it is absolutely hostile to it, and will at last destroy it utterly ; but the process is a long one, so long that many imagine badness and beauty vitally associable. Tom yielded to the haunting, and it was in part the fault of those eyes that he used such hard words to his wife in the morning. Wives have not seldom to suffer sorely for discomforts and wrongs in their husbands of which they know nothing. But the thing will be set right one day, and in a better fashion than if all the woman's-rights' committees in the world had their will of the matter.

About this time, from the top, left-hand corner of the last page of "The Firefly," it appeared that Twilight had given place to Night ; for the first of many verses began to show themselves, in which Twilight, or Hesper, or Vesper, or the Evening Star, was no more once mentioned, but only and always Nox, or Hecate, or the dark Diana. *Tenebrious* was a great word with Tom about this time. He was very fond, also, of the word *interlunar*. I will not trouble my reader with any specimen of the outcome of Tom's new inspiration, partly for this reason, that the verses not unfrequently came so near being good, nay, sometimes were really so good, that I do not choose to set them down where they would be treated with a mockery they do not in themselves deserve. He did not direct his wife's attention to them, nor did he compose them at home or at the office. Mostly he wrote them between acts at the theatre, or in any public place where something in which he was not interested was going on.

Of all that read them, and here was a Nemesis awful in justice, there was not one less moved by them than she who had inspired them. She saw in them, it is true, a reflex of her own power—and that pleased, but it did not move her. She took the devotion and pocketed it, as a greedy boy might an orange or bull's-eye. The verses in which Tom delighted were but the merest noise in the ears of the lady to whom of all he would have had them acceptable. One momentary revelation as to how she regarded them would have been enough to release him from his foolish enthrallment. Indignation, chagrin, and mortification would have soon been the death of such poor love as Tom's.

Mary and Sepia were on terms of politeness—of readiness to help on the one side, and condescension upon the other. Sepia would have condescended to the Mother Mary. The pure human was an idea beyond her, as beyond most people. They have not enough religion toward God to know there is such a thing as *religion* toward their neighbor. But Sepia never made an enemy—if she could help it. She could not afford the luxury of hating—openly, at least. But I imagine she would have hated Mary heartily could she have seen the way she regarded her—the look of pitiful love, of compassionate and waiting helpfulness which her soul would now and then cast upon her. Of all things she would have resented pity ; and she took Mary's readiness to help for servility—and naturally, seeing in herself willingness came from nothing else, though she called it prudence and necessity, and knew no shame because of it. Her children justify the heavenly wisdom, but the worldly wisdom justifies her children. Mary could not but feel how Sepia regarded her service, but service, to be true, must be divine, that is, to the just and the unjust, like the sun and the rain.

Between Sepia and Mr. Redmain continued a distance too great for either difference or misunderstanding. They met with a cold good morning, and parted without any good night. Their few words were polite, and their demeanor was civil. At the breakfast-table, Sepia would silently pass things to Mr. Redmain ; Mr. Redmain would thank her, but never trouble himself to do as much for her. His attentions, indeed, were seldom wasted at home ; but he was not often rude to anybody save his wife and his man, except when he was ill.

It was a long time before he began to feel any interest in Mary. He knew nothing of her save as a nice-looking maid his wife had got—rather a prim-looking puss, he would have said, had he had occasion to describe her. What Mary knew of him was merely the reflection of him in the mind of his wife; but, the first time she saw him, she felt she would rather not have to speak to him.

CHAPTER XXXIV.

A STRAY SOUND.

MARY went to see Letty as often as she could, and that was not seldom; but she had scarcely a chance of seeing Tom; either he was not up, or had gone—to the office, Letty supposed: she had no more idea of where the office was, or of the other localities haunted by Tom, than he himself had of what spirit he was of.

One day, when Mary could not help remarking upon her pale, weary looks, Letty burst into tears, and confided to her a secret of which she was not the less proud that it caused her anxiety and fear. As soon as she began to talk about it, the joy of its hope began to predominate, and before Mary left her she might have seemed to a stranger the most blessed little creature in the world. The greatness of her delight made Mary sad for her. To any thoughtful heart it must be sad to think what a little time the joy of so many mothers lasts—not because their babies die, but because they live; but Mary's mournfulness was caused by the fear that the splendid dawn of mother-hope would soon be swallowed in dismal clouds of father-fault. For mothers and for wives there is no redemption, no unchaining of love, save by the coming of the kingdom—*in themselves.* Oh! why do not mothers, sore-hearted mothers at least, if none else on the face of the earth, rush to the feet of the Son of Mary?

Yet every birth is but another link in the golden chain by which the world shall be lifted to the feet of God. It is only by the birth of new children, ever fresh material for the creative Spirit of the Son of Man to work upon, that the world can finally be redeemed. Letty had no *ideas* about children, only the usual instincts of appropriation and indulgence ; Mary had a few, for she recalled with delight some of her father's ways with herself. Him she knew as, next to God, the source of her life, so well had he fulfilled that first duty of all parents —the transmission of life. About such things she tried to talk to Letty, but soon perceived that not a particle of her thought found its way into Letty's mind : she cared nothing for any duty concerned—only for the joy of being a mother.

She grew paler yet and thinner ; dark hollows came about her eyes ; she was parting with life to give it to her child : she lost the girlish gayety Tom used to admire, and the something more lovely that was taking its place he was not capable of seeing. He gave her less and less of his company. His countenance did not shine on her, in her heart she grew aware that she feared him, and, ever as she shrunk, he withdrew. Had it not now been for Mary, she would likely have died. She did all for her that friend could. As often as she seemed able, she would take her for a drive, or on the river, that the wind, like a sensible presence of God, might blow upon her, and give her fresh life to take home with her. So little progress did she make with Hesper, that she could not help thinking it must have been for Letty's sake she was allowed to go to London.

Mr. and Mrs. Redmain went again to Durnmelling, but Mary begged Hesper to leave her behind. She told her the reason, without mentioning the name of the friend she desired to tend. Hesper shrugged her shoulders, as much as to say she wondered at her taste ; but she did not believe that was in reality the cause of her wish, and, setting herself to find another, concluded she did not choose to show herself at Testbridge in her new position, and, afraid of losing if she opposed her, let her have her way. Nor, indeed, was she so necessary to her at Durnmelling, where there were few visitors, and comparatively little dressing was required : for the mere routine of such ordinary days, Jemima was enough, who, now and then called by Mary to her aid, had proved herself handy and capable, and had learned much.

So, all through the hottest of the late summer and autumn weather, Mary remained in London, where every pavement seemed like the floor of a baker's oven, and, for all the life with which the city swarmed, the little winds that wandered through it seemed to have lost their vitality. How she longed for the common and the fields and the woods, where the very essence of life seemed to dwell in the atmosphere even when stillest, and the joy that came pouring from the throats of the birds seemed to flow first from her own soul into them! The very streets and lanes of Testbridge looked like paradise to Mary in London. But she never wished herself in the shop again, although almost every night she dreamed of the glad old time when her father was in it with her, and when, although they might not speak from morning to night, their souls kept talking across crowd and counters, and each was always aware of the other's supporting presence.

Longing, however, is not necessarily pain—it may, indeed, be intensest bliss; and, if Mary longed for the freedom of the country, it was not to be miserable that she could not have it. Her mere thought of it was to her a greater delight than the presence of all its joys is to many who desire them the most. That such things, and the possibility of such sensations from them, should be in the world, was enough to make Mary jubilant. But, then, she was at peace with her conscience, and had her heart full of loving duty. Besides, an active patience is a heavenly power. Mary could not only walk along a pavement dry and lifeless as the Sahara, enjoying the summer that brooded all about and beyond the city, but she bore the refreshment of blowing winds and running waters into Letty's hot room, with the clanging street in front, and the little yard behind, where, from a cord stretched across between the walls, hung a few pieces of ill-washed linen, motionless in the glare, two plump sparrows picking up crumbs in their shadow —into this live death Mary would carry a tone of breeze, and sailing cloud, and swaying tree-top. In her the life was so concentrated and active that she was capable of communicating life—the highest of human endowments.

One evening, as Letty was telling her how the dressmaker

up stairs had been for some time unwell, and Mary was feeling reproachful that she had not told her before, that she might have seen what she could do for her, they became aware, it seemed gradually, of one softest, sweetest, faintest music-tone coming from somewhere—but not seeming sufficiently of this world to disclose whence. Mary went to the window : there was nothing capable of music within sight. It came again ; and intermittingly came and came. For some time they would hear nothing at all, and then again the most delicate of tones would creep into their ears, bringing with it more, it seemed to Mary in the surprise of its sweetness, than she could have believed single tone capable of carrying. Once or twice a few consecutive sounds made a division strangely sweet : and then again, for a time, nothing would reach them but a note here and a note there of what she was fain to imagine a wonderful melody. The visitation lasted for about an hour, then ceased. Letty went to bed, and all night long dreamed she heard the angels calling her. She woke weeping that her time was come so early, while as yet she had tasted so little of the pleasure of life. But the truth was, she had as yet, poor child, got so little of the *good* of life, that it was not at all time for her to go.

When her hour drew near. Tom condescended—unwillingly, I am sorry to say, for he did not take the trouble to understand her feelings—to leave word where he might be found if he should be wanted. Even this assuagement of her fears Letty had to plead for ; Mary's being so much with her was to him reason, and he made it excuse, for absence ; he had begun to dread Mary. Nor, when at length he was sent for, was he in any great haste ; all was well over ere he arrived. But he was a little touched when, drawing his face down to hers, she feebly whispered, "He's as like to you, Tom, as ever small thing was to great !" She saw the slight emotion, and fell asleep comforted.

It was night when she woke. Mary was sitting by her.

"O Mary !" she cried, "the angels have been calling me again. Did you hear them ?"

"No," answered Mary, a little coldly, for, if ever she was inclined to be hard, it was toward self-sentiment. "Why do you think the angels should call you? Do you suppose them very desirous of your company?"

"They do call people," returned Letty, almost crying; "and I don't know why they mightn't call me. I'm not such a very wicked person!"

Mary's heart smote her; she was refusing Letty the time God was giving her! She could not wake her up, and, while God was waking her, she was impatient!

"I heard the call, too, Letty," she said; "but it was not the angels. It was the same instrument we heard the other night. Who can there be in the house to play like that? It was clearer this time. I thought I could listen to it a whole year."

"Why didn't you wake me?" said Letty.

"Because the more you sleep the better. And the doctor says I mustn't let you talk. I will get you something, and then you must go to sleep again."

Tom did not appear any more that night; and, if they had wanted him now, they would not have known where to find him. He was about nothing very bad—only supping with some friends—such friends as he did not even care to tell that he had a son.

He was ashamed of being in London at this time of the year, and, but that he had not money enough to go anywhere except to his mother's, he would have gone, and left Letty to shift for herself.

With his child he was pleased, and would not seldom take him for a few moments; but, when he cried, he was cross with him, and showed himself the unreasonable baby of the two.

The angels did not want Letty just yet, and she slowly recovered.

For Mary it was a peaceful time. She was able to read a good deal, and, although there were no books in Mr. Redmain's house, she generally succeeded in getting such as she wanted. She was able also to practice as much as she pleased, for now the grand piano was entirely at her service, and she took the opportunity of having a lesson every day.

CHAPTER XXXV.

THE MUSICIAN.

ONE evening, soon after the baby's arrival, as Mary sat with him in her lap, the sweet tones they had heard twice before came creeping into her ears so gently that she seemed to be aware of their presence only after they had been for some time coming and going : she laid the baby down, and, stealing from the room, listened on the landing. Certainly the sounds were born in the house, but whether they came from below or above she could not tell. Going first down the stair, and then up, she soon satisfied herself that they came from above, and thereupon ventured a little farther up the stair.

She had already been to see the dressmaker, whom she had come to know through the making of Hesper's twilight robe of cloud, had found her far from well, and had done what she could for her. But she was in no want, and of more than ordinary independence—a Yorkshire woman, about forty years of age, delicate, but of great patience and courage ; a plain, fair, freckled woman, with a belief in religion rather than in God. Very strict, therefore, in her observances, she thought a great deal more of the Sabbath than of man, a great deal more of the Bible than of the truth, and ten times more of her creed than of the will of God ; and, had she heard any one utter such words as I have just written, would have said he was an atheist. She was a worthy creature, notwithstanding, only very unpleasant if one happened to step on the toes of a pet ignorance Mary soon discovered that there was no profit in talking with her on the subjects she loved most : plainly she knew little about them, except at second hand—that is, through the forms of other minds than her own. Such people seem intended for the special furtherance of the saints in patience ; being utterly unassailable by reason, they are especially trying to those who desire to stand on brotherly terms with all men, and so are the more sensitive to the rudeness that always goes with moral stupidity ; intellectual stupidity may coexist with the loveliness of an angel It is one of the blessed hopes of the world to

come, that there will be none such in it. But why so many
words ? I say to myself, Will one of such as I mean recognize
his portrait in my sketch ? Many such have I met in my
young days, and in my old days I find they swarm still. I
could wish that all such had to earn their own bread like Ann
Byrom : had she been rich, she would have been unbearable.
Women like her, when they are well to do, walk with a manly
stride, make the tails of their dresses go like the screw of a
steamer behind them, and are not unfrequently Scotch.

As Mary went up, the music ceased ; but, hoping Miss Byrom would be able to enlighten her concerning its source, she
continued her ascent, and knocked at her door. A voice,
rather wooden, yet not without character, invited her to enter.

Ann sat near the window, for, although it was quite dusk,
a little use might yet be made of the lingering ghost of the daylight. Almost all Mary could see of her was the reflection
from the round eyes of a pair of horn spectacles.

"How do you do, Miss Byrom ?" she said.

"Not at all well," answered Ann, almost in a tone of offense.

"Is there nothing I can do for you ?" asked Mary.

"We are to owe no man anything but love, the apostle
tells us."

"You must owe a good deal of that, then," said Mary, one
part vexed, and two parts amused, "for you don't seem to pay
much of it."

She was just beginning to be sorry for what she had said
when she was startled by a sound, very like a little laugh,
which seemed to come from behind her. She turned quickly,
but, before she could see anything through the darkness, the
softest of violin-tones thrilled the air close beside her, and then
she saw, seated on the corner of Ann's bed, the figure of a man
—young or old, she could not tell. How could he have kept
so still ! His bow was wandering slowly about over the strings
of his violin ; but presently, having overcome, as it seemed,
with the help of his instrument, his inclination to laugh, he
ceased, and all was still.

"I came," said Mary, turning again to Ann, "hoping you

might be able to tell me where the sweet sounds came from which we have heard now two or three times: but I had no idea there was any one in the room besides yourself.—They come at intervals a great deal too long," she added, turning toward the figure in the darkness.

"I am afraid my ear is out sometimes," said the man, mistaking her remark. "I think it comes of the anvil."

The voice was manly, though gentle, and gave an impression of utter directness and simplicity. It was Mary's turn, however, not to understand, and she made no answer.

"I am very sorry," the musician went on, "if I annoyed you, miss."

Mary was hastening to assure him that the fact was quite the other way, when Ann prevented her.

"I told you so!" she said; "*you* make an idol of your foolish plaything, but other people take it only for the nuisance it is."

"Indeed, you never were more mistaken," said Mary. "Both Mrs. Helmer and myself are charmed with the little that reaches us. It is, indeed, seldom one hears tones of such purity."

The player responded with a sigh of pleasure.

"Now there you are, miss," cried Ann, "a-flattering of his folly till not a word I say will be of the smallest use!"

"If your words are not wise," said Mary, with suppressed indignation, "the less he heeds them the better."

"It ain't wise, to my judgment, miss, to make a man think himself something when he is nothing. It's quite enough a man should deceive his own self, without another to come and help him."

"To speak the truth is not to deceive," replied Mary. "I have some knowledge of music, and I say only what is true."

"What good can it be spending his time scraping horsehair athort catgut?"

"They must fancy some good in it up in heaven," said Mary, "or they wouldn't have so much of it there."

"There ain't no fiddles in heaven," said Ann, with indignation; "they've nothing there but harps and trumpets."

Mary turned to the man, who had not said a word.

"Would you mind coming down with me," she said, "and playing a little, very softly, to my friend ? She has a little baby, and is not strong. It would do her good."

"She'd better read her Bible," said Ann, who, finding she could no longer see, was lighting a candle.

"She does read her Bible," returned Mary ; "and a little music would, perhaps, help her to read it to better purpose."

"There, Ann !" cried the player.

The woman replied with a scornful grunt.

"Two fools don't make a wise man, for all the franchise," she said.

But Mary had once more turned toward the musician, and in the light of the candle was met by a pair of black eyes, keen yet soft, looking out from under an overhanging ridge of forehead. The rest of the face was in shadow, but she could see by the whiteness, through a beard that clouded all the lower part of it, that he was smiling to himself : Mary had said what pleased him, and his eyes sought her face, and seemed to rest on it with a kind of trust, and a look as if he was ready to do whatever she might ask of him.

"You will come ?" said Mary.

"Yes, miss, with all my heart," he replied, and flashed a full smile that rested upon Ann, and seemed to say he knew her not so hard as she looked.

Rising, he tucked his violin under his arm, and showed himself ready to follow.

"Good night, Miss Byrom," said Mary.

"Good night, miss," returned Ann, grimly. "I'm sorry for you both, miss. But, until the spirit is poured out from on high, it's nothing but a stumbling in the dark."

This last utterance was a reflection rather than a remark.

Mary made no reply. She did not care to have the last word ; nor did she fancy her cause lost when she had not at hand the answer that befitted folly. She ran down the stair, and at the bottom stood waiting her new acquaintance, who descended more slowly, careful not to make a noise.

She could now see, by the gaslight that burned on the

landing, a little more of what the man was. He was powerfully built, rather over middle height, and about the age of
thirty. His complexion was dark, and the hand that held the
bow looked grimy. He bore himself well, but a little stiffly,
with a care over his violin like that of a man carrying a baby.
He was decidedly handsome, in a rugged way—mouth and chin
but hinted through a thick beard of darkest brown.

"Come this way," said Mary, leading him into Letty's
parlor "I will tell my friend you are come. Her room, you
see, opens off this, and she will hear you delightfully. Pray,
take a seat."

"Thank you, miss," said the man, but remained standing.

"I have caught the bird, Letty," said Mary, loud enough
for him to hear; "and he is come to sing a little to you—if you
feel strong enough for it."

"It will do me good," said Letty. "How kind of him!"

The man, having heard, was already tuning his violin when
Mary came from the bedroom, and sat down on the sofa. The
instant he had got it to his mind, he turned, and, going to the
farthest corner of the room, closed his eyes tight, and began
to play.

But how shall I describe that playing? how convey an idea
of it, however remote? I fear it is nothing less than presumption in me, so great is my ignorance, to attempt the thing.
But would it be right, for dread of bringing shame upon me
through failure, to leave my readers without any notion of it
at all? On the other hand, I shall, at least, have the merit of
daring to fail—a merit of which I could well be ambitious.

If, then, my reader will imagine some music-loving sylph
attempting to guide the wind among the strings of an Æolian
harp, every now and then for a moment succeeding, and then
again for a while the wind having its own way, he will gain, I
think, something like a dream-notion of the man's playing.
Mary tried hard to get hold of some clew to the combinations
and sequences, but the motive of them she could not find.
Whatever their source, there was, either in the composition
itself or in his mode of playing, not a little of the inartistic,
that is, the lawless. Yet every now and then would come a

passage of exquisite melody, owing much, however, no doubt, to the marvelous delicacy of the player's tones, and the utterly tender expression with which he produced them. But ever as she thought to get some insight into the movement of the man's mind, still would she be swept away on the storm of some change, seeming of mood incongruous.

At length came a little pause. He wiped his forehead with a blue cotton handkerchief, and seemed ready to begin again. Mary interrupted him with the question :

"Will you please tell me whose music you have been playing ?"

He opened his eyes, which had remained closed even while he stood motionless, and, with a smile sweeter than any she had ever seen on such a strong face, answered :

"It's nobody's, miss."

"Do you mean you have been extemporizing all this time ?"

"I don't know exactly what that means."

"You must have learned it from notes ?"

"I couldn't read them if I had any to read," he answered.

"Then what an ear and what a memory you must have ! How often have you heard it ?"

"Just as often as I've played it, and no oftener. Not being able to read, and seldom hearing any music I care for, I'm forced to be content with what runs out at my fingers when I shut my eyes. It all comes of shutting my eyes. I couldn't play a thing but for shutting my eyes. It's a wonderful deal that comes of shutting your eyes ! Did you never try it, miss ?"

Mary was so astonished both by what he said and the simplicity with which he said it, having clearly no notion that he was uttering anything strange, that she was silent, and the man, after a moment's retuning, began again to play. Then did Mary gather all her listening powers, and brace her attention to the tightest—but at first with no better success. And, indeed, that was not the way to understand. It seems to me, at least, in my great ignorance, that one can not understand music unless he is humble toward it, and consents, if need be, not to understand. When one is quiescent, submissive, opens the ears of the mind, and demands of them nothing more than the hearing—when the rising waters of question retire to their bed, and individuality is still, then the dews and rains of music, finding the way clear for them, soak and sink through the sands of the mind, down, far down, below the thinking-place, down to the region of music, which is the hidden workshop of the soul, the place where lies ready the divine material for man to go making withal.

Weary at last with vain effort, she ceased to endeavor, and in a little while was herself being molded by the music unconsciously received to the further understanding of it. It wrought in her mind pictures, not thoughts. It is possible, however, my later knowledge may affect my description of what Mary then saw with her mind's eye.

First there was a crowd in slow, then rapid movement. Arose cries and entreaties. Came hurried motions, disruption, and running feet. A pause followed. Then woke a lively melody, changing to the prayer of some soul too grateful to find words. Next came a bar or two of what seemed calm, lovely speech, then a few slowly delivered chords, and all was still.

She came to herself, and then first knew that, like sleep, the music had seized her unawares, and she had been understanding, or at least enjoying, without knowing it. The man was approaching her from his dark corner. His face was shining, but plainly he did not intend more music, for his violin was already under his arm. He made her a little awkward bow—not much more than a nod, and turned to the door. He had it half open, and not yet could Mary speak. For Letty, she was fast asleep.

From the top of the stair came the voice of Ann, screaming:

"Here's your hat, Joe. I knew you'd be going when you played that. You'd have forgotten it, *I* know!"

Mary heard the hat come tumbling down the stair.

"Thank you, Ann," returned Joe. "Yes, I'm going. The ladies don't care much for my music. Nobody does but myself. But then it's good for me."

The last two sentences were spoken in soliloquy, but Mary heard them, for he stood with the handle of the door in his hand. He closed it, picked up his hat, and went softly down the stair.

The spell was broken, and Mary darted to the door. But, just as she opened it, the outer door closed behind the strange musician, and she had not even learned his name.

CHAPTER XXXVI.

A CHANGE.

As soon as Letty had strength enough to attend to her baby without help, Mary, to the surprise of her mistress, and the destruction of her theory concerning her stay in London, presented herself at Durnmelling, found that she was more welcome than looked for, and the same hour resumed her duties about Hesper.

It was with curiously mingled feelings that she gazed from her window on the chimneys of Thornwick. How much had come to her since first, in the summer-seat at the end of the yew-hedge, Mr. Wardour opened to her the door of literature! It was now autumn, and the woods, to get young again, were dying their yearly death. For the moment she felt as if she, too, had begun to grow old. Ministration had tired her a little—but, oh! how different its weariness from that which came of labor amid obstruction and insult! Her heart beat a little slower, perhaps, but she could now be sad without losing a jot of hope. Nay, rather, the least approach of sadness would begin at once to wake her hope. She regretted nothing that had come, nothing that had gone. She believed more and more that not anything worth having is ever lost; that even the most evanescent shades of feeling are safe for those who grow after their true nature, toward that for which they were made—in other and higher words, after the will of God.

But she did for a moment taste some bitterness in her cup, when, one day, on the footpath of Testbridge, near the place where, that memorable Sunday, she met Mr. Wardour, she met him again, and, looking at her, and plainly recognizing her, he passed without salutation. Like a sudden wave the blood rose to her face, and then sank to the deeps of her heart ; and from somewhere came the conviction that one day the destiny of Godfrey Wardour would be in her hands : he had done more for her than any but her father ; and, when that day was come, he should not find her fail him !

She was then on her way to the shop. She did not at all relish entering it, but, as she had a large money-interest in the business, she ought at least, she said to herself, to pay the place a visit. When she went in, Turnbull did not at first recognize her, and, taking her for a customer, blossomed into repulsive suavity. The change that came over his countenance, when he knew her, was a shadow of such mingled and conflicting shades that she felt there was something peculiar in it which she must attempt to analyze. It remained hardly a moment to encounter question, but was almost immediately replaced with a politeness evidently false. Then, first, she began to be aware of distrusting the man.

Asking a few questions about the business, to which he gave answers most satisfactory, she kept casting her eyes about the shop, unable to account for the impression the look of it made upon her. Either her eyes had formed for themselves another scale, and could no more rightly judge between past and present, or the aspect of the place was different, and not so satisfactory. Was there less in it? she asked herself—or was it only not so well kept as when she left it ? She could not tell. Neither could she understand the profound but distant consideration with which Mr. Turnbull endeavored to behave to her, treating her like a stranger to whom he must, against his inclination, manifest all possible respect, while he did not invite her even to call at *the villa*. She bought a pair of gloves of the young woman who seemed to occupy her place, paid for them, and left the shop without speaking to any one else. All the time, George was standing behind the opposite counter, staring at her; but, much to her relief, he showed no other sign of recognition.

Before she went to find Beenie, who was still at Testbridge, in a cottage of her own, she felt she must think over these things, and come, if possible, to some conclusion about them. She left the town, therefore, and walked homeward.

What did it all mean? She knew very well they must look down on her ten times more than ever, because of the *menial* position in which she had placed herself, sinking thereby beyond all pretense to be regarded as their equal. But, if that was what the man's behavior meant, why was he so studiously—not so much polite as respectful? That did not use to be Mr. Turnbull's way where he looked down upon one. And, then, what did the shadow preceding this behavior mean? Was there not in it something more than annoyance at the sight of her? It was with an effort he dismissed it! She had never seen that look upon him!

Then there was the impression the shop made on her! Was there anything in that? Somehow it certainly seemed to have a shabby look! Was it possible anything was wrong or going wrong with the concern? Her father had always spoken with great respect of Mr. Turnbull's business faculties, but she knew he had never troubled himself to look into the books or know how they stood with the bank. She knew also that Mr. Turnbull was greedy after money, and that his wife was ambitious, and hated the business. But, if he wanted to be out of it, would he not naturally keep it up to the best, at least in appearance, that he might part with his share in it to the better advantage?

She turned, and, walking back to the town, sought Beenie.

The old woman being naturally a gossip, Mary was hardly seated before she began to pour out the talk of the town, in which came presently certain rumors concerning Mr. Turnbull —mainly hints at speculation and loss.

The result was that Mary went from Beenie to the lawyer in whose care her father had left his affairs. He was an old man, and had been ill; had no suspicion of anything being wrong, but would look into the matter at once. She went home, and troubled herself no more.

She had been at Durnmelling but a few days, when Mr. Redmain, wishing to see how things were on his estate in Cornwall, and making up his mind to run down, carelessly asked his wife if she would accompany him : it would be only for a few days, he said ; but a breeze or two from the Atlantic would improve her complexion. This was gracious ; but he was always more polite in the company of Lady Margaret, who continued to show him the kindness no one else dared or was inclined to do. For some years he had suffered increasingly from recurrent attacks of the disease to which I have already referred ; and, whatever might be the motive of his mother-in-law's behavior, certainly, in those attacks, it was a comfort to him to be near her. On such occasions in London, his sole attendant was his man Mewks.

Mary was delighted to see more of her country. She had traveled very little, but was capable of gathering ten times more from a journey to Cornwall than most travelers from one through Switzerland itself. The place to which they went was lonely and lovely, and Mary, for the first few days, enjoyed it unspeakably.

But then, suddenly, as was not unusual, Mr. Redmain was taken ill. For some reason or other, he had sent his man to London, and the only other they had with them, besides the coachman, was useless in such a need, while the housekeeper who lived at the place was nearly decrepit ; so that of the household Mary alone was capable of fit attendance in the sick-room. Hesper shrunk, almost with horror, certainly with disgust, from the idea of having anything to do with her husband as an invalid. When she had the choice of her company, she said, she would not choose his. Mewks was sent for at once, but did not arrive before the patient had had some experience of Mary's tendance ; nor, after he came, was she altogether without opportunity of ministering to him. The attack was a long and severe one, delaying for many weeks their return to London, where Mr. Redmain declared he must be, at any risk, before the end of November.

CHAPTER XXXVII.

LYDGATE STREET.

LETTY's whole life was now gathered about her boy, and she thought little, comparatively, about Tom. And Tom thought so little about her that he did not perceive the difference. When he came home, he was always in a hurry to be gone again. He had always something important to do, but it never showed itself to Letty in the shape of money. He gave her a little now and then, of course, and she made it go incredibly far, but it was ever with more of a grudge that he gave it. The influence over him of Sepia was scarcely less now that she was gone ; but, if she cared for him at all, it was mainly that, being now not a little stale-hearted, his devotion reminded her pleasurably of a time when other passions than those of self-preservation were strongest in her ; and her favor even now tended only to the increase of Tom's growing disappointment, for, like Macbeth, he had begun already to consider life but a poor affair. Across the cloud of this death gleamed, certainly, the flashing of Sepia's eyes, or the softly infolding dawn of her smile, but only, the next hour, nay, the next moment, to leave all darker than before. Precious is the favor of any true, good woman, be she what else she may ; but what is the favor of one without heart or faith or self-giving ? Yet is there testimony only too strong and terrible to the demoniacal power, enslaving and absorbing as the arms of the kraken, of an evil woman over an imaginative youth. Possibly, did he know beforehand her nature, he would not love her, but, knowing it only too late, he loves and curses ; calls her the worst of names, yet can not or will not tear himself free ; after a fashion he still calls love, he loves the demon, and hates her thralldom. Happily Tom had not reached this depth of perdition ; Sepia was prudent for herself, and knew, none better, what she was about, so far as the near future was concerned, therefore held him at arm's length, where Tom basked in a light that was of hell—for what is a hell, or a woman like Sepia, but an inverted creation ?

His nature, in consequence, was in all directions dissolving. He drank more and more strong drink, fitting fuel to such his passion, and Sepia liked to see him approach with his eyes blazing. There are not many women like her; she is a rare type—but not, therefore, to be passed over in silence. It is little consolation that the man-eating tiger is a rare animal, if one of them be actually on the path : and to the philosopher a possibility is a fact. But the true value of the study of abnormal development is that, in the deepest sense, such development is not abnormal at all, but the perfected result of the laws that avenge law-breach. It is in and through such that we get glimpses, down the gulf of a moral volcano, to the infernal possibilities of the human—the lawless rot of that which, in its *attainable* idea, is nothing less than divine, imagined, foreseen, cherished, and labored for, by the Father of the human. Such inverted possibility, the infernal possibility, I mean, lies latent in every one of us, and, except we stir ourselves up to the right, will gradually, from a possibility, become an energy. The wise man dares not yield to a temptation, were it only for the terror that, if he do, he will yield the more readily again. The commonplace critic, who recognizes life solely upon his own conscious level, mocks equally at the ideal and its antipode, incapable of recognizing the art of Shakespeare himself as true to the human nature that will not be human.

I have said that Letty did her best with what money Tom gave her; but when she came to find that he had not paid the lodging for two months ; that the payment of various things he had told her to order and he would see to had been neglected, and that the tradespeople were getting persistent in their applications; that, when she told him anything of the sort, he treated it at one time as a matter of no consequence which he would speedily set right, at another as behavior of the creditor hugely impertinent, which he would punish by making him wait his time—her heart at length sank within her, and she felt there was no bulwark between her and a sea of troubles; she felt as if she lay already in the depths of a debtor's jail. Therefore, sparing as she had been from the first, she was more sparing than ever. Not only would she buy nothing for which she could not pay down, having often in consequence to go without proper food, but, even when she had a little in hand, would live like an anchorite. She grew very thin; and, indeed, if she had not been of the healthiest, could not have stood her own treatment many weeks.

Her baby soon began to show suffering, but this did not make her alter her way, or drive her to appeal to Tom. She was ignorant of the simplest things a mother needs to know, and never imagined her abstinence could hurt her baby. So long as she went on nursing him, it was all the same, she thought. He cried so much, that Tom made it a reason with himself, and indeed gave it as one to Letty, for not coming home at night: the child would not let him sleep; and how was he to do his work if he had not his night's rest? It mattered little with semi-mechanical professions like medicine or the law, but how was a man to write articles such as he wrote, not to mention poetry, except he had the repose necessary to the redintegration of his exhausted brain? The baby went on crying, and the mother's heart was torn. The woman of the house said he must be already cutting his teeth, and recommended some devilish sirup. Letty bought a bottle with the next money she got, and thought it did him good—because, lessening his appetite, it lessened his crying, and also made him sleep more than he ought.

At last one night Tom came home very much the worse of drink, and in maudlin affection insisted on taking the baby from its cradle. The baby shrieked. Tom was angry with the weakling, rated him soundly for ingratitude to "the author of his being," and shook him roughly to teach him the good manners of the world he had come to.

Thereat in Letty sprang up the mother, erect and fierce. She darted to Tom, snatched the child from his arms, and turned to carry him to the inner room. But, as the mother rose in Letty, the devil rose in Tom. If what followed was not the doing of the real Tom, it was the doing of the devil to whom the real Tom had opened the door. With one stride he overtook his wife, and mother and child lay together on the floor. I must say for him that, even in his drunkenness, he

did not strike his wife as he would have struck a man ; it was
an open-handed blow he gave her, what, in familiar language,
is called a box on the ear, but for days she carried the record
of it on her cheek in five red finger-marks.

When he saw her on the floor, Tom's bedazed mind came
to itself; he knew what he had done, and was sobered. But,
alas! even then he thought more of the wrong he had done to
himself as a gentleman than of the grievous wound he had
given his wife's heart. He took the baby, who had ceased to
cry as soon as he was in his mother's arms, and laid him on the
rug, then lifted the bitterly weeping Letty, placed her on the
sofa, and knelt beside her—not humbly to entreat her pardon, but, as was his wont, to justify himself by proving that all
the blame was hers, and that she had wronged him greatly in
driving him to do such a thing. This for apology poor Letty,
never having had from him fuller acknowledgment of wrong,
was fain to accept. She turned on the sofa, threw her arms
about his neck, kissed him, and clung to him with an utter
forgiveness. But all it did for Tom was to restore him his
good opinion of himself, and enable him to go on feeling as
much of a gentleman as before.

Reconciled, they turned to the baby. He was pale, his eyes
were closed, and they could not tell whether he breathed. In
a horrible fright, Tom ran for the doctor. Before he returned
with him, the child had come to, and the doctor could discover
no injury from the fall they told him he had had. At the
same time, he said he was not properly nourished, and must
have better food.

This was a fresh difficulty to Letty : it was a call for more
outlay. And now their landlady, who had throughout been
very kind, was in trouble about her own rent, and began to
press for part at least of theirs. Letty's heart seemed to labor
under a stone. She forgot that there was a thing called joy.
So sad she looked that the good woman, full of pity, assured
her that, come what might, she should not be turned out,
but at the worst would only have to go a story higher, to
inferior rooms. The rent should wait, she said, until better days. But this kindness relieved Letty only a little, for

the rent past and the rent to come hung upon her like a cloak
of lead.

Nor was even debt the worst that now oppressed her. For,
possibly from the fall, but more from the prolonged want of
suitable nourishment and wise treatment, after that terrible
night, the baby grew worse. Many were the tears the sleepless
mother shed over the sallow face and wasted limbs of her slumbering treasure—her one antidote to countless sorrows; and
many were the foolish means she tried to restore his sinking
vitality.

Mary had written to her, and she had written to Mary;
but she had said nothing of the straits to which she was re-
duced; that would have been to bring blame upon Tom. But
Mary, with her fine human instinct, felt that things must be
going worse with her than before; and, when she found that
her return was indefinitely postponed by Mr. Redmain's illness,
she ventured at last in her anxiety upon a daring measure : she
wrote to Mr. Wardour, telling him she had reason to fear
things were not going well with Letty Helmer, and suggesting,
in the gentlest way, whether it might not now be time to let
bygones be bygones, and make some inquiry concerning her.

To this letter Godfrey returned no answer. For all her denial, he had never ceased to believe that Mary had been Letty's
accomplice throughout that miserable affair; and the very
name—the Letty and the Helmer—stung him to the quick.
He took it, therefore, as a piece of utter presumption in Mary to
write to him about Letty, and that in the tone, as he interpreted it, of one reading him a lesson of duty. But, while he was
thus indignant with Mary, he was also vexed with Letty that
she should not herself have written to him if she was in any
need, forgetting that he had never hinted at any door of communication open between him and her. His heart quivered at
the thought that she might be in distress; he had known for
certain, he said, the fool would bring her to misery ! For himself, the thought of Letty was an ever-open wound—with an
ever-present pain, now dull and aching, now keen and stinging. The agony of her desertion, he said, would never cease
gnawing at his heart until it was laid in the grave; like most

heathen Christians, he thought of death as the end of all the joys, sorrows, and interests generally of this life. But, while thus he brooded, a fierce and evil joy awoke in him at the thought that now at last the expected hour had come when he would heap coals of fire on her head. He was still fool enough to think of her as having forsaken him, although he had never given her ground for believing, and she had never had conceit enough to imagine, that he cared the least for her person. If he could but let her have a glimmer of what she had lost in losing him! She knew what she had gained in Tom Helmer.

He passed a troubled night, dreamed painfully, and started awake to renewed pain. Before morning he had made up his mind to take the first train to London. But he thought far more of being her deliverer than of bringing her deliverance.

CHAPTER XXXVIII.

GODFREY AND LETTY.

IT was a sad, gloomy, kindless November night, when Godfrey arrived in London. The wind was cold, the pavements were cold, the houses seemed to be not only cold but feeling it. The very dust that blew in his face was cold. Now cold is a powerful ally of the commonplace, and imagination therefore was not very busy in the bosom of Godfrey Wardour as he went to find Letty Helmer, which was just as well, in the circumstances. He was cool to the very heart when he walked up to the door indicated by Mary, and rung the bell: Mrs. Helmer was at home: would he walk up stairs?

It was not a house of ceremonies; he was shown up and up and into the room where she sat, without a word carried before to prepare her for his visit. It was so dark that he could see nothing but the figure of one at work by a table, on which stood a single candle. There was but a spark of fire in the dreary grate and Letty was colder than any one could know, for she was at the moment making down the last woolly garment she had, in the vain hope of warming her baby.

She looked up. She had thought it was the landlady, and had waited for her to speak. She gazed for a moment in bewilderment, saw who it was, and jumped up half frightened, half ready to go wild with joy. All the memories of Godfrey rushed in a confused heap upon her, and overwhelmed her. She ran to him, and the same moment was in his arms, with her head on his shoulder, weeping tears of such gladness as she had not known since the first week of her marriage.

Neither spoke for some time; Letty could not because she was crying, and Godfrey would not because he did not want to cry. Those few moments were pure, simple happiness to both of them; to Letty, because she had loved him from childhood, and hoped that all was to be as of old between them; to Godfrey, because, for the moment, he had forgotten himself, and had neither thought of injury nor hope of love, remembering only the old days and the Letty that used to be. It may seem strange that, having never once embraced her all the time they lived together, he should do so now; but Letty's love would any time have responded to the least show of affection, and when, at the sight of his face, into which memory had called up all his tenderness, she rushed into his arms, how could he help kissing her? The pity was that he had not kissed her long before. Or was it a pity? I think not.

But the embrace could not be a long one. Godfrey was the first to relax its strain, and Letty responded with an instant collapse; for instantly she feared she had done it all, and disgusted Godfrey. But he led her gently to the sofa, and sat down beside her on the hard old slippery horsehair. Then first he perceived what a change had passed upon her. Pale was she, and thin, and sad, with such big eyes, and the bone tightening the skin upon her forehead! He felt as if she were a spectre-Letty, not the Letty he had loved. Glancing up, she caught his troubled gaze.

"I am not ill, Cousin Godfrey," she said. "Do not look at me so, or I shall cry again. You know you never liked to see me cry."

"My poor girl !" said Godfrey, in a voice which, if he had not kept it lower than natural, would have broken, "you are suffering."

"Oh, no, I'm not," replied Letty, with a pitiful effort at the cheerful ; "I am only so glad to see you again, Cousin Godfrey."

She sat on the edge of the sofa, and had put her open hands, palm to palm, between her knees, in a childish way, looking like one chidden, who did not deserve it, but was ready to endure. For a moment Godfrey sat gazing at her, with troubled heart and troubled looks, then between his teeth muttered, "Damn the rascal !"

Letty sat straight up, and turned upon him eyes of appeal, scared, yet ready to defend. Her hands were now clinched, one on each side of her ; she was poking the little fists into the squab of the sofa.

"Cousin Godfrey !" she cried, "if you mean Tom, you must not, you must not. I will go away if you speak a word against him. I will ; I will —I *must*, you know !"

Godfrey made no reply—neither apologized nor sought to cover.

"Why, child !" he said at last, "you are half starved !"

The pity and tenderness of both word and tone were too much for her. She had not been at all pitying herself, but such an utterance from the man she loved like an elder brother so wrought upon her enfeebled condition that she broke into a cry. She strove to suppress her emotion ; she fought with it ; in her agony she would have rushed from the room, had not Godfrey caught her, drawn her down beside him, and kept her there.

"You shall not leave me !" he said, in that voice Letty had always been used to obey. "Who has a right to know how things go with you, if I have not ? Come, you must tell me all about it."

"I have nothing to tell, Cousin Godfrey," she replied with some calmness, for Godfrey's decision had enabled her to conquer herself, "except that baby is ill, and looks as if he would never get better, and it is like to break my heart. Oh, he is such a dar"

"Let me see him," said Godfrey, in his heart detesting the child—the visible sign that another was nearer to Letty than he.

She jumped up, almost ran into the next room, and, coming back with her little one, laid him in Godfrey's arms. The moment he felt the weight of the little, sad-looking, sleeping thing, he grew human toward him, and saw in him Letty and not Tom.

"Good God! the child is starving, too," he exclaimed.

"Oh, no, Cousin Godfrey!" cried Letty; "he is not starving. He had a fresh-laid egg for breakfast this morning, and some arrowroot for dinner, and some bread and milk for tea—"

"London milk!" said Godfrey.

"Well, it is not like the milk in the dairy at Thornwick," admitted Letty. "If he had milk like that, he would soon be well!"

But Godfrey dared not say, "Bring him to Thornwick": he knew his mother too well for that!

"When were you anywhere in the country?" he asked. In a negative kind of way he was still nursing the baby.

"Not since we were married," she answered, sadly. "You see, poor Tom can't afford it."

Now Godfrey happened to have heard, "from the best authority," that Tom's mother was far from illiberal to him.

"Mrs. Helmer allows him so much a year—does she not?" he said.

"I know he gets money from her, but it can't be much," she answered.

Godfrey's suspicions against Tom increased every moment. He must learn the truth. He *would* have it, if by an even cruel experiment! He sat a moment silent—then said, with assumed cheerfulness:

"Well, Letty, I suppose, for the sake of old times, you will give me some dinner?"

Then, indeed, her courage gave way. She turned from him, laid her head on the end of the sofa, and sobbed so that the room seemed to shake with the convulsions of her grief.

"Letty," said Godfrey, laying his hand on her head, "it is
no use any more trying to hide the truth. I don't want any
dinner; in fact, I dined long ago. But you would not be open
with me, and I was forced to find out for myself: you have
not enough to eat, and you know it. I will not say a word
about who is to blame—for anything I know, it may be no one
—I am sure it is not you. But this must not go on! See, I
have brought you a little pocket-book. I will call again to-
morrow, and you will tell me then how you like it."

He laid the pocket-book on the table. There was ten times
as much in it as ever Letty had had at once. But she never
knew what was in it. She rose with instant resolve. All the
woman in her waked at once. She felt that a moment was come
when she must be resolute, or lose her hold on life.

"Cousin Godfrey," she said, in a tone he scarcely recognized
as hers—it frightened him as if it came from a sepulchre—"if
you do not take that purse away, I will throw it in the fire
without opening it! If my husband can not give me enough
to eat, I can starve as well as another. If you loved Tom, it
would be different, but you hate him, and I will have nothing
from you. Take it away, Cousin Godfrey."

Mortified, hurt, miserable, Godfrey took the purse, and,
without a word, walked from the room. Somewhere down in
his secret heart was dawning an idea of Letty beyond anything
he used to think of her, but in the mean time he was only
blindly aware that his heart had been shot through and through.
Nor was this the time for him to reflect that, under his training, Letty, even if he had married her, would never have grown
to such dignity.

It was, indeed, only in that moment she had become capable of the action. She had been growing as none, not Mary,
still less herself, knew, under the heavy snows of affliction, and
this was her first blossom. Not many of my readers will mistake me, I trust. Had it been in Letty pride that refused help
from such an old friend, that pride I should count no blossom,
but one of the meanest rags that ever fluttered to scare the
birds. But the dignity of her refusal was in this—that she
would accept nothing in which her husband had and could

have no human, that is, no spiritual share. She had married him because she loved him, and she would hold by him wherever that might lead her: not wittingly would she allow the finest edge, even of ancient kindness, to come between her Tom and herself! To accept from her cousin Godfrey the help her husband ought to provide her, would be to let him, however innocently, step into his place! There was no reasoning in her resolve: it was allied to that spiritual insight which, in simple natures, and in proportion to their simplicity, approaches or amounts to prophecy. As the presence of death will sometimes change even an ordinary man to a prophet, in times of sore need the childlike nature may well receive a vision sufficing to direct the doubtful step. Letty felt that the taking of that money would be the opening of a gulf to divide her and Tom for ever.

The moment Godfrey was out of the room she cast herself on the floor, and sobbed as if her heart must break. But her sobs were tearless. And, oh, agony of agonies! unsought came the conviction, and she could not send it away—to this had sunk her lofty idea of her Tom!—that he would have had her take the money! More than once or twice, in the ill-humors that followed a forced hilarity, he had forgotten his claims to being a gentleman so far as—not exactly to reproach her with having brought him to poverty—but to remind her that, if she was poor, she was no poorer than she had been when dependent on the charity of a distant relation!

The baby began to cry. She rose and took him from the sofa where Godfrey had laid him when he was getting out the pocket-book, held him fast to her bosom, as if by laying their two aching lives together they might both be healed, and, rocking him to and fro, said to herself, for the first time, that her trouble was greater than she could bear. "O baby! baby! baby!" she cried, and her tears streamed on the little wan face. But, as she sat with him in her arms, the blessed sleep came, and the storm sank to a calm.

CHAPTER XXXIX.

RELIEF.

It was dark, utterly dark, when she woke. For a minute she could not remember where she was. The candle had burned out: it must be late. The baby was on her lap—still, very still. One faint gleam of satisfaction crossed her "during dark" at the thought that he slept so peacefully, hidden from the gloom which, somehow, appeared to be all the same gloom outside and inside of her. In that gloom she sat alone.

Suddenly a prayer was in her heart. It was moving there as of itself. It had come there by no calling of it thither, by no conscious will of hers. "O God," she cried, "I am desolate! —Is there no help for me?" And therewith she knew that she had prayed, and knew that never in her life had she prayed before.

She started to her feet in an agony: a horrible fear had taken possession of her. With one arm she held the child fast to her bosom, with the other hand searched in vain to find a match. And still, as she searched, the baby seemed to grow heavier upon her arm, and the fear sickened more and more at her heart.

At last she had light! and the face of the child came out of the darkness. But the child himself had gone away into it. The Unspeakable had come while she slept—had come and gone, and taken her child with him. What was left of him was no more good to kiss than the last doll of her childhood!

When Tom came home, there was his wife on the floor as if dead, and a little way from her the child, dead indeed, and cold with death. He lifted Letty and carried her to the bed, amazed to find how light she was: it was long since he had had her thus in his arms. Then he laid her dead baby by her side, and ran to rouse the doctor. He came, and pronounced the child quite dead—from lack of nutrition, he said. To see Tom, no one could have helped contrasting his dress and appearance with the look and surroundings of his wife; but, no one would have been ready to lay blame on him; and, as for himself, he was not in the least awake to the fact of his guilt.

The doctor gave the landlady, who had responded at once to Tom's call, full directions for the care of the bereaved mother; Tom handed her the little money he had in his pocket, and she promised to do her best. And she did it; for she was one of those, not a few, who, knowing nothing of religion toward God, are yet full of religion toward their fellows, and with the Son of Man that goes a long way. As soon as it was light, Tom went to see about the burying of his baby.

He betook himself first to the editor of " The Firefly," but had to wait a long time for his arrival at the office. He told him his baby was dead, and he wanted money. It was forth-coming at once; for literary men, like all other artists, are in general as ready to help each other as the very poor themselves. There is less generosity, I think, among business-men than in any other class. The more honor to the exceptions!

"But," said the editor, who had noted the dry, burning palm, and saw the glazed, fiery eye of Tom, "my dear fellow, you ought to be in bed yourself. It's no use taking on about the poor little kid: *you* couldn't help it. Go home to your wife, and tell her she's got you to nurse; and, if she's in any fix, tell her to come to me."

Tom went home, but did not give his wife the message. She lay all but insensible, never asked for anything, or refused anything that was offered her, never said a word about her baby, or about Tom, or seemed to be more than when she lay in her mother's lap. Her baby was buried, and she knew no-thing of it. Not until nine days were over did she begin to revive.

For the first few days, Tom, moved with undefined remorse, tried to take a part in nursing her. She took things from him, as she did from the landlady, without heed or recognition. Just once, opening suddenly her eyes wide upon him, she ut-tered a feeble wail of " *Baby!* " and, turning her head, did not look at him again. Then, first, Tom's conscience gave him a sharp sting.

He was far from well. The careless and in many respects

dissolute life he had been leading had more than begun to tell on a constitution by no means strong, but he had never become aware of his weakness nor had ever felt really ill until now.

But that sting, although the first sharp one, was not his first warning of a waking conscience. Ever since he took his place at his wife's bedside, he had been fighting off the conviction that he was a brute. He would not, he could not believe it. What! Tom Helmer, the fine, indubitable fellow! such as he had always known himself!—he to cower before his own consciousness as a man unworthy, and greatly to be despised! The chaos was come again! And, verily, chaos was there, but not by any means newly come. And, moreover, when chaos begins to be conscious of itself, then is the dawn of an ordered world at hand. Nay, the creation of it is already begun, and the pangs of the waking conscience are the prophecy of the new birth.

With that pitiful cry of his wife after her lost child, disbelief in himself got within the lines of his defense; he could do no more, and began to loathe that conscious self which had hitherto been his pride.

Whatever the effect of illness may be upon the temper of some, it is most certainly an ally of the conscience. All pains, indeed, and all sorrows, all demons, yea, and all sins themselves under the suffering care of the highest minister, are but the ministers of truth and righteousness. I never came to know the condition of such as seemed exceptionally afflicted but I seemed to see reason for their affliction, either in exceptional faultiness of character or the greatness of the good it was doing them.

But conscience reacts on the body—for sickness until it is obeyed, for health thereafter. The moment conscience spoke thus plainly to Tom, the little that was left of his physical endurance gave way, his illness got the upper hand, and he took to his bed—all he could have for bed, that is—namely, the sofa in the sitting-room, widened out with chairs, and a mattress over all. There he lay, and their landlady had enough to do. Not that either of her patients was exacting; they were both too ill and miserable for that. It is the self-pitiful self-coddling invalid that is exacting. Such, I suspect, require something sharper still.

Tom groaned and tossed, and cursed himself, and soon passed into delirium. Straightway his visions, animate with shame and confusion of soul, were more distressing than even his ready tongue could have told. Dead babies and ghastly women pursued him everywhere. His fever increased. The cries of terror and dismay that he uttered reached the ears of his wife, and were the first thing that roused her from her lethargy. She rose from her bed, and, just able to crawl, began to do what she could for him. If she could but get near enough to him, the husband would yet be dearer than any child. She had him carried to the bed, and thereafter took on the sofa what rest there was for her. To and fro between bed and sofa she crept, let the landlady say what she might, gave him all the food he could be got to take, cooled his burning hands and head, and cried over him because she could not take him on her lap like the baby that was gone. Once or twice, in a quieter interval, he looked at her pitifully, and seemed about to speak ; but the back-surging fever carried far away the word of love for which she listened so eagerly. The doctor came daily, but Tom grew worse, and Letty could not get well.

CHAPTER XL.

GODFREY AND SEPIA.

WHEN the Redmains went to Cornwall, Sepia was left at Durnmelling, in the expectation of joining them in London within a fortnight at latest. The illness of Mr. Redmain, however, caused her stay to be prolonged, and she was worn out with *ennui*. The self she was so careful over was not by any means good company : not seldom during her life had she found herself capable of almost anything to get rid of it, short of suicide or repentance. This autumn, at Durnmelling, she would even, occasionally, with that object, when the weather was fine, go

for a solitary walk—a thing, I need not say, she hated in itself,
though now it was her forlorn hope, in the poor possibility of
falling in with some distraction. But the hope was not altogether a vague one ; for was there not a man somewhere under-
neath those chimneys she saw over the roof of the laundry ?
She had never spoken to him, but Hesper and she had often
talked about him, and often watched him ride—never man
more to her mind. In her wanderings she had come upon the
breach in the ha-ha, and, clambering up, found herself on the
forbidden ground of a neighbor whom the family did not visit.
To no such folly would Sepia be a victim.

The analysis of such a nature as hers, with her story to set
it forth, would require a book to itself, and I must happily content myself with but a fact here and there in her history.

In one of her rambles on his ground she had her desire,
and met Godfrey Wardour. He lifted his hat, and she stopped
and addressed him by way of apology.

"I am afraid you think me very rude, Mr. Wardour," she
said. "I know I am trespassing, but this field of yours is
higher than the ground about Durnmelling, and seems to take
pounds off the weight of the atmosphere."

For all he had gone through, Godfrey was not yet less than
courteous to ladies. He assured Miss Yolland that Thornwick
was as much at her service as if it were a part of Durnmelling.
"Though, indeed," he added, with a smile, "it would be
more correct to say, 'as if Durnmelling were a part of Thornwick'—for that was the real state of the case once upon a
time."

The statement interested or seemed to interest Miss Yolland, giving rise to many questions ; and a long conversation
ensued. Suddenly she woke, or seemed to wake, to the consciousness that she had forgotten herself and the proprieties
together : hastily, and to all appearance with some confusion,
she wished him a good morning ; but she was not too much
confused to thank him again for the permission he had given
her to walk on his ground.

It was not by any intention on the part of Godfrey that
they met, little

conversation before they parted ; nor did Sepia find any difficulty in getting him sufficiently within their range to make
him feel the power of her eyes.   She was too prudent, however, to bring to bear upon any man all at once the full play
of her mesmeric battery ; and things had got no further when
she went to London—a week or two before the return of the
Redmains, ostensibly to get things in some special readiness
for Hesper ; but that this may have been a pretense appears
possible from the fact that Mary came from Cornwall on the
same mission a few days later.

I have just mentioned an acquaintance of Sepia's, who attracted the notice and roused the peculiar interest of Mr.
Redmain, because of a look he saw pass betwixt them.   This
man spoke both English and French with a foreign accent,
and gave himself out as a Georgian—Count Galofta, he called
himself : I believe he was a prince in Paris.   At this time
he was in London, and, during the ten days that Sepia was
alone, came to see her several times—called early in the fore-
noon first, the next day in the evening, when they went together to the opera, and once came and staid late.   Whether
from her dark complexion making her look older than she
was, or from the subduing air which her experience had given
her, or merely from the fact that she belonged to nobody much,
Miss Yolland seemed to have *carte blanche* to do as she pleased,
and come and go when and where she liked, as one knowing
well enough how to take care of herself.

Mary, arriving unexpectedly at the house in Glammis
Square, met him in the hall as she entered : he had just taken
leave of Sepia, who was going up the stair at the moment.
Mary had never seen him before, but something about him
caused her to look at him again as he passed.

Somehow, Tom also had discovered Sepia's return, and had
gone to see her more than once.

When Mr. and Mrs Redmain arrived, there was so much
to be done for Hesper's wardrobe that, for some days, Mary
found it impossible to go and see Letty.   Her mistress seemed
harder to please than usual, and more doubtful of humor than
ever before   This may have arisen—but I doubt it—from the

fact that, having gone to church the Sunday before they left, she had there heard a different sort of sermon from any she had heard in her life before . sermons have something to do with the history of the world, however many of them may be no better than a withered leaf in the blast.

The morning after her arrival, Hesper, happening to find herself in want of Mary's immediate help, instead of calling her as she generally did, opened the door between their rooms, and saw Mary on her knees by her bedside. Now, Hesper had heard of saying prayers—night and morning both—and, when a child, had been expected, and indeed compelled, to say her prayers ; but to be found on one's knees in the middle of the day looked to her a thing exceedingly odd. Mary, in truth, was not much in the way of kneeling at such a time : she had to pray much too often to kneel always, and God was too near her, wherever she happened to be, for the fancy that she must seek him in any particular place ; but so it happened now. She rose, a little startled rather than troubled, and followed her mistress into her room.

"I am sorry to have disturbed you, Mary," said Hesper, herself a little annoyed, it is not quite easy to say why ; "but people do not generally say their prayers in the middle of the day."

"I say mine when I need to say them," answered Mary, a little cross that Hesper should take any notice. She would rather the thing had not occurred, and it was worse to have to talk about it.

"For my part, I don't see any good in being righteous overmuch," said Hesper.

I wonder if there was another saying in the Bible she would have been so ready to quote !

"I don't know what that means," returned Mary. "I believe it is somewhere in the Bible, but I am sure Jesus never said it, for he tells us to be righteous as our Father in heaven is righteous."

"But the thing is impossible," said Hesper. "How is one, with such claims on her as I have, to attend to these things ? Society has claims

"And has God none?" asked Mary.

"Many people think now there is no God at all," returned Hesper, with an almost petulant expression.

"If there is no God, that settles the question," answered Mary. "But, if there should be one, how then?"

"Then I am sure he would never be hard on one like me. I do just like other people. One must do as people do. If there is one thing that must be avoided more than another, it is peculiarity. How ridiculous it would be of any one to set herself against society!"

"Then you think the Judge will be satisfied if you say, 'Lord, I had so many names in my visiting-book, and so many invitations I could not refuse, that it was impossible for me to attend to those things'?"

"I don't see that I'm at all worse than other people," persisted Hesper. "I can't go and pretend to be sorry for sins I should commit again the next time there was a necessity. I don't see what I've got to repent of."

Nothing had been said about repentance: here, I imagine, the sermon may have come in.

"Then, of course, you can't repent," said Mary.

Hesper recovered herself a little.

"I am glad you see the thing as I do," she said.

"I don't see it at all as you do, ma'am," answered Mary, gently.

"Why!" exclaimed Hesper, taken by surprise, "what have I got to repent of?"

"Do you really want me to say what I think?" asked Mary.

"Of course, I do," returned Hesper, getting angry, and at the same time uneasy: she knew Mary's freedom of speech upon occasion, but felt that to draw back would be to yield the point. "What have I done to be ashamed of, pray?"

Some ladies are ready to plume themselves upon not having been guilty of certain great crimes. Some thieves, I dare say, console themselves that they have never committed murder.

"If I had married a man I did not love," answered Mary, "I should be more ashamed of myself than I can tell."

"That is the way of looking at such things in the class you

belong to, I dare say," rejoined Hesper; "but with us it is quite different. There is no necessity laid upon *you. Our* position obliges us."

"But what if God should not see it as you do?"

"If that is all you have got to bring against me!—" said Hesper, with a forced laugh.

"But that is not all," replied Mary. "When you married, you promised many things, not one of which you have ever done."

"Really, Mary, this is intolerable!" cried Hesper.

"I am only doing what you asked me, ma'am," said Mary. "And I have said nothing that every one about Mr. Redmain does not know as well as I do."

Hesper wished heartily she had never challenged Mary's judgment.

"But," she resumed, more quietly, "how could you, how could any one, how could God himself, hard as he is, ask me to fulfill the part of a loving wife to a man like Mr. Redmain? —There is no use mincing matters with *you*, Mary."

"But you promised," persisted Mary. "It belongs, besides, to the very idea of marriage."

"There are a thousand promises made every day which nobody is expected to keep. It is the custom, the way of the world! How many of the clergy, now, believe the things they put their names to?"

"They must answer for themselves. We are not clergymen, but women, who ought never to say a thing except we mean it, and, when we have said it, to stick to it."

"But just look around you, and see how many there are in precisely the same position! Will you dare to say they are all going to be lost because they do not behave like angels to their brutes of husbands?"

"I say, they have got to repent of behaving to their husbands as their husbands behave to them."

"And what if they don't?"

Mary paused a little.

"Do you expect to go to heaven, ma'am?" she asked.

"I hope

"Do you think you will like it?"

"I must say, I think it will be rather dull."

"Then, to use your own word, you must be very like lost anyway. There does not seem to be a right place for you anywhere, and that is very like being lost—is it not?"

Hesper laughed.

"I am pretty comfortable where I am," she said.

"Husband and all!" thought Mary, but she did not say that. What she did say was:

"But you know you can't stay here. God is not going to keep up this way of things for you; can you ask it, seeing you don't care a straw what he wants of you? But I have sometimes thought, What if hell be just a place where God gives everybody everything she wants, and lets everybody do whatever she likes, without once coming nigh to interfere! What a hell that would be! For God's presence in the very being, and nothing else, is bliss. That, then, would be altogether the opposite of heaven, and very much the opposite of this world. Such a hell would go on, I suppose, till every one had learned to hate every one else in the same world with her."

This was beyond Hesper, and she paid no attention to it.

"You can never, in your sober senses, Mary," she said, "mean that God requires of me to do things for Mr. Redmain that the servants can do a great deal better! That would be ridiculous—not to mention that I oughtn't and couldn't and wouldn't do them for any man!"

"Many a woman," said Mary, with a solemnity in her tone which she did not intend to appear there, "has done many more trying things for persons of whom she knew nothing."

"I dare say! But such women go in for being saints, and that is not my line. I was not made for that."

"You were made for that, and far more," said Mary.

"There are such women, I know," persisted Hesper; "but I do not know how they find it possible."

"I can tell you how they find it possible. They love every human being just because he is human. Your husband might be a demon from the way you behave to him."

"I suppose *you* find it agreeable to wait upon him : he is civil to you, I dare say !"

"Not very," replied Mary, with a smile ; "but the person who can not bear with a sick man or a baby is not fit to be a woman."

"You may go to your own room," said Hesper

For the first time, a feeling of dislike to Mary awoke in the bosom of her mistress—very naturally, *all* my readers will allow. The next few days she scarcely spoke to her, sending directions for her work through Sepia, who discharged the office with dignity.

CHAPTER XLI.

THE HELPER.

AT length one morning, when she believed Mrs. Redmain would not rise before noon, Mary felt she must go and see Letty. She did not find her in the quarters where she had left her, but a story higher, in a mean room, sitting with her hands in her lap. She did not lift her eyes when Mary entered : where hope is dead, curiosity dies. Not until she had come quite near did she raise her head, and then she seemed to know nothing of her. When she did recognize her, she held out her hand in a mechanical way, as if they were two specters met in a miserable dream, in which they were nothing to each other, and neither could do, or cared to do, anything for the other.

"My poor Letty!" cried Mary, greatly shocked, "what has come to you? Are you not glad to see me? Has anything happened to Tom?"

She broke into a low, childish wail, and for a time that was all Mary heard. Presently, however, she became aware of a feeble moaning in the adjoining chamber, the sound of a human sea in trouble—mixed with a wandering babble, which to Letty was but as the voice of her own despair, and to Mary was a cry for he   hing from Letty, and went into the next room, the door of which stood wide. There lay Tom, but so changed that Mary took a moment to be certain it was he. Going softly to him, she laid her hand on his head. It was burning. He opened his eyes, but she saw their sense was gone. She went back to Letty, and, sitting down beside her, put her arm about her, and said :

"Why didn't you send for me, Letty ? I would have come to you at once. I will come now, to-night, and help you to nurse him. Where is the baby ?"

Letty gave a shriek, and, starting from her chair, walked wildly about the room, wringing her hands. Mary went after her, and taking her in her arms, said :

"Letty, dear, has God taken your baby ?"

Letty gave her a lack-luster look.

"Then," said Mary, "he is not far away, for we are all in God's arms."

But what is the use of the most sovereign of medicines while they stand on the sick man's table ? What is the mightiest of truths so long as it is not believed ? The spiritually sick still mocks at the medicine offered ; he will not know its cure. Mary saw that, for any comfort to Letty, God was nowhere. It went to her very heart. Death and desolation and the enemy were in possession. She turned to go, that she might return able to begin her contest with ruin. Letty saw that she was going, and imagined her offended and abandoning her to her misery. She flew to her, stretching out her arms like a child, but was so feeble that she tripped and fell. Mary lifted her, and laid her wailing on her couch.

"Letty," said Mary, "you didn't think I was going to leave you ! But I must go for an hour, perhaps two, to make arrangements for staying with you till Tom is over the worst."

Then Letty clasped her hands in her old, beseeching way, and looked up with a faint show of comfort.

"Be courageous, Letty," said Mary. "I shall be back as soon as ever I can. God has sent me to you."

She drove straight home, and heard that Mrs. Redmain was annoyed that she had gone out.

"I offered to dress her," said Jemima ; "and she knows I

can quite well ; but she would not get up till you came, and made me fetch her a book. So there she is, a-waiting for you !"

"I am sorry," said Mary ; "but I had to go, and she was fast asleep."

When she entered her room, Hesper gave her a cold glance over the top of her novel, and went on with her reading. Mary proceeded to get her things ready for dressing. But by this time she had got interested in the story.

"I shall not get up yet," she said

"Then, please, ma'am," replied Mary, "would you mind letting Jemima dress you ? I want to go out again, and should be glad if you could do without me for some days. My friend's baby is dead, and both she and her husband are very ill."

Hesper threw down her book, and her eyes flamed.

"What do you mean by using me so, Miss Marston ?" she said.

"I am very sorry to put you to inconvenience," answered Mary ; "but the husband seems dying, and the wife is scarcely able to crawl."

"I have nothing to do with it," interrupted Hesper. "When you made it necessary for me to part with my maid, you undertook to perform her duties. I did not engage you as a sick-nurse for other people."

"No, ma'am," replied Mary ; "but this is an extreme case, and I can not believe you will object to my going."

"I do object. How, pray, is the world to go on, if this kind of thing be permitted ! I may be going out to dinner, or to the opera to-night, for anything you know, and who is there to dress me ? No ; on principle, and for the sake of ex- ample, I will not let you go."

"I thought," said Mary, not a little disappointed in Hes- per, "I did not stand to you quite in the relation of an ordi- nary servant."

"Certainly you do not : I look for a little more devotion from you than from a common, ungrateful creature who thinks only of herself. But you are all alike."

More and more distressed to find one she had loved so

long show herself so selfish, Mary's indignation had almost got
the better of her. But a little heightening of her color was
all the show it made.

"Indeed, it is quite necessary, ma'am," she persisted, "that
I should go."

"The law has fortunately made provision against such behavior," said Hesper. "You can not leave without giving me
a month's notice."

". The understanding on which I came to you was very different," said Mary, sadly.

"It was; but, since then, you consented to become my
maid."

"It is ungenerous to take advantage of that," returned
Mary, growing angry again.

"I have to protect myself and the world in general from
the consequences that must follow were such lawless behavior
allowed to pass."

Hesper spoke with calm severity, and Mary, making up her
mind, answered now with almost equal calmness.

". The law was made for both sides, ma'am; and, as you
bring the law to me, I will take refuge in the law. It is, I believe, a month's warning or a month's wages; and, as I have
never had any wages, I imagine I am at liberty to go. Good-
by, ma'am."

Hesper made her no answer, and Mary left the room. She
went to her own, stuffed her immediate necessities into a bag,
let herself out of the house, called a cab, and, with a great
lump in her throat, drove to the help of Letty.

First she had a talk with the landlady, and learned all she
could tell. Then she went up, and began to make things as
comfortable as she could : all was in sad disorder and neglect.

With the mere inauguration of cleanliness, and the first
dawn of coming order, the courage of Letty began to revive a
little. The impossibility of doing all that ought to be done,
had, in her miserable weakness, so depressed her that she had
not done even as much as she could—except where Tom was
immediately concerned : there she had not failed of her utmost.

Mary next went to the doctor to get instructions, and then

to buy what things were most wanted. And now she almost wished Mrs. Redmain had paid her for her services, for she must write to Mr. Turnbull for money, and that she disliked. But by the very next post she received, inclosed in a business memorandum in George's writing, the check for fifty pounds she had requested.

She did not dare write to Tom's mother, because she was certain, were she to come up, her presence would only add to the misery, and take away half the probability of his recovery and of Letty's, too. In the case of both, nourishment was the main thing; and to the fit providing and the administering of it she bent her energy.

For a day or two, she felt at times as if she could hardly get through what she had undertaken; but she soon learned to drop asleep at any moment, and wake immediately when she was wanted; and thereafter her strength was by no means so sorely tried.

Under her skillful nursing—skillful, not from experience, but simply from her faith, whence came both conscience of and capacity for doing what the doctor told her—things went well. It is from their want of this faith, and their consequent arrogance and conceit, that the ladies who aspire to help in hospitals give the doctors so much trouble: they have not yet learned *obedience*, the only path to any good, the one essential to the saving of the world. One who can not obey is the merest slave—essentially and in himself a slave. The crisis of Tom's fever was at length favorably passed, but the result remained doubtful. By late hours and strong drink, he had done not a little to weaken a constitution, in itself, as I have said, far from strong; while the unrest of what is commonly and foolishly called a bad conscience, with misery over the death of his child and the conduct which had disgraced him in his own eyes and ruined his wife's happiness, combined to retard his recovery.

While he was yet delirious, and grief and shame and consternation operated at will on his poetic nature, the things he kept saying over and over were very pitiful; but they would have sounded more miserable by much in the ears of one who did not look so far ahead as Mary. She, trained to regard all things in their true import, was rejoiced to find him loathing his former self, and beyond the present suffering saw the gladness at hand for the sorrowful man, the repenting sinner. Had she been mother or sister to him, she could hardly have waited on him with more devotion or tenderness.

One day, as his wife was doing some little thing for him, he took her hand in his feeble grasp, and pressing it to his face, wet with the tears of reviving manhood, said :

"We might have been happy together, Letty, if I had but known how much you were worth, and how little I was worth myself !—Oh me ! oh me !"

He burst into an uncontrollable wail that tortured Letty with its likeness to the crying of her baby.

"Tom ! my own darling Tom !" she cried, "when you speak as if I belonged to you, it makes me as happy as a queen. When you are better, you will be happy, too, dear. Mary says you will."

"O Letty !" he sobbed—"the baby !"

"The baby's all right, Mary says ; and, some day, she says, he will run into your arms, and know you for his father."

"And I shall be ashamed to look at him !" said Tom.

An hour or so after, he woke from a short sleep, and his eyes sought Letty's watching face.

"I have seen baby," he said, "and he has forgiven me. I dare say it was only a dream," he added, "but somehow it makes me happier. At least, I know how the thing might be."

"It was true, whether it was but a dream or something more," said Mary, who happened to be by.

"Thank you, Mary," he returned. "You and Letty have saved me from what I dare not think of ! I could die happy now—if it weren't for one thing."

"What is that ?" asked Mary.

"I am ashamed to say," he replied, "but I ought to say it and bear the shame, for the man who does shamefully ought to be ashamed. It is that, when I am in my grave—or somewhere else, for I know Mary does not like people to talk about being in their graves—you say it is heathenish, don't you,

Mary ?—when I am where they can't find me, then, it is horrid to think that people up here will have a hold on me and a right over me still, because of debts I shall never be able to pay them."

" Don't be too sure of that, Tom." said Mary, cheerfully. "I think you will pay them yet.—But I have heard it said," she went on, " that a man in debt never tells the truth about his debts—as if he had only the face to make them, not to talk about them : can you make a clean breast of it, Tom ?"

" I don't exactly know what they are ; but I always did mean to pay them, and I have some idea about them. I don't think they would come to more than a hundred pounds."

" Your mother would not hesitate to pay that for you ?" said Mary.

" I know she wouldn't ; but, then, I'm thinking of Letty." He paused, and Mary waited.

" You know, when I am gone," he resumed. " there will be nothing for her but to go to my mother ; and it breaks my heart to think of it. Every sin of mine she will lay to her charge ; and how am I to lie still in my grave—oh, I beg your pardon, Mary."

"I will pay your debts. Tom, and gladly," said Mary, "if they don't come to much more than you say—than you *think*, I mean."

" But, don't you see, Mary, that would be only a shifting of my debt from them to you ? Except for Letty, it would not make the thing any better."

" What !" said Mary, " is there no difference between owing a thing to one who loves you and one who does not ? to one who would always be wishing you had paid him and one who is glad to have even the poor bond of a debt between you and her ? All of us who are sorry for our sins are brothers and sisters."

"O Mary !" said Tom.

" But I will tell you what will be better : let your mother pay your debts, and I will look after Letty. I will care for her like my own sister. Tom "

"Then I shall die happy," said Tom ; and from that day began to recover.

Many who would pay money to keep a man alive or to deliver him from pain would pay nothing to take a killing load off the shoulders of his mind. Hunger they can pity—not mental misery.

Tom would not hear of his mother being written to.

"I have done Letty wrong enough already," he said, "without subjecting her to the cruel tongue of my mother. I have conscience enough left not to have anybody else abuse her."

"But, Tom," expostulated Mary, "if you want to be good, one of your first duties is to be reconciled to your mother."

"I am very sorry things are all wrong between us, Mary," said Tom. "But, if you want her to come here, you don't know what you are talking about. She must have everything her own way, or storm from morning to night. I would gladly make it up with her, but live with her, or die with her, I could *not*. To make either possible, you must convert her, too. When you have done that, I will invite her at once."

"Never mind me, Tom," said Letty. "So long as you love me, I don't care what even your mother thinks of me. I will do everything I can to make her comfortable, and satisfied with me."

"Wait till I am better, anyhow, Letty ; for I solemnly assure you I haven't a chance if my mother comes. I will tell you what, Mary : I promise you, if I get better, I will do what is possible to be a son to my mother ; and for the present I will dictate a letter, if you will write it, bidding her good-by, and asking her pardon for everything I have done wrong by her, which you will please send if I should die. I can not and I will not promise more."

He was excited and exhausted, and Mary dared not say another word. Nor truly did she at the moment see what more could be said. Where all relation has been perverted, things can not be set right by force. Perhaps all we can do sometimes is to be willing and wait.

The letter was dictated and written—a lovely one, Mary thought—and it made her weep as she wrote it. Tom signed it with his own hand. Mary folded, sealed, addressed it, and laid it away in her desk.

The same evening Tom said to Letty, putting his thin, long hand in hers—

"Mary thinks we shall know each other there, Letty."

"Tom!" interrupted Letty, "don't talk like that; I *can't* bear it. If you do, I shall die before you."

"All I wanted to say," persisted Tom, "was, that I should sit all day looking out for you, Letty."

CHAPTER XLII.

THE LEPER.

THE faint, sweet, luminous jar of bow and string, as betwixt them they tore the silky air into a dying sound, came hovering—neither could have said whether it was in the soul only, or there and in the outer world too.

"What *is* that?" said Tom.

"Mary!" Letty called into the other room, "there is our friend with the violin again! Don't you think Tom would like to hear him?"

"Yes, I do," answered Mary.

"Then would you mind asking him to come and play a little to us? It would do Tom good, I do think."

Mary went up the one stair—all that now divided them, and found the musician with his sister—his half-sister she was.

"I thought we should have you in upon us!" said Ann. "Joe thinks he can play so as nobody can hear him; and I was fool enough to let him try. I am sorry."

"I am glad," rejoined Mary, "and am come to ask him down stairs; for Mrs. Helmer and I think it will do her husband good to hear him. He is very fond of music."

"Much help music will be to him, poor young man!" said Ann, scornfully.

"Wouldn't you give a sick man a flower, even if it only

made him a little happier for a moment with its scent and its loveliness ? " asked Mary.

"No, I wouldn't. It would only be to help the deceitful heart to be more desperately wicked."

I will not continue the conversation, although they did a little longer. Ann's father had been a preacher among the followers of Whitefield, and Ann was a follower of her father. She laid hold upon the garment of a hard master, a tyrannical God. Happy he who has learned the gospel according to Jesus, as reported by John—that God is light, and in him is no darkness at all ! Happy he who finds God his refuge from all the lies that are told for him, and in his name ! But it is love that saves, and not opinion that damns ; and let the Master himself deal with the weeds in his garden as with the tares in his field.

"I read my Bible a good deal," said Mary, at last, "but I never found one of those things you say in it."

"That's because you were never taught to look for them," said Ann.

"Very likely," returned Mary. "In the mean time I prefer the violin—that is, with one like your brother to play it."

She turned to the door, and Joseph Jasper, who had not spoken a word, rose and followed her. As soon as they were outside, Mary turned to him, and begged he would play the same piece with which he had ended on the former occasion.

"I thought you did not care for it ! I am so glad !" he said.

"I care for it very much," replied Mary, "and have often thought of it since. But you left in such haste ! before I could find words to thank you !"

"You mean the ten lepers, don't you ? " he said. "But of course you do. I always end off with them."

"Is that how you call it ? " returned Mary. "Then you have given me the key to it, and I shall understand it much better this time, I hope."

"That is what I call it," said Joseph, " —to myself, I mean, not to Ann. She would count it blasphemy. God has

made so many things that she thinks must not be mentioned
in his hearing !"

When they entered the room, Joseph, casting a quick look
round it, made at once for the darkest corner. Three swift
strides took him there ; and, without more preamble than if he
had come upon a public platform to play, he closed his eyes
and began.

And now at last Mary understood at least this specimen of
his strange music, and was able to fill up the blanks in the
impression it formerly made upon her. Alas, that my helpless ignorance should continue to make it impossible for me to
describe it !

A movement even and rather slow, full of unexpected
chords, wonderful to Mary, who did not know that such things
could be made on the violin, brought before her mind's eye
the man who knew all about everything, and loved a child
more than a sage, walking in the hot day upon the border between Galilee and Samaria. Sounds arose which she interpreted as the stir of village life, the crying and calling of do-
mestic animals, and of busy housewives at their duties, carried
on half out of doors, in the homeliness of country custom.
Presently the instrument began to tell the gathering of a
crowd, with bee-like hum, and the crossing of voice with
voice—but, at a distance, the sounds confused and obscure.
Swiftly then they seemed to rush together, to blend and lose
themselves in the unity of an imploring melody, in which she
heard the words, uttered afar, with uplifted hands and voices,
drawing nearer and nearer as often repeated, "Jesus, Master,
have mercy on us." Then came a brief pause, and then what,
to her now fully roused imagination, seemed the voice of the
Master, saying, "Go show yourselves unto the priests." Then
followed the slow, half-unwilling, not hopeful march of time-
less feet ; then a clang as of something broken, then a silence
as of sunrise, then air and liberty—long-drawn notes divided
with quick, hurried ones ; then the trampling of many feet,
going farther and farther—merrily, with dance and song ; once
more a sudden pause—and a melody in which she read the
awe-struck joyous return of one. Steadily yet eagerly the feet

drew nigh, the melody growing at once in awe and jubilation, as the man came nearer and nearer to him whose word had made him clean, until at last she saw him fall on his face before him, and heard his soul rushing forth in a strain of adoring thanks, which seemed to end only because it was choked in tears.

The violin ceased, but, as if its soul had passed from the instrument into his, the musician himself took up the strain, and in a mellow tenor voice, with a mingling of air and recitative, and an expression which to Mary was entrancing, sang the words, "And he was a Samaritan."

At the sound of his own voice, he seemed to wake up, hung his head for a moment, as if ashamed of having shown his emotion, tucked his instrument under his arm, and walked from the room, without a word spoken on either side. Nor, while he played, had Mary once seen the face of the man; her soul sat only in the porch of her ears, and not once looked from the windows of her eyes.

CHAPTER XLIII.

MARY AND MR. REDMAIN.

A FEW rudiments of righteousness lurked, in their original undevelopment, but still in a measure active, in the being of Mr. Redmain: there had been in the soul of his mother, I suspect, a strain of generosity, and she had left a mark of it upon him, and it was the best thing about him. But in action these rudiments took an evil shape.

Preferring inferior company, and full of that suspicion which puts the last edge upon what the world calls knowledge of human nature, he thought no man his equal in penetrating the arena of motive, and reading actions in the light of motive; and, that the fundamental principle of all motive was self-interest, he assumed to be beyond dispute. With this candle, not that of the Lord, he searched the dark places of the soul;

but, where the soul was light, his candle could show him no-thing—served only to blind him yet further, if possible, to what was there present. And, because he did not seek the good, never yet in all his life had he come near enough to a righteous man to recognize that in something or other that man was dif-ferent from himself. As for women—there was his wife—of whom he was willing to think as well as she would let him! And she, firmly did he believe, was an angel beside Sepia!—of whom, bad as she was, it is quite possible he thought yet worse than she deserved · alas for the woman who is not good, and falls under the judgment of a bad man!—the good woman he can no more hurt than the serpent can bite the adamant. He believed he knew Sepia's self, although he did not yet know her history; and he scorned her the more that he was not a hair better himself. He had regard enough for his wife, and what virtue his penetration conceded her, to hate their inti-macy; and ever since his marriage had been scheming how to get rid of Sepia—only, however, through finding her out: he must unmask her · there would be no satisfaction in getting rid of her without his wife's convinced acquiescence. He had been, therefore, almost all the time more or less on the watch to uncover the wickedness he felt sure lay at no great depth be-neath her surface: and in the mean time, and for the sake of this end, he lived on terms of decent domiciliation with her. She had no suspicion how thin was the crust between her and the lava.

In Cornwall, he began at length to puzzle himself about Mary. Of course she was just like the rest! but he did not at once succeed in fitting what he saw to what he entirely believed of her. She remained, like Sepia, a riddle to be solved. He was not so ignorant as his wife concerning the relations of the different classes, and he felt certain there must be some reason, of course a discreditable one, for her leaving her former, and taking her present, position. The attack he had in Cornwall afforded him unexpected opportunity of making her out, as he called it.

Upon this occasion it was also that Mary first ventured to expostulate with her mistress on her neglect of her husband.

She heard her patiently ; and the same day, going to his room, paid him some small attention—handed him his medicine, I believe, but clumsily, because ungraciously. The next moment, one of his fits of pain coming on, he broke into such a torrent of cursing as swept her in stately dignity from the room. She would not go near him again.

"Brought up as you have been, Mary," she said, "you can not enter into the feelings of one in my position, to whom the very tone even of coarse language is unspeakably odious. It makes me sick with disgust. Coarseness is what no lady can endure. I beg you will not mention Mr. Redmain to me again."

"Dear Mrs. Redmain," said Mary, "ugly as such language is, there are many things worse. It seems to me worse that a wife should not go near her husband when he is suffering than that he should in his pain speak bad words."

She had been on the point of saying that a thin skin was not purity, but bethought herself in time.

"You are scarcely in a position to lay down the law for me, Mary," said Hesper. "We will, if you please, drop the subject."

Mary's words were overheard, as was a good deal in the house more than was reckoned on, and reached Mr. Redmain, whom they perplexed : what could the young woman hope from taking his part ?

One morning, after the arrival of Mewks, his man, Mary heard Mr. Redmain calling him in a tone which betrayed that he had been calling for some time : the house was an old one, and the bells were neither in good trim, nor was his in a convenient position. She thought first to find Mewks, but pity rose in her heart. She ran to Mr. Redmain's door, which stood half open, and showed herself.

"Can *I* not do something for you, sir ?" she said.

"Yes, you can. Go and tell that lumbering idiot to come to me instantly. No ! here, you !—there's a good girl !—Oh, damn !—Just give me your hand, and help me to turn an inch or two."

Change of posture relieved him a little.

"Thank you," he said. "That is better. Wait a few moments, will you—till the rascal comes?"

Mary stood back, a little behind him, thinking not to annoy him with the sight of her.

"What are you doing there?" he cried "I like to see what people are about in my room. Come in front here, and let me look at you."

Mary obeyed, and with a smile took the position he pointed out to her. Immediately followed another agony of pain, in which he looked beset with demons, whom he not feared but hated. Mary hurried to him, and, in the compassion which she inherited long back of Eve, took his hand, the fingers of which were twisting themselves into shapes like tree-roots. With a hoarse roar, he dashed hers from him, as if it had been a serpent. She returned to her place, and stood.

"What did you mean by that?' he said, when he came to himself. "Do you want to make a fool of me?"

Mary did not understand him, and made no reply. Another fit came. This time she kept her distance.

"Come here," he howled; "take my head in your hands." She obeyed.

"Damned nice hands you've got!" he gasped; "much nicer than your mistress's."

Mary took no notice. Gently she withdrew her hands, for the fit was over.

"I see! that's the way of you!" he said, as she stepped back. "But come now, tell me how it is that a nice, well-behaved, handsome girl like you, should leave a position where, they tell me, you were your own mistress, and take a cursed place as lady's maid to my wife."

"It was because I liked Mrs. Redmain so much," answered Mary. "But, indeed, I was not very comfortable where I was."

"What the devil did you see to like in her? I never saw anything!"

"She is so beautiful!" said Mary.

"Is she! ho! ho!" he laughed. "What is that to another woman! You are new to the trade, my girl, if you think

that will go down! One woman taking to another because
'she's so beautiful'! Ha! ha! ha!"

He repeated Mary's words with an indescribable contempt,
and his laugh was insulting to a degree; but it went off in a
cry of suffering.

"Hypocrisy mustn't be too barefaced," he resumed, when
again his torture abated. "I didn't make you stop to amuse
me! It's little of that this beastly world has got for me!
Come, a better reason for waiting on my wife?"

"That she was kind to me," said Mary, "may be a better
reason, but it is not a truer."

"It's more than ever she was to me! What wages does she
give you?"

"We have not spoken about that yet, sir."

"You haven't had any?"

"I haven't wanted any yet."

"Then what the deuce ever made you come to this house?"

"I hoped to be of some service to Mrs. Redmain," said
Mary, growing troubled.

"And you ain't of any? Is that why you don't want
wages?"

"No, sir. That is not the reason."

"Then what *is* the reason? Come! Trust me. I will be
much better to you than your mistress. Out with it! I knew
there was something!"

"I would rather not talk more about it," said Mary, knowing that her feeling in relation to Hesper would be altogether
incredible, and the notion of it ridiculous to him.

"You needn't mind telling *me!* I know all about such
things.—Look here! Give me that pocket-book on the
table."

Mary brought him the pocket-book. He opened it, and,
taking from it some notes, held them out to her.

"If your mistress won't pay you your wages, I will. There!
take that. You're quite welcome. What matter which pays
you? It all comes out of the same stocking-foot."

"I don't know yet," answered Mary, "whether I shall accept wages from Mrs. Redmain. Something might happen to

make it impossible ; or, if I had taken money, to make me regret it."

"I like that ! There you keep a hold on her !" said Mr. Redmain, in a confidential tone, while in his heart he was more puzzled than ever. "There's no occasion, though, for all that," he went on, "to go without your money when you can have it and she be nothing the wiser. There—take it. I will swear you any oath you like not to tell my stingy wife."

"She is not stingy," said Mary : "and, if I don't take wages from her, I certainly shall not from any one else —Besides," she added, "it would be dishonest."

"Oh ! that's the dodge !" said Mr. Redmain to himself ; but aloud, "Where would be the dishonesty, when the money is mine to do with as I please ?"

"Where the dishonesty, sir !" exclaimed Mary, astounded. "To take wages from you, and pretend to Mrs. Redmain I was going without !"

"Ha ! ha ! The first time, no doubt, you ever pretended anything !"

"It would be," said Mary, "so far as I can, at the moment, remember."

"Go along," cried Mr. Redmain, losing, or pretending to lose, patience with her ; "you are too unscrupulous a liar for me to deal with."

Mary turned and left the room. As she went, his keen glance caught the expression of her countenance, and noted the indignant red that flushed her cheeks, and the lightning of wronged innocence in her eyes

"I ought not to have said it," he remarked to himself.

He did not for a moment fancy she had spoken the truth ; but the look of her went to a deeper place in him than he knew even the existence of.

"Hey ! stop," he cried, as she was disappearing. "Come back, will you ?"

"I will find Mr. Mewks," she answered, and went.

After this, Mary naturally dreaded conference with Mr. Redmain ; and he, thinking she must have time to get over the offense he had given her, made for the present no fresh attempt to come, by her own aid, at a bird's-eye view of her character and scheme of life. His curiosity, however, being in no degree assuaged concerning the odd human animal whose spoor he had for the moment failed to track, he meditated how best to renew the attempt in London. Not small, therefore, was his annoyance to find, a few days after his arrival, that she was no longer in the house. He questioned his wife as to the cause of her absence, and told her she was utterly heartless in refusing her leave to go and nurse her friend; whereupon Hesper, neither from desire to do right nor from regard to her husband's opinion, but because she either saw or fancied she saw that, now Mary did not dress her, she no longer caused the same sensation on entering a room, resolved to write to her—as if taking it for granted she had meant to return as soon as she was able. And to prick the sides of this intent came another spur, as will be seen from the letter she wrote:

"Dear Mary, can you tell me what is become of my large sapphire ring? I have never seen it since you brought my case up with you from Cornwall. I have been looking for it all the morning, but in vain. You *must* have it. I shall be lost without it, for you know it has not its equal for color and brilliance. I do not believe you intended for a moment to keep it, but only to punish me for thinking I could do without you. If so, you have your revenge, for I find I can not do without either of you—you or the ring—so you will not carry the joke further than I can bear. If you can not come at once, write and tell me it is safe, and I shall love you more than ever. I am dying to see you again. Yours faithfully, H. R."

By this time, Letty was much better, and Tom no longer required such continuous attention; Mary, therefore, betook herself at once to Mr. Redmain's. Hesper was out shopping, and Mary went to her own room to wait for her, where she was glad of the opportunity of getting at some of the things she had left behind her.

While she was looking for what she wanted, Sepia entered, and was, or pretended to be, astonished to see her. In a strange, sarcastic tone:

"Ah, you there!" she said. "I hope you will find it."

"If you mean the ring, that is not likely, Miss Yolland," Mary answered.

Sepia was silent a moment or two, then said :

"How is your cousin ?"

"I have no cousin," replied Mary.

"The person, I mean, you have been staying with ? "

"Better, thank you."

"Almost a pity, is it not—if there should come trouble about this ring ?"

"I do not understand you. The ring will, of course, be found," returned Mary.

"In any case the blame will come on you : it was in your charge."

"The ring was in the case when I left."

"You will have to prove that."

"I remember quite well."

"That no one will question."

Beginning at last to understand her insinuations, Mary was so angry that she dared not speak.

"But it will hardly go to clear you," Sepia went on. "Don't imagine I mean you have taken it, I am only warning you how the matter will look, that you may be prepared. Mr. Redmain is one to believe the worst things of the best people."

"I am obliged to you," said Mary, "but I am not anxious "

"It is necessary you should know also," continued Sepia, "that there is some suspicion attaching to a female friend of yours as well, a young woman who used to visit you—the wife of the other, it is supposed. She was here, I remember, one night there was a party ; I saw you together in my cousin's bedroom. She had just dressed and gone down."

"I remember," said Mary. "It was Mrs. Helmer. Well ?"

"It is very unfortunate, certainly ; but the truth must be told : a few days before you left, one of the servants, hearing some one in the house in the middle of the night, got up and went down, but only in time to hear the front door open and shut. In the morning a hat was found in the drawing-room, with the name *Thomas Helmer* in it : that is the name of your friend's husband, I believe ?"

"I am aware Mr. Helmer was a frequent visitor," said Mary, trying to keep cool for what was to come.

This that Sepia told her was true enough, though she was not accurate as to the time of its occurrence. I will relate briefly how it came about.

Upon a certain evening, a few days before Mary's return from Cornwall, Tom would have gone to see Miss Yolland had he not known that she meant to go to the play with a Mr. Emmet, a cousin of the Redmains. Before the hour arrived, however, Count Galofta called, and Sepia went out with him, telling the man who opened the door to ask Mr. Emmet to wait. The man was rather deaf, and did not catch with certainty the name she gave. Mr. Emmet did not appear, and it was late before Sepia returned.

Tom, jealous even to hatred, spent the greater part of his evening in a tavern on the borders of the city—in gloomy solitude, drinking brandy-and-water, and building castles of the most foolish type—for castles are as different as the men that build them. Through all the rooms of them glided the form of Sepia, his evil genius. He grew more and more excited as he built, and as he drank. He rose at last, paid his bill, and, a little suspicious of his equilibrium, stalked into the street. There, almost unconsciously, he turned and walked westward. It was getting late ; before long the theatres would be emptying : he might have a peep of Sepia as she came out !—but where was the good when that fellow was with her ! "But," thought Tom, growing more and more daring as in an adventurous dream, " why should I not go to the house, and see her after he has left her at the door ?"

He went to the house and rang the bell. The man came, and said immediately that Miss Yolland was out, but had desired him to ask Mr. Helmer to wait ; whereupon Tom walked in, and up the stair to the drawing-room, thence into a second and a third drawing-room, and from the last into the conservatory. The man went down and finished his second pint of ale. From the conservatory, Tom, finding himself in danger of havoc among the flower-pots, turned back into the third room, threw himself on a couch, and fell fast asleep.

He woke in the middle of the night in pitch darkness: and it was some time before he could remember where he was. When he did, he recognized that he was in an awkward predicament. But he knew the house well, and would make the attempt to get out undiscovered. It was foolish, but Tom was foolish. Feeling his way, he knocked down a small table with a great crash of china, and, losing his equanimity, rushed for the stair. Happily the hall lamp was still alight, and he found no trouble with bolts or lock: the door was not any way secured.

The first breath of the cold night-air brought with it such a gush of joy as he had rarely experienced; and he trod the silent streets with something of the pleasure of an escaped criminal, until, alas! the wind, at the first turning, let him know that he had left his hat behind him! He felt as if he had committed a murder, and left his card-case with the body. A vague terror grew upon him as he hurried along. Justice seemed following on his track. He had found the door on the latch: if anything was missing, how should he explain the presence of his hat without his own? The devil of the brandy he had drunk was gone out of him, and only the gray ashes of its evil fire were left in his sick brain, but it had helped first to kindle another fire, which was now beginning to glow unsuspected—that of a fever whose fuel had been slowly gathering for some time.

He opened the door with his pass-key, and hurried up the stair, his long legs taking three steps at a time. Never before had he felt as if he were fleeing to a refuge when going home to his wife.

He opened the door of the sitting-room—and there on the floor lay Letty and little Tom, as I have already told.

" Why have I heard nothing of this before ? " said Mary

" I am not aware of any right you have to know what happens in this house."

" Not to   M   not

from Mrs. Redmain ; but the servants talk of most things, and
I have not heard a word—"

"How could you," interrupted Sepia, when you were not
in the house ?—And, so long as nothing was missed, the thing
was of no consequence," she added. "Now it is different."

This confused Mary a little. She stopped to consider. One
thing was clear—that, if the ring was not lost till after she left
—and of so much she was sure—it could not be Tom that had
taken it, for he was then ill in bed. Something to this effect
she managed to say.

"I told you already," returned Sepia, "that I had no suspicion of him—at least, I desire to have none, but you may be
required to prove all you say ; and it is as well to let you understand—though there is no reason why *I* should take the trouble
—that your going to those very people at the time, and their
proving to be friends of yours, adds to the difficulty."

"How ?" asked Mary.

"I am not on the jury," replied Sepia, with indifference.

The scope of her remarks seemed to Mary intended to show
that any suspicion of her would only be natural. For the moment the idea amused her. But Sepia's way of talking about
Tom, whatever she meant by it, was disgraceful !

"I am astonished you should seem so indifferent," she said,
"if the character of a gentleman with whom you have been so
intimate is so seriously threatened as you would imply. I know
he has been to see you more than once while Mr. and Mrs. Redmain were not yet returned."

Sepia's countenance changed ; an evil fire glowed in her
eyes, and she looked at Mary as if she would search her to the
bone. The poorer the character, the more precious the repute !

"The foolish fellow," she returned, with a smile of contempt, "chose to fall in love with me !—A married man, too !"

"If you understood that, how did he come to be here so
often ?" asked Mary, looking her in the face.

But Sepia knew better than declare war a moment before it
was unavoidable.

"Have I not just told you," she said, in a haughty tone,
"that the man was in love with me ?"

"And have you not just told me he was a married man? Could he have come to the house so often without at least your permission?"

Mary was actually taking the upper hand with her! Sepia felt it with scarcely repressible rage.

"He deserved the punishment," she replied, with calmness.

"You do not seem to have thought of his wife!"

"Certainly not. She never gave me offense."

"Is offense the only ground for casting a regard on a fellow-creature?"

"Why should I think of her?"

"Because she was your neighbor, and you were doing her a wrong."

"Once for all, Marston," cried Sepia, overcome at last, "this kind of thing will not do with me. I may not be a saint, but I have honesty enough to know the genuine thing from humbug. You have thrown dust in a good many eyes in this house, but *none* in mine."

By this time Mary had got her temper quite in hand, taking a lesson from the serpent, who will often keep his when the dove loses hers. She hardly knew what fear was, for she had in her something a little stronger than what generally goes by the name of faith She was therefore able to see that she ought, if possible, to learn Sepia's object in talking thus to her.

"Why do you say all this to me?" she asked, quietly. "I can not flatter myself it is from friendship."

"Certainly not. But the motive may be worthy, for all that. You are not the only one involved. People who would pass for better than their neighbors will never believe any good purpose in one who does not choose to talk their slang."

Sepia had repressed her rage, and through it looked aggrieved. "She confesses to a purpose," said Mary to herself, and waited.

"They are not all villains who are not saints," Sepia went on. "—This man's wife is your friend?"

"She is."

"Well, the man himself is my friend—in a sort of a sense."

A strange shiver went through Mary, and seemed to make her angry. Sepia went on :

"I confess I allowed the poor boy—he is little more—to talk foolishly to me. I was amused at first, but perhaps I have not quite escaped unhurt ; and, as a woman, you must understand that, when a woman has once felt in that way, if but for a moment, she would at least be—sorry—" Here her voice faltered, and she did not finish the sentence, but began afresh : "What I want of you is, through his wife, or any way you think best, to let the poor fellow know he had better slip away—to France, say—and stop there till the thing blow over."

"But why should you imagine he has had anything to do with the matter ? The ring will be found, and then the hat will not signify."

"Well," replied Sepia, putting on an air of openness, and for that sake an air of familiarity, "I see I must tell you the whole truth. I never did for a moment believe Mr. Helmer had anything to do with the business, though, when you put me out of temper, I pretended to believe it, and that you were in it as well : that was mere irritation. But there is sure to be trouble ; for my cousin is miserable about her sapphire, which she values more than anything she has ; and, if it is not found, the affair will be put into the hands of the police, and then what will become of poor Mr. Helmer, be he as innocent as you and I believe him ! Even if the judge should declare that he leaves the court without a blot on his character, Newgate mud is sure to stick, and he will be *half* looked upon as a thief for the rest of his days : the world is so unjust. Nor is that all ; for they will put you in the witness-box, and make you confess the man an old friend of yours from the same part of the country ; whereupon the counsel for the prosecution will not fail to hint that you ought to be standing beside the accused. Believe me, Mary, that, if Mr. Helmer is taken up for this, you will not come out of it clean."

"Still you explain nothing," said Mary. "You would not have me believe it is for my sake you are giving yourself all this trouble ? "

"No. But I thought you would see where I was leading you. For—and now for the *whole* truth—although nothing can touch the character of one in my position, it would be worse than awkward for me to be spoken of in connection with the poor fellow's visits to the house : *my* honesty would not be called in question as yours would, but what is dear to me as my honesty might—nay, it certainly would. You see now why I came to you !—You must go to his wife, or, better still, to Mr. Helmer himself, and tell him what I have been saying to you. He will at once see the necessity of disappearing for a while."

Mary had listened attentively. She could not help fearing that something worse than unpleasant might be at hand ; but she did not believe in Sepia, and in no case could consent that Tom should compromise himself. Danger of this kind must be met, not avoided. Still, whatever could be done ought to be done to protect him, especially in his present critical state. A breath of such a suspicion as this reaching him might be the death of him, and of Letty, too.

"I will think over what you have said," she answered ; "but I can not give him the advice you wish me. What I shall do I can not say—the thing has come upon me with such a shock."

"You have no choice that I see," said Sepia. "It is either what I propose or ruin. I give you fair warning that I will stick at nothing where my reputation is concerned. You and yours shall be trod in the dirt before I allow a spot on my character !"

To Mary's relief they were here interrupted by the hurried entrance of Mrs. Redmain. She almost ran up to her, and took her by both hands.

"You dear creature ' You have brought me my ring !" she cried

Mary shook her head with a little sigh.

"But you have come to tell me where it is ?"

"Alas ! no, dear Mrs. Redmain !" said Mary.

"Then you must find it," she said, and turned away with an ominous-looking frown.

"I will do all I can to help you find it."

"Oh, you *must* find it! My jewel-case was in your charge."

"But there has been time to lose everything in it, the one after the other, since I gave it up. The sapphire ring was there, I know, when I went."

"That can not be. You gave me the box, and I put it away myself, and, the next time I looked in it, it was not there."

"I wish I had asked you to open it when I gave it you," said Mary.

"I wish you had," said Hesper. "But the ring must be found, or I shall send for the police."

"I will not make matters worse, Mrs. Redmain," said Mary, with as much calmness as she could assume, and much was needed, "by pointing out what your words imply. If you really mean what you say, it is I who must insist on the police being sent for."

"I am sure, Mary," said Sepia, speaking for the first time since Hesper's entrance, "that your mistress has no intention of accusing you."

"Of course not," said Hesper; "only, what am I to do? I must have my ring. Why did you come, if you had nothing to tell me about it?"

"How could I stay away when you were in trouble? Have you searched everywhere?"

"Everywhere I can think of."

"Would you like me to help you look? I feel certain it will be found."

"No, thank you. I am sick of looking."

"Shall I go, then?—What would you like me to do?"

"Go to your room, and wait till I send for you."

"I must not be long away from my invalids," said Mary, as cheerfully as she could.

"Oh, indeed! I thought you had come back to your work!"

"I did not understand from your letter you wished that, ma'am—though, indeed, I could not have come just yet in any case."

"Then you mean to go, and leave things just as they are?"

"I am afraid there is no help for it. If I could do anything—. But I will call again to-morrow, and every day till the ring is found, if you like."

"Thank you," said Hesper, dryly : "I don't think that would be of much use."

"I will call anyhow," returned Mary, "and inquire whether you would like to see me.—I will go to my room now, and while I wait will get some things I want."

"As you please," said Hesper.

Scarcely was Mary in her room, however, when she heard the door, which had the trick of falling-to of itself, closed and locked, and knew that she was a prisoner. For one moment a frenzy of anger overcame her : the next, she remembered where her life was hid, knew that nothing could touch her, and was calm. While she took from her drawers the things she wanted, and put them in her hand-bag, she heard the door unlocked, but, as no one entered, she sat down to wait what would next arrive.

Mrs. Redmain, as soon as she was aware of her loss, had gone in her distress to tell her husband, whose gift the ring had been. Unlike his usual self, he had showed interest in the affair. She attributed this to the value of the jewel, and the fact that he had himself chosen it ; he was rather, and thought himself very, knowing in stones ; and the sapphire was in truth a most rare one : but it was for quite other reasons that Mr. Redmain cared about its loss : it would, he hoped, like the famous carbuncle, cast a light all round it.

He was as yet by no means well, and had not been from the house since his return.

The moment Mary was out of the room, Hesper rose.

"I should be a fool to let her leave the house," she said.

"Hesper, you will do nothing but mischief," cried Sepia.

Hesper paid no attention, but, going after Mary, locked the door of her room, and, running to her husband's, told him she had made her a prisoner.

No sooner was she in her husband's room than Sepia hastened to unlock Mary's door : but, just as she did so, she heard some one on the stair above, and retreated without going in. She would then have turned the key again, but now she heard steps on the stair below, and once more withdrew.

Mary heard a knock at her door. Mewks entered. He brought a request from his master that she would go to his room.

She rose and went, taking her bag with her.

"You may go now, Mrs. Redmain," said her husband when Mary entered. "Get out, Mewks," he added; and both lady and valet disappeared.

"So!" he said, with a grin of pleasure. "Here's a pretty business! You may sit down, though. You haven't got the ring in that bag there?"

"Nor anywhere else, sir," answered Mary. "Shall I shake it out on the floor?—or on the sofa would be better."

"Nonsense! You don't imagine me such a fool as to suppose, if you had it, you would carry it about in your bag!"

"You don't believe I have it, sir—do you?" she returned, in a tone of appeal.

"How am I to know what to believe? There is something dubious about you—you have yourself all but admitted that: how am I to know that robbery mayn't be your little dodge? All that rubbish you talked down at Lychford about honesty, and taking no wages, and loving your mistress, and all that rot, looks devilish like something off the square! That ring, now, the stone of it alone, is worth seven hundred pounds: one might let pretty good wages go for a chance like that!"

Mary looked him in the face, and made him no answer. He spied a danger: if he irritated her, he would get nothing out of her!

"My girl," he said, changing his tone, "I believe you know nothing about the ring; I was only teasing you."

Mary could not help a sigh of relief, and her eyes fell, for she felt them beginning to fill. She could not have believed that the judgment of such a man would ever be of consequence to her. But the unity of the race is a thing that can not be broken.

Now, although Mr. Redmain was by no means so sure of her innocence as he had pretended, he did at least wish and hope to find her innocent—from no regard for her, but because there was another he would be more glad to find concerned in the ugly affair.

"Mrs. Redmain," he went on, "would have me hand you over to the police, but I won't. You may go home when you please, and you need fear nothing."

He had the house where the Helmers lodged already watched, and knew this much, that some one was ill there, and that the doctor came almost every day.

"I certainly shall fear nothing," said Mary, not quite trusting him; "my fate is in God's hands."

"We know all about that," said Mr. Redmain; "I'm up to most dodges. But look here, my girl, it wouldn't be prudent in me, lest there should be such a personage as you have just mentioned, to be hard upon any of my fellow-creatures I am one day pretty sure to be in misfortune myself. You mightn't think it of me, but I am not quite a heathen, and do reflect a little at times. You may be as wicked as myself, or as good as Joseph, for anything I know or care, for, as I say, it ain't my business to judge you. Tell me now what you are up to, and I will make it the better for you."

Mary had been trying hard to get at what he was "up to," but found herself quite bewildered.

"I am sorry, sir," she faltered, "but I haven't the slightest idea what you mean."

"Then you go home," he said. "I will send for you when I want you."

The moment she was out of the room, he rang his bell violently. Mewks appeared.

"Go after that young woman—do you hear? You know her—Miss—damn it, what's her name?—Harland or Cranston, or—oh, hang it! you know well enough, you rascal!"

"Do you mean Miss Marston, sir?"

"Of course I do! Why didn't you say so before? Go after her, I tell you; and make haste. If she goes straight home—you know where—come back as soon as she's inside the door."

"Yes, sir."

"Damn you, go, or you'll lose sight of her!"

"I'm a-listenin' after the street-door, sir. It ain't gone yet. There it is now!"

And with the word he left the room.

Mary was too much absorbed in her own thoughts to note that she was followed by a man with the collar of his great-coat up to his eyes, and a woolen comforter round his face. She walked on steadily for home, scarce seeing the people that passed her. It was clear to Mewks that she had not a suspicion of being kept in sight. He saw her in at her own door, and went back to his master.

CHAPTER XLIV.

JOSEPH JASPER.

ANOTHER fact Mewks carried to his master—namely, that, as Mary came near the door of the house, she was met by "a rough-looking man," who came walking slowly along, as if he had been going up and down waiting for her. He made her an awkward bow as she drew near, and she stopped and had a long conversation with him—such at least it seemed to Mewks, annoyed that he could hear nothing of it, and fearful of attracting their attention—after which the man went away, and Mary went into the house. This report made his master grin, for, through the description Mewks gave, he suspected a thief disguised as a workman; but, his hopes being against the supposition, he dwelt the less upon it.

The man who stopped Mary, and whom, indeed, she would have stopped, was Joseph Jasper, the blacksmith. That he was rough in appearance, no one who knew him would have wished himself able to deny, and one less like a thief would have been hard to find. His hands were very rough and in-grained with black; his fingers were long, but chopped off square at the points, and had no resemblance to the long, tapering fingers of an artist or pickpocket. His clothes were of corduroy, not *very* grimy, because of the huge apron of thick leather he wore at his work, but they looked none the better that he had topped them with his tall Sunday hat. His complexion was a mixture of brown and browner; his black eyebrows hung far over the blackest of eyes, the brightest flashing of which was never seen, because all the time he played he kept them closed tight. His face wore its natural clothing—a mustache thick and well-shaped, and a beard not too large, of a color that looked like black burned brown. His hair was black and curled all over his head. His whole appearance was that of a workman; a careless glance could never have suspected him a poet-musician; as little could even such a glance have failed to see in him an honest man. He was powerfully built, over the middle height, but not tall. He spoke very fair old-fashioned English, with the Yorkshire tone and turn. His walk was rather plodding, and his movements slow and stiff; but in communion with his violin they were free enough, and the more delicate for the strength that was in them; at the anvil they were as supple as powerful. On his face dwelt an expression that was not to be read by the indifferent—a waiting in the midst of work, as of a man to whom the sense of the temporary was always present, but present with the constant reminder that, just therefore, work must be as good as work can be that things may last their due time.

The following was the conversation concerning the purport of which Mewks was left to what conjecture was possible to a serving-man of his stamp.

Mary held out her hand to Jasper, and it disappeared in his. He held it for a moment with a great but gentle grasp, and, as he let it go, said:

"I took the liberty of watching for you, miss. I wanted to ask a favor of you. It seemed to me you would take no offense."

"You might be sure of that," Mary answered. "You have a right to anything I can do for you."

He fixed his gaze on her for a moment, as if he did not understand her.

"That's where it is," he said : "I've *done* nothing for your people. It's all very well to go playing and playing, but that's not doing anything ; and, if *he* had done nothing, there would ha' been no fiddling. You understand me, miss, I know : work comes before music, and makes the soul of it ; it's not the music that makes the doing. I'm a poor hand at saying without my fiddle, miss : you'll excuse me."

Mary's heart was throbbing. She had not heard a word like this—not since her father went to what people call the "long home"—as if a home could be too long ! What do we want but an endless home ?—only it is not the grave ! She felt as if the spirit of her father had descended on the strange workman, and had sent him to her. She looked at him with shining eyes, and did not speak. He resumed, as fearing he had not conveyed his thought.

"What I think I mean is, miss, that, if the working of miracles in his name wouldn't do it, it's not likely playing the fiddle will."

"Oh, I understand you so well !" said Mary, in a voice hardly her own, " —so well ! It makes me happy to hear you ! Tell me what I can do for you."

"The poor gentleman in there must want all the help you can give him, and more. There must be something left, surely, for a man to do. He must want lifting at times, for instance, and that's not fit for either of you ladies."

"Thank you," said Mary, heartily. "I will mention it to Mrs. Helmer, and I am sure she will be very glad of your help sometimes."

"Couldn't you ask her now, miss ? I should like to know at what hour I might call. But perhaps the best way would be to walk about here in the evening, after my day's work is over, and then you could run down any time, and look out : that would be enough ; I should be there. Saturday nights I could just as well be there all night."

To Tom and Letty it seemed not a little peculiar that a man so much a stranger should be ready to walk about the street in order to be at hand with help for them ; but Mary was only delighted, not surprised, for what the man had said to her made the thing not merely intelligible, but absolutely reasonable.

Joseph was not, however, allowed to wander the street. The arrangement made was, that, as soon as his work was over, he should come and see whether there was anything he could do for them. And he never came but there was plenty to do. He took a lodging close by, that he might be with them earlier, and stay later ; and, when nothing else was wanted of him, he was always ready to discourse on his violin. Sometimes Tom enjoyed his music much, though he found no little fault with his mode of playing, for Tom knew something about everything, and could render many a reason ; at other times, he preferred having Mary read to him.

On one of these latter occasions, Mary, occupied in cooking something for the invalid, asked Joseph to read for her. He consented, but read very badly—as if he had no understanding of the words, but, on the other hand, stopping every few lines, apparently to think and master what he had read. This was not good reading anyway, least of all for an invalid who required the soothing of half-thought, molten and diluted in sweet, even, monotonous sound, and it was long before Mary asked him again.

Many things showed that he had had little education, and therefore probably the more might be made of him. Mary saw that he must be what men call a genius, for his external history had been, by his own showing, of an altogether commonplace type.

His father, who was a blacksmith before him, and a local preacher, had married a second time, and Joseph was the only child of the second marriage. His father had brought him up to his own trade, and, after his death, Joseph came to work in London, whither his sister had preceded him. He was now thirty, and had from the first been saving what he could of his wages in the hope of one day having a smithy of his own, and his time more at his ordering.

Mary saw too that in his violin he possessed a grand fundamental undeveloped education ; he was like a man going about the world with a ten-thousand-pound-note in his pocket, and not many sixpences to pay his way with. But there was another education working in him far deeper, and already more developed, than that which divine music even was giving him; this also Mary thoroughly recognized; this it was in him that chiefly attracted her; and the man himself knew it as underlying all his consciousness.

Though he could ill read aloud, he could read well for his inward nourishment; he could write tolerably, and, if he could not spell, that mattered a straw, and no more; he had never read a play of Shakespeare—had never seen a play; knew nothing of grammar or geography—or of history, except the one history comprising all. He knew nothing of science; but he could shoe a horse as well as any man in the three Ridings, and make his violin talk about things far beyond the ken of most men of science.

So much of a change had passed upon Tom in his illness, that Mary saw it not unreasonable to try upon him now and then a poem of her favorite singer. Occasionally, of course, the feeling was altogether beyond him, but even then he would sometimes enter into the literary merit of the utterance.

"I had no idea there were such gems in George Herbert, Mary!" he said once. "I declare, some of them are even in their structure finer than many things that have nothing in them to admire except the structure."

"That is not to be wondered at," replied Mary.

"No," said Joseph; "it is not to be wondered at; for it's clear to me the old gentleman plied a good bow. I can see that plain enough."

"Tell us how you see it," said Mary, more interested than she would have liked to show.

"Easily," he answered. "There was one poem "—he pronounced it *pome*—"you read just now—"

"Which? which?" interrupted Mary, eagerly.

"That I can not tell you; but, all the time you were reading it, I heard the gentleman—Mr. George Herbert, you call him—playing the tune to it."

"If you heard him so well," ventured Mary, "you could, I fancy, play the tune over again to us."

"I think I could," he answered, and, rising, went for his instrument, which he always brought, and hung on an old nail in the wall the moment he came in.

He played a few bars of a prelude, as if to get himself into harmony with the recollection of what he had heard the master play, and then began a lively melody, in which he seemed as usual to pour out his soul. Long before he reached the end of it, Mary had reached the poem.

"This is the one you mean, is it not?" she said, as soon as he had finished—and read it again.

In his turn he did not speak till she had ended.

"That's it, miss," he said then: "I can't mistake it; for, the minute you began, there was the old gentleman again with his fiddle."

"And you know now what it says, don't you?" asked Mary.

"I heard nothing but the old gentleman," answered the musician

Mary turned to Tom.

"Would you mind if I tried to show Mr. Jasper what I see in the poem? He can't get a hold of it himself for the master's violin in his ears; it won't let him think about it."

"I should like myself to hear what you have got to say about it, Mary! Go on," said Tom.

Mary had now for a long time been a student of George Herbert; and anything of a similar life-experience goes infinitely further, to make one understand another, than any amount of learning or art. Therefore, better than many a poet, Mary was able to set forth the scope and design of this one. Herself at the heart of the secret from which came all his utterance, she could fit herself into most of the convolutions of the shell of his expression, and was hence able also to make others perceive in his verse not a little of what they were of themselves unable to see.

"We shall have you lecturing at the Royal Institution yet, Mary," said Tom; "only it will be long before its members care for that sort of antique."

Tom's insight had always been ahead of his character, and

of late he had been growing. People do grow very fast in bed sometimes. Also he had in him plenty of material, to which a childlike desire now began to give shapes and sequences.

The musician's remark consisted in taking his violin, and once more giving his idea of the "old gentleman's" music, but this time with a richer expression and fuller harmonics. Mary had every reason to be satisfied with her experiment. From that time she talked a good deal more about her favorite writers, and interested both the critical taste of Tom and the artistic instinct of the blacksmith.

But Joseph's playing had great faults : how could it be otherwise ?—and to Mary great seemed the pity that genius should not be made perfect in faculty, that it should not have that redemption of its body for which unwittingly it groaned. And the man was one of those childlike natures which may indeed go a long time without discovering this or that external fault in themselves, patent to the eye of many an inferior on-looker—for the simple soul is the last to see its own outside—but, once they become aware of it, begin that moment to set the thing right. At the same time he had not enough of knowledge to render it easy to show him by words wherein any fault consisted—the nature, the being of the fault, that is—what it simply was ; but Mary felt confident that, the moment he saw a need, he would obey its law.

She had taken for herself the rooms below, formerly occupied by the Helmers, with the hope of seeing them before long reinstated in them ; and there she had a piano, the best she could afford to hire : with its aid she hoped to do something toward the breaking of the invisible bonds that tied the wings of Jasper's genius.

His great fault lay in his time. Dare I suggest that he contented himself with measuring it to his inner ear, and let his fingers, like horses which he knew he had safe in hand, play what pranks they pleased ? A reader may, I think, be measuring verse correctly to himself, and yet make of it nothing but rugged prose to his hearers. Perhaps this may be how severe masters of quantity in the abstract are so careless of it in the concrete—in the audible, namely, where alone it is of value. Shall I analogize yet a little further, and suggest the many who admire righteousness and work iniquity ; who say, " Lord, Lord," and seldom or never obey ? Anyhow, a man may have a good enough ear, with which he holds all the time a secret understanding, and from carelessness offend grievously the ears he ought to please ; and it was thus with Joseph Jasper.

Mary was too wise to hurry anything. One evening when he came as usual, and she knew he was not at the moment wanted, she asked him to take a seat while she played something to him. But she was not a little disappointed in the reception he gave her offering—a delicate morsel from Beethoven. She tried something else, but with no better result. He showed little interest : he was not a man capable of showing where nothing was, for he never meant to show anything ; his expression was only the ripple of the unconscious pool to the sway and swirl of the fishes below. It seemed as if he had only a narrow entrance for the admission of music into his understanding—but a large outlet for the spring that rose within him, and was, therefore, a somewhat remarkable exception to the common run of mortals : in such, the capacity for reception far exceeds the capability of production. His dominant thoughts were in musical form, and easily found their expression in music : but, mainly no doubt from want of practice in reception, and experience of variety in embodiment, the forms in which others gave themselves utterance could not with corresponding readiness find their way to the sympathetic place in him. But pride or repulsion had no share in this defect. The man was open and inspired, and stupid as a child.

The next time she made the attempt to open this channel between them, something she played did find him, and for a few minutes he seemed lost in listening.

" How nice it would be," she said, " if we could play together sometimes ! "

" Do you mean both at once, miss ? " he asked.

" Yes—you on your violin, and I on the piano."

" That could hardly be, I'm afraid, miss," he answered ;

"for, you see, I don't know always—not exactly—what I'm going to play; and if I don't know, and you don't know, how are we to keep together?"

"Nobody can play your own things but yourself, of course —that is, until you are able to write them down; but, if you would learn something, we could play that together."

"I don't know how to learn. I've heard tell of the notes and all that, but I don't know how to work them."

"You have heard the choir in the church—all keeping with the organ," said Mary.

"Scarcely since I was a child—and not very often then— though my mother took me sometimes. But I was always wanting to get out again, and gave no heed."

"Do you never go to church now?"

"No, miss—not for long. Time's too precious to waste."

"How do you spend it, then?"

"As soon as I've had my breakfast—that's on a Sunday, I mean—I get up and lock my door, and set myself to have a day of it. Then I read the next thing where I stopped last— whether it be a chapter or a verse—till I get the sense of it—if I can't get that, it's no manner of use to me; and I generally know when I've got it by finding the bow in one hand and the fiddle in the other. Then, with the two together, I go stirring and stirring about at the story, and the music keeps coming and coming; and when it stops, which it does sometimes all at once, then I go back to the book."

"But you don't go on like that all day, do you?" said Mary.

"I generally go on till I'm hungry, and then I go out for something to eat. My landlady won't get me any dinner. Then I come back and begin again."

"Will you let me teach you to read music?" said Mary, more and more delighted with him, and desirous of contributing to his growth—the one great service of the universe.

"If you would, miss, perhaps then I might be able to learn. You see, I never was like other people. Mother was the only one that didn't take me for an innocent. She used to talk big things about me, and the rest used to laugh at her. She gave me her large Testament when she was dying, but, if it hadn't been for Ann, I should never have been able to read it well enough to understand it. And now Ann tells me I'm a heathen and worship my fiddle, because I don't go to chapel with her ; but it do seem such a waste of good time. I'll go to church, though, miss, if you tell me it's the right thing to do ; only it's hard to work all the week, and be weary all the Sunday. I should only be longing for my fiddle all the time. You don't think, miss, that a great person like God cares whether we pray to him in a loom or in a church ? "

"No, I don't," answered Mary. " For my own part, I find I can pray best at home."

"So can I," said Joseph, with solemn fervor. " Indeed, miss, I can't pray at all sometimes till I get my fiddle under my chin, and then it says the prayers for me till I grow able to pray myself. And sometimes, when I seem to have got to the outside of prayer, and my soul is hungrier than ever, only I can't tell what I want, all at once I'm at my fiddle again, and it's praying for me. And then sometimes it seems as if I lost myself altogether, and God took me, for I'm nowhere and everywhere all at once."

Mary thought of the "groanings that can not be uttered." Perhaps that is just what music is meant for—to say the things that have no shape, therefore can have no words, yet are intensely alive—the unembodied children of thought, the eternal child. Certainly the musician can groan the better with the aid of his violin. Surely this man's instrument was the gift of God to him. All God's gifts are a giving of himself. The Spirit can better dwell in a violin than in an ark or in the mightiest of temples.

But there was another side to the thing, and Mary felt bound to present it.

" But, you know, Mr. Jasper," she said, " when many violins play together, each taking a part in relation to all the rest, a much grander music is the result than any single instrument could produce."

" I've heard tell of such things, miss, but I've never heard them."

He had never been to concert or oratorio, any more than the play.

"Then you shall hear them," said Mary, her heart filling with delight at the thought. "—But what if there should be some way in which the prayers of all souls may blend like many violins? We are all brothers and sisters, you know—and what if the gathering together in church be one way of making up a concert of souls?—Imagine one mighty prayer, made up of all the desires of all the hearts God ever made, breaking like a huge wave against the foot of his throne!"

"There would be some force in a wave like that, miss!" said Joseph. "But answer me one question: Ain't it Christ that teaches men to pray?"

"Surely," answered Mary. "He taught them with his mouth when he was on the earth; and now he teaches them with his mind."

"Then, miss, I will tell you why it seems to me that churches can't be the places to tune the fiddles for that kind of consort—and that's just why I more than don't care to go into one of them: I never heard a sermon that didn't seem to be taking my Christ from me, and burying him where I should never find him any more. For the somebody the clergy talk about is not only nowise like my Christ, but nowise like a live man at all. It always seemed to me more like a guy they had dressed up and called by his name than the man I read about in my mother's big Testament."

"How my father would have delighted in this man!" said Mary to herself.

"You see, miss," Jasper resumed, "I can't help knowing something about these matters, because I was brought up in it all, my father being a local preacher, and a very good man. Perhaps, if I had been as clever as Sister Ann, I might be thinking now just as she does; but it seems to me a man that is born stupid has much to be thankful for: he can't take in things before his heart's ready for believing them, and so they don't get spoiled, like a child's book before he is able to read it. All that I heard when I went with my father to his preachings was to me no more than one of the chapters full of names in the Book of Chronicles—though I do remember once hearing a Wesleyan clergyman say that he had got great spiritual benefit from those chapters. I wasn't even frightened at the awful things my father said about hell, and the certainty of our going there if we didn't lay hold upon the Saviour; for, all the time, he showed but such a ghost or cloud of a man that he called the Saviour as it wasn't possible to lay hold upon. Not that I reasoned about it that way then; I only felt no interest in the affair; and my conscience said nothing about it. But after my father and mother were gone, and I was at work away from all my old friends—well, I needn't trouble you with what it was that set me a-thinking—it was only a great disappointment, such as I suppose most young fellows have to go through—I shouldn't wonder," he added with a smile, "if that was what you ladies are sent into this world for—to take the conceit out of the likes of us, and give us something to think about. What came of it was, that I began to read my mother's big Testament in earnest, and then my conscience began to speak. Here was a man that said he was God's son, and sent by him to look after us, and we must do what he told us or we should never be able to see our Father in heaven! That's what I made out of it, miss. And my conscience said to me, that I must do as he said, seeing he had taken all that trouble, and come down to look after us. If he spoke the truth, and nobody could listen to him without being sure of that, there was nothing left but just to do the thing he said. So I set about getting a hold of anything he did say, and trying to do it. And then it was that I first began to be able to play on the fiddle, though I had been muddling away at it for a long time before. I knew I could play then, because I understood what it said to me, and got help out of it. I don't really mean that, you know, miss; for I know well enough that the fiddle in itself is nothing, and nothing is anything but the way God takes to teach us. And that's how I came to know you, miss."

"How do you mean that?" asked Mary.

"I used to be that frightened of Sister Ann that, after I came to L · ˑ I ˑ ˑˑ ˑˑ ˑ ˑ ˑ ˑ ˑˑ at I thought Jesus Christ would have me go ; and, if I hadn't gone to see her, I should never have seen you. When I went to see her, I took my fiddle with me to take care of me ; and, when she would be going on at me, I would just give my fiddle a squeeze under my arm, and that gave me patience."

"But we heard you playing to her, you know."

"That was because I always forgot myself while she was talking. The first time, I remember, it was from misery— what she was saying sounded so wicked, making God out not fit for any honest man to believe in. I began to play without knowing it, and it couldn't have been very loud, for she went on about the devil picking up the good seed sown in the heart. Off I went into that, and there I saw no end of birds with long necks and short legs gobbling up the corn. But, a little way off, there was the long beautiful stalks growing strong and high, waving in God's wind ; and the birds did not go near them."

Mary drew a long breath, and said to herself :

"The man is a poet !"—"You're not afraid of your sister now ?" she said to him.

"Not a bit," he answered. "Since I knew you, I feel as if we had in a sort of a way changed places, and she was a little girl that must be humored and made the best of. When she scolds, I laugh, and try to make a bit of fun with her. But she's always so sure she's right, that you wonder how the world got made before she was up."

They parted with the understanding that, when he came next, she should give him his first lesson in reading music. With herself Mary made merry at the idea of teaching the man of genius his letters.

But, when once, through trying to play with her one of his own pieces which she had learned from hearing him play it, he had discovered how imperative it was to keep good time, he set himself to the task with a determination that would have made anything of him that he was only half as fit to become as a musician.

When, however, in a short time, he was able to learn from notes, he grew so delighted with some of the music Mary got for him, entering into every nicety of severest law, and finding therein a better liberty than that of improvisation, that he ceased for long to play anything of his own, and Mary became mortally afraid lest, in developing the performer, she had ruined the composer.

"How can I go playing such loose, skinny things," he would say, "when here are such perfect shapes all ready to my hand!"

But Mary said to herself that, if these were shapes, his were odors.

CHAPTER XLV.

THE SAPPHIRE.

ONE morning, as Mary sat at her piano, Mewks was shown into the room. He brought the request from his master that she would go to him; he wanted particularly to see her. She did not much like it, neither did she hesitate.

She was shown into the room Mr. Redmain called his study, which communicated by a dressing-room with his bedroom. He was seated, evidently waiting for her.

"Ah, Miss Marston!" he said; "I have a piece of good news for you—so good that I thought I should like to give it you myself."

"You are very kind, sir," Mary answered.

"There!" he went on, holding out what she saw at once was the lost ring.

"I am so glad!" she said, and took it in her hand. "Where was it found?"

"There's the point!" he returned. "That is just why I sent for you! Can you suggest any explanation of the fact that it was found, after all, in a corner of my wife's jewel-box? Who searched the box last?"

"I do not know, sir."

"Did you search it?"

"No, sir. I offered to help Mrs. Redmain to look for the ring, but she said it was no use. Who found it, sir?"

"I will tell you who found it, if you will tell me who put it there."

"I don't know what you mean, sir. It must have been there all the time."

"That's the point again! Mrs. Redmain swears it was not, and could not have been, there when she looked for it. It is not like a small thing, you see. There is something mysterious about it."

He looked hard at Mary.

Now, Mary had very much admired the ring, as any one must who had an eye for stones; and had often looked at it—into the heart of it—almost loving it; and while they were talking now, she kept gazing at it. When Mr. Redmain ended, she stood silent. In her silence, her attention concentrated itself upon the sapphire. She stood long, looking closely at it, moving it about a little, and changing the direction of the light; and, while her gaze was on the ring, Mr. Redmain's gaze was on her, watching her with equal attention. At last, with a sigh, as if she waked from a reverie, she laid the ring on the table. But Mr. Redmain still stared in her face.

"Now what is it you've got in your head?" he said at last. "I have been watching you think for three minutes and a half, I do believe. Come, out with it!"

"Hardly *think*, sir,' answered Mary. "I was only plaguing myself between my recollection of the stone and the actual look of it. It is so annoying to find what seemed a clear recollection prove a deceitful one! It may appear a presumptuous thing to say, but my recollection seems of a finer color."

While she spoke, she had again taken the ring, and was looking at it. Mr. Redmain snatched it from her hand.

"The devil!" he cried. "You haven't the face to hint that the stone has been changed?"

Mary laughed.

"Such a thing never came into my head, sir; but now that you have put it there, I could almost believe it."

"Go along with you!" he cried, casting at her a strange

look, which she could not understand, and the same moment pulling the bell hard.

That done, he began to examine the ring intently, as Mary had been doing, and did not speak a word Mewks came.

"Show Miss Marston out," said his master ; "and tell my coachman to bring the hansom round directly."

"For Miss Marston ?" inquired Mewks, who had learned not a little cunning in the service.

"No !" roared Mr. Redmain : and Mewks darted from the room, followed more leisurely by Mary.

"I don't know what's come to master '" ventured Mewks, as he led the way down the stair.

But Mary took no notice, and left the house.

For about a week she heard nothing.

In the mean time Mr. Redmain had been prosecuting certain inquiries he had some time ago begun, and another quite new one besides. He was acquainted with many people of many different sorts, and had been to jewelers and pawnbrokers, gamblers and lodging-house keepers, and had learned some things to his purpose.

Once more Mary received from him a summons, and once more, considerably against her liking, obeyed. She was less disinclined to go this time, however, for she felt not a little curious about the ring.

"I want you to come back to the house," he said, abruptly, the moment she entered his room.

For such a request Mary was not prepared. Even since the ring was found, so long a time had passed that she never expected to hear from the house again. But Tom was now so much better, and Letty so much like her former self, that, if Mrs. Redmain had asked her, she might perhaps have consented.

"Mr. Redmain," she answered, "you must see that I can not do so at your desire."

"Oh, rubbish ! humbug !" he returned, with annoyance. "Don't fancy I am asking you to go fiddle-faddling about my wife again : I don't see how you *can* do that. after the way she has used you ! But I have reasons for wanting to have you within call. Go to Mrs. Perkin I won't take a refusal."

"I can not do it, Mr. Redmain," said Mary; "the thing is impossible." And she turned to leave the room.

"Stop, stop!" cried Mr. Redmain, and jumped from his chair to prevent her.

He would not have succeeded had not Mewks met her in the doorway full in the face. She had to draw back to avoid him, and the man, perceiving at once how things were, closed the door the moment he entered, and stood with his back against it.

"He's in the drawing-room, sir," said Mewks.

A scarcely perceptible sign of question was made by the master, and answered in kind by the man.

"Show him here directly," said Mr. Redmain. Then turning to Mary, "Go out that way, Miss Marston, if you will go," he said, and pointed to the dressing-room.

Mary, without a suspicion, obeyed; but, just as she discovered that the door into the bedroom beyond was locked, she heard the door behind her locked also. She turned, and knocked.

"Stay where you are," said Mr. Redmain, in a low but imperative voice. "I can not let you out till this gentleman is gone. You must hear what passes: I want you for a witness."

Bewildered and annoyed, Mary stood motionless in the middle of the room, and presently heard a man, whose voice seemed not quite strange to her, greet Mr. Redmain like an old friend. The latter made a slight apology for having sent for him to his study—claiming the privilege, he said, of an invalid, who could not for a time have the pleasure of meeting him either at the club or at his wife's parties. The visitor answered agreeably, with a touch of merriment that seemed to indicate a soul at ease with itself and with the world.

But here Mary all at once came to herself, and was aware that she was in quite a false position. She withdrew therefore to the farthest corner, sat down, closed her ears with the palms of her hands, and waited.

She had sat thus for a long time, not weary, but occupied with such thoughts as could hardly for a century or two cross the horizon line of such a soul as Mr. Redmain's, even if he were at once to repent, when she heard a loud voice calling her name from a distance. She raised her head, and saw the white, skin-drawn face of Mr. Redmain grinning at her from the open door. When he spoke again, his words sounded like thunder, for she had removed her hands from her ears.

"I fancy you've had a dose of it !" he said.

As he spoke, she rose to her feet, her countenance illumined both with righteous anger and the tender shine of prayer. Her look went to what he had of a heart, and the slightest possible color rose to his face.

"Gone a step too far, damn it !" he murmured to himself. "There's no knowing one woman by another !"

"I see !" he said ; "it's been a trifle too much for you, and I don't wonder ! You needn't believe a word I said about myself. It was all hum to make the villain show his game."

"I have not heard a word, Mr. Redmain," she said with indignation.

"Oh, you needn't trouble yourself !" he returned. "I meant you to hear it all What did I put you there for, but to get your oath to what I drew from the fellow ? A fine thing if your pretended squeamishness ruin my plot ! What do you think of yourself, hey ?—But I don't believe it."

He looked at her keenly, expecting a response, but Mary made him none. For some moments he regarded her curiously, then turned away into the study, saying :

"Come along. By Jove ! I'm ashamed to say it, but I half begin to believe in you. I did think I was past being taken in, but it seems possible for once again. Of course, you will return to Mrs. Redmain now that all is cleared up."

"It is impossible," Mary answered "I can not live in a house where the lady mistrusts and the gentleman insults me "

She left the room, and Mr. Redmain did not try to prevent her. As she left the house she burst into tears ; and the fact Mewks carried to his master.

The man was the more careful to report everything about Mary, that there was one in the house of whom he never reported anything, but to whom, on the contrary, he told everything he thought she would care to know. Till Sepia came, he had been conventionally faithful—faithful with the faith of a lackey, that is—but she had found no difficulty in making of him, in respect of her, a spy upon his master.

I will now relate what passed while Mary sat deaf in the corner.

Mr. Redmain asked his visitor what he would have, as if, although it was quite early, he must, as a matter of course, stand in need of refreshment. He made choice of brandy and soda-water, and the bell was rung. A good deal of conversation followed about a disputed point in a late game of cards at one of the clubs.

The talk then veered in another direction—that of personal adventure, so guided by Mr. Redmain. He told extravagant stories about himself and his doings, in particular various *ruses* by which he had contrived to lay his hands on money. And whatever he told, his guest capped, narrating trick upon trick to which on different occasions he had had recourse. At all of them Mr. Redmain laughed heartily, and applauded their cleverness extravagantly, though some of them were downright swindling.

At last Mr. Redmain told how he had once got money out of a lady. I do not believe there was a word of truth in it. But it was capped by the other with a narrative that seemed specially pleasing to the listener. In the midst of a burst of laughter, he rose and rang the bell. Count Galofta thought it was to order something more in the way of "refreshment," and was not a little surprised when he heard his host desire the man to request the favor of Miss Yolland's presence. But the Count had not studied non-expression in vain, and had brought it to a degree of perfection not easily disturbed. Casting a glance at him as he gave the message, Mr. Redmain could read nothing; but this was in itself suspicious to him—and justly, for the man ought to have been surprised at such a close to the conversation they had been having.

Sepia had been told that Galofta was in the study, and therefore received the summons thither — a thing that had never happened before—with the greater alarm. She made, consequently, what preparation she could against surprise. Thoroughly capable of managing her features, her anxiety was sufficient nevertheless to deprive her of power over her complexion, and she entered the room with the pallor peculiar to the dark-skinned. Having greeted the Count with the greatest composure, she turned to Mr. Redmain with question in her eyes.

"Count Galofta," said Mr. Redmain in reply, "has just been telling me a curious story of how a certain rascal got possession of a valuable jewel from a lady with whom he pretended to be in love, and I thought the opportunity a good one for showing you a strange discovery I have made with regard to the sapphire Mrs. Redmain missed for so long. Very odd tricks are played with gems—such gems, that is, as are of value enough to make it worth a rogue's while."

So saying, he took the ring from one drawer, and from another a bottle, from which he poured something into a crystal cup. Then he took a file, and, looking at Galofta, in whose well-drilled features he believed he read something that was not mere curiosity, said, "I am going to show you something very curious," and began to file asunder that part of the ring which immediately clasped the sapphire, the setting of which was open.

"What a pity!" cried Sepia; "you are destroying the ring! What will Cousin Hesper say?"

Mr. Redmain filed away, heedless; then with the help of a pair of pincers freed the stone, and held it up in his hand.

"You see this?" he said.

"A splendid sapphire!" answered Count Galofta, taking it in his fingers, but, as Mr. Redmain saw, not looking at it closely.

"I have always heard it called a splendid stone," said Sepia, whose complexion, though not her features, passed through several changes while all this was going on: she was anxious.

Nor did her inquisitor fail to surprise the uneasy glances she threw, furtively though involuntarily, in the face of the Count—who never once looked in hers: tolerably sure of himself, he was not sure of her.

"That ring, when I bought it—the stone of it," said Mr. Redmain, "was a star sapphire, and worth seven hundred pounds; now, the whole affair is worth about ten."

As he spoke, he threw the stone into the cup, let it lie a few moments, and took it out again; when, almost with a touch, he divided it in two, the one a mere scale.

"There!" he said, holding out the thin part on the tip of a finger, "that is a slice of sapphire; and there!" holding out the rest of the seeming stone, "that is glass."

"What a shame!" cried Sepia.

"Of course," said the Count, "you will prosecute the jeweler."

"I will not prosecute the jeweler," answered Mr. Redmain; "but I have taken some trouble to find out who changed the stones."

With that he threw both the bits of blue into a drawer, and the contents of the cup into the fire. A great flame flew up the chimney, and, as if struck at the sight of it, he stood gazing for a moment after it had vanished.

When he turned, the Count was gone, as he had expected, and Sepia stood with eyes full of anger and fear. Her face was set and colorless, and strange to look upon.

"Very odd—ain't it?" said Mr. Redmain, and, opening the door of his dressing-room, called out:

"Miss Marston!"

When he turned, Sepia too was gone.

I would not have my reader take Sepia for an accomplice in the robbery. Even Mr. Redmain did not believe that: she was much too prudent! His idea was, that she had been wearing the ring — Hesper did not mind what she wore of hers—and that (I need not give his conjecture in detail), with or without her knowledge, the fellow had got hold of it and carried it away, then brought it back, treating the thing as a joke, when she was only too glad to restore it to the jewel-case, hoping the loss of it would then pass for an oversight on the part of Hesper. If he was right in this theory of the affair, then the Count had certainly a hold upon her, and she dared not or would not expose him!

He had before discovered that, about the time when the ring disappeared, the Count had had losses, and was supposed unable to meet them, but had suddenly showed himself again "flush of money," and from that time had had an extraordinary run of luck.

When he went out of the door of Mr. Redmain's study, he vanished from the house and from London. Turning the first corner he came to, and the next and the next, he stepped into a mews, the court of which seemed empty, and slipped behind the gate. He wore a new hat, and was clean shaved except his upper lip. Presently a man came out of the mews in a Scotch cap and a full beard.

What had become of him Mr. Redmain did not care. He had no desire to punish him. It was enough he had found him out, proved his suspicion correct, and obtained evidence against Sepia. He did not at once make up his mind how he would act on this last : while he lived, it did not matter so much , and he had besides a certain pleasure in watching his victim. But Hesper, free, rich, and beautiful, and far from wise, with Sepia for counselor, was not an idea to be contemplated with equanimity. Still he shrank from the outcry and scandal of sending her away : for certainly his wife, if it were but to oppose him, would refuse to believe a word against her cousin.

For the present, therefore, the thing seemed to blow over. Mr. Redmain, who had pleasure in behaving handsomely so far as money was concerned, bought his wife the best sapphire he could find, and, for once, really pleased her.

But Sepia knew that Mr. Redmain had now to himself justified his dislike of her ; and, as he said nothing, she was the more certain he meant something. She lived, therefore, in constant dread of his sudden vengeance, against which she could take no precaution, for she had not even a conjecture as to what form it might assume From that hour she was never at peace in his presence, and hardly out of it : from every possible *tête-à-tête* with him she fled as from a judgment.

Nor was it a small addition to her misery that she imagined Mary cog⋯ ⸳ ⸳⸳ f M . P ⸳ ⸳⸳ ⸳ ⸳ ⸳ ⸳⸳ ⸳ ⸳⸳ with regard to her, and holding the worst possible opinion of her. For, whatever had passed first between the Count and Mr. Redmain, she did not doubt Mary had heard, and was prepared to bring against her when the determined moment should arrive. How much the Count might or might not have said, she could not tell; but, seeing their common enemy had permitted him to escape, she more than dreaded he had sold her secret for his own impunity, and had laid upon her a burden of lies as well.

CHAPTER XLVI.

REPARATION.

WITH all Mr. Redmain's faults, there was a certain love of justice in the man; only, as is the case with most of us, it had ten times the reference to the action of other people that it had to his own: I mean, he made far greater demand for justice upon other people than upon himself; and was much more indignant at any shortcoming of theirs which crossed any desire or purpose of his than he was anxious in his own person to fulfill justice when that fulfillment in its turn would cross any wish he cherished. Badly as he had himself behaved to Mary, he was now furious with his wife for having treated her so heartlessly that she could not return to her service; for he began to think she might be one to depend upon, and to desire her alliance in the matter of ousting Sepia from the confidence of his wife.

However indifferent a woman may be to the opinion of her husband, he can nevertheless in general manage to make her uncomfortable enough if he chooses: and Mr. Redmain did choose now, in the event of her opposition to his wishes: when he set himself to do a thing, he hated defeat even more than he loved success.

The moment Mary was out of the study, he walked into his wife's boudoir, and shut the door behind him. His presence there was enough to make her angry, but she took no notice of it.

"I understand, Mrs. Redmain," he began, "that you wish to bring the fate of Sodom upon the house."

"I do not know what you mean," she answered, scarcely raising her eyes from her novel—and spoke the truth, for she knew next to nothing of the Bible, while the Old Testament was all the literature Mr. Redmain was "up in."

"You have turned out of it the only just person in it, and we shall all be in hell soon!"

"How dare you come to my room with such horrid language!"

"You'll hear worse before long, if you keep on at this rate. My language is not so bad as your actions. If you don't have that girl back, and in double-quick time, too, I shall know how to make you!"

"You have taught me to believe you capable of anything."

"You shall at least find me capable of a good deal. Do you imagine, madam, I have found you a hair worse than I expected?'

"I never took the trouble to imagine anything about you."

"Then I need not ask you whether I married you to please you or to please myself?'

"You need not. You can best answer that question yourself."

"Then we understand each other."

"We do not, Mr. Redmain; and, if this occurs again, I shall go to Durnmelling."

She spoke with a vague idea that he also stood in some awe of the father and mother whose dread, however well she hid it, she would never, while she lived, succeed in shaking off. But to the husband it was a rare delight to speak with conscious rectitude in the moral chastisement of his wife. He burst into a loud and almost merry laugh

"Happy they will be to see you there, madam! Why, you goose, if I send a telegram before you, they won't so much as open the door to you! They know better which side their bread is buttered."

Hesper started up in a rage. This was too much—and the more too much, that she believed it would be as he said.

"Mr. Redmain, if you do not leave the room, I will."

"Oh, don't!" he cried, in a tone of pretended alarm. His pleasure was great, for he had succeeded in stinging the impenetrable. "You really ought to consider before you utter such an awful threat! I will go myself a thousand times rather!—But will you not feel the want of pocket-money when you come to pay a rough cabman? The check I gave you yesterday will not last you long."

"The money is my own, Mr. Redmain."

"But you have not yet opened a banking-account in your own name."

"I suppose you have a meaning, Mr. Redmain; but I am not in the habit of using cabs."

"Then you had better get into the habit; for I swear to you, madam, if you don't fetch that girl home within the week, I will, next Monday, discharge your coachman, and send every horse in the stable to Tattersall's! Good morning."

She had no doubt he would do as he said; she knew Mr. Redmain would just enjoy selling her horses. But she could not at once give in. I say "*could* not," because hers was the weak will that can hardly bring itself to do what it knows it must, and is continually mistaken for the strong will that defies and endures. She had a week to think about it, and she would see!

During the interval, he took care not once to refer to his threat, for that would but weaken the impression of it, he knew.

On the Sunday, after service, she knocked at his door, and, being admitted, bade him good morning, but with no very gracious air—as, indeed, he would have been the last to expect.

"We have had a sermon on the forgiveness of injuries, Mr. Redmain," she said.

"By Jove!" interrupted her husband, "it would have been more to the purpose if I, or poor Mary Marston, had had it; for I swear you put our souls in peril!"

"The ring was no common one, Mr. Redmain; and the young woman had, by leaving the house, placed herself in a false position : every one suspected her as much as I did. Besides, she lost her temper, and talked about forgiving *me*, when I was in despair about my ring !"

"And what, pray, was your foolish ring compared to the girl's character ?"

"A foolish ring, indeed !—Yes, it was foolish to let you ever have the right to give it me ! But, as to her character, that of persons in her position is in constant peril. They have to lay their account with that, and must get used to it How was I to know ? We can not read each other's hearts."

"Not where there is no heart in the reader."

Hesper's face flushed, but she did her best not to lose her temper. Not that it would have been any great loss if she had, for there is as much difference in the values of tempers as in those who lose them. She said nothing, and her husband resumed :

"So you came to forgive me ?" he said.

"And Marston," she answered.

"Well, I will accept the condescension—that is, if the terms of it are to my mind."

"I will make no terms. Marston may return when she pleases."

"You must write and ask her."

"Of course, Mr. Redmain It would hardly be suitable that *you* should ask her."

"You must write so as to make it possible to accept your offer."

"I am not deceitful, Mr. Redmain."

"You are not A man must be fair, even to his wife."

"I will show you the letter I write "

"If you please."

She had to show him half a score ere he was satisfied, declaring he would do it himself, if she could not make a better job of it.

At length one was dispatched, received, and answered : Mary would not return. She had lost all hope of being of any true service to Mrs. Redmain, and she knew that, with Tom and Letty, she was really of use for the present.

Mrs. Redmain carried the letter, with ill-concealed triumph, to her husband ; nor did he conceal his annoyance.

"You must have behaved to her very cruelly," he said. "But you have done your best now—short of a Christian apology, which it would be folly to demand of you. I fear we have seen the last of her."—"And there was I," he said to himself, "for the first time in my life, actually beginning to fancy I had perhaps thrown salt upon the tail of that rare bird, an honest woman ! The devil has had quite as much to do with my history as with my character ! Perhaps that will be taken into the account one day."

But Mary lay awake at night, and thought of many things she might have said and done better when she was with Hesper, and would gladly have given herself another chance ; but she could no longer flatter herself she would ever be of any real good to her. She believed there was more hope of Mr. Redmain even. For had she not once, for one brief moment, seen him look a trifle ashamed of himself ? while Hesper was and remained, so far as she could judge, altogether satisfied with herself. Equal to her own demands upon herself, there was nothing in her to begin with—no soil to work upon.

CHAPTER XLVII.

ANOTHER CHANGE.

For some time Tom made progress toward health, and was able to read a good part of the day. Most evenings he asked Joseph to play to him for a while ; he was fond of music, and fonder still of criticism—upon anything. When he had done with Joseph, or when he did not want him, Mary was always ready to give the latter a lesson ; and, had he been a less gifted man than he was, he could not have failed to make progress with such a teacher.

The large - hearted, delicate - souled woman felt nothing strange in the presence of the workingman, but, on the contiary, was comfortably aware of a being like her own, less privileged but more gifted, whose nearness was strength. And no teacher, not to say no woman, could have failed to be pleased at the thorough painstaking with which he followed the slightest of her hints, and the delight his flushed face would reveal when she praised the success he had achieved.

It was not long before he began to write some of the things that came into his mind. For the period of quiescence as to production, which followed the initiation of more orderly study, was, after all, but of short duration, and the return tide of musical utterance was stronger than ever. Mary's delight was great when first he brought her one of his compositions very fairly written out—after which others followed with a rapidity that astonished her. They enabled her also to understand the man better and better ; for to have a thing to brood over which we are capable of understanding must be more to us than even the master's playing of it. She could not be sure this or that was correct, according to the sweet inexorability of musical ordainment, but the more she pondered them, the more she felt that the man was original, that the material was there, and the law at hand, that he brought his music from the only bottomless well of utterance, the truth, namely, by which alone the soul most glorious in gladness, or any other the stupidest of souls, can live.

To the first he brought her she contrived to put a poor little faulty accompaniment : and when she played his air to him so accompanied, his delight was touching, and not a little amusing. Plainly he thought the accompaniment a triumph of human faculty, and beyond anything he could ever develop. Never pupil was more humble, never pupil more obedient ; thinking nothing of himself or of anything he had done or could do, his path was open to the swiftest and highest growth. It matters little where a man may be at this moment ; the point is whether he is growing. The next point will be, whether he is growing at the ratio given him. The key to the whole thing is *obedience*, and nothing else.

What the gift of such an instructor was to Joseph, my reader may be requested to imagine. He was like a man seated

on the grass outside the heavenly gate, from which, slow-open-
ing every evening as the sun went down, came an angel to
teach, and teach, until he too should be fit to enter in : an
hour would arrive when she would no longer have to come out
to him where he sat. Under such an influence all that was
gentlest and sweetest in his nature might well develop with
rapidity, and every accidental roughness—and in him there
was no other—by swift degrees vanish from both speech and
manners. The angels do not want tailors to make their clothes :
their habits come out of themselves. But we are often too
hard upon our fellows ; for many of those in the higher ranks
of life—no, no, I mean of society—whose insolence wakens
ours, as growl wakes growl in the forest, are not yet so far removed from the savage—I mean in their personal history—as
some in the lowest ranks. When a nobleman mistakes the
love of right in another for a hatred of refinement, he can not
be far from mistaking insolence for good manners. Of such a
nobility, good Lord, deliver us from all envy !

As to falling in love with a lady like Mary, such a thing
was as far from Jasper's consciousness as if she had been a
duchess. She belonged to another world from his, a world
which his world worshiped, waiting. He might miss her even
to death ; her absence might, for him, darken the universe as
if the sun had withdrawn his brightness ; but who thinks of
falling in love with the sun, or dreams of climbing nearer to
his radiance ?

The day will one day come—or what of the long-promised
kingdom of heaven ?—when a woman, instead of spending
anxious thought on the adornment of her own outward person,
will seek with might the adornment of the inward soul of
another, and will make that her crown of rejoicing. Nay, are
there none such even now ? The day will come when a man,
rather than build a great house for the overflow of a mighty
hospitality, will give himself, in the personal labor of outgoing
love, to build spiritual houses like St. Paul—a higher art than
any of man's invention. O my brother, what were it not for
thee to have a hand in making thy brother beautiful !

Be not indignant, my reader · not for a moment did I

imagine thee capable of such a mean calling! It is left to
a certain school of weak enthusiasts, who believe that such
growth, such embellishment, such creation, is all God cares
about ; these enthusiasts can not indeed see, so blind have they
become with their fixed idea, how God could care for anything else. They actually believe that the very Son of the
life-making God lived and died for that, and for nothing else.
That such men and women are fools, is and has been so widely
believed, that, to men of the stamp of my indignant reader, it
has become a fact! But the end alone will reveal the beginning. Such a fool was Prometheus, with the vulture at his
heart—but greater than Jupiter with his gods around him.

There soon came a change, however, and the lessons ceased
altogether.

Tom had come down to his old quarters, and, in the arrogance of convalescence, had presumed on his imagined strength,
and so caught cold. An alarming relapse was the consequence,
and there was no more playing ; for now his condition began
to draw to a change, of which, for some time, none of them
had even thought, the patient had seemed so certainly recovering. The cold settled on his lungs, and he sank rapidly.

Joseph, whose violin was useless now, was not the less in
attendance. Every evening, when his work was over, he came
knocking gently at the door of the parlor, and never left until
Tom was settled for the night. The most silently helpful,
undemonstrative being he was, that doctor could desire to wait
upon patient. When it was his turn to watch, he never
closed an eye, but at daybreak—for it was now spring—would
rouse Mary, and go off straight to his work, nor taste food
until the hour for the mid-day meal arrived.

Tom speedily became aware that his days were numbered—
phrase of unbelief, for are they not numbered from the beginning? Are our hairs numbered, and our days forgotten—till
death gives a hint to the doctor? He was sorry for his past
life, and thoroughly ashamed of much of it, saying in all honesty he would rather die than fall for one solitary week into
the old ways—not that he wished to die, for, with the confidence of youth, he did not believe he could fall into the old

ways again. For my part, I think he was taken away to have a little more of that care and nursing which neither his mother nor his wife had been woman enough to give the great baby. After all, he had not been one of the worst of babies.

Is it strange that one so used to bad company and bad ways should have so altered, in so short a time, and without any great struggle? The assurance of death at the door, and a wholesome shame of things that are past, may, I think, lead up to such a swift change, even in a much worse man than Tom. For there is the Life itself, all-surrounding, and ever pressing in upon the human soul, wherever that soul will afford a chink of entrance; and Tom had not yet sealed up all his doors.

When he lay there dead—for what excuse could we have for foolish lamentation, if we did not speak of the loved as *lying dead?*—Letty had him already enshrined in her heart as the best of husbands—as her own Tom, who had never said a hard word to her—as the cleverest as well as kindest of men, who had written poetry that would never die while the English language was spoken. Nor did "The Firefly" spare its dole of homage to the memory of one of its gayest writers. Indeed, all about its office had loved him, each after his faculty. Even the boy cried when he heard he was gone, for to him too he had always given a kind word, coming and going. A certain little runnel of verse flowed no more through the pages of "The Firefly," and in a month there was not the shadow of Tom upon his age. But the print of him was deep in the heart of Letty, and not shallow in the affection of Mary; nor were such as these, insignificant records for any one to leave behind him, as records go. Happy was he to have left behind him any love, especially such a love as Letty bore him! For what is the loudest praise of posterity to the quietest love of one's own generation? For his mother, her memory was mostly in her temper. She had never understood her wayward child, just because she had given him her waywardness, and not parted with it herself, so that between them the two made havoc of love. But she who gives her child all he desires, in the hope of thus binding his love to herself, no less than she who thwarts him in everything, may rest assured of the neglect she has richly earned. When she heard of his death, she howled and cursed her fate, and the woman, meaning poor Letty, who had parted her and her Tom, swearing she would never set eyes upon her, never let her touch a farthing of Tom's money. She would not hear of paying his debts until Mary told her she then would, upon which the fear of public disapprobation wrought for right if not righteousness.

But what was Mary to do now with Letty? She was little more than a baby yet, not silly from youth, but young from silliness. Children must learn to walk, but not by being turned out alone in Cheapside.

She was relieved from some perplexity for the present, however, by the arrival of a letter from Mrs. Wardour to Letty, written in a tone of stiffly condescendent compassion—not so unpleasant to Letty as to her friend, because from childhood she had been used to the nature that produced it, and had her mind full of a vast, undefined notion of the superiority of the writer. It may be a question whether those who fill our inexperienced minds with false notions of their greatness, do us thereby more harm or good; certainly when one comes to understand with what an arrogance and self-assertion they have done so, putting into us as reverence that which in them is conceit, one is ready to be scornful more than enough; but, rather than have a child question such claims, I would have him respect the meanest soul that ever demanded respect, the first shall be last in good time, and the power of revering come forth uninjured; whereas a child judging his elders has already withered the blossom of his being.

But Mrs. Wardour's letter was kind—perhaps a little repentant; it is hard to say, for ten persons will repent of a sin for one who will confess it—I do not mean to the priest—that may be an easy matter, but to the only one who has a claim to the confession, namely, the person wronged. Yet such confession is in truth far more needful to the wronger than to the wronged; it is a small thing to be wronged, but a horrible thing to wrong.

The le⸻   ⸻ sympathy, and an invitation to spend the summer months with them at her old home. It might, the letter said, prove but a dull place to her after the gayety to which she had of late been accustomed, but it might not the less suit her present sad situation, and possibly uncertain prospects.

Letty's heart felt one little throb of gladness at the thought of being again at Thornwick, and in peace. With all the probable unpleasant accompaniments of the visit, nowhere else, she thought, could she feel the same sense of shelter as where her childhood had passed. Mary also was pleased; for, although Letty might not be comfortable, the visit would end, and by that time she might know what could be devised best for her comfort and well-being.

CHAPTER XLVIII.

DISSOLUTION.

It was now Mary's turn to feel that she was, for the first time in her life, about to be cut adrift—adrift, that is, as a world is adrift, on the surest of paths, though without eyes to see. For ten days or so, she could form no idea of what she was likely or would like to do next. But, when we are in such perplexity, may not the fact be accepted as showing that decision is not required of us—perhaps just because our way is at the moment being made straight for us?

Joseph called once or twice, but, for Letty's sake, they had no music. As they met so seldom now, Mary, anxious to serve him as she could, offered him the loan of some of her favorite books. He accepted it with a gladness that surprised her, for she did not know how much he had of late been reading.

One day she received an unexpected visit—from Mr. Brett, her lawyer. He had been searching into the affairs of the shop, and had discovered enough to make him uneasy, and indeed fill him with self-reproach that he had not done so with more thoroughness immediately on her father's death. He had come to tell her all he knew, and talk the matter over with her, that they might agree what proceedings should be taken.

I will not weary myself or my readers with business detail, for which kind of thing I have no great aptitude, and a good deal of incapacitating ignorance : but content myself with the briefest statement of the condition in which Mr. Brett found the affairs of Mr. Turnbull.

He had been speculating in several companies, making haste to be rich, and had periled and lost what he had saved of the profits of the business, and all of Mary's as well that had not been elsewhere secured. He had even trenched on the original capital of the firm, by postponing the payment of moneys due, and allowing the stock to run down and to deteriorate, and things out of fashion to accumulate, so that the business had perceptibly fallen off. But what displeased Mary more than anything was, that he had used money of her father's to speculate with in more than one public-house ; and she knew that, if in her father's lifetime he had so used even his own, it would have been enough to make him insist on dissolving partnership.

It was impossible to allow her money to remain any longer in the power of such a man, and she gave authority to Mr. Brett to make the necessary arrangements for putting an end to business relations between them.

It was a somewhat complicated, therefore tedious business ; and things looked worse the further they were searched into. Unable to varnish the facts to the experience of a professional eye, Mr. Turnbull wrote Mary a letter almost cringing in its tone, begging her to remember the years her father and he had been as brothers ; how she had grown up in the shop, and had been to him, until misunderstandings arose, into the causes of which he could not now enter, in the place of a daughter ; and insisting that her withdrawal from it had had no small share in the ruin of the business. For these considerations, and, more than all, for the memory of her father, he entreated her to leave things as they were, to trust him to see after the interests of the daughter of his old friend, and not insist upon measures which must end in a forced sale, in the shutting up of the shop of Turnbull and Marston, and the disgracing of her father's name along with his.

Mary replied that she was acting by the advice of her father's lawyer, and with the regard she owed her father's memory, in severing all connection with a man in whom she no longer had confidence ; and insisted that the business must be wound up as soon as possible.

She instructed Mr. Brett, at the same time, that, if it could be managed, she would prefer getting the shop, even at considerable loss, into her own hands, with what stock might be in it, when she would attempt to conduct the business on principles her father would have approved, whereby she did not doubt of soon restoring it to repute. While she had no intention, she said, of selling so *well* as Mr. Turnbull would fain have done, she believed she would soon be able to buy to just as good advantage as he. It would be necessary, however, to keep her desire a secret, else Mr. Turnbull would be certain to frustrate it.

Mr. Brett approved of her plan, for he knew she was much respected, and had many friends. Mr. Turnbull would be glad, he said, to give up the whole to escape prosecution—that at least was how Mary interpreted his somewhat technical statement of affairs between them.

The swindler wrote again, begging for an interview—which she declined, except in the presence of her lawyer.

She made up her mind that she would not go near Testbridge till everything was settled, and the keys of the shop in Mr. Brett's hands ; and remained, therefore, where she was— with Letty, who to keep her company delayed her departure as long as she could without giving offense at Thornwick.

A few days before Letty was at last compelled to leave, Jasper called, and heard about as much as they knew themselves of their plans. When Mary said to him she would miss her pupil, he smiled in a sort of abstracted way, as if not quite apprehending what she said, which seemed to Mary a little odd, his manners in essentials being those of a gentleman, as judged by one a little more than a lady ; for there is an unnamed degree higher than the ordinary *lady*.

So Mary was left alone—more alone than she had ever been in her life. But she did not feel lonely, for the best of reasons —that she never fancied herself alone, but knew that she was not. Also she had books at her command, being one of the few who can read ; and there were picture-galleries to go to, and music-lessons to be had. Of these last she crowded in as many as her master could be persuaded to give her—for it would be long, she knew, before she was able to have such again.

Joseph Jasper never came near her. She could not imagine why, and was disappointed and puzzled.

To know that Ann Byrom was in the house was not a great comfort to her—she regarded so much that Mary loved as of earth and not of heaven. God's world even she despised, because men called it nature, and spoke of its influences. But Mary did go up to see her now and then. Very different she seemed from the time when first they were at work together over Hesper's twilight dress! Ever since Mary had made the acquaintance of her brother, she seemed to have changed toward her. Perhaps she was jealous ; perhaps she believed Mary was confirming him in his bad ways. Just where they were all three of one mind—just *there* her rudimentary therefore self-sufficient religion shut them out from her sympathy and fellowship.

Alone, and with her time at her command, Mary was more inclined than she had ever been, except for her father's company, to go to church. The second Sunday after Letty left her, she went to the one nearest, and in the congregation thought she saw Joseph. A week before, she would have waited for him as he came out, but, now that he seemed to avoid her, she would not, and went home neither comforted by the sermon nor comfortable with herself. For the parson, instead of recognizing, through all defects of the actual, the pattern after which God had made man, would fain have him remade after the pattern of the middle-age monk—a being far superior, no doubt, to the most of his contemporaries, but as far from the beauty of the perfect man as the mule is from that of the horse ; and she was annoyed with herself that she was annoy

It was the middle of summer before the affairs of the firm were wound up, and the shop in the hands of the London man whom Mr. Brett had employed in the purchase.

Lawyer as he was, however, Mr. Brett had not been sharp enough for Turnbull. The very next day, a shop in the same street, that had been to let for some time, displayed above its now open door the sign, *John Turnbull, late*—then a very small *of*—*Turnbull and Marston ;* whereupon Mr. Brett saw the oversight of which he had been guilty. There was nothing in the shop when it was opened, but that Turnbull utilized for advertisement : he had so arranged, that within an hour the goods began to arrive, and kept arriving, by every train, for days and days after, while all the time he made public show of himself, fussing about, the most triumphant man in the town. It made people talk, and if not always as he would have liked to hear them talk, yet it was talk, and, in the matter of advertisement, that is the main thing.

When it was told Mary, it gave her not the smallest uneasiness. She only saw what had several times seemed on the point of arriving in her father's lifetime. She would not have moved a finger to prevent it. Let the two principles meet, with what result God pleased !

Whether he had suspected her design, and had determined to challenge her before the public, I can not tell ; but his wife's aversion to shopkeeping was so great, that one who knew what sort of scene passed because of it between them, would have expected that, but for some very strong reason, he would have been glad enough to retire from that mode of gaining a livelihood. As it was, things appeared to go on with them just as before. They still inhabited the villa, the wife scornful of her surroundings, and the husband driving a good horse to his shop every morning. How he managed it all, nobody knew but himself, and whether he succeeded or not was a matter of small interest to any except his own family and his creditors. He was a man nowise beloved, although there was something about him that carried simple people with him—for his ends, not theirs. To those who alluded to the change, he represented it as entirely his own doing, to be rid of the interference of Miss Marston in matters of which she knew nothing. He knew well that a confident lie has all the look of truth, and, while fact and falsehood were disputing together in men's mouths, he would be selling his drapery. The country people were flattered by the confidence he seemed to put in them by this explanation, and those who liked him before sought the new shop as they had frequented the old one.

Unlike most men, not to say lawyers, Mr. Brett was fully recognizant to Mary of his oversight, and was not a little relieved to be assured she would not have had the thing otherwise: she would gladly meet Mr. Turnbull in a fair field—not that she would in the least acknowledge or think of him as a rival; she would simply carry out her own ideas of right, without regard to him or any measures he might take; the result should be as God willed. Mr. Brett shook his head: he knew her father of old, and saw the daughter prepared to go beyond the father. Theirs were principles that did not come within the range of his practice! He said to himself and his wife that the world could not go on for a twelvemonth if such ways were to become universal: whether by the world he meant his own profession, I will not inquire. Certainly he did not make the reflection that the new ways are intended to throw out the old ways; and the worst argument against any way is that the world can not go on so: for that is just what is wanted—that the world should not go on so. Mr. Brett nevertheless admired not only Mary's pluck, but the business faculty which every moment she manifested: there *is* a holy way of doing business, and, little as business men may think it, that is the standard by which they must be tried; for their judge in business affairs is not their own trade or profession, but the man who came to convince the world concerning right and wrong and the choice between them: or, in the older speech—to reprove the world of sin, and of righteousness, and of judgment.

CHAPTER XLIX.

THORNWICK.

It was almost with bewilderment that Mrs. Helmer revisited Thornwick. The near past seemed to have vanished like a dream that leaves a sorrow behind it, and the far past to take its place. She had never been accustomed to reflect on her own feelings; things came, were welcome or unwelcome, proved better or worse than she had anticipated, passed away, and were mostly forgotten. With plenty of faculty, Letty had not yet emerged from the chrysalid condition; she lived much as one in a dream, with whose dream mingle sounds and glimmers from the waking world. Very few of us are awake, very few even alive in true, availing sense. "Pooh! what stuff!" says the sleeper, and will say it until the waking begins to come.

On the threshold of her old home, then, Letty found her old self awaiting her; she crossed it, and was once more just Letty, a Letty wrapped in the garments of sorrow, and with a heaviness at the heart, but far from such a miserable Letty as during the last of her former life there. Little joy had been hers since the terrible night when she fled from its closed doors; and now that she returned, she could take up everything where she had left it, except the gladness. But peace is better than gladness, and she was on the way to find that.

Mrs. Wardour, who, for all her severity, was not without a good-sized heart, and whose conscience had spoken to her in regard of Letty far oftener than any torture would have made her allow, was touched with compassion at sight of her worn and sad look; and, granting to herself that the poor thing had been punished enough, even for her want of respect to the house of Thornwick, broke down a little, though with well-preserved dignity, and took the wandering ewe-lamb to her bosom. Letty, loving and forgiving always, nestled in it for a moment, and in her own room quietly wept a long time. When she came out, Mrs. Wardour pleased herself with the fancy that her eyes were red with the tears of repentance; but

Letty never dreamed of repenting, for that would have been to deny Tom, to cut off her married life, throw it from her, and never more see Tom.

By degrees, rapid yet easy, she slid into all her old ways; took again the charge of the dairy as if she had never left it; attended to the linen, darned the stockings: and in everything but her pale, thin face, and heavy, exhausted heart, was the young Letty again. She even went to the harness-room to look to Cousin Godfrey's stirrups and bits; but finding, morning after morning for a whole week, that they had not once been neglected, dismissed the care—not without satisfaction.

Mrs. Wardour continued kind to her; but every now and then would allow a tone as of remembered naughtiness to be sub-audible in speech or request. Letty, even in her own heart, never re-ented it. She had been so used to it in the old days, that it seemed only natural. And then her aunt considered her health in the kindest way. Now that Letty had known some of the troubles of marriage, she felt more sympathy with her, did not look down upon her from quite such a height, and to Letty this was strangely delightful. Oh, what a dry, hard, cold world this would grow to, but for the blessing of its many sick-nesses!

When Godfrey saw her moving about the house as in former days, but changed, like one of the ghosts of his saddest dreams, a new love began to rise out of the buried seed of the old. In vain he reasoned with himself, in vain he resisted. The image of Letty, with its trusting eyes fixed on him so "solemn sad," and its watching looks full of ministration, haunted him, and was too much for him. She was never the sort of woman he could have fancied himself falling in love with; he did in fact say to himself that she was only *almost* a lady—but at the word his heart rebuked him for a traitor to love and its holy laws. Neither in person was she at all his ideal. A woman like Hesper, uplifted and strong, broad-fronted and fearless, large-limbed, and full of latent life, was more of the ideal he could have written poetry about. But we are deeper than we know. Who is capable of knowing his own ideal? The ideal of a man's self is hid in the bosom of God, and may lie ages away from his

knowledge ; and his ideal of woman is the ideal belonging to
this unknown self : the ideal only can bring forth an ideal.
He can not, therefore, know his own ideal of woman ; it is,
nevertheless—so I presume—this his own unknown ideal that
makes a man choose against his choice. Gladly would Godfrey
now have taken Letty to his arms. It was no longer anything
that from boyhood he had vowed rather to die unmarried, and
let the land go to a stranger, than marry a widow. He had to
recall every restraining fact of his and her position to prevent
him from now precipitating that which he had before too long
delayed. But the gulf of the grave and the jealousy of a mother were between them ; for, if he were again to rouse her suspicions, she would certainly get rid of Letty, as she had before
intended, so depriving her of a home, and him of opportunity.
He kept, therefore, out of Letty's way as much as he could,
went more about the farm, and took long rides.

Nothing was further from Letty than any merest suspicion
of the sort of regard Godfrey cherished for her. There was
in her nothing of the self-sentimental. Her poet was gone
from her, but she did not therefore take to poetry ; nay, what
poetry she had learned to like was no longer anything to her,
now her singing bird had flown to the land of song. To her,
Tom was the greatest, the one poet of the age ; he had been
hers—was hers still, for did he not die telling her that he
would go on watching till she came to him ? He had loved
her, she knew ; he had learned to love her better before he
died. She must be patient ; the day would come when she
should be a Psyche, as he had told her, and soar aloft in search
of her mate. The sense of wifehood had grown one with her
consciousness. It mingled with all her prayers, both in chamber and in church. As she went about the house, she was
dreaming of her Tom—an angel in heaven, she said to herself,
but none the less her husband, and waiting for her. If she
did not read poetry, she read her New Testament ; and if she
understood it only in a childish fashion, she obeyed it in a childlike one, whence the way of all wisdom lay open before her.
It is not where one is, but in what direction he is going. Before her, too, was her little boy—borne in his father's arms, she

pictured him, and hearing from him of the mother who was coming to them by and by, when God had made her good enough to rejoin them !

But, while she continued thus simple, Godfrey could not fail to see how much more of a woman she had grown : he was not yet capable of seeing that she would—could never have got so far with him, even if he had married her.

Love and marriage are of the Father's most powerful means for the making of his foolish little ones into sons and daughters. But so unlike in many cases are the immediate consequences to those desired and expected, that it is hard for not a few to believe that he is anywhere looking after their fate— caring about them at all. And the doubt would be a reasonable one, if the end of things was marriage. But the end is life—that we become the children of God ; after which, all things can and will go their grand, natural course ; the heart of the Father will be content for his children, and the hearts of the children will be content in their Father.

Godfrey indulged one great and serious mistake in reference to Letty, namely, that, having learned the character of Tom through the saddest of personal experience, she must have come to think of him as he did, and must have dismissed from her heart every remnant of love for him. Of course, he would not hint at such a thing, he said to himself, nor would she for a moment allow it, but nothing else could be the state of her mind ! He did not know that in a woman's love there is more of the specially divine element than in a man's— namely, the original, the unmediated. The first of God's love is not founded upon any merit, rests only on being and need, and the worth that is yet unborn.

The Redmains were again at Durnmelling—had been for some weeks ; and Sepia had taken care that she and Godfrey should meet—on the footpath to Testbridge, in the field accessible by the breach in the ha-ha—here and there and anywhere suitable for a little detention and talk that should seem accidental, and be out of sight. Nor was Godfrey the man to be insensible to the influence of such a woman, brought to bear at close quarters. A man less vulnerable—I hate the word, but it's the right one

with Sepia concerned, for she was, in truth, an enemy—might
perhaps have yielded room to the suspicion that these meetings
were not all so accidental as they appeared, and as Sepia treated
them ; but no glimmer of such a thought passed through the
mind of Godfrey. He knew nothing of all that my readers know
to Sepia's disadvantage, and her eyes were enough to subdue most
men from the first—for a time at least. Had it not been for the
return of Letty, she would by this time have had him her slave :
nothing but slavery could it ever be to love a woman like her,
who gave no love in return, only exercised power. But although
he was always glad to meet her, and his heart had begun to beat
a little faster at sight of her approach, the glamour of her presence was nearly destroyed by the arrival of Letty ; and Sepia
was more than sharp enough to perceive a difference in the expression of his eyes the next time she met him. At the very
first glance she suspected some hostile influence at work !—intentionally hostile, for persons with a consciousness like Sepia's
are always imagining enemies. And as the two worst enemies
she could have were the truth and a woman, she was alter-
nately jealous and terrified : the truth and a woman together,
she had not yet begun to fear ; that would, indeed, be too
much !

She soon found there was a young woman at Thornwick,
who had but just arrived ; and ere long she learned who she
was—one, indeed, who had already a shadowy existence in her
life—was it possible the shadow should be now taking solidity,
and threatening to foil her ? Not once did it occur to her that,
were it so, there would be retribution in it. She had heard of
Tom's death through " The Firefly," which had a kind, extravagant article about him, but she had not once thought of his
widow—and there she was, a hedge across the path she wanted
to go ! If the house of Durnmelling had but been one story
higher, that she might see all round Thornwick !

For some time now, as I have already more than hinted,
Sepia had been fashioning a man to her thrall—Mewks, namely, the body-servant of Mr. Redmain. It was a very gradual
process she had adopted, and it had been the more successful.
It had got so far with him that whatever Sepia showed the

least wish to understand, Mewks would take endless trouble to learn for her. The rest of the servants, both at Durnmelling and in London, were none of them very friendly with her— least of all Jemima, who was now with her mistress as lady's-maid, the accomplished attendant whom Hesper had procured in place of Mary being away for a holiday.

The more Sepia realized, or thought she realized, the position she was in, the more desirous was she to get out of it, and the only feasible and safe way, in her eyes, was marriage : there was nothing between that and a return to what she counted slavery. Rather than lift again such a hideous load of irksomeness, she would find her way out of a world in which it was not possible, she said, to be both good and comfortable : she had, in truth, tried only the latter. But if she could, she thought, secure for a husband this gentleman-yeoman, she might hold up her head with the best. Even if Galofta should reappear, she would know then how to meet him : with a friend or two, such as she had never had yet, she could do what she pleased ! It was hard work to get on quite alone—or with people who cared only for themselves ! She must have some love on her side ! some one who cared for *her!*

From all she could learn, there was nothing that amounted even to ordinary friendship between Mr. Wardour and the young widow. She was in the family but as a distant poor relation—" Much as I am myself !" thought Sepia, with a bitter laugh that even in her own eyes she should be comparable to a poor creature like Letty. The fact, however, remained that Godfrey was a little altered toward her · she must have been telling him something against her—something she had heard from that detestable little hypocrite who was turned away on suspicion of theft ! Yes—that was how Sepia talked *to herself* about Mary.

One morning, Letty, finding she had an hour's leisure, for her aunt did not pursue her as of old time. wandered out to the oak on the edge of the ha-ha, so memorable with the shadowy presence of her Tom. She had not been seated under it many minutes before Godfrey caught sight of her from his horse's back `. .` `. .` `. .` `. .` `. .` , he yielded to an urgent longing, took his horse to the stable, and crossed the grass to where she sat.

Letty was thinking of Tom—what else was there of her own to do ?—thinking like a child, looking up into the cloud-flecked sky, and thinking Tom was somewhere there, though she could not see him : she must be good and patient, that she might go up to him, as he could not come down to her—if he could, he would have come long ago ! All the enchantment of the first days of her love had come back upon the young widow ; all the ill that had crept in between had failed from out her memory, as the false notes in music melt in the air that carries the true ones across ravine and river, meadow and grove, to the listening ear. Letty lived in a dream of her husband—in heaven, " yet not from her "—such a dream of bliss and hope as in itself went far to make up for all her sorrows.

She was sitting with her back toward the tree and her face to Thornwick, and yet she did not see Godfrey till he was within a few yards of her. She smiled, expecting his kind greeting, but was startled to hear from behind her instead the voice of a lady greeting him. She turned her head involuntarily : there was the head of Sepia rising above the breach in the ha-ha, and Godfrey had turned aside and run to give her his hand.

Now Letty knew Sepia by sight, from the evening she had spent at the old hall ; more of her she knew nothing. From the mind of Tom, in his illness, her baleful influence had van-ished like an evil dream, and Mary had not thought it neces-sary to let him know how falsely, contemptuously, and con-temptibly, she had behaved toward him. Letty, therefore, had no feeling toward Sepia but one of admiration for her grace and beauty, which she could appreciate the more that they were so different from her own.

" Thank you," said Sepia, holding fast by Godfrey's hand, and coming up with a little pant. " What a lovely day it is for your haymaking ! How can you afford the time to play knight-errant to a distressed damsel ? "

" The hay is nearly independent of my presence," replied Godfrey. " Sun and wind have done their parts too well for my being of much use."

"Take me with you to see how they are getting on. I am as fond of hay as Bottom in his translation."

She had learned Godfrey's love of literature, and knew that one quotation may stand for much knowledge

"I will, with pleasure," said Godfrey, perhaps a little consoled in the midst of his disappointment: and they walked away, neither taking notice of Letty.

"I did not know," she said to herself, "that the two houses had come together at last! What a handsome couple they make!"

What passed between them is scarcely worthy of record. It is enough to say that Sepia found her companion distrait, and he felt her a little invasive. In a short while they came back together, and Sepia saw Letty under the great bough of the Durnmelling oak. Godfrey handed her down the rent, careful himself not to invade Durnmelling with a single foot. She ran home, and up to a certain window with her opera-glass. But the branches and foliage of the huge oak would have concealed pairs and pairs of lovers.

Godfrey turned toward Letty. She had not stirred.

"What a beautiful creature Miss Yolland is!" she said, looking up with a smile of welcome, and a calmness that prevented the slightest suspicion of a flattering jealousy.

"I was coming to *you*," returned Godfrey. "I never saw her till her head came up over the ha-ha.—Yes, she is beautiful —at least, she has good eyes."

"They are splendid! What a wife she would make for you, Cousin Godfrey! I should like to see such a two."

Letty was beyond the faintest suggestion of coquetry. Her words drove a sting to the heart of Godfrey. He turned pale. But not a word would he have spoken then, had not Letty in her innocence gone on to torture him. She sprang from the ground.

"Are you ill, Cousin Godfrey?" she cried in alarm, and with that sweet tremor of the voice that shows the heart is near. "You are quite white!—Oh, dear! I've said something I oughtn't to have said! What can it be? Do forgive me, Cousin Godfrey."

In her childlike anxiety she would have thrown her arms
round his neck, but her hands only reached his shoulders. He
drew back : such was the nature of the man that every sting
tasted of offense. But he mastered himself, and in his turn,
alarmed at the idea of having possibly hurt her, caught her
hands in his. As they stood regarding each other with troubled
eyes, the embankment of his prudence gave way, and the
stored passion broke out.

"You don't *mean* you would like to see me married, Letty ?" he groaned.

"Yes, indeed, I do, Cousin Godfrey! You would make
such a lovely husband !"

"Ah ! I thought as much ! I knew you never cared for
me, Letty !"

He dropped her hands, and turned half aside, like a figure
warped with fire.

" I care for you more than anybody in the world—except,
perhaps, Mary," said Letty : truthfulness was a part of her.

"And I care for you more than all the world !—more than
very being—it is worthless without you. O Letty ! your eyes
haunt me night and day ! I love you with my whole
soul."

"How kind of you, Cousin Godfrey !" faltered Letty,
trembling, and not knowing what she said. She was very
frightened, but hardly knew why, for the idea of Godfrey in
love with her was all but inconceivable. Nevertheless, its approach was terrible. Like a fascinated bird she could not take
her eyes off his face. Her knees began to fail her ; it was all
she could do to stand. But Godfrey was full of himself, and
had not the most shadowy suspicion of how she felt. He took
her emotion for a favorable sign, and stupidly went on :

" Letty, I can't help it ! I know I oughtn't to speak to you
like this—so soon, but I can't keep quiet any longer. I love
you more than the universe and its Maker. A thousand times
rather would I cease to live, than live without you to love me.
I have loved you for years and years—longer than I know. I
was loving you with heart and soul and brain and eyes when
you went away and left me."

"Cousin Godfrey!" shrieked Letty. "don't you know I belong to Tom?"

And she dropped like one lifeless on the grass at his feet.

Godfrey felt as if suddenly damned ; and his hell was death. He stood gazing on the white face. The world, heaven, God, and nature were dead, and that was the soul of it all, dead before him' But such death is never born of love. This agony was but the fog of disappointed self-love , and out of it suddenly rose what seemed a new power to live, but one from a lower world : it was all a wretched dream, out of which he was no more to issue, in which he must go on for ever, dreaming, yet acting as one wide awake! Mechanically he stooped and lifted the death-defying lover in his arms, and carried her to the house. He felt no thrill as he held the treasure to his heart It was the merest material contact. He bore her to the room where his mother sat, laid her on the sofa, said he had found her under the oak-tree—and went to his study, away in the roof. On a chair in the middle of the floor he sat, like a man bereft of all. Nothing came between him and suicide but an infinite scorn. A slow rage devoured his heart. Here he was, a man who knew his own worth, his faithfulness, his unchangeableness, cast over the wall of the universe, into the waste places, among the broken shards of ruin! If there was a God—and the rage in his heart declared his being—why did he make him ? To make him for such a misery was pure injustice, was willful cruelty! Henceforward he would live above what God or woman could do to him! He rose and went to the hay-field, whence he did not return till after midnight.

He did not sleep, but he came to a resolution. In the morning he told his mother that he wanted a change ; now that the hay was safe, he would have a run, he hardly knew where—possibly on the Continent ; she must not be uneasy if she did not hear from him for a week or two ; perhaps he would have a look at the pyramids. The old lady was filled with dismay ; but scarcely had she begun to expostulate when she saw in his eyes that something was seriously amiss, and held her peace—she had had to learn that with both father and son.

Godfrey went, and courted distraction. Ten years before, he would have brooded : that he would not do now : the thing was not worth it! His pride was strong as ever, and both helped him to get over his suffering, and prevented him from gaining the good of it. He intrenched himself in his pride. No one should say he had not had his will! He was a strong man, and was going to prove it to himself afresh!

Thus thought Godfrey ; but he is in reality a weak man who must have recourse to pride to carry him through. Only, if a man has not love enough to make a hero of him, what is he to do ?

He was away a month, and came back in seeming health and spirits. But it was no small relief to him to find on his arrival that Letty was no longer at Thornwick.

She had gone through a sore time. To have made Godfrey unhappy, made her miserable ; but how was she to help it ? She belonged to Tom ! Not once did she entertain the thought of ceasing to be Tom's. She did not even say to herself, what would Tom do if she forgot and forsook him—and for what he could not help ! for having left her because death took him away ! But what was she to do ? She must not remain where she was. No more must she tell his mother why she went.

She wrote to Mary, and told her she could not stay much longer. They were very kind, she said, but she must be gone before Godfrey came back.

Mary suspected the truth. The fact that Letty did not give her any reason was almost enough. The supposition also rendered intelligible the strange mixture of misery and hardness in Godfrey's behavior at the time of Letty's old mishap. She answered, begging her to keep her mind easy about the future, and her friend informed of whatever concerned her.

This much from Mary was enough to set Letty at comparative ease. She began to recover strength, and was able to write a letter to Godfrey, to leave where he would find it, in his study.

It was a lovely letter—the utterance of a simple, childlike spirit—with much in it, too, I confess, that was but prettily childish. She poured out on Godfrey the affection of a woman-child. She told him what a reverence and love he had been to her always; told him, too, that it would change her love into fear, perhaps something worse, if he tried to make her forget Tom. She told him he was much too grand for her to dare love him in that way, but she could look up to him like an angel—only he must not come between her and Tom. Nothing could be plainer, simpler, honester, or stronger, than the way the little woman wrote her mind to the great man. Had he been worthy of her, he might even yet, with her help, have got above his passion in a grand way, and been a great man indeed. But, as so many do, he only sat upon himself, kept himself down, and sank far below his passion.

When he went to his study the day after his return, he saw the letter. His heart leaped like a wild thing in a trap at sight of the ill-shaped, childish writing; but—will my lady reader believe it?—the first thought that shot through it was—" She shall find it too late! I am not one to be left and taken at will!" When he read it, however, it was with a curling lip of scorn at the childishness of the creature to whom he had offered the heart of Godfrey Wardour. Instead of admiring the lovely devotion of the girl-widow to her boy-husband, he scorned himself for having dreamed of a creature who could not only love a fool like Tom Helmer, but go on loving him after he was dead, and that even when Godfrey Wardour had condescended to let her know he loved her. It was thus the devil befooled him. Perhaps the worst devil a man can be possessed withal, is himself. In mere madness, the man is beside himself; but in this case he is inside himself; the presiding, indwelling, inspiring spirit of him is himself, and that is the hardest of all to cast out. Godfrey rose from the reading of that letter *cured*, as he called it. But it was a cure that left the wound open as a door to the entrance of evil things. He tore the letter into a thousand pieces, and threw them into the empty grate—not even showed it the respect of burning it with fire.

Mary had got her affairs settled, and was again in the old place, the hallowed temple of so many holy memories. I do not forget it was a shop I call a temple. In that shop God had been worshiped with holiest worship—that is, obedience—and would be again. Neither do I forget that the devil had been worshiped there too—in what temple is he not? He has fallen like lightning from heaven, but has not yet been cast out of the earth. In that shop, however, he would be worshiped no more for a season.

At once she wrote to Letty, saying the room which had been hers was at her service as soon as she pleased to occupy it· she would take her father's.

Letty breathed a deep breath of redemption, and made haste to accept the offer. But to let Mrs. Wardour know her resolve was a severe strain on her courage.

I will not give the conversation that followed her announcement that she was going to visit Mary Marston. Her aunt met it with scorn and indignation. Ingratitude, laziness, love of low company, all the old words of offense she threw afresh in her face. But Letty could not help being pleased to find that her aunt's storm no longer swamped her boat. When she began, however, to abuse Mary, calling her a low creature, who actually gave up an independent position to put herself at the beck and call of a fine lady, Letty grew angry.

"I must not sit and hear you call Mary names, aunt," she said. "When you cast me out, she stood by me. You do not understand her. She is the only friend I ever had—except Tom."

"You dare, you thankless hussy, to say such a thing in the house where you've been clothed and fed and sheltered for so many years! You're the child of your father with a vengeance! Get out of my sight!"

"Aunt—" said Letty, rising.

"No aunt of yours!" interrupted the wrathful woman.

"Mrs. Wardour," said Letty, with dignity, " you have been my benefactor, but hardly my friend : Mary has taught me the difference. I owe you more than you will ever give me the chance of repaying you. But what friendship could have stood for an hour the hard words you have been in the way of giving me, as far back as I can remember! Hard words take all the sweetness from shelter. Mary is the only Christian I have ever known."

"So we are all pagans, except your low-lived lady's-maid! Upon my word!"

"She makes me feel, often, often," said Letty, bursting into tears. "as if I were with Jesus himself—as if he must be in the room somewhere."

So saying, she left her, and went to put up her things. Mrs. Wardour locked the door of the room where she sat, and refused to see or speak to her again. Letty went away, and walked to Testbridge.

"Godfrey will do something to make her understand," she said to herself, weeping as she walked.

Whether Godfrey ever did, I can not tell.

CHAPTER L.

WILLIAM AND MARY MARSTON.

THE same day on which Turnbull opened his new shop, a man was seen on a ladder painting out the sign above the old one. But the paint took time to dry.

The same day, also, Mary returned to Testbridge, and, going in by the kitchen-door, went up to her father's room, of which and of her own she had kept the keys—to the indignation of Turnbull, who declared he did not know how to get on without them for storage. But, for all his bluster, he was afraid of Mary, and did not dare touch anything she had left.

That night she spent alone in the house. But she could not sleep. She got up and went down to the shop. It was a bright, moonlit night, and all the house, even where the moon could not enter, was full of glimmer and gleam, except the shop. There she lighted a candle, sat down on a pile of goods, and gave herself up to memories of the past. Back and back went her thoughts as far as she could send them. God was everywhere in all the story; and the clearer she saw him there the surer she was that she would find him as she went on. She was neither sad nor fearful.

The dead hours of the night came, that valley of the shadow of death where faith seems to grow weary and sleep, and all the things of the shadow wake up and come out and say, " Here we are, and there is nothing but us and our kind in the universe ! " They woke up and came out upon Mary now, but she fought them off. Either there is mighty, triumphant life at the root and apex of all things, or life is not—and whence, then, the power of dreaming horrors ? It is life alone—life imperfect—that can fear ; death can not fear. Even the terror that walketh by night is a proof that I live, and that it shall not prevail against me. And to Mary, besides her heavenly Father, her William Marston seemed near all the time. Wherever she turned she saw the signs of him, and she pleased herself to think that perhaps he was there to welcome her. But it would not have made her the least sad to know for certain that he was far off, and would never come near her again in this world. She knew that, spite of time and space, she was and must be near him so long as she loved and did the truth. She knew there is no bond so strong, none so close, none so lasting as the truth. In God alone, who is the truth, can creatures meet.

The place was left in sad confusion and dirt, and she did not a little that night to restore order at least. But at length she was tired, and went up to her room.

On the first landing there was a window to the street. She stopped and looked out, candle in hand, but drew back with a start : on the opposite side of the way stood a man, looking up, she thought, at the house ! She hastened to her room, and to bed. If God was not watching, no waking was of use ; and if God was watching, she might sleep in peace. She did sleep, and woke refreshed.

Her first care in the morning was to write to Letty—with the result I have set down. The next thing she did was to go and ask Beenie to give her some breakfast. The old woman was delighted to see her, and ready to lock her door at once and go back to her old quarters. They returned together, while Testbridge was yet but half awake.

Many things had to be done before the shop could be

opened. Beenie went after charwomen, and soon a great bustle of cleaning arose. But the door was kept shut, and the front windows.

In the afternoon Letty came fresh from misery into more than counterbalancing joy. She took but time to put off her bonnet and shawl, and was presently at work helping Mary, cheerful as hope and a good conscience could make her.

Mary was in no hurry to open the shop. There was "stock to be taken," many things had to be rearranged, and not a few things to be added, before she could begin with comfort; and she must see to it all herself, for she was determined to engage no assistant until she could give her orders without hesitation.

She was soon satisfied that she could not do better than make a proposal to Letty which she had for some time contemplated—namely, that she should take up her permanent abode with her, and help her in the shop. Letty was charmed, nor ever thought of the annoyance it would be to her aunt. Mary had thought of that, but saw that, for Letty to allow the prejudices of her aunt to influence her, would be to order her life not by the law of that God whose Son was a workingman, but after the whim and folly of an ill-educated old woman. A new spring of life seemed to bubble up in Letty the moment Mary mentioned the matter; and in serving she soon proved herself one after Mary's own heart. Letty's day was henceforth without a care, and her rest was sweet to her. Many customers were even more pleased with her than with Mary. Before long, Mary, besides her salary, gave her a small share in the business.

Mrs. Wardour carried her custom to the Turnbulls.

When the paint was dry which obliterated the old sign, people saw the new one begin with an *M.*, and the sign-writer went on until there stood in full, *Mary Marston*. Mr. Brett hinted he would rather have seen it without the Christian name; but Mary insisted she would do and be nothing she would not hold just that name to; and on the sign her own name, neither more nor less, should stand. She would have liked, she said, to make it *William and Mary Marston*, for

the business was to go on exactly as her father had taught her ;
the spirit of her father should never be out of the place ; and
if she failed, of which she had no fear, she would fail trying
to carry out his ideas—but people were too dull to understand,
and she therefore set the sign so in her heart only.

Her old friends soon began to come about her again, and
it was not many weeks before she saw fit to go to London to
add to her stock.

The evening of her return, as she and Letty sat over a late
tea, a silence fell, during which Letty had a brooding fit.

"I wonder how Cousin Godfrey is getting on ? " she said
at last, and smiled sadly.

"How do you mean *getting on ?* " asked Mary.

"I was wondering whether Miss Yolland and he—"

Mary started from her seat, white as the table-cloth.

" Letty ! " she said, in a voice of utter dismay, " you don't
mean that woman is—is making friends with *him ?* "

"I saw them together more than once, and they seemed—
well, on very good terms."

" Then it is all over with him ! " cried Mary, in despair.
" O Letty ! what *is* to be done ? Why didn't you tell me
before ? He'll be madly in love with her by this time ! They
always are."

"But where's the harm, Mary ? She's a very handsome
lady, and of a good family."

"We're all of good enough family," said Mary, a little petulantly. " But that Miss Yolland—Letty—that Miss Yolland
—she's a bad woman, Letty."

" I never heard you say such a hard word of anybody before,
Mary ! It frightens me to hear you."

" It's a true word of her, Letty."

" How can you be so sure ? "

Mary was silent. There was that about Letty that made
the maiden shrink from telling the married woman what she
knew. Besides, in so far as Tom had been concerned, she could
not bring herself, even without mentioning his name, to talk
of him to his wife : there was no evil to be prevented and no
good to be done by it. If Letty was ever to know those pas-

sages in his life, she must hear them first in high places, and from the lips of the repentant man himself!

"I can not tell you, Letty," she said. "You know the two bonds of friendship are the right of silence and the duty of speech. I dare say you have some things which, truly as I know you love me, you neither wish nor feel at liberty to tell me."

Letty thought of what had so lately passed between her and her cousin Godfrey, and felt almost guilty. She never thought of one of the many things Tom had done or said that had cut her to the heart; those had no longer any existence. They were swallowed in the gulf of forgetful love—dismissed even as God casts the sins of his children behind his back : behind God's back is just nowhere She did not answer, and again there was silence for a time, during which Mary kept walking about the room, her hands clasped behind her, the fingers interlaced, and twisted with a strain almost fierce.

"There's no time! there's no time!" she cried at length. "How are we to find out? And if we knew all about it, what could we do? O Letty! what *am* I to do?"

"Anyhow, Mary dear, *you* can't be to blame! One would think you fancied yourself accountable for Cousin Godfrey!"

"I *am* accountable for him. He has done more for me than any man but my father; and I know what he does not know, and what the ignorance of will be his ruin. I know that one of the best men in the world "—so in her agony she called him—"is in danger of being married by one of the worst women ; and I can't bear it—I can't bear it!"

"But what can you do, Mary?"

"That's what I want to know," returned Mary, with irritation. "What *am* I to do? What *am* I to do?"

"If he's in love with her, he wouldn't believe a word any one—even you—told him against her."

"That is true, I suppose ; but it won't clear me. I must do something"

She threw herself on the couch with a groan.

"It's horrid!" she cried, and buried her face in the pillow.

All this time Letty had been so bewildered by Mary's agitation, and the cause of it was to her so vague, that apprehension for her cousin did not wake. But when Mary was silent, then came the thought that, if she had not so repulsed him—but she could not help it, and would not think in that direction.

Mary started from the couch, and began again to pace the room, wringing her hands, and walking up and down like a wild beast in its cage. It was so unlike her to be thus seriously discomposed, that Letty began to be frightened. She sat silent and looked at her. Then spoke the spirit of truth in the scholar, for the teacher was too troubled to hear. She rose, and going up to Mary from behind, put her arm round her, and whispered in her ear:

"Mary, why don't you ask Jesus?"

Mary stopped short, and looked at Letty. But she was not thinking about her; she was questioning herself: why had she not done as Letty said? Something was wrong with her: that was clear, if nothing else was! She threw herself again on the couch, and Letty saw her body heaving with her sobs. Then Letty was more frightened, and feared she had done wrong. Was it her part to remind Mary of what she knew so much better than she?

"But, then, I was only referring her to herself!" she thought.

A few minutes, and Mary rose. Her face was wet and white, but perplexity had vanished from it, and resolution had taken its place. She threw her arms round Letty, and kissed her, and held her face against hers. Letty had never seen in her such an expression of emotion and tenderness.

"I have found out, Letty, dear," she said. "Thank you, thank you, Letty! You are a true sister."

"What have you found out, Mary?"

"I have found out why I did not go at once to ask Him what I ought to do. It was just because I was afraid of what he would tell me to do."

And with that the tears ran down her cheeks afresh.

"Then you know now what to do?" asked Letty.

"Yes," answered Mary, and sat down.

CHAPTER LI.

A HARD TASK.

THE next morning, leaving the shop to Letty, Mary set out immediately after breakfast to go to Thornwick. But the duty she had there to perform was so distasteful, that she felt her very limbs refuse the office required of them. They trembled so under her that she could scarcely walk. She sent, therefore, to the neighboring inn for a fly. All the way, as she went, she was hoping she might be spared an encounter with Mrs. Wardour; but the old lady heard the fly, saw her get out, and, imagining she had brought Letty back in some fresh trouble, hastened to prevent either of them from entering the house. The door stood open, and they met on the broad step.

"Good morning, Mrs. Wardour," said Mary, trying to speak without betraying emotion.

"Good morning, Miss Marston," returned Mrs. Wardour, grimly.

"Is Mr. Wardour at home?" asked Mary.

"What is your business with *him*?" rejoined the mother.

"Yes; it is with him," returned Mary, as if she had mistaken her question, and there had been a point of exclamation after the *What*.

"About that hussy?"

"I do not know whom you call by the name," replied Mary, who would have been glad indeed to find a fellow-protector of Godfrey in his mother.

"You know well enough whom I mean. Whom should it be, but Letty Lovel!"

"My business has nothing to do with her," answered Mary.

"Whom has it to do with, then?"

"With Mr. Wardour."

"What is it?"

"Only Mr. Wardour himself must hear it. It is his business, not mine."

"I will have nothing to do with it."

"I have no desire to give you the least trouble about it," rejoined Mary.

"You can't see Mr. Wardour. He's not one to be at the beck and call of every silly woman that wants him."

"Then I will write, and tell him I called, but you would not allow me to see him."

"I will give him a message, if you like."

"Then tell him what I have just said. I am going home to write to him. Good morning."

She was getting into the fly again, when Mrs. Wardour, reflecting that it must needs be something of consequence that brought her there so early in a fly, and made her show such a determined front to so great a personage as herself, spoke again.

"I will tell him you are here; but you must not blame me if he does not choose to see you. We don't feel you have behaved well about that girl."

"Letty is my friend. I have behaved to her as if she were my sister."

"You had no business to behave to her as if she were your sister. You had no right to tempt her down to your level."

"Is it degradation to earn one's own living?"

"You had nothing to do with her. She would have done very well if you had but let her alone."

"Excuse me, ma'am, but I have *some* right in Letty. I am sorry to have to assert it, but she would have been dead long ago if I had behaved to her as you would have me."

"That was all her own fault."

"I will not talk with you about it: you do not know the circumstances to which I refer. I request to see Mr. Wardour. I have no time to waste in useless altercation."

Mary was angry, and it did her good; it made her fitter to face the harder task before her.

That moment they heard the step of Godfrey approaching through a long passage in the rear. His mother went into the parlor, leaving the door, which was close to where Mary stood, ajar. Godfrey, reaching the hall, saw Mary, and came up to her with a formal bow, and a face flushed with displeasure.

"May I speak to you alone, Mr. Wardour?" said Mary.

"Can you not say what you have to say here?"

"It is impossible."

"Then I am curious to know—"

"Let your curiosity plead for me, then."

With a sigh of impatience he yielded, and led the way to the drawing-room, which was at the other end of the hall. Mary turned and shut the door he left open.

"Why all this mystery, Miss Marston?" he said. "I am not aware of anything between you and me that can require secrecy."

He spoke with unconcealed scorn.

"When I have made my communication, you will at least allow secrecy to have been necessary."

"Some objects may require it!" said Wardour, in a tone itself an insult.

"Mr. Wardour," returned Mary, "I am here for your sake, not my own. May I beg you will not render a painful duty yet more difficult?"

"May *I* beg, then, that you will be as brief as possible? I am more than doubtful whether what you have to say will seem to me of so much consequence as you suppose."

"I shall be very glad to find it so."

"I can not give you more than ten minutes."

Mary looked at her watch.

"You have lately become acquainted with Miss Yolland, I am told," she began.

"Whew!" whistled Godfrey, yet hardly as if he were surprised.

"I have been compelled to know a good deal of that lady."

"As lady's-maid in her family, I believe."

"Yes," said Mary—then changing her tone after a slight pause, went on · "Mr. Wardour, I owe you more than I can ever thank you for. I strongly desire to fulfill the obligation your goodness has laid upon me, though I can never discharge it. For the sake of that obligation—for your sake, I am risking much—namely, your opinion of me."

He made a gesture of impatience.

"I *know* Miss Yolland to be a woman without principle.

I know it by the testimony of my own eyes, and from her own confession. She is capable of playing a cold-hearted, cruel game for her own ends. Be persuaded to consult Mr. Redmain before you commit yourself. Ask him if Miss Yolland is fit to be the wife of an honest man."

There was nothing in Godfrey's countenance but growing rage. Turning to the door, Mary would have gone without another word.

"Stay!" cried Godfrey, in a voice of suppressed fury. "Do not dare to go until I have told you that you are a vile slanderer. I knew something of what I had to expect, but you should never have entered this room had I known how far your effrontery could carry you. Listen to me : if anything more than the character of your statement had been necessary to satisfy me of the falsehood of every word of it, you have given it me in your reference to Mr. Redmain—a man whose life has rendered him unfit for the acquaintance, not to say the confidence of any decent woman. This is a plot—for what final object, God knows—between you and him ! I should be doing my duty were I to expose you both to the public scorn you deserve."

"Now I am clear !" said Mary to herself, but aloud, and stood erect, with glowing face and eyes of indignation : "Then why not do your duty, Mr. Wardour ? I should be glad of anything that would open your eyes. But Miss Yolland will never give Mr. Redmain such an opportunity. Nor does he desire it, for he might have had it long ago, by the criminal prosecution of a friend of hers. For my part, I should be sorry to see her brought to public shame."

"Leave the house !" said Godfrey through his teeth, and almost under his breath.

"I am sorry it is so hard to distinguish between truth and falsehood," said Mary, as she went to the door.

She walked out, got into the fly, and drove home ; went into the shop, and served the rest of the morning ; but in the afternoon was obliged to lie down, and did not appear again for three days.

The reception she had met with did not much surprise her :

plainly Sepia had been before her. She had pretended to make
Godfrey her confidant, had invented, dressed, and poured out
injuries to him, and so blocked up the way to all testimony un-
favorable to her. Was there ever man in more pitiable position?

It added to Godfrey's rage that he had not a doubt Mary
knew what had passed between Letty and him. That, he reasoned, was at the root of it all: she wanted to bring them
together yet: it would be a fine thing for her to have her
bosom-friend mistress of Thornwick! What a cursed thing
he should ever have been civil to her! And what a cursed
fool he was ever to have cared a straw for such a low-
minded creature as that Letty! Thank Heaven, he was cured
of that!

Cured?—He had fallen away from love—that was all the
cure!

Like the knight of the Red Cross, he was punished for
abandoning Una, by falling in love with Duessa. His rage
against Letty, just because of her faithfulness, had cast him an
easy prey into the arms of the clinging Sepia.

And now what more could Mary do? Just one thing was
left: Mr. Redmain could satisfy Mr. Wardour of the fact he
would not hear from her!—so, at least, thought Mary yet. If
Mr Redmain would take the trouble to speak to him, Mr.
Wardour must be convinced! However true might be what
Mr. Wardour had said about Mr. Redmain, fact remained fact
about Sepia!

She sat down and wrote the following letter:

"Sir: I hardly know how to address you without seeming
to take a liberty; at the same time I can not help hoping you
trust me enough to believe that I would not venture such a request as I am about to make, without good reason. Should
you kindly judge me not to presume, and should you be well
enough in health, which I fear may not be the case, would you
mind coming to see me here in my shop? I think you must
know it—it used to be Turnbull and Marston—the Marston
was my father. You will see my name over the door. Any

hour from morning to night will do for me ; only please let it be as soon as you can make it convenient.

"I am, sir,

"Your humble and grateful servant,

"MARY MARSTON."

"What the deuce is she grateful to me for ?" grumbled Mr. Redmain when he read it. "I never did anything for her ! By Jove, the gypsy herself wouldn't let me ! I vow she's got more brains of her own than any half-dozen women I ever had to do with before !"

The least thing bearing the look of plot, or intrigue, or secret to be discovered or heard, was enough for Mr. Redmain. What he had of pride was not of the same sort as Wardour's : it made no pretense to dignity, and was less antagonistic, so long at least as there was no talk of good motive or righteous purpose. Far from being offended with Mary's request, he got up at once, though indeed he was rather unwell and dreading an attack, ordered his brougham, and drove to Testbridge. There, careful of secrecy, he went to several shops, and bought something at each, but pretended not to find the thing he wanted.

He then said he would lunch at the inn, told his coachman to put up, and, while his meal was getting ready, went to Mary's shop, which was but a few doors off. There he asked for a certain outlandish stuff, and insisted on looking over a bale not yet unpacked. Mary understood him, and, whispering Letty to take him to the parlor, followed a minute after.

As soon as she entered—

"Come, now, what's it all about ?" he said.

Mary began at once to tell him, as directly as she could, that she was under obligation to Mr. Wardour of Thornwick, and that she had reason to fear Miss Yolland was trying to get a hold of him—"And you know what that would be for any man !" she said.

"No, by Jove ! I don't," he answered. "What would it be ?"

"Utter ruin," replied Mary.

"Then go and tell him so, if you want to save him."

"I have told him. But he does not like me, and won't believe me."

"Then let him take his own course, and be ruined."

"But I have just told you, sir, I am under obligation to him—great obligation!"

"Oh! I see! you want him yourself!—Well, as you wish it, I would rather you should have him than that she-devil. But come, now, you must be open with me."

"I am. I will be."

"You say so, of course. Women do.—But you confess you want him yourself?"

Mary saw it would be the worst possible policy to be angry with him, especially as she had given him the trouble to come to her, and she must not lose this her last chance. .

"I do not want him," she answered, with a smile; "and, if I did, he would never look at one in my position. He would as soon think of marrying the daughter of one of his laborers —and quite right, too—for the one might just be as good as the other."

"Well, now, that's a pity. I would have done a good deal for *you*—I don't know why, for you're a little humbug if ever there was one! But, if you don't care about the fellow, I don't see why I should take the trouble Confess—you're a little bit in love with him—ain't you, now? Confess to that, and I will do what I can"

"I can't confess to a lie. I owe Mr. Wardour a debt of gratitude—that is all—but no light thing, you will allow, sir!"

"I don't know; I never tried its weight. Anyhow, I should make haste to be rid of it."

"I have sought to make him this return, but he only fancies me a calumniator. Miss Yolland has been beforehand with me."

"Then, by Jove! I don't see but you're quits with him. If he behaves like that to you, don't you see, it wipes it all out? Upon my soul! I don't see why you should trouble your head about him. Let him take his way, and go to—Sepia."

"But, sir, what a dreadful thing it would be, knowing what she is, to let a man like him throw himself away on her!"

"I don't see it. I've no doubt he's just as bad as she is. We all are; we're all the same. And, if he weren't, it would be the better joke. Besides, you oughtn't to keep up a grudge, don't you know; you ought to let the—the *woman* have a chance. If he marries her—and that must be her game this time—she'll grow decent, and be respectable ever after, you may be sure—go to church, as you would have her, and all that—never miss a Sunday, I'll lay you a thousand."

"He's of a good old family!" said Mary, foolishly, thinking that would weigh with him.

"Good old fiddlestick! Damned old worn-out broom-end! *She's* of a good old family—quite good enough for his, you may take your oath! Why, my girl! the thing's not worth burning your fingers with. You've brought me here on a goose-errand. I'll go and have my lunch."

He rose.

"I'm sorry to have vexed you, sir," said Mary, greatly disappointed.

"Never mind.—I'm horribly sold," he said, with a tight grin. "I thought you must have some good thing in hand to make it worth your while to send for me."

"Then I must try something else," reflected Mary aloud.

"I wouldn't advise you. The man's only the surer to hate you and stick to her. Let him alone. If he's a stuck-up fellow like that, it will take him down a bit—when the truth comes out, that is, as come out it must. There's one good thing in it, my wife'll get rid of her. But I don't know! there's an enemy, as the Bible says, that sticketh closer than a brother. And they'll be next door when Durnmelling is mine! But I can sell it."

"If he *should* come to you, will you tell him the truth?"

"I don't know that. It might spoil my own little game."

"Will you let him think me a liar and slanderer?"

"No, by Jove! I won't do that. I don't promise to tell him all the truth, or even that what I do tell him shall be exactly true; but I won't let him think ill of my little puritan; that would spoil *your* game. Ta, ta!"

He went out, with his curious grin, amused, and enjoying

the idea of a proud fellow like that being taken in with Sepia.

"I hope devoutly he'll marry her!" he said to himself as he went to his luncheon. "Then I shall hold a rod over them both, and perhaps buy that miserable little Thornwick. Mortimer would give the skin off his back for it."

The thing that ought to be done had to be done, and Mary had done it—alas! to no purpose for the end desired: what was left her to do further? She could think of nothing. Sepia, like a moral hyena, must range her night. She went to bed, and dreamed she was pursued by a crowd, hooting after her, and calling her all the terrible names of those who spread evil reports. She woke in misery, and slept no more.

CHAPTER LII.

A SUMMONS.

One hot Saturday afternoon, in the sleepiest time of the day, when nothing was doing, and nobody in the shop, except a poor boy who had come begging for some string to help him fly his kite, though for the last month wind had been more scarce than string, Jemima came in from Durnmelling, and, greeting Mary with the warmth of the friendship that had always been true between them, gave her a letter.

"Whom is this from?" asked Mary, with the usual human waste of inquiry, seeing she held the surest answer in her hand.

"Mr. Mewks gave it me," said Jemima. "He didn't say whom it was from."

Mary made haste to open it: she had an instinctive distrust of everything that passed through Mewks's hands, and greatly feared that, much as his master trusted him, he was not true to him. She found the following note from Mr. Redmain:

"Dear Miss Marston : Come and see me as soon as you can ; I have something to talk to you about. Send word by the bearer when I may look for you. I am not well.
'"Yours truly,
"F. G. Redmain."

Mary went to her desk and wrote a reply, saying she would be with him the next morning about eleven o'clock. She would have gone that same night, she said, but, as it was Saturday, she could not, because of country customers, close in time to go so far.

"Give it into Mr. Redmain's own hand, if you can, Jemima," she said.

"I will try ; but I doubt if I can, miss," answered the girl

"Between ourselves, Jemima," said Mary, "I do not trust that man Mewks."

"Nobody does, miss, except the master and Miss Yolland."

"Then," thought Mary, "the thing is worse than I had supposed."

"I'll do what I can, miss," Jemima went on. "But he's so sharp !—Mr. Mewks, I mean."

After she was gone, Mary wished she had given her a verbal message ; that she might have insisted on delivering in person.

Jemima, with circumspection, managed to reach Mr. Redmain's room unencountered, but just as she knocked at the door, Mewks came behind her from somewhere, and snatching the letter out of her hand, for she carried it ready to justify her entrance to the first glance of her irritable master, pushed her rudely away, and immediately went in. But as he did so he put the letter in his pocket.

"Who took the note ?" asked his master.

"The girl at the lodge, sir."

"Is she not come back yet ?"

"No, sir, not yet. She'll be in a minute, though. I saw her coming up the avenue."

"Go and bring her here."

"Yes, sir."

Mewks went, and in two minutes returned with the letter, and the message that Miss Marston hadn't time to direct it.

"You damned rascal! I told you to bring the messenger here."

"She ran the whole way, sir, and not being very strong, was that tired, that, the moment she got in, the poor thing dropped in a dead faint. They ain't got her to yet."

His master gave him one look straight in the eyes, then opened the letter, and read it.

"Miss Marston will call here to-morrow morning," he said; "see that *she* is shown up at once—here, to my sitting-room. I hope I am explicit."

When the man was gone, Mr. Redmain nodded his head three times, and grinned the skin tight as a drum-head over his cheek-bones.

"There isn't a damned soul of them to be trusted!" he said to himself, and sat silently thoughtful.

Perhaps he was thinking how often he had come short of the hope placed in him; times of reflection arrive to most men; and a threatened attack of the illness he believed must one day carry him off, might well have disposed him to think.

In the evening he was worse.

By midnight he was in agony, and Lady Margaret was up with him all night. In the morning came a lull, and Lady Margaret went to bed. His wife had not come near him. But Sepia might have been seen, more than once or twice, hovering about his door

Both she and Mewks thought, after such a night, he must have forgotten his appointment with Mary.

When he had had some chocolate, he fell into a doze. But his sleep was far from profound. Often he woke and again dozed off.

The clock in the dressing-room struck eleven.

"Show Miss Marston up the moment she arrives," he said —and his voice was almost like that of a man in health.

"Yes, sir," replied the startled Mewks, and felt he must obey.

So Mary was at once shown to the chamber of the sick man.

To her surprise (for Mewks had given her no warning), he was in bed, and looking as ill as ever she had seen him. His small head was like a skull covered with parchment. He made the slightest of signs to her to come nearer—and again. She went close to the bed. Mewks sat down at the foot of it, out of sight. It was a great four-post-bed, with curtains.

" I'm glad you're come," he said, with a feeble grin, all he had for a smile. " I want to have a little talk with you. But I can't while that brute is sitting there. I have been suffering horribly. Look at me, and tell me if you think I am going to die—not that I take your opinion for worth anything. That's not what I wanted you for, though. I wasn't so ill then. But I want you the more to talk to now. *You* have a bit of a heart, even for people that don't deserve it—at least I'm going to believe you have ; and, if I am wrong, I almost think I would rather not know it till I'm dead and gone !—Good God ! where shall I be then ?"

I have already said that, whether in consequence of remnants of mother-teaching or from the movements of a conscience that had more vitality than any of his so-called friends would have credited it with, Mr. Redmain, as often as his sufferings reached a certain point, was subject to fits of terror—horrible anguish it sometimes amounted to—at the thought of hell. This, of course, was silly, seeing hell is out of fashion in far wider circles than that of Mayfair ; but denial does not alter fact, and not always fear. Mr. Redmain laughed when he was well, and shook when he was suffering. In vain he argued with himself that what he held by when in health was much more likely to be true than a dread which might be but the suggestion of the disease that was slowly gnawing him to death : as often as the sickness returned, he received the suggestion afresh, whatever might be its source, and trembled as before. In vain he accused himself of cowardice—the thing was there—*in him*—nothing could drive it out. And, verily, even a madman may be wiser than the prudent of this world ; and the courage of not a few would forsake them if they dared but look the danger in the face. I pity the poor ostrich, and

must I admire the man of whose kind he is the type, or take
him in any sense for a man of courage ? Wait till the thing
stares you in the face, and then, whether you be brave man or
coward, you will at all events care little about courage or cowardice. The nearer a man is to being a true man, the sooner
will conscience of wrong make a coward of him ; and herein
Redmain had a far-off kindred with the just. After the night
he had passed, he was now in one of his terror-fits ; and this
much may be said for his good sense—that, if there was anywhere a hell for the use of anybody, he was justified in antici-
pating a free entrance.

"Mewks !" he called, suddenly, and his tone was loud and
angry.

Mewks was by his bedside instantly.

"Get out with you! If I find you in this room again,
without having been called, I will kill you ! I am strong
enough for that, even without this pain. They won't hang a
dying man, and where I am going they will rather like it."

Mewks vanished.

"You need not mind, my girl," he went on, to Mary.
"Everybody knows I am ill—very ill. Sit down there, on the
foot of the bed, only take care you don't shake it, and let me
talk to you. People, you know, say nowadays there ain't any
hell—or perhaps none to speak of ?"

"I should think the former more likely than the latter,"
said Mary.

"You don't believe there is any ? I *am* glad of that ! for
you are a good girl, and ought to know."

"You mistake me, sir. How can I imagine there is no
hell, when *he* said there was ?"

"Who's *he* ?"

"The man who knows all about it, and means to put a stop
to it some day."

"Oh, yes ; I see ! Hm !—But I don't for the life of me see
what a fellow is to make of it all—don't you know ? Those
parsons ! They will have it there's no way out of it but theirs,
and I never could see a handle anywhere to that door !"

"I don't see what the parsons have to do with it," or, at

least, what you have got to do with the parsons. If a thing is true, you have as much to do with it as any parson in England ; if it is not true, neither you nor they have anything to do with it."

"But, I tell you, if it be all as true as—as—that we are all sinners, I don't know what to do with it !"

"It seems to me a simple thing. *That* man as much as said he knew all about it, and came to find men that were lost, and take them home."

"He can't well find one more lost than I am ! But how am I to believe it ? How *can* it be true ? It's ages since he was here, if ever he was at all, and there hasn't been a sign of him ever since, all the time ! "

"There you may be quite wrong. I think I could find you some who believe him just as near them now as ever he was to his own brothers—believe that he hears them when they speak to him, and heeds what they say."

"That's bosh. You would have me believe against the evidence of my senses ! "

"You must have strange senses, Mr. Redmain, that give you evidence where they can't possibly know anything ! If that man spoke the truth when he was in the world, he is near now ; if he is not near us, there is an end of it all."

" The nearer he is, the worse for me !" sighed Mr. Redmain.

"The nearer he is, the better for the worst man that ever breathed."

" That's queer doctrine ! Mind you, I don't say it mayn't be all right. But it does seem a cowardly thing to go asking him to save you, after you've been all your life doing what ought to damn you—if there be a hell, mind you, that is."

"But think," said Mary, " if that should be your only chance of being able to make up for the mischief you have done ? No punishment you can have will do anything for that. No suffering of yours will do anything for those you have made suffer. But it is so much harder to leave the old way than to go on and let things take their chance ! "

" There may be something in what you say ; but still I can't see it anything better than sneaking, to do a world of mischief, and then slink away into heaven, leaving all the poor wretches to look after themselves."

"I don't think Jesus Christ is worse pleased with you for feeling like that," said Mary.

"Eh ? What ? What's that you say ?—Jesus Christ worse pleased with me ? That's a good one ! As if he ever thought about a fellow like me !"

"If he did not, you would not be thinking about him just this minute, I suspect. There's no sense in it, if he does not think about you. He said himself he didn't come to call the righteous, but sinners to repentance."

" I wish I could repent."

" You can, if you will."

" I can't make myself sorry for what's gone and done with."

"No ; it wants him to do that. But you can turn from your old ways, and ask him to take you for a pupil Aren't you willing to learn, if he be willing to teach you ? "

" I don't know. It's all so dull and stupid ! I never could bear going to church."

"It's not one bit like that ! It's like going to your mother, and saying you're going to try to be a good boy, and not vex her any more."

"I see. It's all right, I dare say ! But I've had as much of it as I can stand ! You see, I'm not used to such things. You go away, and send Mewks. Don't be far off, though, and mind you don't go home without letting me know. There ! Go along."

She had just reached the door, when he called her again.

"I say ! Mind whom you trust in this house. There's no harm in Mrs. Redmain ; she only grows stupid directly she don't like a thing. But that Miss Yolland !—that woman's the devil. I know more about her than you or any one else. I can't bear her to be about Hesper : but, if I told her the half I know, she would not believe the half of that. I shall find a way, though. But I am forgetting ! you know her as well as I do—that is, you would, if you were wicked enough to understand. I will tell you one of these days what I am going to do. There! don't say a word. I want no advice on *such* things. Go along, and send Mewks."

With all his suspicion of the man, Mr. Redmain did not suspect *how* false Mewks was : he did not know that Miss Yolland had bewitched him for the sake of having an ally in the enemy's camp. All he could hear—and the dressing-room door was handy—the fellow duly reported to her. Already, instructed by her fears, she had almost divined what Mr. Redmain meant to do.

Mary went and sat on the lowest step of the stair just outside the room.

"What are you doing there ?" said Lady Margaret, coming from the corridor.

"Mr. Redmain will not have me go yet, my lady," answered Mary, rising. "I must wait first till he sends for me."

Lady Margaret swept past her, murmuring, "Most peculiar !" Mary sat down again.

In about an hour, Mewks came and said his master wanted her.

He was very ill, and could not talk, but he would not let her go. He made her sit where he could see her, and now and then stretched out his hand to her. Even in his pain he showed a quieter spirit. "Something may be working—who can tell !" thought Mary.

It was late in the afternoon when at length he sought further conversation.

"I have been thinking, Mary," he said, "that if I do wake up in hell when I die, no matter how much I deserve it, nobody will be the better for it, and I shall be all the worse."

He spoke with coolness, but it was by a powerful effort : he had waked from a frightful dream, drenched from head to foot. Coward ? No. He had reason to fear.

"Whereas," rejoined Mary, taking up his clew, "everybody will be the better if you keep out of it—everybody," she repeated, "—God, and Jesus Christ, and all their people."

"How do you make that out ?" he asked. "God has more to do than look after such as me."

"You think he has so many worlds to look to—thousands

of them only making ? But why does he care about his worlds ? Is it not because they are the schools of his souls ? And why should he care for the souls ? Is it not because he is making them children—his own children to understand him, and be happy with his happiness ?"

"I can't say I care for his happiness. I want my own. And yet I don't know any that's worth the worry of it. No : I would rather be put out like a candle."

"That's because you have been a disobedient child, taking your own way, and turning God's good things to evil. You don't know what a splendid thing life is. You actually and truly don't know, never experienced in your being the very thing you were made for."

"My father had no business to leave me so much money."

"You had no business to misuse it "

"I didn't *quite* know what I was doing "

"You do now."

Then came a pause.

"You think God hears prayer—do you ?"

"I do."

"Then I wish you would ask him to let me off—I mean, to let me die right out when I do die. What's the good of making a body miserable ?"

"That, I am sure it would be of no use to pray for. He certainly will not throw away a thing he has made, because that thing may be foolish enough to prefer the dust-hole to a cabinet."

"Wouldn't you do it now, if I asked you ?"

"I would not. I would leave you in God's hands rather than inside the gate of heaven."

"I don't understand you. And you wouldn't say so if you cared for me ! Only, why should you care for me ?"

"I would give my life for you."

"Come, now ! I don't believe that."

"Why, I couldn't be a Christian if I wouldn't !"

"You are getting absurd !" he cried. But he did not look exactly as if he thought it.

"Ab . . . . him

our Saviour ?   How could I be his disciple, if I wouldn't do as
he did ? "

"You are saying a good deal !"

"Can't you see that I have no choice ? "

"*I* wouldn't do that for anybody under the sun ! "

"You are not his disciple.   You have not been going about
with him."

"And you have ? "

"Yes—for many years.   Besides, I can not help thinking
there is one for whom you would do it."

"If you mean my wife, you never were more mistaken.   I
would do nothing of the sort."

"I did not mean your wife.   I mean Jesus Christ."

"Oh, I dare say ! Well, perhaps ; if I knew him as you do,
and if I were quite sure he wanted it done for him."

"He does want it done for him—always and every day—
not for his own sake, though it does make him very glad.   To
give up your way for his is to die for him ; and, when any one
will do that, then he is able to do everything for him ; for then,
and not till then, he gets such a hold of him that he can lift
him up, and set him down beside himself.   That's how my
father used to teach me, and now I see it for myself to be
true."

"It's all very grand, no doubt ; but it ain't nowhere, you
know.   It's all in your own head, and nowhere else.   You
don't, you *can't* positively believe all that ! "

"So much, at least, that I live in the strength and hope it
gives me, and order my ways according to it."

"Why didn't you teach my wife so ? "

"I tried, but she didn't care to think.   I could not get
any further with her.   She has had no trouble yet to make her
listen."

"By Jove ! I should have thought marrying a fellow like
me might have been trouble enough to make a saint of her."

It was impossible to fix him to any line of thought, and
Mary did not attempt it.   To move the child in him was more
than all argument.

A pause followed.

"I don't love God," he said.

"I dare say not," replied Mary. "How should you, when you don't know him?"

"Then what's to be done? I can't very well show myself where I hate the master of the house!"

"If you knew him, you would love him."

"You are judging by yourself. But there is as much difference between you and me as between light and darkness."

"Not quite that," replied Mary, with one of those smiles that used to make her father feel as if she were that moment come fresh from God to him. "If you knew Jesus Christ, you could not help loving him, and to love him is to love God."

"You wear me out! Will you never come to the point? *Know Jesus Christ!* How am I to go back two thousand years?"

"What he was then he is now," answered Mary. "And you may even know him better than they did at the time who saw him; for it was not until they understood him better, by his being taken from them, that they wrote down his life."

"I suppose you mean I must read the New Testament?" said Mr. Redmain, pettishly.

"Of course!" answered Mary, a little surprised; for she was unaware how few have a notion what the New Testament is, or is meant for.

"Then why didn't you say so at first? There I have you! That's just where I learn that I must be damned for ever!"

"I don't mean the Epistles. Those you can't understand —yet."

"I'm glad you don't mean *them.* I hate them."

"I don't wonder. You have never seen a single shine of what they are; and what most people think them is hardly the least like them. What I want you to read is the life and death of the son of man, the master of men."

"I can't read. I should only make myself twice as ill. I won't try."

"But I will read to you, if you will let me."

"How comes it you are such a theologian ? A woman is not expected to know about that sort of thing."

"I am no theologian. There just comes one of the cases in which those who call themselves his followers do not believe what the Master said : he said God hid these things from the wise and prudent, and revealed them to babes. I had a father who was child enough to know them, and I was child enough to believe him, and so grew able to understand them for myself. The whole secret is to do the thing the Master tells you : then you will understand what he tells you. The opinion of the wisest man, if he does not do the things he reads, is not worth a rush. He may be partly right, but you have no reason to trust him."

"Well, you shall be my chaplain. To-morrow, if I'm able to listen, you shall see what you can make of the old sinner."

Mary did not waste words : where would have been the use of pulling up the poor spiritual clodpole at every lumbering step, at any word inconsistent with the holy manners of the high countries ? Once get him to court, and the power of the presence would subdue him, and make him over again from the beginning, without which absolute renewal the best observance of religious etiquette is worse than worthless. Many good people are such sticklers for the proprieties ! For myself, I take joyous refuge with the grand, simple, every-day humanity of the man I find in the story—the man with the heart like that of my father and my mother and my brothers and sisters. If I may but see and help to show him a little as he lived to show himself, and not as church talk and church ways and church ceremonies and church theories and church plans of salvation and church worldliness generally have obscured him for hundreds of years, and will yet obscure him for hundreds more !

Toward evening, when she had just rendered him one of the many attentions he required, and which there was no one that day but herself to render, for he would scarcely allow Mewks to enter the room, he said to her :

"Thank you ; you are very good to me. I shall remember you. Not that I think I'm going to die just yet ; I've often been as bad as this, and got quite well again. Besides, I want to show that I have turned over a new leaf. Don't you think God will give me one more chance, now that I really mean it? I never did before."

"God can tell whether you mean it without that," she answered, not daring to encourage him where she knew nothing. "But you said you would remember me, Mr. Redmain : I hope you didn't mean in your will."

"I did mean in my will," he answered, but in a tone of displeasure. "I must say, however, I should have preferred you had not *shown* quite such an anxiety about it. I sha'n't be in my coffin to-morrow ; and I'm not in the way of forgetting things."

"I *beg* you," returned Mary, flushing, "to do nothing of the sort. I have plenty of money, and don't care about more. I would much rather not have any from you."

"But think how much good you might do with it!" said Mr. Redmain, satirically "—It was come by honestly—so far as I know."

"Money can't do half the good people think. It is stubborn stuff to turn to any good. And in this case it would be directly against good"

"Nobody has a right to refuse what comes honestly in his way. There's no end to the good that may be done with money—to judge, at least, by the harm I've done with mine," said Mr. Redmain, this time with seriousness.

"It is not in it," persisted Mary. "If it had been, our Lord would have used it, and he never did."

"Oh, but he was all an exception !"

"On the contrary, he is the only man who is no exception. We are the exceptions. Every one but him is more or less out of the straight. Do you not see ?—he is the very one we must all come to be the same as, or perish ! No, Mr. Redmain ! don't leave me any money, or I shall be altogether bewildered what to do with it. Mrs. Redmain would not take it from me. Miss Yolland might, but I dared not give it to her. And for societies, I have small faith in them."

"Well, well! I'll think about it," said Mr Redmain, who

had now got so far on the way of life as to be capable of believing that when Mary said a thing she meant it, though he
was quite incapable of understanding the true relations of
money. Few indeed are the Christians capable of that! The
most of them are just where Peter was, when, the moment
after the Lord had honored him as the first to recognize him
as the Messiah, he took upon him to object altogether to his
Master's way of working salvation in the earth. The Roman
emperors took up Peter's plan, and the devil has been in the
church ever since—Peter's Satan, whom the Master told to get
behind him. They are poor prophets, and no martyrs, who
honor money as an element of any importance in the salvation of the world. Hunger itself does incomparably more to
make Christ's kingdom come than ever money did, or ever
will do while time lasts. Of course money has its part, for
everything has; and whoever has money is bound to use it as
best he knows; but his best is generally an attempt to do
saint-work by devil-proxy.

"I can't think where on earth you got such a sackful of
extravagant notions!" Mr. Redmain added.

"I told you before, sir, I had a father who set me thinking!" answered Mary.

"I wish I had had a father like yours," he rejoined.

"There are not many such to be had."

"I fear mine wasn't just what he ought to be, though he
can't have been such a rascal as his son: he hadn't time; he
had his money to make."

"He had the temptation to make it, and you have the
temptation to spend it: which is the more dangerous, I don't
know. Each has led to many crimes."

"Oh, as to crimes—I don't know about that! It depends
on what you call crimes."

"It doesn't matter whether men call a deed a crime or a
fault; the thing is how God regards it, for that is the only
truth about it. What the world thinks, goes for nothing, because it is never right. It would be worse in me to do some
things the world counts perfectly honorable, than it would be
for this man to commit a burglary, or that a murder. I mean

my guilt might be greater in committing a respectable sin, than theirs in committing a disreputable one."

Had Mary known anything of science, she might have said that, in morals as in chemistry, the qualitative analysis is easy, but the quantitative another affair.

The latter part of this conversation, Sepia listening heard, and misunderstood utterly.

All the rest of the day Mary was with Mr. Redmain, mostly by his bedside, sitting in silent watchfulness when he was unable to talk with her. Nobody entered the room except Mewks, who, when he did, seemed to watch everything, and try to hear everything, and once Lady Margaret. When she saw Mary seated by the bed, though she must have known well enough she was there, she drew herself up with grand English repellence, and looked scandalized. Mary rose, and was about to retire. But Mr. Redmain motioned her to sit still.

"This is my spiritual adviser, Lady Margaret," he said

Her ladyship cast a second look on Mary, such as few but her could cast, and left the room.

On into the gloom of the evening Mary sat. No one brought her anything to eat or drink, and Mr Redmain was too much taken up with himself, soul and body, to think of her. She was now past hunger, and growing faint, when, through the settled darkness, the words came to her from the bed :

"I should like to have you near me when I am dying, Mary."

The voice was a softer than she had yet heard from Mr. Redmain, and its tone went to her heart.

"I will certainly be with you, if God please," she answered.

"There is no fear of God," returned Mr. Redmain ; "it's the devil will try to keep you away. But never you heed what any one may do or say to prevent you. Do your very best to be with me. By that time I may not be having my own way any more. Be sure, the first moment they can get the better of me, they will. And you mustn't place confidence in a single soul in this house. I don't say my wife would play me false so long as I was able to swear at her, but I wouldn't trust her one moment longer. You come and be with me in spite of the whole posse of them."

"I will try, Mr. Redmain," she answered, faintly. "But indeed you must let me go now, else I may be unable to come to-morrow."

"What's the matter?" he asked hurriedly, half lifting his head with a look of alarm. "There's no knowing," he went on, muttering to himself, "what may happen in this cursed house."

"Nothing," replied Mary, "but that I have not had anything to eat since I left home. I feel rather faint." .

"They've given you nothing to eat!" cried Mr. Redmain, but in a tone that seemed rather of satisfaction than displeasure. "Ring—no, don't."

"Indeed, I would rather not have anything now till I get home," said Mary. "I don't feel inclined to eat where I am not welcome."

"Right! right! right!" said Mr. Redmain. "Stick to that. Never eat where you are not welcome. Go home directly. Only say when you will come to-morrow."

"I can't very well during the day," answered Mary. "There is so much to be done, and I have so little help. But, if you should want me, I would rather shut up the shop than not come."

"There is no need for that! Indeed, I would much rather have you in the evening. The first of the night is worst of all. It's then the devils are out.—Look here," he added, after a short pause, during which Mary, for as unfit as she felt, hesitated to leave him, "—being in business, you've got a lawyer, I suppose?"

"Yes," she answered.

"Then you go to him to-night the first thing, and tell him to come to me to-morrow, about noon. Tell him I am ill, and in bed, and particularly want to see him; and he mustn't let anything they say keep him from me, not even if they tell him I am dead."

"I will," said Mary, and, stroking the thin hand that lay outside the counterpane, turned and left him.

" Don't tell any one you are gone," he called after her, with a voice far from feeble. "I don't want any of their damned company."

— · ·

CHAPTER LIII.

A FRIEND IN NEED.

MARY left the house, and saw no one on her way. But it was better, she said to herself, that he should lie there untended, than be waited on by unloving hands.

The night was very dark. There was no moon, and the stars were hidden by thick clouds. She must walk all the way to Testbridge. She felt weak, but the fresh air was reviving. She did not know the way so familiarly as that between Thornwick and the town, but she would enter the latter before arriving at the common.

She had not gone far when the moon rose, and from behind the clouds diminished the darkness a little. The first part of her journey lay along a narrow lane, with a small ditch, a rising bank, and a hedge on each side. About the middle of the lane was a farmyard, and a little way farther a cottage. Soon after passing the gate of the farmyard, she thought she heard steps behind her, seemingly soft and swift, and naturally felt a little apprehension ; but her thoughts flew to the one hiding-place for thoughts and hearts and lives, and she felt no terror. At the same time something moved her to quicken her pace. As she drew near the common, she heard the steps more plainly, still soft and swift, and almost wished she had sought refuge in the cottage she had just passed—only it bore no very good character in the neighborhood. When she reached the spot where the paths united, feeling a little at home, she stopped to listen. Behind her were the footsteps plain enough ! The same moment the clouds thinned about the moon, and a pale light came filtering through upon the common in front of her. She

cast one look over her shoulder, saw something turn a corner
in the lane, and sped on again. She would have run, but there
was no place of refuge now nearer than the corner of the turn-
pike-road, and she knew her breath would fail her long before
that. How lonely and shelterless the common looked! The
soft, swift steps came nearer and nearer.

Was that music she heard? She dared not stop to listen.
But immediately, thereupon, was poured forth on the dim air
such a stream of pearly sounds as if all the necklaces of some
heavenly choir of woman-angels were broken, and the beads
came pelting down in a cataract of hurtless hail. From no
source could they come save the bow and violin of Joseph Jasper! Where could he be? She was so rejoiced to know that
he must be somewhere near, that, for very delight of unsecured
safety, she held her peace, and had almost stopped. But she
ran on again.

She was now nigh the ruined hut with which my narrative
has made the reader acquainted. In the mean time the moon
had been growing out of the clouds, clearer and clearer. The
hut came in sight. But the look of it was somehow altered
—with an undefinable change, such as might appear on a familiar object in a dream; and leaning against the side of the
door stood a figure she could not mistake for another than her
musician. Absorbed in his music, he did not see her. She
called out, "Joseph! Joseph!" He started, threw his bow
from him, tucked his violin under his arm, and bounded to
meet her. She tried to stop, and the same moment to look
behind her. The consequence was that she fell—but safe in
the smith's arms. That instant appeared a man running. He
half stopped, and, turning from the path, took to the common.
Jasper handed his violin to Mary, and darted after him. The
chase did not last a minute; the man was nearly spent. Joseph seized him by the wrist, saw something glitter in his
other hand, and turned sick. The fellow had stabbed him.
With indignation, as if it were a snake that had bit him, the
blacksmith flung from him the hand he held. The man gave
a cry, staggered, recovered himself, and ran. Joseph would
have followed again, but fell, and for a minute or two lost con-

sciousness. When he came to himself, Mary was binding up his arm.

"What a fool I am!" he said, trying to get up, but yielding at once to Mary's prevention. "Ain't it ridic'lous now, miss, that a man of my size. and ready to work a sledge with any smith in Yorkshire, should turn sick for a little bit of a job with a knife? But my father was just the same, and he was a stronger man than I'm like to be. I fancy."

"It is no such wonder as you think," said Mary: "you have lost a good deal of blood."

Her voice faltered. She had been greatly alarmed—and the more that she had not light enough to get the edges of the wound properly together.

"You've stopped it—ain't you, miss?"

"I think so."

"Then I'll be after the fellow "

"No. no: you must not attempt it. You must lie still awhile. But I don't under-tand it at all! That cottage used to be a mere hovel, without door or window! It can't be you live in it?"

"Ay, that I do! and it's not a bad place either," answered Joseph. "That's what I went to Yorkshire to get my money for. It's mine—bought and paid for "

"But what made you think of coming here?"

"Let's go into the smithy—hou-e I won't presume to call it." said Joseph, "though it has a lean-to for the smith—and I'll tell you everything about it But really, miss, you oughtn't to be out like this after dark. There's too many vagabonds about."

With but little need of the help Mary yet gave him. Joseph got up, and led her to what was now a respectable little smithy, with forge and bellows and anvil and bucket. Opening a door where had been none, he brought a chair, and making her sit down, began to blow the covered fire on the hearth, where he had not long before "boiled his kettle" for his tea. Then closing the door, he lighted a candle, and Mary looking about her could scarcely believe the change that had come upon the mise '   '   J   l, and begged to know where she had just been, and how far she had run from the rascal. When he had learned something of the peculiar relations in which Mary stood to the family at Durnmelling, he began to think there might have been something more in the pursuit than a chance ruffianly assault, and the greater were his regrets that he had not secured the miscreant.

"Anyhow, miss," he said, "you'll never come from there alone in the dark again !"

"I understand you, Joseph," answered Mary, "for I know you would not have me leave doing what I can for the poor man up there, because of a little danger in the way."

"No, that I wouldn't, miss. That would be as much as to say you would do the will of God when the devil would let you. What I mean is, that here am I—your slave, or servant, or soldier, or whatever you may please to call me, ready at your word."

"I must not take you from your work, you know, Joseph."

"Work's not everything, miss," he answered; "and it's seldom so pressing but that—except I be shoeing a horse—I can leave it when I choose. Any time you want to go anywhere, don't forget as you've got enemies about, and just send for me. You won't have long to wait till I come. But I am main sorry the rascal didn't have something to keep him in mind of his manners."

Part of this conversation, and a good deal more, passed on their way to Testbridge, whither, as soon as Joseph seemed all right, Mary, who had forgotten her hunger and faintness, insisted on setting out at once. In her turn she questioned Joseph, and learned that, as soon as he knew she was going to settle at Testbridge, he started off to find if possible a place in the neighborhood humble enough to be within his reach, and near enough for the hope of seeing her sometimes, and having what help she might please to give him. The explanation afforded Mary more pleasure than she cared to show. She had a real friend near her—one ready to help her on her own ground —one who understood her because he understood the things she loved ! He told her that already he had work enough to keep him going; that the horses he once shod were always brought to him again ; that he was at no expense such as in a town ; and that he had plenty of time both for his violin and his books.

When they came to the suburbs, she sent him home, and went straight to Mr. Brett with Mr. Redmain's message. He undertook to be at Durnmelling at the time appointed, and to let nothing prevent him from seeing his new client.

CHAPTER LIV.

THE NEXT NIGHT.

Mr. BRETT found no difficulty in the way of the interview, for Mr. Redmain had given Mewks instructions he dared not disobey : his master had often ailed, and recovered again, and he must not venture too far ! As soon as he had shown the visitor into the room, he was dismissed, but not before he had satisfied himself that he was a lawyer. He carried the news at once to Sepia, and it wrought no little anxiety in the house. There was a will already in existence, and no ground for thinking a change in it boded anything good Mr. Mortimer never deigned to share his thoughts, anxieties, or hopes with any of his people ; but the ladies met in deep consultation, although of course there was nothing to be done. The only operative result was that it let Sepia know how, though for reasons somewhat different, her anxiety was shared by the others : unlike theirs, her sole desire was—*not* to be mentioned in the will : that could only be for the sake of leaving her a substantial curse ! Mr. Redmain's utter silence, after, as she well knew, having gathered damning facts to her discredit, had long convinced her he was but biding his time. Certain she was he would not depart this life without leaving his opinion of her and the proofs of its justice behind him, carrying weight as the affidavit of a dying man. Also she knew Hesper well enough to be certain that, however she might delight in opposition to the desire of her husband, she would for the sake of no one carry that opposition to a point where it became injurious to her interests. Sepia's one thought therefore was: could not something be done to prevent the making of another will, or the leaving of any fresh document behind him? What he might already have done, she could nowise help; what he might yet do, it would be well to prevent. Once more, therefore, she impressed upon Mewks, and that in the names of Mrs. Redmain and Lady Margaret, as well as in her own person, the absolute necessity of learning as much as possible of what might pass between his master and the lawyer.

Mewks was driven to the end of his wits, and they were not a few, to find excuses for going into the room, and for delaying to go out again, while with all his ears he listened. But both client and lawyer were almost too careful for him; and he had learned positively nothing when the latter rose to depart. He instantly left the room, with the door a trifle ajar, and listening intently, heard his master say that Mr. Brett must come again the next morning; that he felt better, and would think over the suggestions he had made; and that he must leave the memoranda within his reach, on the table by his bedside. Ere the lawyer issued, Mewks was on his way with all this to his tempter.

Sepia concluded there had been some difference of opinion between Mr. Redmain and his adviser, and hoped that nothing had been finally settled. Was there any way to prevent the lawyer from seeing him again? Could she by any means get a peep at the memoranda mentioned? She dared not suggest the thing to Hesper or Lady Malice—of all people they were those in relation to whom she feared their possible contents—and she dared not show herself in Mr. Redmain's room. Was Mewks to be trusted to the point of such danger as grew in her thought?

The day wore on. Toward evening he had a dreadful attack. Any other man would have sent before now for what medical assistance the town could afford him, but Mr. Redmain hated having a stranger about him, and, as he knew how to treat himself, it was only when very ill that he would send for his own doctor to the country, fearing that otherwise he

might give him up as a patient, such visits, however well re-
munerated, being seriously inconvenient to a man with a large
London practice. But now Lady Margaret took upon herself
to send a telegram.

An hour before her usual time for closing the shop, Mary
set out for Durnmelling; and, at the appointed spot on the
way, found her squire of low degree in waiting. At first sight,
however, and although she was looking out for him, she did
not certainly recognize him. I would not have my reader imagine Joseph one of those fools who delight in appearing something else than they are; but while every workman ought to
look a workman, it ought not to be by looking less of a man,
or of a *gentleman* in the true sense; and Joseph, having, out
of respect to her who would honor him with her company,
dressed himself in a new suit of unpretending gray, with a
wide-awake hat, looked at first sight more like a country gentleman having a stroll over his farm, than a man whose hands
were hard with the labors of the forge. He took off his hat as
she approached—if not with ease, yet with the clumsy grace
peculiar to him; for, unlike many whose manners are unobjec-
tionable, he had in his something that might be called his own.
But the best of it was, that he knew nothing about his manners, beyond the desire to give honor where honor was due.

He walked with her to the door of the house; for they had
agreed that, from whatever quarter had come the pursuit, and
whatever might have been its object, it would be well to show
that she was attended. They had also arranged at what hour,
and at what spot close at hand, he was to be waiting to accompany her home. But, although he said nothing about it, Joseph was determined not to leave the place until she rejoined
him.

It was nearly dark when he left her; and when he had
wandered up and down the avenue awhile, it seemed dark
enough to return to the house, and reconnoiter a little.

He had already made the acquaintance of the farmer who
occupied a portion of the great square, behind the part where
the family lived: he had had several of his horses to shoe, and
had not only given satisfaction by the way in which he shod

them, but had interested their owner with descriptions of more
than one rare mode of shoeing to which he had given attention ; he was, therefore, the less shy of being discovered about
the place.

From the back he found his way into the roofless hall, and
there paced quietly up and down, measuring the floor, and
guessing at the height and thickness of the walls, and the sort
of roof they had borne. He noted that the wall of the house
rose higher than those of the ruin with which it was in contact ; and that there was a window in it just over one of those
walls. Thinking whether it had been there when the roof was
on, he saw through it the flickering of a fire, and wondered
whether it could be the window of Mr. Redmain's room.

Mary, having resolved not to give any notice of her arrival,
if she could get in without it, and finding the hall-door on the
latch, entered quietly, and walked straight to Mr. Redmain's
bedroom. When she opened the door of it, Mewks came hurriedly to meet her, as if he would have made her go out again,
but she scarcely looked at him, and advanced to the bed. Mr.
Redmain was just waking from the sleep into which he had
fallen after a severe paroxysm.

"Ah, there you are ! " he said, smiling her a feeble welcome.
" I am glad you are come. I have been looking out for you.
I am very ill. If it comes again to-night, I think it will make
an end of me."

She sat down by the bedside. He lay quite still for some
time, breathing like one very weary. Then he seemed to grow
easier, and said, with much gentleness :

"Can't you talk to me ? "

"Would you like me to read to you ? " she asked.

"No," he answered ; " I can't bear the light ; it makes my
head furious."

" Shall I talk to you about my father ? " she asked.

"I don't believe in fathers," he replied.   " They're always
after some notion of their own. It's not their children they
care about."

" That may be true of some fathers," answered Mary ; "but
it is not the least true of mine."

" Where is he ? Why don't you bring him to see me, if he is such a good man ? He might be able to do something for me."

" There is none but your own father can do anything for you," said Mary. " My father is gone home to him, but if he were here, he would only tell you about *him*."

There was a moment's silence.

" Why don't you talk ? " said Mr. Redman, crossly. " What's the good of sitting there saying nothing ! How am I to forget that the pain will be here again, if you don't say a word to help me ? "

Mary lifted up her heart, and prayed for something to say to the sad human soul that had never known the Father. But she could think of nothing to talk about except the death of William Marston. So she began with the dropping of her watch, and, telling whatever seemed at the moment fit to tell, ended with the dream she had the night of his funeral. By that time the hidden fountain was flowing in her soul, and she was able to speak straight out of it.

" I can not tell you, sir," she said, closing the story of her dream, " what a feeling it was ! The joy of it was beyond all expression."

" You're not surely going to offer me a dream in proof of anything ! " muttered the sick man.

" Yes," answered Mary—" in proof of what it can prove. The joy of a child over a new toy, or a colored sweetmeat, shows of what bliss the human soul is made capable."

" Oh, capable, I dare say ! "

" And more than that," Mary went on, adding instead of replying, " no one ever felt such gladness without believing in it. There must be somewhere the justification of such gladness. There must be the father of it somewhere."

" Well ! I don't like to say, after your kindness in coming here to take care of me, that you talk the worst rubbish I ever heard ; but just tell me of what use is it all to me, in the state I am in ! What I want is to be free of pain, and have some pleasure in life—not to be told about a father."

" But what if the father you don't want is determined you

shall not have what you do want ? What if your desire is not worth keeping you alive for ? And what if he is ready to help your smallest effort to be the thing he wants you to be—and in the end to give you your heart's desire ? "

"It sounds very fine, but it's all so thin, so up in the clouds ! It don't seem to have a leg to stand upon. Why, if that were true, everybody would be good ! there would be none but saints in the world ! What's in it, I'm sure I don't know."

"It will take ages to know what is in it ; but, if you should die now, you will be glad to find, on the other side, that you have made a beginning. For my part, if I had everything my soul could desire, except God with me, I could but pray that he would come to me, or not let me live a moment longer ; for it would be but the life of a devil."

"What do you mean by a devil ? "

"A power that lives against its life," said Mary.

Mr. Redmain answered nothing. He did not perceive an atom of sense in the words. They gave him not a glimmer. Neither will they to many of my readers ; while not a few will think they see all that is in them, and see nothing.

He was silent for a long time—whether he waked or slept she could not tell.

The annoyance was great in the home conclave when Mewks brought the next piece of news—namely, that there was that designing Marston in the master's room again, and however she got into the house he was sure *he* didn't know.

"All the same thing over again, miss !—hard at it a-tryin' to convert 'im !—And where's the use, you know, miss ? If a man like my master's to be converted and get off, I don't for my part see where's the good o' keepin' up a devil."

"I am quite of your opinion, Mewks," said Sepia.

But in her heart she was ill at ease.

All day long she had been haunted with an ever-recurring temptation, which, instead of dismissing it, she kept like a dog in a string. Different kinds of evil affect people differently. Ten thousand will do a dishonest thing, who would indignantly reject the dishonest thing favored by another ten thousand. They are not sufficiently used to its ugly face not to dislike it, though it may not be quite so ugly as their *protégé*. A man will feel grandly honest against the dishonesties of another trade than his, and be eager to justify those of his own. Here was Sepia, who did not care the dust of a butterfly's wing for causing any amount of family misery, who would without a pang have sacrificed the genuine reputation of an innocent man to save her own false one—shuddering at an idea as yet bodiless in her brain—an idea which, however, she did not dismiss, and so grew able to endure!

I have kept this woman—so far as personal acquaintance with her is concerned—in the background of my history. For one thing, I am not fond of *post-mortem* examinations; in other words, I do not like searching the decompositions of moral carrion. Analysis of such is, like the use of reagents on dirt, at least unpleasant. Nor was any true end to be furthered by a more vivid presentation of her. Nosology is a science doomed, thank God, to perish! Health alone will at last fill the earth. Or, if there should be always the ailing to help, a man will help them by being sound himself, not by knowing the ins and outs of disease. Diagnosis is not therapy.

Sepia was unnatural—as every one is unnatural who does not set his face in the direction of the true Nature; but she had gone further in the opposite direction than many people have yet reached. At the same time, whoever has not faced about is on the way to a capacity for worse things than even our enemies would believe of us.

Her very existence seemed to her now at stake. If by his dying act Mr. Redmain should drive her from under Hesper's roof, what was to become of her! Durnmelling, too, would then be as certainly closed against her, and she would be compelled to take a situation, and teach music, which she hated, and French and German, which gave her no pleasure apart from certain strata of their literature, to insolent girls whom she would be constantly wishing to strangle, or stupid little boys who would bore her to death. Her very soul sickened at the thought—as well it might, for to have to do such service with such a heart as hers, must indeed be torment. All hope of marrying Godfrey Wardour would be gone, of course. Did he but remain uncertain as to the truth or falsehood of a third part of what Mr. Redmain would record against her, he would never meet her again !

Since the commencement of this last attack of Mr. Redmain's malady, she had scarcely slept ; and now what Mewks reported rendered her nigh crazy. For some time she had been generally awake half the night, and all the last night she had been wandering here and there about the house, not unfrequently couched where she could hear every motion in Mr. Redmain's room. Haunted by fear, she in turn haunted her fear. She could not keep from staring down the throat of the pit. She was a slave of the morrow, the undefined, awful morrow, ever about to bring forth no one knows what. That morrow could she but forestall !

If any should think that anxiety and watching must have so wrought on Sepia that she came to be no longer accountable for her actions, I will not oppose the kind conclusion. For my own part, until I shall have seen a man absolutely one with the source of his being, I do not believe I shall ever have seen a man absolutely sane. What many would point to as plainest proofs of sanity, I should regard as surest signs of the contrary.

A sign of my own insanity is it ?

Your insanity may be worse than mine, for you are aware of none, and I with mine do battle. I believe all insanity has moral as well as physical roots. But enough of this. There are questions we can afford to leave.

Sepia had got very thin during these trying days. Her great eyes were larger yet, and filled with a troubled anxiety. Not paleness, for of that her complexion was incapable, but a dull pallor possessed her cheek. If one had met her as she roamed the house that night, he might well have taken her for some naughty ancestor, whose troubled conscience, not yet able to shake off the madness of some evil deed, made her wander still about the place where she had committed it.

She believed in no supreme power who cares that right should be done in his worlds. Here, it may be, some of my unbelieving acquaintances, foreseeing a lurid something on the horizon of my story, will be indignant that the capacity for crime should be thus associated with the denial of a Live Good. But it remains a mere fact that it is easier for a man to commit a crime when he does not fear a willed retribution. Tell me there is no merit in being prevented by fear; I answer, the talk is not of merit. As the world is, that is, as the race of men at present is, it is just as well that the man who has no merit, and never dreamed of any, should yet be a little hindered from cutting his neighbor's throat at his evil pleasure.—No ; I do not mean hindered by a lie—I mean hindered by the poorest apprehension of the grandest truth.

Of those who do not believe, some have never had a noble picture of God presented to them ; but whether their phantasm is of a mean God because they refuse him, or they refuse him because their phantasm of him is mean, who can tell ? Anyhow, mean notions must come of meanness, and, uncharitable as it may appear, I can not but think there is a moral root to all chosen unbelief. But let God himself judge his own

With Sepia, what was *best* meant what was best for her, and *best for her* meant *most after her liking.*

She had in her time heard a good deal about *euthanasia*, and had taken her share in advocating it. I do not assume this to be anything additional against her ; one who does not believe in God, may in such an advocacy indulge a humanity pitiful over the irremediable ills of the race ; and, being what she was, she was no worse necessarily for advocating that than for advocating cremation, which she did—occasionally, I must confess, a little coarsely. But the notion of *euthanasia* might well work for evil in a mind that had not a thought for the case any more than for the betterment of humanity, or indeed for anything but its own consciousness of pleasure or comfort. Opinions, like drugs, work differently on different constitutions. Hence the man is foolish who goes scattering vague notions regardless of the soil on which they may fall

She was used to asking the question, What's the good ? but always in respect of something she wanted out of her way.

"What's the good of an hour or two more if you're not

enjoying it ?" she said to herself again and again that Monday. "What's the good of living when life is pain—or fear of death, from which no fear can save you ?" But the question had no reference to her own life . she was judging for another—and for another not for his sake, or from his point of view, but for her own sake, and from where she stood.

All the day she wandered about the house, such thoughts as these in her heart, and in her pocket a bottle of that concentrated which Mr. Redmain was taking much diluted for medicine. But she *hoped not to have to use it.* If only Mr. Redmain would yield the conflict, and depart without another interview with the lawyer !

But if he would not, and two drops from the said bottle, not taken by herself, but by another, would save her, all her life to come, from endless anxiety and grinding care, from weariness and disgust, and indeed from want ; nor that alone, but save likewise that other from an hour, or two hours, or perhaps a week, or possibly two weeks, or—who could tell ?— it might be a month of pain and moaning and weariness, would it not be well ?—must it not be more than well ?

She had not learned to fear temptation ; she feared poverty, dependence, humiliation, labor. *ennui,* misery. The thought of the life that must follow and wrap her round in the case of the dreaded disclosure was unendurable ; the thought of the suggested frustration was not *so* unendurable—was not absolutely unendurable—was to be borne—might be permitted to come—to return—was cogitated—now with imagined resistance, now with reluctant and partial acceptance, now with faint resolve, and now with determined resolution—now with the beaded drops pouring from the forehead, and now with a cold, scornful smile of triumphant foil and success.

Was she so very exceptionally bad, however ? You who hate your brother or your sister—you do not think yourself at all bad ! But you are a murderer, and she was only a murderer. You do not feel wicked ? How do you know she did ? Besides, you hate, and she did not hate ; she only wanted to take care of herself. Lady Macbeth did not hate Duncan ; she only wanted to give her husband his crown. You only hate your brother ; you would not, you say, do him any harm ; and I believe you would not do him mere bodily harm ; but, were things 'changed, so that hate-action became absolutely safe, I should have no confidence what you might not come to do. No one can tell what wreck a gust of passion upon a sea of hate may work. There are men a man might well kill, if he were anything less than ready to die for them. The difference between the man that hates and the man that kills may be nowhere but in the courage. These are *grewsome* thinkings : let us leave them—but hating with them.

All the afternoon Sepia hovered about Mr. Redmain's door, down upon Mewks every moment he appeared. Her head ached ; she could hardly breathe. Rest she could not. Once when Mewks, coming from the room, told her his master was asleep, she crept in, and, softly approaching the head of the bed, looked at him from behind, then stole out again.

" He seems dying, Mewks," she said.

" Oh, no, miss ! I've often seen him as bad. He's better."

" Who's that whispering ?" murmured the patient, angrily, though half asleep.

Mewks went in, and answered :

" Only me and Jemima, sir."

" Where's Miss Marston ?"

" She's not come yet, sir."

" I want to go to sleep again. You must wake me the moment she comes."

" Yes, sir."

Mewks went back to Sepia.

" His voice is much altered," she said.

" He most always speaks like that now, miss, when he wakes—very different from I used to know him ! He'd always swear bad when he woke ; but Miss Marston do seem t' 'ave got a good deal of that out of him. Anyhow, this last two days he's scarce swore enough to make it feel home-like."

" It's death has got it out of him," said Sepia. " I don't think he can last the night through. Fetch me at once if— And don't let that Marston into the room again, whatever you do."

She spoke with the utmost emphasis, plainly clinching instructions previously given, then went slowly up the stair to her own room. Surely he would die to-night, and she would not be led into temptation! She would then have but to get a hold of the paper! What a hateful and unjust thing it was that her life should be in the power of that man—a miserable creature, himself hanging between life and death!—that such as he should be able to determine her fate, and say whether she was to be comfortable or miserable all the rest of a life that was to outlast his so many years! It was absurd to talk of a Providence! She must be her own providence!

She stole again down the stair. Her cousin was in her own room safe with a novel, and there was Mewks fast asleep in an easy-chair in the study, with the doors of the dressing-room and chamber ajar! She crept into the sick-room. There was the tumbler with the medicine! and her fingers were on the vial in her pocket. The dying man slept.

She drew near the table by the bed. He stirred as if about to awake. Her limbs, her brain seemed to rebel against her will.—But what folly it was! the man was not for this world a day longer; what could it matter whether he left it a few hours earlier or later? The drops on his brow rose from the pit of his agony; every breath was a torture; it were mercy to help him across the verge; if to more life, he would owe her thanks; if to endless rest, he would never accuse her.

She took the vial from her pocket. A hand was on the lock of the door! She turned and fled through the dressing-room and study, waking Mewks as she passed. He, hurrying into the chamber, saw Mary already entered.

When Sepia learned who it was that had scared her, she felt she could kill her with less compunction than Mr. Redmain. She hated her far worse.

"You *must* get the viper out of the house, Mewks," she said. "It is all your fault she got into the room."

"I'm sure I'm willing enough," he answered, "—even if it wasn't you as as't me, miss! But what am I to do? She's that brazen, you wouldn' believe, miss! It wouldn' be becomin' to tell you what I think that young woman fit to do."

"I don't doubt it," responded Sepia. "But surely," she went on, "the next time he has an attack, and he's certain to have one soon, you will be able to get her hustled out!"

"No, miss—least of all just then. She'll make that a pretense for not going a yard from the bed—as if me that's been about him so many years didn't know what ought to be done with him in his paroxes of pain better than the likes of her! Of all things I do loathe a row, miss—and the talk of it after; and sure I am that without a row we don't get her out of that room. The only way is to be quiet, and seem to trust her, and watch for the chance of her going out—then shut her out, and keep her out."

"I believe you are right," returned Sepia, almost with a hope that no such opportunity might arrive, but at the same time growing more determined to take advantage of it if it should.

Hence partly it came that Mary met with no interruption to her watching and ministering. Mewks kept coming and going—watching her, and waiting his opportunity. Mr Redmain scarcely heeded him, only once and again saying in sudden anger, "What can that idiot be about? He might know by this time I'm not likely to want *him* so long as *you* are in the room!"

And said Mary to herself: "Who knows what good the mere presence of one who trusts may be to him, even if he shouldn't seem to take much of what she says! Perhaps he may think of some of it after he is dead—who knows?" Patiently she sat and waited, full of help that would have flowed in a torrent, but which she felt only trickle from her heart like a stream that is lost on the face of the rock down which it flows.

All at once she bethought herself, and looked at her watch. Joseph had been waiting for her more than an hour, and would not, she knew, if he stopped all night, go away without her! And for her, she could not forsake the poor man her presence seemed to comfort! He was now lying very still: she would slip out and send Joseph away, and be back before the patient or any one else should miss her!

She went softly from the room, and glided down the stairs,

and out of the house, seeing no one—but not unseen : hardly was she from the room, when the door of it was closed and locked behind her, and hardly from the house, when the house-door also was closed and locked behind her. But she heard nothing, and ran, without the least foreboding of mishap, to the corner where Joseph was to meet her.

There he was, waiting as patiently as if the hour had not yet come.

"I can't leave him, Joseph. My heart won't let me," she said. "I can not go back before the morning. I will look in upon you as I pass."

So saying, and without giving him time to answer, she bade him good night, and ran back to the house, hoping to get in as before without being seen. But to her dismay she found the door already fast, and concluded the hour had arrived when the house was shut up for the night. She rang the bell, but there was no answer—for there was Mewks himself standing close behind the door, grinning like his master an evil grin. As she knocked and rang in vain, the fact flashed upon her that she was intentionally excluded. She turned away, overwhelmed with a momentary despair. What was she to do ? There stood Joseph ! She ran back to him, and told him they had shut her out.

"It makes me miserable," she went on, "to think of the poor man calling me, and me nowhere to answer. The worst of it is, I seem the only person he has any faith in, and what I have been telling him about the father of us all, whose love never changes, will seem only the idler tale, when he finds I am gone, and nowhere to be found—as they're sure to tell him. There's no saying what lies they mayn't tell him about my going ! Rather than go, I will sit on the door-step all night, just to be able to tell him in the morning that I never went home."

"Why have they done it, do you think ?" asked Joseph.

"I dare hardly allow myself to conjecture," answered Mary. "None of them like me but Jemima—not even Mrs. Redmain now, I am afraid ; for you see I never got any of the good done her I wanted, and, till something of that was done, she could not know how I felt toward her. I shouldn't a bit wonder if they fancy I have a design on his money—as if anybody fit to call herself a woman would condescend to such a thing! But when a woman would marry for money, she may well think as badly of another woman."

"This is a serious affair," said Joseph. "To have a dying man believe you false to him would be dreadful! We must find some way in. Let us go to the kitchen-door."

"If Jemima happened to be near, then, perhaps!" rejoined Mary; "but if they want to keep me out, you may be sure Mewks has taken care of one door as well as another. He knows I'm not so easy to keep out."

"If you did get in," said Joseph, speaking in a whisper as they went, "would you feel quite safe after this?"

"I have no fear. I dare say they would lock me up somewhere if they could, before I got to Mr. Redmain's room. once in, they would not dare touch me."

"I shall not go out of hearing so long as you are in that house," said Joseph, with decision. "Not until I have you out again do I leave the premises. If anything should make you feel uncomfortable, you cry out, miss, and I'll make a noise at the door that everybody at Thornwick over there shall hear me."

"It is a large house, Joseph: one might call in many a part of it, and never be heard out of doors. I don't think you could hear me from Mr. Redmain's room," said Mary, with a little laugh, for she was amused as well as pleased at the protection Joseph would give her; "it is up two flights, and he chose it himself for the sake of being quiet when he was ill!"

As she spoke, they reached the door they sought—the most likely of all to be still open · it was fast and dark as if it had not been unbolted for years. One or two more entrances they tried, but with no better success.

"Come this way," whispered Joseph. "I know a place where we shall at least be out of their sight, and where we can plan at our leisure."

He led her to the back entrance to the old hall. Alas! even that was closed.

"This *is* disappointing," he said; "for, if we were only in there, I think something might be done."

"I believe I know a way," said Mary, and led him to a place near, used for a wood-shed.

At the top of a great heap of sticks and fagots was an opening in the wall, that had once been a window, or perhaps a door.

"That, I know, is the wall of the tower," she said ; "and there can be no difficulty in getting through there. Once in, it will be easy to reach the hall—that is, if the door of the tower is not locked."

In an instant Joseph was at the top of the heap, and through the opening, hanging on, and feeling with his feet. He found footing at no great distance, and presently Mary was beside him. They descended softly, and found the door into the hall wide open.

"Can you tell me what window is that," whispered Joseph, "just above the top of the wall ? "

"I can not," answered Mary. "I never could go about this house as I did about Mr. Redmain's ; my lady always looked so fierce if she saw me trying to understand the place. But why do you ask ? "

"You see the flickering of a fire ? Could it be Mr. Redmain's room ? "

"I can not tell. I do not think it. That has no window in this direction, so far as I know. But I could not be certain."

"Think how the stairs turn as you go up, and how the passages go to the room. Think in what direction you look every corner you turn. Then you will know better whether or not it might be."

Mary was silent, and thought. In her mind she followed every turn she had to take from the moment she entered the house till she got to the door of Mr. Redmain's room, and then thought how the windows lay when she entered it. Her conclusion was that one side of the room must be against the hall, but she could remember no window in it.

"But," she added, "I never was in that room when I was here before, and, the twice I have now been in it, I was too much occupied to take much notice of things about me. Two windows, I know, look down into a quiet little corner of the courtyard, where there is an old pump covered with ivy. I remember no other."

"Is there any way of getting on to the top of that wall from this tower?" asked Joseph.

"Certainly there is. People often walk round the top of those walls. They are more than thick enough for that."

"Are you able to do it?"

"Yes, quite. I have been round them more than once. But I don't like the idea of looking in at a window."

"No more do I, miss: but you must remember, if it is his room, it will only be your eyes going where the whole of you has a right to be; and, if it should not be that room, they have driven you to it: such a necessity will justify it."

"You must be right," answered Mary, and, turning, led the way up the stair of the tower, and through a gap in the wall out upon the top of the great walls.

It was a sultry night. A storm was brooding between heaven and earth. The moon was not yet up, and it was so dark that they had to feel their way along the wall, glad of the protection of a fence of thick ivy on the outer side. Looking down into the court on the one hand, and across the hall to the lawn on the other, they saw no living thing in the light from various windows, and there was little danger of being discovered. In the gable was only the one window for which they were making. Mary went first, as better knowing the path, also as having the better right to look in. Through the window, as she went, she could see the flicker, but not the fire. All at once came a great blaze. It lasted but a moment— long enough, however, to let them see plainly into a small closet, the door of which was partly open.

"That is the room, I do believe," whispered Mary. "There is a closet, but I never was in it."

"If only the window be not bolted!" returned Joseph.

The same instant Mary heard the voice of Mr. Redmain call in a tone of annoyance—"Mary! Mary Marston! I want you. Who is that in the room?—Damn you! who are you?"

"Le' ..." ... "..." ... hold to

the ivy, here spread on to the gable, he got between Mary and the window. The blaze was gone, and the fire was at its old flicker. The window was not bolted. He lifted the sash. A moment and he was in. The next, Mary was beside him.

Something, known to her only as an impulse, induced Mary to go softly to the door of the closet, and peep into the room. She saw Hesper, as she thought, standing—sidewise to the closet—by a chest of drawers invisible from the bed. A candle stood on the farther side of her. She held in one hand the tumbler from which, repeatedly that evening, Mary had given the patient his medicine : into this she was pouring, with an appearance of care, something from a small dark bottle.

With a sudden suspicion of foul play, Mary glided swiftly into the room, and on to where she stood. It was Sepia ! She started with a smothered shriek, turned white, and almost dropped the bottle ; then, seeing who it was, recovered herself. But such a look as she cast on Mary ! such a fire of hate as throbbed out of those great black eyes ! Mary thought for a moment she would dart at her. But she turned away, and walked swiftly to the door. Joseph, however, peeping in behind Mary, had caught a glimpse of the bottle and tumbler, also of Sepia's face. Seeing her now retiring with the bottle in her hand, he sprang after her, and, thanks to the fact that she had locked the door, was in time to snatch it from her. She turned like a wild beast, and a terrible oath came hissing as from a feline throat. When, however, she saw, not Mary, but the unknown figure of a powerful man, she turned again to the door and fled. Joseph shut and locked it, and went back to the closet. Mary drew near the bed.

" Where have you been all this time ? " asked the patient, querulously ; "and who was that went out of the room just now ? What's all the hurry about ? "

Anxious he should be neither frightened nor annoyed, Mary replied to the first part of his question only.

" I had to go and tell a friend, who was waiting for me, that I shouldn't be home to-night. But here I am now, and I will not leave you again."

"How did the door come to be locked ? And who was that went out of the room ?"

While he was thus questioning, Joseph crept softly out of the window ; and all the rest of the night he lay on the top of the wall under it.

"It was Miss Yolland," answered Mary.

"What business had she in my room ?"

"She shall not enter it again while I am here."

"Don't let Mewks in either," he rejoined. "I heard the door unlock and lock again : what did it mean ?"

"Wait till to-morrow. Perhaps we shall find out then."

He was silent a little.

"I must get out of this house, Mary," he sighed at length.

"When the doctor comes, we shall see," said Mary.

"What ! is the doctor coming ? I am glad of that. Who sent for him ?"

"I don't know ; I only heard he was coming."

"But your lawyer, Mary—what's his name ?—will be here first : we'll talk the thing over with him, and take his advice. I feel better, and shall go to sleep again."

All night long Mary sat by him and watched. Not a step, so far as she knew, came near the door ; certainly not a hand was laid upon the lock. Mr. Redmain slept soundly, and in the morning was beyond a doubt better.

But Mary could not think of leaving him until Mr. Brett came. At Mr. Redmain's request she rang the bell. Mewks made his appearance, with the face of a ghost. His master told him to bring his breakfast.

"And see, Mewks," he added, in a tone of gentleness that terrified the man, so unaccustomed was he to such from the mouth of his master—"see that there is enough for Miss Marston as well. She has had nothing all night. Don't let my lady have any trouble with it.—Stop," he cried, as Mewks was going. "I won't have you touch it either ; I am fastidious this morning. Tell the young woman they call Jemima to come here to Miss Marston."

Mewks slunk away. Jemima came, and Mr. Redmain ordered her to get breakfast for himself and Mary. It was done speedily, and Mary remained in the sick-chamber until the lawyer arrived.

CHAPTER LV.

DISAPPEARANCE.

"I AM afraid I must ask you to leave us now, Miss Marston," said Mr. Brett, seated with pen, ink, and paper, to receive his new client's instructions.

"No," said Mr. Redmain ; "she must stay where she is. I fancy something happened last night which she has got to tell us about."

"Ah ! What was that ?" asked Mr. Brett, facing round on her.

Mary began her story with the incident of her having been pursued by some one, and rescued by the blacksmith, whom she told her listeners she had known in London. Then she narrated all that had happened the night before, from first to last, not forgetting the flame that lighted the closet as they approached the window.

"Just let me see those memoranda," said Mr. Brett to Mr. Redmain, rising, and looking for the paper where he had left it the day before.

"It was of that paper I was this moment thinking," answered Mr. Redmain.

"It is not here !" said Mr. Brett.

"I thought as much ! The fool ! There was a thousand pounds there for her ! I didn't want to drive her to despair : a dying man must mind what he is about. Ring the bell and see what Mewks has to say to it."

Mewks came, in evident anxiety.

I will not record his examination. Mr. Brett took it for granted he had deliberately and intentionally shut out Mary, and Mewks did not attempt to deny it, protesting he believed she was boring his master. The grin on that master's face at hearing this was not very pleasant to behold. When examined as to the missing paper, he swore by all that was holy he knew nothing about it.

Mr. Brett next requested the presence of Miss Yolland. She was nowhere to be found The place was searched throughout, but there was no trace of her.

When the doctor arrived, the bottle Joseph had taken from her was examined, and its contents discovered.

Lady Malice was grievously hurt at the examination she found had been going on.

"Have I not nursed you like my own brother, Mr. Redman?" she said.

"You may be glad you have escaped a coroner's inquest in your house, Lady Margaret!" said Mr. Brett.

"For me," said Mr. Redman, "I have not many days left me, but somehow a fellow does like to have his own!"

Hesper sought Mary, and kissed her with some appearance of gratitude. She saw what a horrible suspicion, perhaps even accusation, she had saved her from. The behavior and disappearance of Sepia seemed to give her little trouble.

Mr. Brett got enough out of Mewks to show the necessity of his dismissal, and the doctor sent from London a man fit to take his place.

Almost every evening, until he left Durnmelling, Mary went to see Mr. Redman. She read to him, and tried to teach him, as one might an unchildlike child. And something did seem to be getting into, or waking up in, him. The man had never before in the least submitted: but now it looked as if the watching spirit of life were feeling through the dust-heap of his evil judgments, low thoughts, and bad life, to find the thing that spirit had made, lying buried somewhere in the frightful tumulus: when the two met and joined, then would the man be saved: God and he would be together. Sometimes he would utter the strangest things—such as if all the old evil modes of thinking and feeling were in full operation again; and sometimes for days Mary would not have an idea what was going on in him. When suffering, he would occasionally break into fierce and evil language, then be sud-

denly silent. God and Satan were striving for the man, and
victory would be with him with whom the man should side.

For some time it remained doubtful whether this attack was
not, after all, going to be the last : the doctor himself was doubtful, and, having no reason to think his death would be a great
grief in the house, did not hesitate much to express his doubt.
And, indeed, it caused no gloom. For there was little love in
the attentions the Mortimers paid him ; and in what other
hope could Hesper have married, than that one day she would
be free, with a freedom informed with power, the power of
money ! But to the mother's suggestions as to possible changes
in the future, the daughter never responded : she had no
thought of plans in common with her.

Strange rumors came abroad. Godfrey Wardour heard
something of them, and laughed them to scorn. There was a
conspiracy in that house to ruin the character of the loveliest
woman in creation ! But when week after week passed, and he
heard nothing of or from her, he became anxious, and at last
lowered his pride so far as to call on Mary, under the pretense
of buying something in the shop.

His troubled look filled her with sympathy, but she could
not help being glad afresh that he had escaped the snares laid
for him. He looked at her searchingly, and at last murmured
a request that she would allow him to have a little conversation
with her.

She led the way to her parlor, closed the door, and asked
him to take a seat. But Godfrey was too proud or too agi-
tated to sit.

" You will be surprised to see me on such an errand,
Miss Marston !" he said.

" I do not yet know your errand," replied Mary ; " but I
may not be so much surprised as you think."

" Do not imagine," said Godfrey, stiffly, " that I believe a
word of the contemptible reports in circulation. I come only
to ask you to tell me the real nature of the accusations brought
against Miss Yolland : your name is, of course, coupled with
them."

" Mr. Wardour," said Mary, " if I thought you would believe what I told you, I would willingly do as you ask me. As it is, allow me to refer you to Mr. Brett, the lawyer, whom I dare say you know."

Happily, the character of Mr. Brett was well known in Testbridge, and all the country round ; and from him Godfrey Wardour learned what sent him traveling on the Continent again—not in the hope of finding Sepia What became of her, none of her family ever learned.

Some time after, it came out that the same night on which the presence of Joseph rescued Mary from her pursuer, a man speaking with a foreign accent went to one of the surgeons in Testbridge to have his shoulder set, which he said had been dislocated by a fall. When Joseph heard it, he smiled, and thought he knew what it meant.

Hesper was no sooner in London, than she wrote to Mary, inviting her to go and visit her. But Mary answered she could no more leave home, and must content herself with the hope of seeing Mrs. Redmain when she came to Durnmelling.

So long as her husband lived, the time for that did not again arrive ; but when Mary went to London, she always called on her, and generally saw Mr. Redmain. But they never had any more talk about the things Mary loved most. That he continued to think of those things, she had one ground of hoping, namely, the kindness with which he invariably received her, and the altogether gentler manner he wore as often and as long as she saw him. Whether the change was caused by something better than physical decay, who knows save him who can use even decay for redemption ? He lived two years more, and died rather suddenly. After his death, and that of her father, which followed soon, Hesper went again to Durnmelling, and behaved better to her mother than before. Mary sometimes saw her, and a flicker of genuine friendship began to appear on Hesper's part.

Mr. Turnbull was soon driving what he called a roaring trade. He bought and sold a great deal more than Mary, but she had business sufficient to employ her days, and leave her nights free, and bring her and Letty enough to live on as comfortably as they desired—with not a little over, to use, when occasion was, for others, and something to lay by for the time of lengthening shadows.

Turnbull seemed to have taken a lesson from his late narrow escape, for he gave up the worst of his speculations, and confined himself to "*genuine business-principles*"—the more contentedly that, all Marston folly swept from his path, he was free to his own interpretation of the phrase. He grew a rich man, and died happy—so his friends said, and said as they saw. Mrs. Turnbull left Testbridge, and went to live in a small county-town where she was unknown. There she was regarded as the widow of an officer in her Majesty's service, and, as there was no one within a couple of hundred miles to support an assertion to the contrary, she did not think it worth her while to make one : was not the supposed brevet a truer index to her consciousness of herself than the actual ticket by ill luck attached to her—Widow of a linen-draper ?

George carried on the business ; and, when Mary and he happened to pass in the street, they nodded to each other.

Letty was diligent in business, but it never got into her heart. She continued to be much liked, and in the shop was delightful. If she ever had another offer of marriage, the fact remained unknown. She lived to be a sweet, gracious little old lady—and often forgot that she was a widow, but never that she was a wife. All the days of her appointed time she waited till her change should come, and she should find her Tom on the other side, looking out for her, as he had said he would. Her mother-in-law could not help dying ; but she never "forgave" her—for what, nobody knew.

After a year or so, Mrs. Wardour began to take a little notice of her again ; but she never asked her to Thornwick until she found herself dying. Perhaps she then remembered a certain petition in the Lord's prayer. But will it not be rather a dreadful thing for some people if they are forgiven as they forgive ?

Old Mr. Duppa died, and a young man came to minister to his congregation who thought the baptism of the spirit of more importance than the most correct of opinions concerning even the baptizing spirit. From him Mary found she could learn, and would be much to blame if she did not learn. From him Letty also heard what increased her desire to be worth something before she went to rejoin Tom.

Joseph Jasper became once more Mary's pupil. She was now no more content with her little cottage piano, but had an instrument of quite another capacity on which to accompany the violin of the blacksmith.

To him trade came in steadily, and before long he had to build a larger shoeing-shed From a wide neighborhood horses were brought him to be shod, cart-wheels to be tired, axles to be mended, plowshares to be sharpened, and all sorts of odd jobs to be done. He soon found it necessary to make arrangement with a carpenter and wheelwright to work on his premises. Before two years were over, he was what people call a flourishing man, and laying by a little money.

" But," he said to Mary, " I can't go on like this, you know, miss. I don't want money. It must be meant to do something with, and I must find out what that something is."

CHAPTER LVI

A CATASTROPHE.

One winter evening, as soon as his work was over for the day, Joseph locked the door of his smithy, washed himself well, put on clean clothes, and, taking his violin, set out for Test-bridge · Mary was expecting him to tea. It was the afternoon of a holiday, and she had closed early.

Was there ever a happier man than Joseph that night as he strode along the footpath ? A day of invigorating and manly toil behind him, folded up in the sense of work accomplished ; a clear sky overhead, beginning to breed stars ; the pale amber hope of to-morrow's sunrise low down in the west ; a frosty air around him, challenging to the surface the glow of the forge which his day's labor had stored in his body ; his heart and brain at rest with his father in heaven ; his precious violin under his arm ; before him the welcoming parlor, where two sweet women waited his coming, one of them the brightest angel, in or out of heaven, to him ; and the prospect of a long evening of torrent-music between them—who, I repeat, could have been more blessed, heart, and soul, and body, than Joseph Jasper ? His being was like an all-sided lens concentrating all joys in the one heart of his consciousness. God only knows how blessed he could make us if we would but let him ! He pressed his violin-case to his heart, as if it were a living thing that could know that he loved it.

Before he reached the town, the stars were out, and the last of the sunset had faded away. Earth was gone, and heaven was all. Joseph was now a reader, and read geology and astronomy : "I've got to do with them all !" he said to himself, looking up. "There lie the fields of my future, when this chain of gravity is unbound from my feet ! Blessed am I here now, my God, and blessed shall I be there then."

When he reached the suburbs, the light of homes was shining through curtains of all colors. "Every nest has its own birds," said Joseph ; "every heart its own joys !" Just then, he was in no mood to think of the sorrows. But the sorrows are sickly things and die, while the joys are strong divine children, and shall live for evermore.

When he reached the streets, all the shops he passed were closed, except the beer-shops and the chemists'. "The nettle and the dock !" said Joseph.

When he reached Mary's shop, he turned into the court to the kitchen-door. "Through the kitchen to the parlor !" he said. "Through the smithy to the presence-chamber ! O my God—through the mud of me, up to thy righteousness !"

He was in a mood for music—was he not ? One might imagine the violin under his arm was possessed by an angel, and, ignoring his ears, was playing straight into his heart !

Beenie let him in, and took him up to the parlor. Mary came half-way to meet him. The pressure as of heaven's atmosphere fell around him, calming and elevating. He stepped across the floor, still, stately, and free. He laid down his violin, and seated himself where Mary told him, in her father's arm-chair by the fire. Gentle nothings with a down of rainbows were talked until tea was over, and then without a word they set to their music—Mary and Joseph, with their own hearts and Letty for their audience.

They had not gone far on the way to fairyland, however, when Beenie called Letty from the room, to speak to a friend and customer, who had come from the country on a sudden necessity for something from the shop. Letty, finding herself not quite equal to the emergency, came in her turn to call Mary ; she went as quietly as if she were leaving a tiresome visitor. The music was broken, and Joseph left alone with the dumb instruments.

But in his hands solitude and a violin were sure to marry in music. He began to play, forgot himself utterly, and, when the customer had gone away satisfied, and the ladies returned to the parlor, there he stood with his eyes closed, playing on, nor knowing they were beside him. They sat down, and listened in silence.

Mary had not listened long before she found herself strangely moved. Her heart seem'd to swell up into her throat, and it was all she could do to keep from weeping. A little longer and she was compelled to yield, and the silent tears flowed freely. Letty, too, was overcome—more than ever she had been by music. She was not so open to its influences as Mary, but her eyes were full, and she sat thinking of her Tom, far in the regions that are none the less true that we can not see them.

A mood had taken shape in the mind of the blacksmith, and wandered from its home, seeking another country. It is not the ghosts of evil deeds that alone take shape, and go forth to wander the earth. Let but a mood be strong enough, and the soul, clothing itself in that mood as with a garment, can walk abroad and haunt the world. Thus, in a garment of mood whose color and texture was music, did the soul of Joseph Jasper that evening, like a homeless ghost, come knocking at the door of Mary Marston. It was the very being of the man, praying for admittance, even as little Abel might have crept up to the gate from which his mother had been driven, and, seeing nothing of the angel with the flaming sword, knocked and knocked, entreating to be let in, pleading that all was not right with the world in which he found himself. And there Mary saw Joseph stand, thinking himself alone with his violin; and the violin was his mediator with her, and was pleading and pleading for the admittance of its master. It prayed, it wept, it implored. It cried aloud that eternity was very long, and like a great palace without a quiet room. "Gorgeous is the glory," it sang; "white are the garments, and lovely are the faces of the holy; they look upon me gently and sweetly, but pitifully, for they know that I am alone—yet not alone, for I love. Oh, rather a thousand-fold let me love and be alone, than be content and joyous with them all, free of this pang which tells me of a bliss yet more complete, fulfilling the gladness of heaven!"

All the time Joseph knew nothing of where his soul was; for he thought Mary was in the shop, and beyond the hearing of his pleader. Nor was this exactly the shape the thing took to the consciousness of the musician. He seemed to himself to be standing alone in a starry and moonlit night, among roses, and sweet-peas, and apple-blossoms—for the soul cares little for the seasons, and will make its own month out of many. On the bough of an apple-tree, in the fair moonlight, sat a nightingale, swaying to and fro like one mad with the wine of his own music, singing as if he wanted to break his heart and have done, for the delight was too much for mortal creature to endure. And the song of the bird grew the prayer of a man in the brain and heart of the musician, and thence burst, through the open fountain of the violin, and worked what it could work, in the world of forces. "I love thee! I love thee! I love thee!" cried the violin; and the worship was entreaty that knew not itself. On and on it went, ever beginning ere it ended, as if it could never come to a close; and the two sat listening as if they cared but to hear, and would listen for ever—listening as if, when the sound ceased, all would be at an end, and chaos come again.

Ah, do not blame, thou who lovest God, and fearest the love of the human! Hast thou yet to learn that the love of the human is love, is divine, is but a lower form of a part of the love of God ? When thou lovest man, or woman, or child, yea, or even dog, aright, then wilt thou no longer need that I tell thee how God and his Christ would not be content with each other alone in the glories even of the eternal original love, because they could create more love. For that more love, together they suffered and patiently waited. He that loveth not his brother whom he hath seen, how shall he love God whom he hath not seen ?

A sob, like a bird new-born, burst from Mary's bosom. It broke the enchantment in which Joseph was bound. That enchantment had possessed him, usurping as it were the throne of his life, and displacing it ; when it ceased, he was not his own master. He started—to conscious confusion only, neither knowing where he was nor what he did. His limbs for the moment were hardly his own. How it happened he never could tell, but he brought down his violin with a crash against the piano, then somehow stumbled and all but fell. In the act of recovering himself, he heard the neck of his instrument part from the body with a tearing, discordant cry, like the sound of the ruin of a living world. He stood up, understanding now, holding in his hand his dead music, and regarding it with a smile sad as a winter sunset gleaming over a grave. But Mary darted to him, threw her arms round him, laid her head on his bosom, and burst into tears. Tenderly he laid his broken violin on the piano, and, like one receiving a gift straight from the hand of the Godhead, folded his arms around the woman— enough, if music itself had been blotted from his universe ! His violin was broken, but his being was made whole ! his treasure taken—type of his self, and a woman given him instead !

"It's just like him !" he murmured.

He was thinking of him who, when a man was brought him to be delivered from a poor palsy, forgave him his sins.

CHAPTER LVII.

THE END OF THE BEGINNING.   .

JOSEPH JASPER and Mary Marston were married the next summer. Mary did not leave her shop, nor did Joseph leave his forge. Mary was proud of her husband, not merely because he was a musician, but because he was a blacksmith. For, with the true taste of a right woman, she honored the manhood that could do hard work. The day will come, and may I do something to help it hither, when the youth of our country will recognize that, taken in itself, it is a more manly, and therefore in the old true sense a more *gentle* thing, to follow a good handicraft, if it make the hands black as a coal, than to spend the day in keeping books, and making up accounts, though therein the hands should remain white—or red, as the case may be. Not but that, from a higher point of view still, all work, set by God, and done divinely, is of equal honor ; but, where there is a choice, I would gladly see boy of mine choose rather to be a blacksmith, or a watchmaker, or a bookbinder, than a clerk. Production, making, is a higher thing in the scale of reality, than any mere transmission, such as buying and selling. It is, besides, easier to do honest work than to buy and sell honestly. The more honor, of course, to those who are honest under the greater difficulty ! But the man who knows how needful the prayer, "Lead us not into temptation," knows that he must not be tempted into temptation even by the glory of duty under difficulty. In humility we must choose the easiest, as we must hold our faces unflinchingly to the hardest, even to the seeming impossible, when it is given us to do.

I must show the blacksmith and the shopkeeper once more —two years after marriage—time long enough to have made common people as common to each other as the weed by the roadside ; but these are not common to each other yet, and never will be They will never complain of being *désillusionnés,* for they have never been illuded. They look up each to the other still, because they were right in looking up each to the other from the first. Each was, and therefore each is and will be, real.

" . . . . The man is honest."
"Therefore he will be, Timon."

It was a lovely morning in summer. The sun was but a little way above the horizon, and the dew-drops seemed to have come scattering from him as he shook his locks when he rose. The foolish larks were up, of course, for they fancied, come what might of winter and rough weather, the universe founded in eternal joy, and themselves endowed with the best of all rights to be glad, for there was the gladness inside, and struggling to get outside of them. And out it was coming in a divine profusion! How many baskets would not have been wanted to gather up the lordly waste of those scattered songs! in all the trees, in all the flowers, in every grass-blade, and every weed, the sun was warming and coaxing and soothing life into higher life. And in those two on the path through the fields from Testbridge, the same sun, light from the father of lights, was nourishing highest life of all—that for the sake of which the Lord came, that he might set it growing in hearts of whose existence it was the very root.

Joseph and Mary were taking their walk together before the day's work should begin. Those who have a good conscience, and are not at odds with their work, can take their pleasure any time—as well before their work as after it. Only where the work of the day is a burden grievous to be borne, is there cause to fear being unfitted for duty by antecedent pleasure. But the joy of the sunrise would linger about Mary all the day long in the gloomy shop; and for Joseph, he had but to lift his head to see the sun hastening on to the softer and yet more hopeful splendors of the evening. The wife, who had not to begin so early, was walking with her husband, as was her custom, even when the weather was not of the best, to see him fairly started on his day's work. It was with something very like pride, yet surely nothing evil, that she would watch the quick blows of his brawny arm, as he beat the cold iron on the anvil till it was all aglow like the sun that lighted the world—then stuck it into the middle of his coals, and blew softly with his bellows till the flame on the altar of his work-offering was awake and keen. The sun might shine or forbear, the wind might blow or be still, the path might be crisp with frost or soft with mire, but the lighting of her husband's forge-fire, Mary, without some forceful reason, never omitted to turn by her presence into a holy ceremony. It was to her the "Come let us worship and bow down" of the daily service of God-given labor. That done, she would kiss him, and leave him : she had her own work to do. Filled with prayer she would walk steadily back the well-known way to the shop, where, all day long, ministering with gracious service to the wants of her people, she would know the evening and its service drawing nearer and nearer, when Joseph would come, and the delights of heaven would begin afresh at home, in music, and verse, and trustful talk. Every day was a life, and every evening a blessed death—type of that larger evening rounding our day with larger hope. But many Christians are such awful pagans that they will hardly believe it possible a young loving pair should think of that evening, except with misery and by rare compulsion !

That morning, as they went, they talked—thus, or something like this :

"O Mary !" said Joseph, "hear the larks ! They are all saying : 'Jo-seph ! Jo-seph ! Hearkentome, Joseph ! What-wouldyouhavebeenbutforMa-ry, Jo-seph ?' That's what they keep on singing, singing in the ears of my heart, Mary !"

"You would have been a true man, Joseph, whatever the larks may say."

"A solitary melody, praising without an upholding harmony, at best, Mary !"

"And what should I have been, Joseph ? An inarticulate harmony—sweetly mumbling, with never a thread of soaring song !"

A pause followed.

"I shall be rather shy of your father, Mary," said Joseph. "Perhaps he won't be content with me."

"Even if you weren't what you are, my father would love you because I love you. But I know my father as well as I know you ; and I know you are just the man it must make him happy afresh, even in heaven, to think of his Mary marrying. You two can hardly be of two minds in anything !"

"That was a curious speech of Letty's yesterday ! You heard her say, did you not, that, if everybody was to be so very good in heaven, she was afraid it would be rather dull ?"

"We mustn't make too much of what Letty says, either when she's merry or when she's miserable. She speaks both times only out of half-way down."

"Yes, yes ! I wasn't meaning to find any fault with her : I was only wishing to hear what you would say. For nobody can make a story without somebody wicked enough to set things wrong in it, and then all the work lies in setting them right again, and, as soon as they are set right, then the story stops."

"There's nothing of the sort in music, Joseph, and that makes one happy enough."

"Yes, there is, Mary. There's strife and difference and compensation and atonement and reconciliation."

"But there's nothing wicked."

"No, that there is not."

"Well !" said Mary, "perhaps it may only be because we know so little about good, that it seems to us not enough. We know only the beginnings and the fightings, and so write and talk only about them. For my part, I don't feel that strife of any sort is necessary to make me enjoy life : of all things it is what makes me miserable. I grant you that effort and strug-gle add immeasurably to the enjoyment of life, but those I look upon as labor, not strife. There may be whole worlds for us to help bring into order and obedience. And I suspect there must be no end of work in which is strife enough—and that of a kind hard to bear. There must be millions of spirits in prison that want preaching to ; and whoever goes among them will have that which is behind of the afflictions of Christ to fill up. Any-how there will be plenty to do, and that's the main thing. Seeing we are made in the image of God, and he is always working, we could not be happy without work."

"Do you think we shall get into any company we like up there ?"

"I must think a minute. When I want to understand, I find myself listening for what my father would say. Yes, I think I know what he would say to that: 'Yes; but not till you are fit for it; and then the difficulty would be to keep out of it. For all that is fit must come to pass in the land of fitnesses—that is, the land where all is just as it ought to be.'—That's how I could fancy I heard my father answer you."

"With that answer I am well content," said Joseph.—"But you don't want to die, do you, Mary?"

"No; I want to live. And I've got such a blessed plenty of life while waiting for more, that I am quite content to wait. But I do wonder that some people I know, should cling to what they call life as they do. It is not that they are comfortable, for they are constantly complaining of their sufferings; neither is it from submission to the will of God, for to hear them talk you must think they imagine themselves hardly dealt with; they profess to believe the Gospel, and that it is their only consolation; and yet they speak of death as the one paramount evil. In the utmost weariness, they yet seem incapable of understanding the apostle's desire to depart and be with Christ, or of imagining that to be with him can be at all so good as remaining where they are. One is driven to ask whether they can be Christians any further than anxiety to secure whatever the profession may be worth to them will make them such."

"Don't you think, though," said Joseph, "that some people have a trick of putting on their clothes wrong side out, and so making themselves appear less respectable than they are? There was my sister Ann: she used to go on scolding at people for not believing, all the time she said they could not believe till God made them—if she had said *except* God made them, I should have been with her there!—and then talking about God so, that I don't see how, even if they could, any one would have believed in such a monster as she made of him; and then, if you objected to believe in such a God, she would tell you it was all from the depravity of your own heart you could not believe in him; and yet this sister Ann of mine, I know, once went for months without enough to eat—without more than just kept body and soul together, that she might feed the children of a neighbor, of whom she knew next to nothing, when their father lay ill of a fever, and could not provide for them. And she didn't look for any thanks neither, except it was from that same God she would have to be a tyrant from the beginning—one who would calmly behold the unspeakable misery of creatures whom he had compelled to exist, whom he would not permit to cease, and for whom he would do a good deal, but not all that he could. Such people, I think, are nearly as unfair to themselves as they are to God."

"You're right, Joseph," said Mary. "If we won't take the testimony of such against God, neither must we take it against themselves. Only, why is it they are always so certain they are in the right?"

"For the perfecting of the saints," suggested Joseph, with a curious smile.

"Perhaps," answered Mary. "Anyhow, we may get that good out of them, whether they be here for the purpose or not. I remember Mr. Turnbull once accusing my father of irreverence, because he spoke about God in the shop. Said my father, 'Our Lord called the old temple his father's house and a den of thieves in the same breath.' Mr. Turnbull saw nothing but nonsense in the answer. Said my father then, 'You will allow that God is everywhere?' 'Of course,' replied Mr. Turnbull. 'Except in this shop, I suppose you mean?' said my father. 'No, I don't. That's just why I wouldn't have you do it.' 'Then you wouldn't have me think about him either?' 'Well! there's a time for everything.' Then said my father, very solemnly, 'I came from God, and I'm going back to God, and I won't have any gaps of death in the middle of my life.' And that was nothing to Mr. Turnbull either."

To one in ten of my readers it may be something.

Just ere they came in sight of the smithy, they saw a lady and gentleman on horseback flying across the common.

"There go Mrs. Redmain and Mr. Wardour!" said Joseph. "They're to be married next month, they say. Well, it's a handsome couple they'll make! And the two properties together'll make a fine estate!"

"I hope she'll learn to like the books he does," said Mary.

"I never could get her to listen to anything for more than three minutes."

Though Joseph generally dropped work long before Mary shut the shop, she yet not unfrequently contrived to meet him on his way home ; and Joseph always kept looking out for her as he walked.

That very evening they were gradually nearing each other —the one from the smithy, the other from the shop—with another pair between them, however, going toward Testbridge —Godfrey Wardour and Hesper Redmain.

"How strange," said Hesper, "that after all its chances and breakings, old Thornwick should be joined up again at last !"

Partly by a death in the family, partly through the securities her husband had taken on the property, partly by the will of her father, the whole of Durnmelling now belonged to Hesper.

"It is strange," answered Godfrey, with an involuntary sigh.

Hesper turned and looked at him.

It was not merely sadness she saw on his face. There was something there almost like humility, though Hesper was not able to read it as such. He lifted his head, and did not avoid her gaze.

"You are wondering, Hesper," he said, "that I do not respond with more pleasure. To tell you the truth, I have come through so much that I am almost afraid to expect the fruition of any good. Please do not imagine, you beautiful creature ! it is of the property I am thinking. In your presence that would be impossible. Nor, indeed, have I begun to think of it. I shall, one day, come to care for it, I do not doubt—that is, when once I have you safe ; but I keep looking for the next slip that is to come—between my lip and this full cup of happiness. I have told you all, Hesper, and I thank you that you do not despise me. But it may well make me solemn and fearful, to think, after all the waves and billows that have gone over me, such a splendor should be mine !—But, do you really love me, Hesper—or am I walking in my sleep ? I had thought,

'Surely now at last I shall never love again!'—and instead of that, here I am loving, as I never loved before!—and doubting whether I ever did love before!'"

"I never loved before," said Hesper. "Surely to love must be a good thing, when it has made you so good! I am a poor creature beside you, Godfrey, but I am glad to think whatever I know of love you have taught me. It is only I who have to be ashamed!"

"That is all your goodness!" interrupted Godfrey. "Yet, at this moment, I can not quite be sorry for some things I ought to be sorry for: but for them I should not be at your side now—happier than I dare allow myself to feel. I dare hardly think of those things, lest I should be glad I had done wrong."

"There are things I am compelled to know of myself, Godfrey, which I shall never speak to you about, for even to think of them by your side would blast all my joy. How plainly Mary used to tell me what I was! I scorned her words! It seemed, then, too late to repent. And now I am repenting! I little thought ever to give in like this! But of one thing I am sure—that, if I had known you, not all the terrors of my father would have made me marry the man."

Was this all the feeling she had for her dead husband? Although Godfrey could hardly at the moment feel regret she had not loved him, it yet made him shiver to hear her speak of him thus. In the perfected grandeur of her external womanhood, she seemed to him the very ideal of his imagination, and he felt at moments the proudest man in the great world; but at night he would lie in torture, brooding over the horrors a woman such as she must have encountered, to whom those mysteries of our nature, which the true heart clothes in abundant honor, had been first presented in the distortions of a devilish caricature. There had been a time in Godfrey's life when, had she stood before him in all her splendor, he would have turned from her, because of her history, with a sad disgust. Was he less pure now? He was more pure, for he was humbler. When those terrible thoughts would come, and the darkness about him grow billowy with black flame, "God help me," he would cry, "to make the buffeted angel forget the past!"

They had talked of Mary more than once, and Godfrey, in part through what Hesper told him of her, had come to see that he was unjust to her. I do not mean he had come to know the depth and extent of his injustice—that would imply a full understanding of Mary herself, which was yet far beyond him. A thousand things had to grow, a thousand things to shift and shake themselves together in Godfrey's mind, before he could begin to understand one who cared only for the highest.

Godfrey and Hesper made a glorious pair to look at—but would theirs be a happy union?—Happy, I dare say—and not too happy. He who sees to our affairs will see that the *too* is not in them. There were fine elements in both, and, if indeed they loved, and now I think, from very necessity of their two hearts, they must have loved, then all would, by degrees, by slow degrees, most likely, come right with them.

If they had been born again both, before they began, so to start fresh, then like two children hand in hand they might have run in through the gates into the city. But what is love, what is loss, what defilement even, what are pains, and hopes, and disappointments, what sorrow, and death, and all the ills that flesh is heir to, but means to this very end, to this waking of the soul to seek the home of our being—the life eternal? Verily we must be born from above, and be good children, or become, even to our self-loving selves, a scorn, a hissing, and an endless reproach.

If they had had but Mary to talk to them! But they did not want her: she was a good sort of creature, who, with all her disagreeableness, meant them well, and whom they had misjudged a little and made cry! They had no suspicion that she was one of the lights of the world—one of the wells of truth, whose springs are fed by the rains on the eternal hills.

Turning a clump of furze-bushes on the common, they met Mary. She stepped from the path. Mr. Wardour took off his hat. Then Mary knew that his wrath was past, and she was glad.

They stopped.

"Well, Mary," said Hesper, holding out her hand, and speaking in a tone from which both haughtiness and condescension had vanished, "where are you going?"

"To meet my husband," answered Mary. "I see him coming."

With a deep, loving look at Hesper, and a bow and a smile to Godfrey, she left them, and hastened to meet her working-man.

Behind Godfrey Wardour and Hesper Redmain walked Joseph Jasper and Mary Marston, a procession of love toward a far-off, eternal goal. But which of them was to be first in the kingdom of heaven, Mary or Joseph or Hesper or Godfrey, is not to be told : they had yet a long way to walk, and there are first that shall be last, and last that shall be first.

THE END.

CPSIA information can be obtained
at www.ICGtesting.com
Printed in the USA
LVHW080211031219
639247LV00011B/108/P